If There Is No Struggle
There Is No Progress

If There Is No Struggle There Is No Progress

Black Politics in Twentieth-Century Philadelphia

EDITED BY JAMES WOLFINGER

With a Foreword by Heather Ann Thompson

TEMPLE UNIVERSITY PRESS
Philadelphia • Rome • Tokyo

TEMPLE UNIVERSITY PRESS
Philadelphia, Pennsylvania 19122
tupress.temple.edu

Copyright © 2022 by Temple University—Of The Commonwealth System of Higher Education
All rights reserved
Published 2022

Library of Congress Cataloging-in-Publication Data

Names: Wolfinger, James, editor. | Thompson, Heather Ann, 1963– writer of supplementary textual content.
Title: If there is no struggle there is no progress : Black politics in twentieth-century Philadelphia / edited by James Wolfinger ; with a foreword by Heather Ann Thompson.
Description: Philadelphia : Temple University Press, 2022. | Includes bibliographical references and index. | Summary: "An edited collection exploring the development of African American political engagement in Philadelphia and how Philadelphia has served as a critical site for Black politics over the last century"— Provided by publisher.
Identifiers: LCCN 2021051886 (print) | LCCN 2021051887 (ebook) | ISBN 9781439919262 (cloth) | ISBN 9781439919279 (paperback) | ISBN 9781439919286 (pdf)
Subjects: LCSH: African Americans—Pennsylvania—Philadelphia—Politics and government—20th century. | African Americans—Political activity—Pennsylvania—Philadelphia—20th century. | African American political activists—Pennsylvania—Philadelphia—History—20th century. | Philadelphia (Pa.)—Politics and government—20th century. | Philadelphia (Pa.)—Race relations—History—20th century.
Classification: LCC F158.9.N4 I43 2022 (print) | LCC F158.9.N4 (ebook) | DDC 323.1196/073074811—dc23/eng/20220207
LC record available at https://lccn.loc.gov/2021051886
LC ebook record available at https://lccn.loc.gov/2021051887

Printed in the United States of America

9 8 7 6 5 4 3 2 1

Contents

	Maps of Philadelphia	vi
	Foreword / Heather Ann Thompson	ix
	Acknowledgments	xiii
	Introduction / James Wolfinger	1
1	Old Philadelphians, the Great Migration, and the Irony of Progressive Politics / Clem Harris	13
2	Building Black Philadelphia / David A. Canton	48
3	The Great Depression and World War II / Stanley Keith Arnold	76
4	Postwar Philadelphia / Abigail Perkiss	95
5	The 1960s and Expanding Ideas of Black Rights / Clem Harris	113
6	African American Politics in Frank Rizzo's Philadelphia / Timothy J. Lombardo	136
7	Taking Political Power / Alyssa Ribeiro	162
8	The Insurgent Nature of Black Politics in Contemporary Philadelphia / Stephen J. McGovern	189
	Appendix	227
	List of Contributors	229
	Illustration Credits	231
	Index	233

Map 1 Map of Philadelphia.

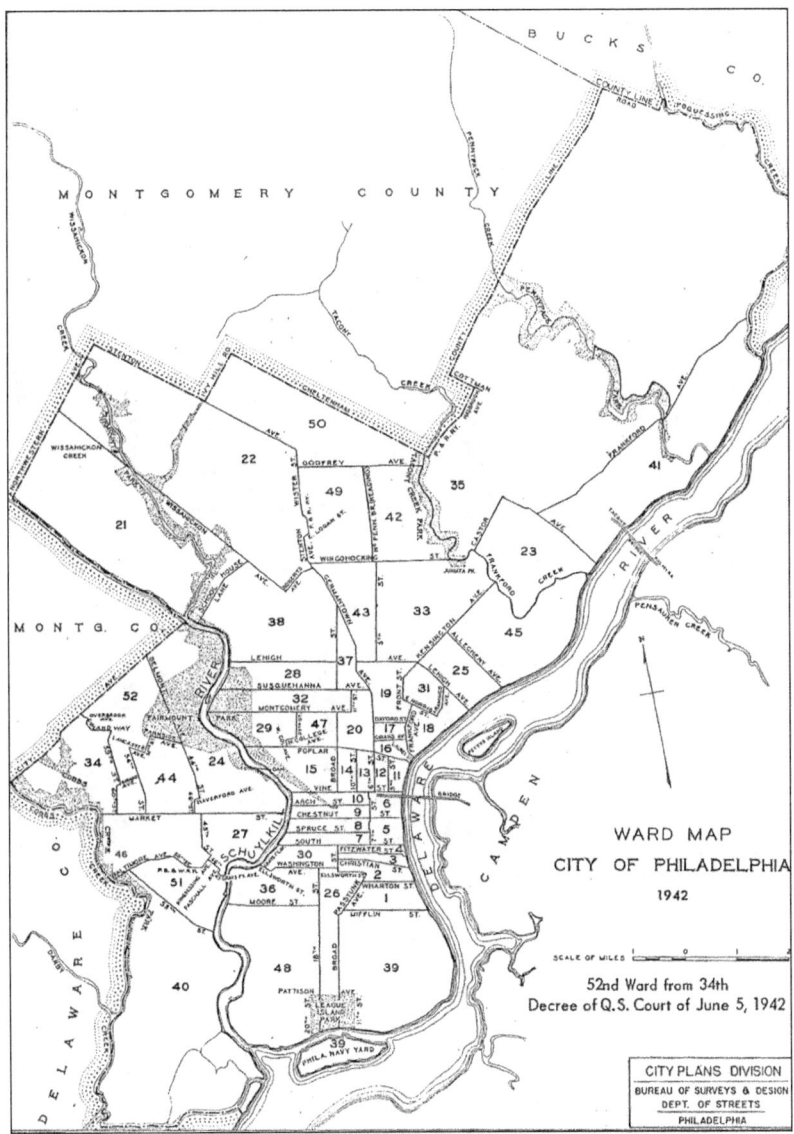

Map 2 Ward Map of Philadelphia, 1942. Note that this map captures the city's wards in midcentury, but boundaries did change over time. More information is available at https://www.phila.gov/phils/Docs/Inventor/graphics/wards/wards.htm.

Foreword

HEATHER ANN THOMPSON

On May 12, 1985, Philadelphians from across the City of Brotherly Love walked down neighborhood streets, boarded SEPTA trains, and drove their cars on I-95 or I-76, to join their families for Mother's Day. None had any idea that something unimaginable was about to happen in their city the very next day. And yet, the Black residents of Osage Avenue on the city's west side at least had an inkling. The night before, these Philadelphians had been told that they must all leave their homes. Dutifully, they packed up a few things and left. But, as they drove away, the scene unfolding over their shoulders was more than unnerving. Barricades were being erected, ominous-looking equipment was being set up, and, perhaps most disturbing, hundreds of armed police officers were assembling. Notably, all of those officers' attention was fixed on one specific row house in the middle of the block.

But even these Philadelphians had no clue what horror was actually about to unfold.

On May 13, 1985, after many hours of first attempting to get at the inhabitants of that rowhouse by breaching its neighboring walls with explosives and shooting rounds of live ammunition, the Philadelphia Police Department ultimately decided to drop a bomb onto its roof. As the Philadelphia Fire Department just looked on, the dwelling immediately became an inferno. Still trapped inside were seven adults and six children. Despite their agonized screams and desperate attempts to get out, by day's end all but two of these residents of 6221 Osage had been burned alive. As incredibly, almost two entire city blocks had also been utterly incinerated. The more than 160 people who had been instructed to evacuate their homes had lost everything they owned.

Images of the charred bodies of so many children and adults, of the neighborhood streets that looked like the cities of World War II Europe after an air raid, and of the tear-stained and bewildered faces of the now homeless neighbors, for a moment, shocked the country. But, in time, the astonishing fact that city officials had dropped a package of military-grade explosives on their own residents in the so-called MOVE bombing of 1985, largely faded from memory, both locally and nationally. In some ways such a collective "forgetting" was not a surprise given that no city official or police officer was ever held legally responsible for what had taken place on Osage Avenue, and the MOVE organization has always been dismissed as the lunatic fringe by the media.

And yet, for not a few residents of the city, particularly the Black working- and middle-class residents of the streets that had been reduced to rubble, it had remained impossible to forget. Indeed, it was utterly incomprehensible *why* the Philadelphia Police Department had chosen to drop a bomb on such a vibrant neighborhood that day, and more to the point, how such a decision had even been *allowed* to happen. And yet, in some ways it was not all that hard to understand. These were Philadelphians who had come of age in a city so discriminatory that their generation had eventually exploded in 1964 and had fought ever since to secure a meaningful voice and presence in the city at every level, agency, and office. Many of them now openly wondered if this horrific tragedy had been allowed to happen, and had also been so easily forgotten, simply because the victims—all of the dead children, the dead adults, and even themselves the now homeless neighbors—were Black. After all, was it even conceivable that Black cops would have been allowed to drop a bomb on a white neighborhood, let alone to escape prosecution had they killed the white men, women, and children who lived there, leaving the hard-earned and well-kept homes of so many white families in ashes? Would America have forgotten that event so quickly?

But, Philadelphia, like all American cities, has always had a most complicated history—one that simply reversing the racial identity of the players involved in this brutal conflagration obscures. In fact, the mayor who had overseen that assault, the one who had allowed it, was W. Wilson Goode, a Black man. What is more, many of the other city officials on whose watch this happened, were also Black, and these leaders had enjoyed tremendous support from the same African American working- and middle-class Philadelphians rendered homeless by all they had unleashed. Over the course of the twentieth century, the rise of Black electoral power in cities across the

United States not only shaped the history of urban America in profound and powerful ways; it did so in ways profoundly complex.

Philadelphia over the long twentieth century was at once a city with staggering inequality and racial injustice and a city where African Americans resisted abuse and marginalization with startling passion and determination, and enjoyed significant electoral success. Diving deeply into this history, and specifically into the history of how Black political activism shaped and impacted Philadelphia over time, allows us to better understand not only this one major American city but also the importance of, and complex role played by, Black politics in urban America writ large. That history is rife with episodes of inequality, injustice, and uneven development. But it is also filled with periods of powerful resistance to each of these realities—at times successful, at times not, but always shaping and reshaping the urban political landscape in ways that neither the city's white elites and the white voting base nor the Black politicians and their voters could predict or control.

This volume offers a much-needed new exploration of African American urban political history, in all of its complexity, with all of its contestation, and with all of its predicted as well as utterly unpredictable fallout. Indeed, by zeroing in on the history of Black politics in the City of Brotherly Love over the long twentieth century, the essays in this collection, together, not only powerfully rescue and reassess the past of this particular urban center but also help us better understand America itself in these critical decades. We come to see, with new clarity, why Philadelphia, as well as every other major U.S. city, has never quite managed to realize truly equal representation nor to ever really include in the social compact all who actually contributed to its growth and wealth. And yet, we also come to appreciate in new ways what it has meant that in this city, as in all others, African Americans have always mobilized to be heard, to be included, and to be recognized, and, therefore, have always placed a powerful check on civic injustice and inequality.

As this history of Black politics in Philadelphia makes clear, Black Philadelphians, like everywhere, have always endured repression but have also actively resisted it at every turn. And, in doing so, Black people have directly shaped the economic and political landscape of the city in which they too live. This collection of essays makes equally clear that no history of any American city can be complete until its African American political history is acknowledged, understood, and reckoned with fully.

Acknowledgments

This book began, as they so often do, with a conversation. Sara Cohen, an editor at Temple University Press, asked if we could meet at the American Historical Association conference to discuss what great new works I knew were emerging about Philadelphia's history. We had a stimulating conversation over coffee, trading insights about what inspired us in the newest histories of the city. At some point, I suggested that someone should bring these scholars together, put their contributions under a single cover. Temple should produce a book that examined the history of Black politics in Philadelphia throughout the long twentieth century. Sara paused, looked at me, and said, "When do we get started?" A book was born.

Of course, it takes significantly more than a cup of coffee to bring an edited collection together. First and foremost, it takes the support of an editorial team. Sara played a central role in getting this book off the ground, but after about a year she left Temple for other opportunities. When the original editor leaves, a project can easily die. I had the good fortune to have Aaron Javsicas see the innate value of this book, and he seamlessly picked up where Sara left off. It never hurts to have the editor-in-chief at a prominent university press champion your book. Aaron secured strong anonymous external reviewers who offered trenchant critiques. I greatly appreciate all of the input these external reviewers have offered; this book is stronger because of them. Aaron also shepherded the book through the approval process with the press's board of trustees. And he acted as a partner in pulling the chapters together and getting them through the production process. My thanks to Aaron, as well as his team at Temple University Press, for all he has done to carry this project forward.

As my thinking about this book project came into focus, I assembled a team of authors who contributed their vast historical knowledge and intellectual creativity to this collective effort. To a person, they had something fresh and provocative to say about Black Philadelphia's past, its race and politics, class and gender, formal party allegiance and grassroots insurgency. Philadelphia's past is a messy place, and the team that wrote the chapters of this book are sure-footed guides who routinely and clearly reveal the unexpected. I have learned much from them in putting this book together. My thanks to Heather Ann Thompson, Clem Harris, David Canton, Stanley Arnold, Abigail Perkiss, Timothy Lombardo, Alyssa Ribeiro, and Stephen McGovern for all they have contributed. This has been a collective effort. Each chapter on its own makes a significant contribution to our understanding of Philadelphia's history. But the whole of the collection is even stronger than the sum of its parts.

If There Is No Struggle
There Is No Progress

Introduction

JAMES WOLFINGER

If there is no struggle there is no progress. Those who profess to favor freedom and yet deprecate agitation are men who want crops without plowing up the ground; they want rain without thunder and lightning. They want the ocean without the awful roar of its many waters. This struggle may be a moral one, or it may be a physical one, and it may be both moral and physical, but it must be a struggle. Power concedes nothing without a demand. It never did and it never will.
—Frederick Douglass, West India Emancipation Speech (1857)

African American politics has always had a fierce urgency. The third decade of the twenty-first century has only underscored that fact. The killings of George Floyd, Breonna Taylor, and Walter Wallace Jr. and many other violent incidents have roiled the United States. The COVID-19 pandemic and its attendant economic dislocations have had a clearly disproportionate impact on the African American community. These may have been new events, but, in many ways, they served more as a culmination of centuries of unequal and racist treatment. Well before 2020, African Americans had less access to adequate medical care, lower life expectancies, and poorer health outcomes related to environmental racism. They faced higher unemployment rates and held less wealth than white Americans. And they too often found social systems such as education, public health, and law enforcement arrayed against them as they sought fair treatment in American society. Former president Donald Trump at best showed a callous disregard for the needs of the African American community. At worst, he fomented racial divisions that recalled some of the worst moments in American history.[1]

This state of affairs has been particularly bitter, coming on the heels of the presidency of Barack Obama who had brought great hope to millions of Americans who dared to believe that a new order had arrived. A nation founded on racial hierarchy and Black exploitation had finally begun to atone for its original sin by electing as president a man of African descent. Few truly believed the United States had entered a postracial society, but hope for advancement abounded. Under President Barack Obama, African Americans obtained a depth and diversity of political representation that they had not previously held.[2]

Yet, despite the hopefulness of the Obama era, African Americans always understood that politics did not stop at the White House door. Throughout the years of the Trump administration, African Americans expanded the Black Lives Matter movement, campaigned for a living wage (Fight for 15), protested police abuse across the country, and organized to support a new wave of women and minority candidates who remade the House of Representatives in the 2018 elections. For four long years, African Americans exercised their political rights in innumerable ways as they continued their demand for equitable treatment in American society.

In 2020, African Americans helped lead a historic wave of voter turnout that won the election for Joseph Biden and Kamala Harris. In Philadelphia, more than 749,000 voters cast ballots—the highest turnout since 1984—with 81 percent of the vote going to Joe Biden and 18 percent to Donald Trump. In a city where African Americans make up 44 percent of the population and exit polls showed Trump improved his performance in white and Latino neighborhoods, Black Philadelphians clearly played a pivotal role in securing a key swing state for the Democrats. Across Pennsylvania, polls showed that some 92 percent of Black voters went for Biden. The election of a woman of color to the second highest office in the land was certainly a major point of pride for many African Americans. Yet, Black Philadelphians expressed tempered feelings about the outcome. Black voters told reporters that, more than anything, voting Trump out of office fueled their desire to cast a ballot. "I was proud of us for [coming out to vote], I was proud of Black people," said Carmela Dow. "I was proud of Philadelphia, but I wasn't impressed with Biden winning. I was relieved but I wasn't celebrating." "We get married to these images and these people," added community organizer Walter Palmer, "but they don't live where we live and they don't come from where we come from." Some regretted that Bernie Sanders did not head the ticket. Others expressed concern about Biden's and Harris's criminal justice background. Many questioned how strong of an ally they had in the White House. Lamont Steptoe, who recalled efforts to suppress the Black vote in the 1950s and 1960s, summarized these views: "I was glad to hear President-elect Biden say that he thanked Black people for having his back and that he would have our back, but governments are governments," he said. "So, there's only so much expectation. For those of us who are proponents of reparations and other progressive agendas for people of color, you just have to realize that it's a long distance run that requires stamina and endurance."[3]

Despite the understandable wariness of Black voters, the kind of activism that takes on police abuse, pushes education reform, challenges environmental racism, and puts presidents in office demonstrates the real power of Black politics. Historically and today, Philadelphia is one of the most important sites for the expression of that Black political power. By focusing on Philadelphia's past, *If There Is No Struggle There Is No Progress: Black Politics in Twentieth-Century Philadelphia* gives readers a deep historical sense of the people and movements that made the city a center of political activism for more than a century. In doing so, it forcefully makes the case for why Philadelphia must be central to any analysis of African American political history.

In the decades after the Civil War, Philadelphia had a small but highly politically engaged Black population that numbered some twenty-two thousand people in 1870 (3.3 percent of the population). African Americans, led by Octavius V. Catto, pushed to obtain the right to vote, end segregation of the city's schools, and desegregate the streetcars. In response, the Pennsylvania state legislature passed laws ending segregation on the street railways in 1867 and in the education system in 1881. Many white Philadelphians recoiled at such changes: the schools remained segregated by custom for decades afterward, and Catto was shot and killed attempting to vote in 1871. Despite racial violence, the Black community continued to grow, reaching nearly thirty-two thousand people in 1880. They supported hundreds of Black-owned businesses, the *Philadelphia Tribune*, and Frederick Douglass Memorial Hospital. By 1900, the number of Black Philadelphians had nearly doubled to 62,613 people, and the population was large enough to merit the attention of a young scholar investigating the Black experience in America. W.E.B. Du Bois, in his classic study, *The Philadelphia Negro*, not only found African Americans confronting many social problems related to education, employment, and the police but also recounted a vitality, a resilience, that suggested the world could change, that such circumstances were not immutable. This tension between social problems and African Americans' will to overcome them emerged as a central theme of the twentieth century and continues today.[4]

In the late nineteenth and early twentieth centuries, African Americans employed what Clem Harris in Chapter 1 calls civil rights liberalism. This combination of electoral and protest activism in the pursuit of equal political and civil rights, focused on obtaining voting rights, protection from police brutality and extralegal violence, and equal opportunity in the workplace, city school system, and public accommodations. In this campaign,

African Americans used the ballot in tandem with protests to hold onto their rights of citizenship within a system of de facto segregation in Philadelphia and across the industrialized urban North. The fight against extralegal violence and legal disenfranchisement was not just a Southern story but an American one. At a time when the Republican Party had developed urban machines and pulled away from its Civil War–era radical egalitarian impulses and the Democratic Party represented the Jim Crow South, Black Philadelphians found the principles of white Progressives appealing. African American political leaders such as Harry Bass and George White quickly learned, however, that Progressives were at best unsteady allies. African Americans could draw on some of the Progressives' arguments about the need to end machine politics and use "scientific" approaches to solving problems as a way to combat racialized thinking, but they understood Black politics would only truly advance if they were rooted in the community and based on the needs of the people.

The Great Migration of the World War I era spurred the development of Black politics in Philadelphia and across the urban North. The city's African American population surged to 134,229 people in 1920, giving Philadelphia a larger number of Black residents than Chicago, Baltimore, or any other city except New York City, which had 152,467 African Americans. Women played a significant role in this chain migration, establishing kin networks that attracted so many migrants that Black Philadelphians expanded from their South Philadelphia enclave to neighborhoods in the northern and western parts of the city. New arrivals supported the local chapter of the National Association for the Advancement of Colored People (NAACP) and the National Urban League as well as the *Tribune*. Most newly arrived African Americans were "working poor," and they sought employment at the area's major companies such as the Pennsylvania and Reading Railroads, Baldwin Locomotive, Midvale Steel, Cramps Shipyard, and the Philadelphia Rapid Transit Company.[5]

As African Americans moved into new neighborhoods and took jobs historically regarded as reserved for white men, they encountered significant resistance. Like Chicago, Tulsa, Springfield, Illinois, and numerous other cities, Philadelphia exploded in racial violence. The shootings of people and destruction of property resulted in four deaths and many injuries as well as many buildings destroyed across the city in 1918. In response, many African Americans came together to form the Colored Protective Association. They also supported Black attorney John Asbury for state senate, and he made the passage of an equal rights bill one of his first orders of business. White senators ultimately defeated the bill, but it was a harbinger of further activism to come.[6]

A larger population with greater financial resources led to a flowering of African American culture as well as politics, as David Canton examines in Chapter 2. By 1930, the city's Black population had reached almost 220,000 people. They frequented venues such as the Dunbar Theater at Broad and Lombard Streets and read the works of author Jessie Redmon Fauset as the city enjoyed a Renaissance that resembled more than rivaled Harlem's. Passage of the Nineteenth Amendment in 1920 opened greater space for women such as Sadie Tanner Mossell Alexander to join her husband Raymond Pace Alexander and other men as leaders in the community. This generation of urban African Americans, termed the "New Negro," made greater demands for the dignity and equality they deserved. Although they continued to support the Republican Party throughout the 1920s at higher levels than Black voters in Chicago and New York City, their demands gained them little with Philadelphia's GOP.[7]

The Great Depression threw Philadelphia, like every American city, into turmoil. In the early 1930s, Philadelphia's unemployment rate exceeded 25 percent and another 35 percent of workers in the city only worked part-time. As usual, when times were bad for white workers, they were rotten for their Black counterparts. African Americans, who always faced the cliché, "last hired, first fired," had their unemployment rate crest at 61 percent. Tens of thousands of Black Philadelphians lost their homes, making a mockery of the city's nickname, "City of Homes." Even more stood in breadlines, trying to stave off starvation.[8]

Desperation led to political realignment. Stanley Arnold details in Chapter 3 how the city's entrenched Republican machine ignored African Americans' plight. Frustrated Black Philadelphians turned from the GOP to other political organizations. Many African Americans ignored generations of Southern Democratic politics to join the Roosevelt coalition. Some turned to liberal interracial activism advocated by the interfaith center, Fellowship House. Others wanted more militant representation, and they found a home in the left-leaning National Negro Congress (which held its 1937 convention in Philadelphia) or in the Communist Party. Black activists engaged in rent strikes and demanded that the government provide decent public housing, which led to the construction of the James Weldon Johnson and Richard Allen Homes. They also protested employers' discriminatory policies with "Don't Buy Where You Can't Work" campaigns. A generation of Black political activists led by Arthur Huff Fauset and his wife Crystal Bird Fauset, Marshall Shepard, and Hobson Reynolds emerged in the 1930s and dominated the scene for nearly thirty years. Shepard and Reynolds worked together to pass the Pennsylvania Equal Rights Law in 1935. Yet, despite this victory, many Black political leaders wondered just how much power they held within the Democratic Party to actually transform Philadelphia's politics. Over time, however, they saw few options better than the Democratic Party and decided to make their political home there. That shift, begun in the 1930s, set the contours for African American politics for the next century.[9]

World War II brought a Second Great Migration of African Americans to Philadelphia. The city's Black population, which stood at 250,880 in 1940, grew by 50 percent, to 376,041, by the decade's end. Philadelphia reached its highest population in 1950 at 2,071,605 people, and nearly every new resident the city gained over that decade was African American. Federal funds granted to industries across the city during the war served as a siren song for Black migrants. They came to work at the shipyards and munitions plants, the textile mills and locomotive works. In doing so, they joined an enormous demographic wave that, between 1941 and 1979, sent some five million people from the South to the cities of the Northeast, Midwest, and West.[10]

Despite the nation's need for their labor, African Americans encountered deep racism. Philadelphia, and many other cities, like Detroit and Mobile, Alabama, saw conflicts flare as new Black residents sought equal access to housing and jobs. After the hard years of the Depression, African Americans were, at first, happy that they could find work, but they quickly learned that employers and, too often, unions relegated them to segregated facilities and menial labor. Across the nation, African Americans waged the Double V campaign: victory over Fascism abroad and racism at home. Labor leader and political activist A. Philip Randolph led the March on Washington movement that demanded the federal government prohibit discrimination in hiring at industries receiving defense contracts. This effort led President Franklin Roosevelt to issue Executive Order 8802, banning racial and ethnic discrimination in defense industries and establishing the Fair Employment Practices Committee (FEPC). In Philadelphia, Carolyn Moore emerged as a strong leader of the NAACP, and she used her office to campaign for public housing and the end of employment discrimination at area munitions factories, shipyards, and, most notably, the Philadelphia Transportation Company. The transit company became one of the most notable flash points in war-era race relations when white workers walked off the job just two months after D-Day rather than accept African Americans in driving positions. The federal government, fearing the walkout would hamper war production, put down the strike by sending five thousand armed troops into the city. Luckily, Philadelphia did not explode in violence, but the strike highlighted the city's simmering racial tensions that could easily boil over.[11]

In the postwar period, Philadelphia politics underwent a sea change. The Republican Party that had dominated the city's politics for generations had a widely held and well-deserved reputation for corruption. Liberal politicians Joseph Clark and Richardson Dilworth, with significant support from a Black population that, by 1960, grew to 529,240 people (for the first time over a quarter of the population), led a Democratic surge that threw out the Republican machine and realigned the city's politics. In 1958, Black voters rejoiced when they elected Robert N. C. Nix Sr. as the first African American representative from Philadelphia in Congress, where he joined William Dawson of Illinois, Adam Clayton Powell Jr. of New York, and Charles Diggs Jr. of Michigan. Despite this significant advance, Black Philadelphians knew that Clark, Dilworth, and other white Democratic leaders produced mixed results for the African American community. On the one hand, they increased civil service opportunities and implemented a Home Rule Charter that provided for a Commission on Human Relations, which was one of the first agencies in the nation dedicated to fighting discrimination. On the other hand, they participated in a nationwide urban renewal program that had a disproportionate impact on African American communities in Chicago, New York City, and other major urban areas. They also failed to halt realtors' blockbusting practices that roiled neighborhoods across the city, and they were powerless to arrest the deindustrialization that claimed some 250,000 jobs from the 1950s to the 1980s.[12]

Although many white communities in Philadelphia and its suburbs, such as Levittown, reacted with violence to African Americans seeking housing, others came together with a different vision for postwar living. As Abigail Perkiss examines in Chapter 4, some white Philadelphians, particularly in the upscale northwest Philadelphia community of West Mount Airy, joined with Black neighbors to emphasize cosmopolitan liberalness, class commonality, and economic self-interest over racial difference. Black Philadelphians in the professional class, notably led by Raymond Pace and Sadie Alexander, spearheaded the development of a coalition that pushed an agenda of equality of opportunity. That political strategy was a clear product of the liberal interracialism that dominated the era.[13]

Cecil B. Moore highlighted the obvious limitations of the liberal strategy. Arriving in Philadelphia after serving in World War II, Moore headed the NAACP in the 1960s and established himself as the local leader of a national radical political impulse typified by Malcolm X and the Black Panther Party. To Moore, the older generation of Black political leaders, epitomized by the Alexanders, lacked authenticity or a real connection to the African American community. As Clem Harris argues in Chapter 5, Moore, the Reverend Leon Sullivan, and other local leaders in the 1960s believed the key to racial advancement and true equality lay not in integrating West Mount Airy but in building grassroots movements that featured women organizing for adequate state support, men demanding the integration of companies that had "whites only" employment policies, and young people protesting for equal educational opportunities. African Americans demonstrated at construction sites, boycotted Tasty Baking Company over its hiring policies, demanded that publicly run Girard College desegregate after more than a century of following its original benefactor's mandate to educate white male orphans, and launched a major protest at the board of education to challenge inferior schools for Black students, the prohibition of traditional African dress, and a curriculum that ignored African American history.[14]

African American protest politics in the 1960s engendered a sharp white reaction that often centered on interactions with the police. By 1970, the city's Black population stood at 653,791 people, just over one-third of all Philadelphia residents. This many people largely pressed into the city's worst and most run-down neighborhoods, and facing an economy that provided too few opportunities for working people, created a tinderbox. The police had two major clashes with Black Philadelphians in this era, the first in August 1964 following a traffic stop in North Philadelphia and the second at board of education protests in 1967. Conflicts such as these helped fuel the rise of Frank Rizzo, first as police commissioner and then as mayor. Rizzo, who liked to think of himself as one of the nation's toughest cops in Richard Nixon's law-and-order era, routinely provoked confrontations with the city's Black population. In Chapter 6, Timothy Lombardo highlights how Rizzo used these confrontations to build a loyal base in the city's white working-class neighborhoods that exacerbated long-standing racial tensions.[15]

In the 1970s and 1980s, African American communities and their political leaders challenged Rizzo's politics by building a local political movement that finally brought them significant formal power. They formed alliances with other minority populations, especially Puerto Ricans, and backed a number of candidates who won office. In the early 1970s, David Richardson won a seat in the Pennsylvania House of Representatives and C. Delores Tucker became the first Black female secretary of state. Charles Bowser made an unsuccessful run for mayor, but he paved the way for the electoral successes of W. Wilson Goode, who rose from the city's religious establishment, and John Street and Michael Nutter in subsequent years. Goode's election placed Philadelphia in the same ranks as Chicago, Atlanta, Cleveland, and Gary, Indiana, in selecting African Americans as mayors in the era.[16]

Black Philadelphians finally had formal political power, but it came just as cities across the United States faced some of the most significant problems in their history. As Alyssa Ribeiro examines in Chapter 7, fiscal troubles, abandoned housing and aging infrastructure, public health crises stemming from crack cocaine and AIDS, and hostile police-community relations all challenged Philadelphia. The city had increasing needs and a shrinking tax base just as the federal government reduced its support of urban communities. At the same time, Philadelphia residents staunchly opposed tax hikes that could have helped lower-income populations. Despite a common desire to bolster Black neighborhoods, African American politicians had to practice an austerity that severely limited their freedom to act. Nonetheless, multiracial coalition building based on neighborhood issues and opposition to the Rizzo administration laid the foundation for African Americans to gain and keep political power into the twenty-first century.[17]

Although African Americans finally obtained and now continue to wield political power, grassroots organizations still push for a more egalitarian city in the first decades of the twenty-first century. Founded by six women in northeast Philadelphia, the Kensington Welfare Rights Union, for example, campaigns for social justice and fair treatment for poor and homeless people. The Black Lives Matter movement calls attention to abusive police practices and demands reform. Black politicians, religious leaders, and community organizers as well as ordinary people in the city's neighborhoods deplore the impact of the carceral state and push political leaders to dismantle it. With the city's African American population stabilizing at about 660,000 people in 2010 (43 percent of the population) and estimates showing that number will grow to about 690,000 in the 2020 census, Black Philadelphians have the population base to hold any politician accountable. As Stephen McGovern recounts in Chapter 8, mass mobilization in opposition to law enforcement policies that disproportionately target individuals and neighborhoods of color helped propel James Kenney, a longtime city council member who had become increasingly sensitive to demands for reforming the criminal justice system, to the mayor's office in 2015. They also played a large role in Larry Krasner's unexpected victory in the district attorney race in 2017. Grassroots activism and the election of politicians critical of police practices and the carceral state have yielded real political change in the contemporary era. African American activists make it clear that they plan to continue to apply pressure to make sure politicians meet the needs of their community.

Looking back over the long history of Philadelphia's African American political experience, it is clear that elections and political offices matter. The importance of electing Wilson Goode, John Street, Michael Nutter, and Robert N. C. Nix Sr. to the mayor's office and Congress cannot be underestimated. But politics means something deeper than elected office. It is embedded in the city's social movements that drew on class, gender, and other markers of identity to mobilize Black Philadelphians throughout the twentieth century. Women and men, poor people, and those in the professional class, all engaged in political activism. They did not always agree with each other and at times the infighting could be severe. But their mobilizations ultimately led to advocacy for a wide array of changes in the city and beyond: job rights, access to housing, equal educational opportunities, fair treatment by the police, and many other goals. Taken as a whole, their campaigns that played out over more than a century of Philadelphia's history highlight the interplay between activism and the broader political context that shaped developments in the African American community and the larger city.

In the end, *If There Is No Struggle There Is No Progress: Black Politics in Twentieth-Century Philadelphia* comes out at a time when African Americans and their allies have rightful concerns about their future in the United States, and this book allows readers to place activists and their causes today in historical context. Times may be hard today, but they often have been. Politically active African Americans, like all people, have made mistakes, have missed opportunities, have confronted situations with no good solutions. But this book shows how they have also displayed creativity, tenacity, and discipline. This is a complicated history, one neither triumphalist nor nihilist. This is a history for our difficult time. This is a history from which we can learn, grow, and face new challenges with a timeless spirit born of a faith that political activism can make the world a better place.

NOTES

1. Jenny Gross, "What We Know about the Death of Walter Wallace Jr. in Philadelphia," *New York Times*, October 29, 2021, accessed November 1, 2021, available at https://www.nytimes.com/article/walter-wallace-jr-philadelphia.html; Jonathan Kozol, *Savage Inequalities: Children in America's Schools* (New York: Crown, 1991); Robert D. Bullard and Benjamin Chavis Jr., eds., *Confronting Environmental Racism: Voices from the Grassroots* (Boston: South End, 1999).

2. Jim Wallis, *America's Original Sin: Racism, White Privilege, and the Bridge to a New America* (Grand Rapids, MI: Brazos, 2016); Ibram Kendi, *Stamped from the Beginning: The Definitive History of Racist Ideas in America* (New York: Nation Books, 2016).

3. All quotes in this paragraph from Sojourner Ahebee, "Philadelphia's Black Voters Reflect on the 2020 Election," Votebeat, November 19, 2020, accessed January 15, 2021, available at https://patch.com/pennsylvania/across-pa/philadelphias-black-voters-reflect-2020-election; "Exit Poll Results and Analysis from Pennsylvania" November 9, 2020, accessed January 15, 2021, available at https://www.washingtonpost.com/elections/interactive/2020/exit-polls/pennsylvania-exit-polls/; Layla A. Jones, "Philadelphia Turnout for the 2020 Election Was the Highest in 25 Years," November 17, 2020, accessed January 15, 2021, available at https://billypenn.com/2020/11/17/philly-turnout-2020-lower-obama-trump-biden/; Jonathan Tamari, Chris Brennan, Sean Collins Walsh, and Jonathan Lai, "Philly Was Supposed to Turn Out Huge for Biden. It Didn't. What Happened?," November 15, 2020, accessed January 15, 2021, available at https://www.inquirer.com/politics/election/philadelphia-2020-election-turnout-biden-trump-20201115.html; "Exit Polls," undated, accessed January 15, 2021, available at https://www.cnn.com/election/2020/exit-polls/president/pennsylvania; "Philadelphia Election Results," November 4, 2020, accessed January 15, 2021, available at https://results.philadelphiavotes.com/ResultsSW.aspx?type=FED&map=CTY.

4. Daniel Biddle and Murray Dubin, *Tasting Freedom: Octavius Catto and the Battle for Equality in Civil War America* (Philadelphia: Temple University Press, 2010); James Wolfinger and Stanley Keith Arnold, "Civil Rights (African American)," accessed October 20, 2020, available at https://philadelphiaencyclopedia.org/archive/civil-rights-afri can-american/; W.E.B. Du Bois, *The Philadelphia Negro: A Social Study* (1899; repr., Philadelphia: University of Pennsylvania Press, 1996).

5. James Wolfinger, "African American Migration," accessed October 20, 2020, available at https://philadelphiaencyclopedia.org/archive/african-american-migration/.

6. William M. Tuttle, *Race Riot: Chicago in the Red Summer of 1919* (Urbana: University of Illinois Press, 1970).

7. David Levering Lewis, *When Harlem Was in Vogue* (New York: Knopf, 1981); Wolfinger and Arnold, "Civil Rights (African American)"; Alain Locke, *The New Negro: An Interpretation* (New York: Boni, 1925).

8. Wolfinger and Arnold, "Civil Rights (African American)"; Margaret B. Tinkcom, "Depression and War, 1929–1946," in *Philadelphia: A 300-Year History*, ed. Russell F. Weigley (New York: Norton, 1982).

9. James Wolfinger, *Philadelphia Divided: Race and Politics in the City of Brotherly Love* (Chapel Hill: University of North Carolina Press, 2007); Stanley Keith Arnold, *Building the Beloved Community: Philadelphia's Interracial Civil Rights Organizations and Race Relations, 1930–1970* (Jackson: University Press of Mississippi, 2014); Erik Gellman, *Death Blow to Jim Crow: The National Negro Congress and the Rise of Militant Civil Rights* (Chapel Hill: University of North Carolina Press, 2012); John Bauman, *Public Housing, Race, and Renewal: Urban Planning in Philadelphia, 1920–1974* (Philadelphia: Temple University Press, 1987).

10. James N. Gregory, "The Second Great Migration: A Historical Overview," in *African American Urban History since World War II*, ed. Kenneth L. Kusmer and Joe W. Trotter (Chicago: University of Chicago Press, 2009).

11. Wolfinger, *Philadelphia Divided*, chs. 4–6; Thomas Sugrue, *The Origins of the Urban Crisis: Race and Inequality in Postwar Detroit* (Princeton, NJ: Princeton University Press, 1996); Bruce Nelson, "Organized Labor and the Struggle for Black Equality in Mobile during World War II," *Journal of American History* 80 (December 1993): 952–988; James Wolfinger, "'We Are in the Front Lines in the Battle for Democracy': Carolyn Moore and Black Activism in World War II Philadelphia," *Pennsylvania History* 72 (January 2005): 1–23; James Wolfinger, *Running the Rails: Capital and Labor in the Philadelphia Transit Industry* (Ithaca, NY: Cornell University Press, 2016), ch. 5.

12. Roger Simon, *Philadelphia: A Brief History* (University Park: Pennsylvania Historical Association, 2003), 110–113; Wolfinger and Arnold, "Civil Rights (African American)"; Robert Nelson Cornelius Nix Sr., biography, History, Art and Archives, United States House of Representatives, accessed January 15, 2021, available at https://history .house.gov/People/Detail/18971; Bauman, *Public Housing, Race, and Renewal*; David McAllister, "Realtors and Racism in Working-Class Philadelphia, 1945–1970," in *African American Urban History since World War II*, ed. Kenneth L. Kusmer and Joe W. Trotter (Chicago: University of Chicago Press, 2009); Beryl Satter, *Family Properties: How the Struggle over Race and Real Estate Transformed Chicago and Urban America* (New York: Metropolitan Books, 2009).

13. James Wolfinger, "'The American Dream—For All Americans': Race, Politics, and the Campaign to Desegregate Levittown," *Journal of Urban History* 38 (May 2012): 430–451; Abigail Perkiss, *Making Good Neighbors: Civil Rights, Liberalism, and Inte-

gration in Postwar Philadelphia (Ithaca, NY: Cornell University Press, 2014); Gunnar Myrdal, *An American Dilemma: The Negro Problem and Modern Democracy* (New York: Harper, 1944).

14. Manning Marable, *Malcolm X: A Life of Reinvention* (New York: Viking, 2011); Matthew Countryman, *Up South: Civil Rights and Black Power in Philadelphia* (Philadelphia: University of Pennsylvania Press, 2007); Lisa Levenstein, *A Movement without Marches: African American Women and the Politics of Poverty in Postwar Philadelphia* (Chapel Hill: University of North Carolina Press, 2009); Wolfinger and Arnold, "Civil Rights (African American)"; Thomas Sugrue, "Affirmative Action from Below: Civil Rights, the Building Trades, and the Politics of Racial Equality in the Urban North, 1945–1969," *Journal of American History* 91 (June 2004): 145–173.

15. Guian McKee, *The Problem of Jobs: Liberalism, Race, and Deindustrialization in Philadelphia* (Chicago: University of Chicago Press, 2008); Wolfinger and Arnold, "Civil Rights (African American)"; Timothy J. Lombardo, *Blue-Collar Conservatism: Frank Rizzo's Philadelphia and Populist Politics* (Philadelphia: University of Pennsylvania Press, 2018).

16. Wolfinger and Arnold, "Civil Rights (African American)"; Alyssa Ribeiro, "'Asking Them and Protesting': Black and Puerto Rican Leadership in Philadelphia Neighborhoods, 1960s–1970s," *Pennsylvania History* 86 (Summer 2019): 359–382.

17. Simon, *Philadelphia*, ch. 4; Buzz Bissinger, *A Prayer for the City* (New York: Vintage, 1997); Ribeiro, "Asking Them and Protesting," 359–382.

1

Old Philadelphians, the Great Migration, and the Irony of Progressive Politics

CLEM HARRIS

During the last two decades of the nineteenth century, Philadelphia's African American community grew by 60.4 percent as Southern Black migrants made their way North from the Upper South, mostly Virginia and Maryland, to resettle in the City of Brotherly Love. By 1890, there were nearly forty thousand Black people in Philadelphia and, by 1900, well over sixty-two thousand African Americans, approximately 5 percent of the total population, called Philadelphia home. Between 1910 and 1920, this pattern of growth continued as the Black community in Philadelphia grew by 58.9 percent, with nearly forty thousand Southern Black migrants, mainly from rural areas in the Lower South, the Carolinas, Georgia, and Florida, entering the city during the World War I and postwar eras. The migration of Southern Black people into Philadelphia can be explained by two major factors. First, as the largest industrial urban center just north of the Mason-Dixon Line, the city had, since the antebellum era, been a beacon for Black people seeking to escape slavery and the harsh conditions of the South. Second, once immigration of western and southeastern Europeans, who had since the post–Civil War era responded to the labor needs of the city, was suspended during World War I, Northern white labor agents turned their recruitment focus toward the vast supply of Black labor in the South to meet the industrial demands of the war economy. African American women played a crucial role in the migration to Philadelphia. Between 1890 and World War I, employment opportunities as domestics and personal service employees increasingly turned in favor of Black women. As a result, opportunities as domestic servants not only allowed Black women a chance to establish stable employment; it also helped them facilitate the migration of Southern Black people through the development of kinship and communal networks.[1] (See Fig. 1.1.)

Although Philadelphia previously had a large Black population, prior to the war, as a result of the Great Migration between 1910 and 1920 the city became home to one of the largest African American populations in the industrialized urban North. This period of dramatic racial and ethnic demographic transformation triggered several important changes to Philadelphia's social and economic structures all of which held important political implications regarding the African American struggle for freedom, jobs, and social justice. These changes also developed new patterns of race, class, and ethnic relations that remain with the city today. While Black settlement occurred across southern, western, and northern regions of the city, between 1890 and the 1920s most Southern Black migrants resided in South Philadelphia's African American community concentrated in three wards: the Seventh, Thirtieth, and Thirty-Sixth. For most newcomers, this was a period of poverty and despair marked by overcrowded housing, workplace discrimination, a rise in slums, and increased crime. As Southern Black migrants entered the city's changing political economy, a minority of older,

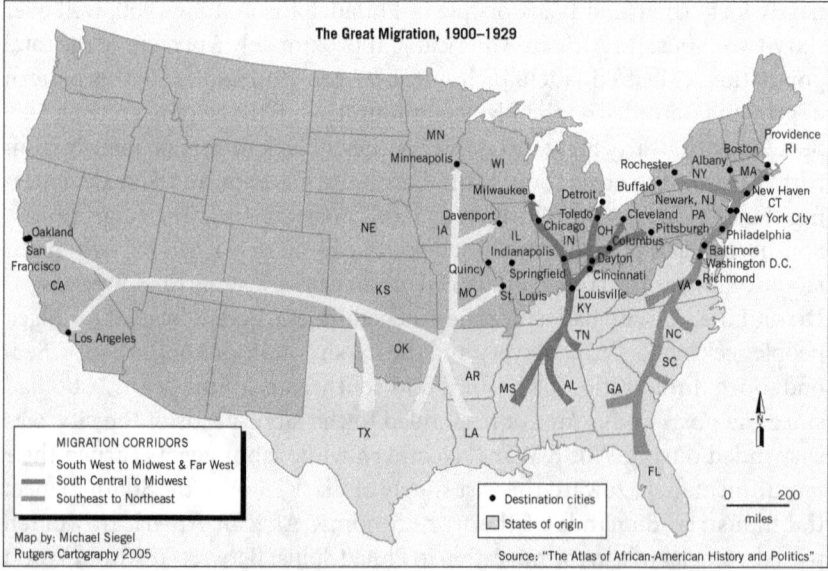

Figure 1.1 Philadelphia was a key destination for African American migrants during the Great Migration.

established middle-class Black Philadelphians recognized that a larger African American community would yield greater political power in the long run. However, the immediate reaction from many native Black Philadelphians, often referred to as the Old Philadelphians, was less optimistic, as most Southern Black migrants were resented because they lacked urbane qualities. Additionally, during the last half of the nineteenth century, changes to the racial and ethnic demography of the city coincided with the rise of Philadelphia's powerful GOP machine, whose political bosses gained power by extending jobs, food, and, at times, money to poor Black people and European immigrants in exchange for their vote. The combination of widespread corruption, poverty, vice, and crime ignited a movement to reform Philadelphia's negative national image and the dominant power local GOP bosses held over the city's wards and municipal institutions. Changes in the city's demography also heightened preexisting levels of anti-Black racism and extralegal violence toward African Americans, which local Black leaders viewed as a crucial failure of the Republican Party to protect the civil rights of Philadelphia's burgeoning Black community and African Americans nationally. During the mayoral elections of 1881 and 1911, these tensions ultimately produced factional divisions within the electorate and spurred an insurgency among Black voters, who on two occasions helped shift the balance of power for control of the city from white GOP managers to white antiestablishment reformers.[2] (See Fig. 1.2.)

This chapter traces the role of electoral and protest activism in the foundation of civil rights liberalism in Philadelphia. By civil rights liberalism, this chapter explicitly means the pursuit of equal political and civil rights for African Americans, including: protection from police brutality, lynching, and all forms of white extralegal violence; voting, to include racial representation in party structures and formal operations of government as well

Figure 1.2
Southern Black migrants heading North.

as equal opportunity in all areas of life, such as the workplace, public education, and all forms of public consumption. More broadly, this case study on Philadelphia makes a larger argument about the making of Black political culture in the industrial urban North during the latter two decades of the nineteenth century and the Progressive Era of the early twentieth century. It reveals how independent Black Progressives resisted political domination by local white Republican ward bosses and how they used balance of power strategies in pursuit of a civil rights agenda. It also reveals why white political reformers failed among Black people, and it uncovers the central role that community-based electoral politics and protests played as tools for preserving local Black political power during a period when political reform by white Northern Progressives mimicked the disenfranchisement strategies of white Southern Democrat segregationists. This chapter builds on what W.E.B. Du Bois called the "paradox of reform" in which he argued that entrenched racist attitudes of white political reformers hindered the growth of higher political morality for Black Philadelphians. African Americans found the egalitarian principles of urban progressivism persuasive and appreciated the use of expertise and high levels of grassroots organizing to reform socioeconomic and sociopolitical inequality but, ultimately, realized that white Social Progressives too readily used antidemocratic urban reforms such as disenfranchisement to control African Americans and the urban poor.[3]

This story of political transformation that gave rise to Black progressives in Philadelphia reflected national trends during the period. Local actions to preserve the ballot held national implications in the fight against disenfranchisement and continued erosion of civil rights protections, on the one hand, and the fight for Black respectability, on the other. Most studies have tended to see the political realignment of Black people to the Democratic Party in 1936 and the post–World War II era worthy of historical analysis, however, the shift of African Americans away from the GOP to reform organizations, while not sustained, remains understudied. The Black political insurgency during the Great Migration of the early twentieth century grew out of a period of cultural and political redefinition known as the New Negro movement. While earlier studies examining the effect of the ballot in this era have mostly focused on the South, this chapter positions Philadelphia and the larger urban North as a critical site for the development of Black politics. From the post–Reconstruction era through the post–World War II period, violent political repression in the South and continued migration of Southern Black people to large industrial urban centers in the North made Northern localities like Philadelphia key places where the ballot was used as a tool for racial reform. These factors not only made Northern localities excellent sites for examining race and democracy; the North is also important if we are to understand the critical role African Americans played as liberal swing voters and why the Progressive political reform movement in the urban North failed among Black people during the period. This moment foreshadowed Black progressive strategies that later defined the African American struggle for political power and civil rights well into the late twentieth century.[4]

By the start of the 1880s, the dual effects of disaffection and insurgency among Black Philadelphians toward the Republican Party could be measured by their responses to the presidential election of 1880 and city elections during the same year. Throughout the presidential campaign Black people across the country were urged to stay "Faithful in the Cornfield, Brave on the Battlefield, Solid for Garfield." Yet, in the years following the Hayes compromise of 1877, this slogan did little to reproduce the type of faithfulness that previously held Black Philadelphians tightly within the party as in the years immediately following the Civil War. For example, while reactions to 1877 did not eliminate Black participation in annual Republican celebrations of the Emancipation Proclamation and Fifteenth Amendment, after 1877 these events no longer possessed their postwar luster. In early 1879, the committee for the Fifteenth Amendment, which included William Still and other notable Black Philadelphia leaders, suggested that passage of the amendment had been a political necessity for the Republican Party rather than a question of rights. The sign of disaffection was undeniable a decade later. In 1889, during the twenty-fifth annual celebration of the Pennsylvania Abolition Society, dubbed an Anniversary of Freedom, the small audience that gathered at Association Hall was two-thirds white despite the presence of Black luminaries like Frederick Douglass, Frances Ellen Watkins Harper, Booker T. Washington, and Still. The event became a moment of embarrassment for white people when Black abolition leader Robert Purvis rose to deliver prepared remarks, threw away the traditional script, and began to criticize a Republican leader of the Philadelphia Department of Public Works for discriminatory treatment of a Black applicant seeking employment within the department. By 1894, the anti-lynching campaign of Ida B. Wells came to Philadelphia's Association Hall. The event drew an overflow crowd, composed of a large percentage of the city's Black population, but event organizers provided no support for partisan politics and relegated white people to seats in the audience rather than on the podium. Throughout the 1890s, Southern violence against African Americans had inspired the national anti-lynching campaign led by Wells and helped propel the Great Migration of Southern Black people into Northern urban industrial centers. It also launched an emerging generation of Black women and men activists who relied on an array of Black urban institutions like the African American press, Black women's clubs, and Black churches to push an agenda for racial justice and social reforms within a new era of American racism labeled the nadir.[5]

As Philadelphia's local elections of 1880–1881 unfolded, growing antipathy among Black voters manifested chiefly over the Republican Party's utter refusal to break the color line in the hiring of Black police officers. During the deeply contested mayoral race, in which Black people and others like the Committee of One Hundred, a group of reform-minded Republican businessmen, and independent Democrats, attempted to stop GOP mayor Bill Stokely from achieving a fourth consecutive term, George Keim, a Republican rival to Stokely indicated to several Black leaders that African Americans who supported the party should receive jobs within the public sector, which included the police department. Keim possessed virtually no credentials within the Black community, but he knew that the issue of breaking the color line in the police department had roots that preceded his campaign. It also persisted well after his campaign collapsed in the beginning of the new year. Prominent Black political leaders, who were courted by all sides, refused to forget the matter. Democrats, independents, and the Committee of One Hundred nominated Samuel L. King, a reform Democratic candidate, to oppose Stokely. King defeated Stokely by five thousand votes. According to historian Harry Silcox, King's victory can be partly attributed to his presence as the lone Democrat to attend the funeral of slain civil rights leader Octavius V. Catto in 1871. Additionally, King's victory suggests insurgent Black voters played a role in shifting the balance of power to a reform Democrat who was willing to honor their demands. By August 1881, King appointed four African Americans to the police department—a move that surprised Democratic supporters and brought joy throughout the Black community.[6]

By 1884, the Republican Party recaptured city hall and successfully relegated the Democratic Party to the margins of Philadelphia's political structure until the presidential election of Franklin Delano Roosevelt in 1932. Equally important, by eliminating the Democratic Party and by opening up a modicum of city jobs, in part through appointments and in part through civil service reforms, as well as supporting Black people for elective posts in the common council, the GOP was able to quell a Black insurgency that led to the first and only reform administration of the nineteenth century. By the time Du Bois completed his study of Philadelphia in 1899, he could point to significant gains. Twenty-nine years after the Fifteenth Amendment was adopted by Congress, Du Bois observed sixty-two Black people who were employed in the city's police department and on patrol in or mostly near Black neighborhoods, although none were promoted; eleven Black people in various municipal departments, for example, one in the customhouse, seventeen in the post office—although none were able to deliver mail in white neighborhoods—and one in the navy yard. Additionally, Philadelphia's African American community was not subjected to racial pogroms and daily breakdowns in law and order that Southern Black people faced. Nor were they subjected to the types of racial segregation in the public schools and transportation system that defined the antebellum period. The progress Du Bois observed was the result of Black electoral and protest activism and grew out of the Fifteenth Amendment. Yet, the political atmosphere Du Bois observed in Philadelphia was anything but rosy. By the time of Du Bois's study, Philadelphia's municipal government and political structure had long gained infamy as one of the most corrupt in the nation. This along with widespread anti-Black discrimination in Philadelphia's industrial landscape led Du Bois to see how most Black voters were vulnerable to the hegemony of white party bosses who instructed them to blindly support the GOP ticket and accept the emoluments of office, a type of indirect bribe, in return for party loyalty. He concluded that any hope for continued racial reform through the ballot resided in a small group of independent Black voters. However, by 1898, Black representation in the common council went from three to one and the nadir of Black independent politics and nullification of Black voting power had been almost totally achieved.[7]

As African American political power receded into the nadir of the late nineteenth century, the level of anti-Black sentiment increased. The dialectical relationship between the loss of political power and an increase in racial hostility toward Black people that unfolded in Philadelphia was part of a broader national story that occurred throughout the industrialized urban North and across the South. Indeed, as the Republican Party, at the local, state, and national levels, continued its retreat from Black civil rights in favor of industrial capitalism and sectional reconciliation, anti-Black racism steadily increased in large Northern urban industrial centers. This was largely due to several key factors. First, the Great Migration of Southern Black people and immigration of Western and Eastern Europeans to Philadelphia's industrial landscape increased competition for jobs and housing between working-class Black people and white people. Second, the inability of African Americans to leverage their voting power for the enforcement of civil rights protections coupled with the absence of a dedicated political ally left them highly vulnerable, especially to the global proliferation of racist and sexist theories, in the form of social Darwinism, which justified racism, political conservatism, and imperialism, and discouraged intervention and reform. Additionally, the Fourteenth Amendment, which extended citizenship to African Americans, provided little consolation when it came to constitutional protection. This might be attributed to the vagueness of language within the Constitution itself. Unlike the Fifteenth Amendment, which clearly prohibited the federal government and states from denying a citizen the right to vote based on race, color, or previous servitude, the Fourteenth Amendment was less clear. Adopted in July 1868, the Fourteenth Amendment declared that "no state shall make or enforce any law which shall abridge the privileges or immunities of citizens of the United States; nor shall any state deprive any person of life, liberty, or property, without due process of law, nor deny to any person within its jurisdiction the equal protection of the laws." The ambiguity associated with what "equal protection under the law" meant presented major challenges during the late nineteenth century, and it remains an unresolved question regarding Black struggles for civil rights protections well into the first two decades of the twenty-first century. This combination of local, regional, and national trends along with the Republican Party's retreat from civil rights set the stage for disaffection among Black voters in the GOP and political factionalism within the Republican Party and triggered some Black people in Philadelphia to turn toward political reform organizations in the early decades of the twentieth century.[8]

During the months leading up to the local elections of 1909, Black political workers who had previously supported the Republican Party aligned with the William Penn Party, an independent reform organization, and actively organized in wards throughout the city. In the Second Division of the Seventh Ward, independent political action by Black people became the target of anti-reform politics and voter intimidation when three Black political workers for the William Penn Party, Edward McKenzie, Garrett Welsh, and Solomon Cole were essentially kidnapped by members of the Philadelphia Police Department. In the case of McKenzie, police entered his home at 707 Lombard Street without a warrant in the early morning before the polls opened on Election Day and placed him under arrest. Welsh and Cole were picked up as they rushed to notify political friends of his jailing. All three were ultimately released half an hour before the polls closed. The following day, the *Philadelphia Inquirer* reported that "Republicans are jubilant over the election and reformers were keenly disappointed." An extreme version of this type of Black voter intimidation and political corruption stretched back to the early period of Reconstruction when the police, working on behalf of Democratic Party ward bosses in the south wards, failed to protect Black voters from hostile political operatives in the Democratic Party during the initial Black vote in 1870 and the assassination of Octavius V. Catto in 1871. From the late nineteenth century through the early decades of the twentieth century, GOP leaders often relied on corrupt elements in police districts who, at times, used violent means to intimidate and control the electorate by suppressing political opposition within the ward. The key to this process resided in the tendering of political assessments, a monetary duty frequently paid by police officers, members of the fire department, and other municipal employees to ward-based political bosses. The collection of political assessments represented how the role of money and the promise of a paid "place" of employment in city government led to a system of corruption and voter intimidation all of which served to regenerate boss control within the GOP and cement their power over the city's vast bureaucracy. This explains the connection between the police department and Thomas S. Duffy, a white GOP leader of the notoriously corrupt Second Division of the Seventh Ward. Duffy orchestrated the kidnapping of Black political workers for organizing against the Republican organization. Furthermore, the suppression of independent Black political activity in the Seventh Ward can be attributed to the gradual development of a small independent political faction among Black voters in the city. This group had become disaffected with the GOP and began a turn toward Philadelphia's political reform movement that expanded after Progressive presidential candidate, Theodore Roosevelt, received unprecedented majorities in Philadelphia and Pennsylvania during the November election of 1904. By 1905, the majorities Roosevelt generated led to a series of local victories by the City Party, the leading reform organization at the time, and triggered a period of insurgency in Philadelphia politics that lasted for a decade.[9]

The following year, insurgents within Philadelphia's Progressive political reform movement set their sights on the gubernatorial election as well as the GOP's tight grip over the state's political structure and economy. Along with reformers throughout Pennsylvania, Progressives mounted challenges to GOP control of the state committee, both houses within the legislature, the governor's office in Harrisburg, and congressional districts across the state. For the first time since the post–Civil War period, the gubernatorial election of 1910 revealed major fault lines in the Republican Party's dominance of the Keystone state's political infrastructure. Pennsylvania had enjoyed a long history as a critical swing state in national elections. Additionally, the state's top GOP leaders held a national reputation as kingmakers when it came to presidential elections. Hence, Republican Party leaders understood the gubernatorial election held important consequences for the 1912 presidential election. They also understood that their success depended on Philadelphia's south wards, a strong Republican base since the late nineteenth century, with large numbers of Jewish and Italian voters and the greatest concentration of Black voters in Pennsylvania.

The election featured a three-way contest between Republican John K. Tener, Democrat Webster Grim, and William H. Berry, representing the state's newest bipartisan reform organization, the Keystone Party, whose headquarters was in Philadelphia. Most African American voters and Black political leaders across the city, particularly in places like the historic Seventh Ward, remained in the Republican Party. Their support for the GOP candidate was not merely tied to blind party loyalty or the dictates of party bosses; African American leaders linked their support in part to the historic relationship they shared with the GOP, their desire for Black representation in the Pennsylvania State House of Representatives, reform of the state's 1887 civil rights law, and an opportunity to reshape the racial power structure with the election of Harry W. Bass.[10]

Bass, who resided at 1426 Lombard Street, was a member of the Pennsylvania Bar and an established political leader among Black Republican voters in the Seventh Ward. Throughout the first decade of the twentieth century, he worked his way up within the GOP organization holding several positions. As a result, Bass became well known among white Republican Party bosses like U.S. senator Boise Penrose, the most powerful GOP leader in the city and state. Born into an old aristocratic family, Penrose was the boss of Philadelphia's Republican Party. His rise to power atop the state's GOP organization was largely due to his close association with nineteenth-century political boss Matthew Quay, who died in 1904. In April 1910, Bass convinced Penrose to support his candidacy in Pennsylvania's Sixth State Legislative District. It is likely that some concern over the threat of factionalism within the Black vote was a decisive factor for Penrose. In addition to the political reform movement, internal tensions for control of the GOP organization were building between Penrose and three brothers: George, William, and Edwin Vare, all of whom were corrupt contractor-politicians popularly known as the "Dukes of South Philadelphia." Bass's nomination, therefore, could have also been part of a power play to redirect Black political support away from the Vares. The GOP's nomination of Bass was the first time in the history of Pennsylvania politics that an African American received the party's nomination for State Assembly, but it was not the first time Black Philadelphians from the Seventh Ward sought racial representation in the state legislature. Nor was it the first time Bass pursued the office. In 1886, Stephen Gipson, a Black candidate for State Assembly from the Seventh Ward, campaigned during the primary for the Republican Party's nomination. Failure of white party leaders to support Gipson's nomination during the convention triggered an insurgency led by the most powerful Black political leader in the Seventh Ward, Gilbert Ball. Ball, a saloon owner and founder of the Matthew S. Quay Club, threatened to run Gipson as an independent during the general election. In 1896, Bass attempted to accomplish what Gipson and Ball failed to achieve. Running as an independent, he only received 590 votes. Two years later, after graduating from the University of Pennsylvania Law School, Bass ran again on the People's Independent Party ticket and lost. The successive losses Bass sustained as a Black independent candidate were the capstone of an African American independent political movement that began in the early 1870s, following passage of the Fifteenth Amendment. Bass's losses also represented the GOP machine's dominance over Philadelphia's political landscape and the nadir of Black independent politics, both of which were fully achieved by the late 1890s. Additional factors such as the death of Ball, in 1890, who had guided expansion of Black political power in the Seventh Ward, from 900 to 2,600 voters, and the gradual increase of Jewish and Italian immigrants into the historic Seventh Ward, indicated that Black Philadelphians, by the beginning of the twentieth century, had lost the ability to leverage their voting strength. With such limited political opportunities for aspiring Black leaders such as Bass, the decision to work within the GOP organization represented a rational choice.[11]

Election results on November 9, 1910, revealed that Bass had beaten his Democratic and Keystone Party challengers by a landslide. He obtained a total of 4,466 votes while his closest competitor, the Keystone candidate, received 581 votes. Additionally, Penrose and the GOP were victorious in their efforts to hold the governorship in Harrisburg. Tener's victory resulted from support he received from the state's two largest cities: Philadelphia and Pittsburgh. However, it was the support he received in Philadelphia, and South Philadelphia in particular, that proved to be pivotal. Republican forces from South Philadelphia produced twenty-one thousand of the thirty-four thousand vote majority Tener received. Given the steady flow of Southern Black people and European immigrants into the wards of South Philadelphia, it is highly likely that the GOP victory in Harrisburg was tied to the nomination of Bass, the African American vote, and that of Eastern and Western Europeans.[12]

Bass's arrival in Harrisburg in January 1911 was met with much pomp and pageantry. According to the *Philadelphia Tribune*, Black Philadelphia's newspaper, approximately 365 African Americans from Philadelphia, who formed the Harry W. Bass Republican Club, formed a long processional that escorted Bass to the state capital. This included a quasimilitary escort by the famous old Grey Invincibles, Pennsylvania's only Black militia. Bass was keenly aware of the historic significance his position held for Black Philadelphians and African Americans throughout the state. He also knew that Black voters from the Seventh Ward expected him to be a champion of civil rights. He immediately set his sights on reforming the state's civil rights law of 1887. Bass recognized that the state's civil rights law held two key flaws when it came to African Americans. First, the law stipulated that plaintiffs could only be awarded up to $100, which was not a significant penalty. Second, Black plaintiffs often encountered steep challenges in court largely because white people denied charges of racism and judges tended to side with them. Ice cream parlors and drugstores, which by the turn of the century were quite popular, were key locales of anti-Black discrimination in the city. As a result, Bass proposed to expand the 1887 statute to include them. The Bass Amendment, or House Bill 298, was first introduced on March 9, 1911. On the bill's second reading on March 22, Bass sought to strengthen the enforcement mechanism. He changed the amendment to state that when "an unusual or excessive price is charged [it] shall be evidence of a purpose and intent to violate the provisions of this Act" and also that establishments having a rule that "persons of a particular color or race are required to sit in or occupy particular or special isolated seats shall be evidence of an intent or purpose to violate the provision of this Act." In early April, House Bill 298 was defeated 71–49 and the Bass Amendment died. The *Pittsburgh Courier*, one of the few nationally syndicated African American newspapers, was quick to issue a strong rebuke of the GOP. According to the editor, failure to support the Bass Amendment was the epitome of Republican hypocrisy: "Credit must be given Speaker Cox, Allen, . . . Halferty, and Geary, who stood up like real Republicans for the Amendment, but they did not control the majority. This is the first time the sincerity of the Republicans has had a test and we need no further proof of the so-called loyalty of the Republican Party. The Negro will have to be shown better and more substantial evidence of a bona fide interest than that manifested in the Bass Amendment before we will follow the red fire of Republican campaign leaders any more. Not that we love the Republican party less but our rights more." For the editor of the *Courier*, the GOP's desertion of the Bass Amendment would not be forgotten.[13]

The introduction of legislation by Bass represented the first attempt to strengthen the state's civil rights laws for African Americans since Reconstruction and the devastating national impact of the 1896 decision *Plessy v. Ferguson*, which nullified the role of federal civil rights protections in public accommodations and legalized the separate but equal doctrine. Equally important, the GOP's failure to support the Bass amendment reflected a continuation of the Republican Party's retreat from Black civil rights that began with the U.S. Supreme Court's nullification of the 1875 Civil Rights Act. Even more disturbing was the lynching of Zachariah Walker, an African American, during the evening of August 13, 1911, in Coatesville, a neighboring city in Chester County. Walker, who had been accused of killing a white police officer, was brutally beaten, dragged from his hospital bed, and burned alive in front of thousands. The Coatesville lynching shocked the nation and ignited an immediate response from the national office of the recently formed NAACP. On June 10, the NAACP sent a committee under the direction of Dr. William A. Sinclair, also from the Seventh Ward, to see President Taft in Washington and request that he strongly denounce lynching in his regular message to Congress. As historian James Campbell has shown, the lynching of Walker represented the continuation of racialized violence and failure of law enforcement to protect African Americans. For Black people in the urban North, the lynching of Walker was a national concern rather than a distinct feature of the Jim Crow South.[14]

As men and women within Philadelphia's Black activist community began mounting grassroots responses to increasing levels of anti-Black discrimination and racial hostility, African American political leaders and voters were also becoming more divided over their relationship with the local Republican Party. It is highly likely that the GOP's refusal to back the Bass Amendment was a key factor but by no means the sole reason. Equally significant, the GOP's narrow victory over the Keystone Party in the elections of 1910 signaled that Progressives intended to launch a strong challenge to Republicans for control of city hall during the mayoral election of 1911. Additionally, the strong showing by Progressives during the elections of 1910 forced Penrose and Philadelphia's GOP organization to embrace a reform agenda. During the GOP primary, Penrose's decision to embrace reform exacerbated preexisting tensions with the Vare brothers when William openly challenged Penrose for dominance by declaring himself a candidate for mayor. The division between Penrose and the Vares also reflected an expanding factional divide among African American political leaders and voters within the Republican Party, the majority of whom backed Penrose's swing toward reform. The general election, which featured two different reform candidates, Rudolph Blankenburg for the Keystone Party and George H. Earle Jr. for the GOP, was a hotly contested battle over ideas of how best to manage the city's government and economy and to eliminate corruption. Penrose had been right to embrace reform, but he underestimated the impact of the power struggle with the Vares and the growing disaffection of Black voters who were angry with the GOP's retreat from civil rights. When the polls closed in November, they revealed that Blankenburg narrowly won by a slim margin of 3,333 votes.[15]

Under the mantra of municipal reform, a renewed spirit of Rooseveltian Progressivism weakened the GOP's grip over city hall and helped usher into power the Keystone Party during the fall elections of 1911. Based on a philosophy that Philadelphia required a form of government whose budget reflected rational economic expenditures and efficient operations, Keystone reformers decried the economic impact of corruption, patronage, and special privilege long associated with municipal government under GOP machine managers. Their reforms focused on two key areas. The first involved the curtailment of the city's annual expenses by creating savings through forced reductions in the municipal workforce, which included the elimination of certain bureaus deemed no longer cost effective. The second involved a call for "pure elections" by systemically eliminating what was seen as special privilege for political operatives (i.e., officeholders whose first loyalty was to partisan organizations) from all areas of municipal service that fell under the control of the mayor. This reflected the ideology of Philadelphia's industrial white elites within the third-party movement who worked hard to develop what sociologist Jerome Hodos calls "a new comprehensive cultural bias for Republican rule, one that resided in a consensual or hegemonic arrangement," the goal of which was to resolve decades of social and political factionalism through uniting the wings of the party, enabling cooperation between elites and professional politicians and promoting harmony between the social classes. While white political reformers in Philadelphia's third-party movement deeply opposed corruption (i.e., the use of patronage and favoritism in city contracts), nearly all saw their political universe within exclusively Republican terms. They were interested in the construction of a new political regime; Black civil rights had not been part of the Keystone Party platform. However, their call for a rational form of municipal government representing the common interests of taxpaying citizens rather than the parochial interests of city ward heelers successfully induced political support from antiorganization Black independents across the city, to include those within Philadelphia's south wards like the Seventh Ward, which had long been considered central to the Republican base. According to the *Philadelphia Inquirer*, in early December, as an estimated twenty-five thousand people marched up Broad Street in Center City to greet Blankenburg, the following observation was made: "The Seventh and Eighth Wards were also united and in their ranks were a good many colored voters."[16]

Blankenburg was not the only person who received the public trust. Richard A. Cooper, a prominent local businessman from the Seventh Ward, had been reelected on the Republican ticket to his third term and received the oath of office as Philadelphia's only African American member of the common council. Cooper was one of several African American leaders whose star was on the rise. One month earlier African Americans throughout Pennsylvania learned that Governor Tener appointed Bass to lead a statewide commission on the Emancipation Proclamation celebration in 1913. Additionally, through the sponsorship of Penrose, Everett J. Waring, an attorney from the Seventh Ward who received distinction as the first African American to appear before the U.S. Supreme Court while arguing for the defense of Black men accused of murder on Navassa Island in 1889, became the first African American appointed as counsel for the Pennsylvania Department of Factory Inspection. This was an important moment in the history of African American political leadership from the Seventh Ward. With the city's only African American representative in the common council and the state's only African American member in the Pennsylvania House of Representatives, the Seventh Ward had emerged as the most important Black political power base simultaneously in Pennsylvania and, arguably, in the urban North.[17]

The Progressive movement and Black insurgency that ushered the Keystone Party into power dramatically shifted the city's political paradigm. For the first time in Philadelphia's twentieth-century political history, control of the city was split between a reform administration in city hall and a Republican machine that controlled the select and common councils. The emergence of a new coalition between a minority of Philadelphia's Black voters and white reformers not only suggested a loss of faith in Republican leadership; it also signaled the arrival of a new form of political optimism. But it remained an open question what it meant for a city whose social and political structures had become increasingly divided over racial issues. Philadelphia's Black voters and political leaders faced this key question during the presidential, congressional, and state elections the following year.[18]

In January 1912, Dr. Richard R. Wright Jr., a nationally renowned Black activist from South Philadelphia and one of the city's most influential scholars, delivered the first of a series of highly publicized lectures at the University of Pennsylvania on what was popularly termed the "Negro problems." Wright claimed that what African Americans faced were not Negro problems but instead a larger societal problem rooted in maladjustment to the American urban environment. The problem, he continued, was not one of ignorance, illiteracy, poverty, vice, immorality, or industrial inefficiency, for these were conditions shared by large numbers of white immigrants who, like Southern Black migrants, were drawn to Philadelphia's industrial landscape. The problem, he concluded, was racial prejudice. Wright drew attention to what Du Bois, in 1900, called the problem of the "color line."[19]

Within days of Wright's first lecture, Mrs. Lela Walker-Bryan discussed the status of African American citizenship in a public forum sponsored by the American Negro Historical Society (ANHS). The ANHS was an important part of Black Philadelphia's public sphere and first emerged in 1897 as an offshoot of the Banneker Literary Institute, which traced its origins back to 1819. The ANHS had roots that connected to free institutions such as the African Methodist Episcopal Church and Prince Hall Masons in the late eighteenth and early nineteenth centuries. It was also part of a rich intellectual tradition within African American political history and an important tool when it came to intellectual combat for the collective advancement of the race. Walker-Bryan falls squarely within this tradition. Although the Fifteenth Amendment denied women the right to vote, since the post–Revolution era in the North and the post–Emancipation era in the South, Black women had actively participated in shaping notions of freedom and political participation within the African American community by engaging in debates, mass meetings, rallies, and parades. As historians Elsa Barkley-Brown and Steven Hahn have observed, institutions like the Black church and ANHS were part of an internal political arena wherein Black women could engage despite being barred from external political spaces. This suggests that Black electoral politics in late nineteenth and early twentieth century Philadelphia, and arguably across the industrialized urban North, was very much viewed as a collective rather than solely male responsibility.[20]

Talks such as those by Wright and Walker-Bryan addressing the lynching of Walker, the growing hostility toward African Americans, and the deterioration of civil rights protections demonstrates that the problem of the color line had reached an epidemic scale during the Progressive Era of the early twentieth century. They also served as a counterbalance to popular as well as academic discourse by white scholars, politicians, journalists, law enforcement officials, and social reformers, all of whom constructed theories to corroborate claims of Black criminality within large Northern urban industrial centers as biological proof of racial inferiority. This type of discourse tended to excuse the Walker lynching as a justifiable response to the "Negro problem." It also led to increased racial tensions between African Americans and European immigrants in both Philadelphia and the city's neighboring communities.[21]

Between 1880 and 1900, the Black population in Philadelphia increased by 60.4 percent and between 1910 and 1920 by 58.9 percent as Southern African American migrants entered the city seeking relief from the vice grip of the Jim Crow South. African American clergy, politicians, activists, social workers, professionals, clubwomen, and intellectuals were acutely aware of the increase in their constituencies—especially in the Seventh and Thirtieth Wards. Wright and Walker-Bryan symbolized the growing presence of a small highly educated, loosely organized vocal faction of politically independent Black elites in South Philadelphia who reached political maturity during the Progressive Era of Theodore Roosevelt. They were essentially Republican in their political principles but antiorganization in political practice and thus held no fealty to the GOP. This group favored resolving racial inequality in ways that differed strategically from the Black Republican faithful. An example of this can been seen in early February 1912, when members of an interracial delegation of clergy and civic leaders amplified Wright and Walker-Bryan's message during a meeting with Blankenburg. They discussed the economic condition of the city's African American community and increasing levels of anti-Black hostility. Led by Black independents James Samuel Stemons and G. Edward Dickerson along with prominent Black pastors C. Albert Tindley, William A. Creditt, and E. W. Moore, the delegation declared: "We affirm that the cumulative effects of high-handed antagonism to the social order have been unbounded in augmenting popular feeling against the entire colored race, with the concomitant hardships of lynching, mob violence, segregation and exclusion from the broad fields of labor." They went on to call for citywide mobilization of the entire African American congregational community to agitate for greater civic decency and political honesty. Black Progressives saw the reform coalition as an opportunity to leverage votes they influenced to advance a liberal racial agenda that had gone unsupported under previous conservative Republican administrations. Like their white contemporaries, Black Progressives were concerned with what Robert Wiebe identified as the inability of piecemeal local government to manage a range of urban issues with a level of expertise and economy that an articulate citizenry had come to expect. Black Progressives also deeply believed that government had a primary responsibility to protect the civil rights of African Americans. That belief was amplified during a mass protest meeting in mid-February.[22]

During the evening of Lincoln's birthday, the local chapter of the National Independent Political League convened a large rally of Black Progressive leaders, some of whom were tightly aligned with the Niagara movement and others who tended to support the theories of Booker T. Washington at the Zion Baptist Church. The rally was largely a response to the lynching of Zachariah Walker. Under the banner "Lynch Law Must Go," an interracial lineup of speakers, including those from the national NAACP office in New York, were joined by local Black leaders such as former North Carolina congressman George H. White as well as Black independents such as Dr. Sinclair, Reverend Creditt, and Reverend Moore to discuss strategies for improving Black civil and political rights.[23]

Moore opened the meeting with a fiery condemnation of mob violence and Jim Crow culture. Several speakers in succession echoed his rebuke. According to Creditt's account, all speakers argued for the elimination of lynching and were prepared to do everything in their power to persuade the federal government to protect the civil rights of African Americans. "We believe," he said, "that the General Government at Washington has the power to put an end to this iniquity and disgrace—lynch law."[24]

Like Moore and Creditt, Sinclair saw lynching as a failure of the federal government to protect African Americans, but he also viewed it as a major crisis of Black political leadership—namely that of Booker T. Washington. He argued that the nation's most recognized African American leader did not speak out boldly on important questions that affected the race for fear that "Negro-haters" would burn down the Tuskegee Institute. For Sinclair, a leader who could not speak out boldly could not in turn successfully lead their people. A leader should be free to champion the cause of his people and cannot do so if he has a padded mouth, Sinclair claimed. He further stated that Washington's attitude had been revealed in numerous public declarations and conclusively showed that the "Sage from Tuskegee" did not possess the will to represent the political and civil aspirations of African Americans. African Americans did not need, he continued, a full-time officeholder, someone who dispensed a few political jobs. Nor did Black people need a remorseless political boss or manager. What the nation's African American community needed, he claimed, was a leadership structure that would be free and untrammeled to "cry out from the housetops against the terrible wrongs and inhumanities which are daily inflicted on our people."[25]

Sinclair provided four points to support his argument. None seemed more devastating than his indictment of Washington's views on the role of the ballot. Washington, he claimed, had taken a position that it was a mistake to have given suffrage to the Black race. This, he believed, was a position that flew in the face of history: "As everyone who has studied the history of Reconstruction knows, there was no other possible way to establish Free Government in the Seceding States, except through the Negro ballot. The temper of the white people of the South made the accomplishment by any other means absolutely impossible." In addition, Sinclair argued, "He has declared that the ballot is unnecessary for the Negro's success and prosperity, and he has advised that the Negro should retire from politics. This position is monstrous. It appears to me to be self-evident that practically all that the colored people have gained in education, culture, material prosperity, religious freedom, and potency, and in sum total of life during the last fifty years of pathetic and heroic struggle, have come to them through the gateway of politics. If the gateway of politics is closed against the colored race, in a hundred years they would be doomed to a worse fate than their fathers in the days of slavery. They would become serfs and pariahs—an outcast people."[26]

Sinclair's critique of Washington was not unique. Such critiques occurred in many urban centers across the country and reflected a fluid moment in African American political culture during the early twentieth century. At the center was a generational divide between two competing forms of Black progressivism: between Booker T. Washington, an older Southerner born into slavery, and W.E.B. Du Bois, a younger New England–born elite of free ancestry who came of age during the post–Reconstruction era. These tensions were further complicated by the ways in which Black migration from rural to urban centers, northern migration of Southern African Americans, European immigration, and the expansion of urban industrialization intersected with the proliferation of Jim Crow and the ongoing problem of racial violence in the nation's cities. In an examination of the NAACP and race relations in the United States in the early twentieth century, historian Charles Kellogg documented the intense racial violence African Americans faced in the South and North during the period of the Great Migration from the Gilded Age through the post–World War I era. In three decades, from 1889 to 1918, a total of 3,224 persons, including 61 women, were lynched. And yet, while the vast majority of lynchings occurred in the South, the North, especially the Midwestern region, also adhered to what historian John Hope Franklin termed "this ancient barbaric ritual of total disregard for the law."[27]

An epidemic of race riots, white-led attacks against communities of color, further complicated the lawlessness of lynching. As lynching as a practice of mob law decreased, race riots increased. In the South, the most sensational race riot took place in Atlanta during the early fall of 1906. For several days, the riot paralyzed the city, factories closed, and virtually all transportation came to a halt. By its conclusion, four African Americans, all of whom were middle class, were killed, many more were injured, and the homes of African Americans were looted and burned. The North was just as hostile. As the migration of African Americans into Northern cities continued, they faced frequent attacks from white mobs. Franklin noted on several occasions white people dragged Black people off streetcars in Philadelphia, with cries of "Lynch him! Kill him!" The riot in Abraham Lincoln's hometown, Springfield, Illinois, in August 1908 was by far the most notorious. Two days after the riot began, order within the city was only restored after the governor mobilized more than five thousand national guardsmen. However, before it was over two African Americans were lynched, one of the murders occurring within a half mile of the only home Lincoln owned and within two miles of the great emancipator's final resting place. Additionally, four white men were killed and more than seventy persons were injured. Even though police made more than one hundred arrests and a grand jury handed down over fifty indictments, the alleged leaders of the mob that began the riot went unpunished.[28]

International events such as the political mobilization of American Jews around the pogroms against Russian Jews also shaped local efforts to find an appropriate political solution to the growing problem of the color line and the devastating impact of white supremacy that Black people encountered in Philadelphia as well as the rest of the nation. For leaders like Creditt, the political response of American Jews to the violent persecution of Russian Jews offered an important lesson concerning the plight of African Americans. In a letter to the editor of the *Philadelphia Tribune* in March 1912, Creditt argued that while African Americans were blocked because of skin color and, therefore, incapable of fully developing themselves into an economic force as had American Jews, Black people in the North could develop into a powerful political force. "The Negroes in this section of the country where they have the right of franchise have a mighty power in the ballot. Let them, as the Hebrew, remember that, no matter how high they themselves may develop, their development, opportunities and successes are only theirs in order to help their suffering brethren, and that they are connected by blood with the Negroes who suffer in certain sections of our country. If the Hebrews in America can succeed in having America protect the Hebrews in Russia, why may not the Negroes of the North so use their political power as to cause the statesmen of this section to come boldly out in their utterances and say, 'Lynch Law Must Go.'"[29]

Creditt had reacted in part to the strategic way American Jews used their political power to pressure the federal government to abrogate the Treaty of 1832 that regulated trade with Russia. Seeking to end the violent persecution of Russian Jews that began during the late nineteenth century, local leaders of Philadelphia's Jewish American community like Judge Mayer Sulzberger successfully lobbied President Taft not to renew the treaty when it expired on January 1, 1913.[30]

The efforts of Sulzberger and the Jewish American Committee proved instructive. They illustrated how a minority group could use its political power to marshal government resources to act on its behalf. Creditt's decision to publish his thoughts in the *Tribune* underscored use of the ballot as a key tactic for resolving issues of lynching and other forms of white vigilante injustice. The publication of Creditt's letter in March 1912 coincided with the beginning of an important political cycle on federal, state, and local levels. The most important of these races involved the presidency, Congress, and the state legislature. A mass protest rally at Zion Baptist Church and the debates that followed indicated how Black political leaders intended to use the ballot as a central tool in the fight against racial inequality in upcoming elections.

The appeal of progressivism in Philadelphia expanded within the African American community during the presidential campaign of 1912 when the major candidates, William Howard Taft, Theodore Roosevelt, and Woodrow Wilson, turned their attention to Philadelphia. Roosevelt ran on the Progressive Party ticket, while Wilson, a Northern Progressive Democrat with Southern roots, embraced many of Roosevelt's domestic reforms in his campaign. The campaign generated heated debates in a city torn between a strong Republican machine and an emerging progressive reform organization. Progressives were energized by Teddy Roosevelt and saw an opportunity to challenge the political establishment. The key to their success was African American voters, who, as a voting bloc, held the balance of power. In 1910, of the three largest cities north of the Mason-Dixon Line, Philadelphia's African American community constituted the largest percentage of Black people per capita. According to the 1910 U.S. Census, Philadelphia's African American community totaled 84,459 or 5.5 percent of the total population, whereas New York City's African American community totaled 91,709 or 1.9 percent of the total population, Chicago's African American community totaled 44,103 or 2.0 percent of the total population, Boston's Black community totaled 13,564 or 2.0 percent of the total population, and

Detroit's Black community totaled 5,741 or 1.2 percent of the total population. When it came to electoral politics, Philadelphia's Black voters held a significant share of the balance of power in the urban North.[31]

Until this point, most Black voters had been loyal to the GOP. However, because the party was increasingly resistant to addressing the escalating concerns of African Americans regarding protection of their political and civil rights, during the presidential election Black Progressives turned toward the reform candidates, Roosevelt and Wilson.

Early polling revealed that Roosevelt and Wilson were outpacing Taft, the Republican incumbent, and other lesser-known presidential candidates. The Keystone Party's postcard campaign suggested that Roosevelt had a commanding lead over Wilson. The returns also revealed that Wilson had outperformed Taft, Robert La Follette, and other candidates. By the end of February, Penrose acknowledged that the Republicans had a problem, admitting that Roosevelt and the Progressive forces behind him posed a serious threat to Taft. Despite Roosevelt's decision during the days leading up to the primary to keep the Southern wing of the Progressive Party lily-white by excluding Southern Black delegates from the national convention, a significant number of rank-and-file voters within Philadelphia's African American community were willing to support him. They were drawn to the former Republican president's national reform agenda, which offered a chance for full political recognition to Northern Black people. A smaller number of Philadelphia's Black Progressives turned to Wilson. They did not believe in the Democratic Party or dislike Roosevelt. Instead, they supported Wilson because of a deep desire for political independence and a belief that the Southern Democrat and president of Princeton University did not possess the type of provincialism that symbolized the new South.[32]

Tensions in urban politics over the presidential campaign played out in a congressional race as well. On March 30, George H. White, an African American attorney who worked in the banking industry, announced his candidacy for Congress in the city's First Congressional District, which was holding a special election to fill a vacancy caused by the recent death of Civil War hero General Henry Bingham. White, who represented North Carolina's Second Congressional District from 1897 to 1901, was an experienced politician. Migrating from North Carolina shortly after the turn of the century, White took up residence at 1508 Lombard Street, in the heart of the African American community's Seventh Ward. In addition to establishing himself as a member of the Pennsylvania Bar, White was president of the People's Savings Bank, the first, and at the time only, local Black-owned banking institution in the Seventh Ward, and a member of the Citizens Republican Club (CRC). His two terms in the House of Representatives coincided with the decline of Black political power from its zenith in the

1870s, when sixteen Black people served in Congress and many others were elected to various state legislatures across the country. In 1901, White, hailing from North Carolina's "Black Second," held the distinction as the nation's last Black member of Congress. He also held a national reputation as a fighter for his race. During White's final year in Congress, three years after the Wilmington, North Carolina, massacre of 1898 in the state's Sixth Congressional District, where an angry mob of white men seeking to end African American participation in politics killed nearly three hundred Black people, he introduced the first piece of legislation that sought to make lynching a federal crime. Before departing, White informed his colleagues that his departure would not be the end of Black representation in Congress when he declared, "This, Mr. Chairman, is perhaps the Negroes' temporary farewell to the American Congress; but . . . phoenix-like he will rise up some day and come again."[33] (See Fig. 1.3.)

White was Philadelphia's first Black congressional candidate. His campaign marked the first serious attempt by African Americans to regenerate Black political power in Congress since the Gilded Age, and he made federal protection from racism, lynching, and mob violence central to his platform. White reminded local and state party leaders of the value of the Black vote when he told them: "In Pennsylvania, in many of the Congressional districts, they hold the balance of power and have uniformly thrown that power to the nominee of the Republican party." With the primary scheduled for April 12, White extended the protest campaign against lynching that

Figure 1.3 Former congressman George White campaigned for Philadelphia's First Congressional District to restore Black representation to the U.S. House of Representatives.

began at Zion Baptist Church in early February, and he made Philadelphia a key site for the regeneration of Black political power in Congress. Black congressional power was now a campaign issue, one that affected ten million Black citizens, and one he strategically forced local and state Republican leaders to address.[34]

Although White was widely considered to be one of the most capable statesmen of his race, his campaign failed. The absence of a Black belt of voters in the First Congressional District greatly hurt his chances. Additionally, Republican Party leaders were not supportive of his campaign. South Philadelphia Republican boss, William Vare, had little interest in supporting White or his campaign for Black civil rights. After losing a brutal campaign that severely divided the local Republican Party and resulted in Progressives claiming the mayoralty, Vare set his eyes on the vacancy in the First Congressional District. The state's Republican boss Penrose, whose constituency included working-class African Americans but also a large number of white ethnic Irish, Italians, and Jews, many of whom held deep anti-Black sentiments and opposed African American political interests, also refused to support White's candidacy. This was another moment when the GOP could have signaled its intentions to strengthen its relationship with the city's Black voters. Instead, the Republican organization's leaders decided they had more to gain by supporting the congressional aspirations of Vare and solidifying the party against the growing power of Progressive forces.[35]

Unlike 1896, when White was elected to Congress by an interracial coalition of Republicans and Populists in North Carolina's "Black Second," the political landscape of Philadelphia during the presidential election of 1912 offered no such opportunity. As an African American, he found no space in local party politics to regenerate Black political power on the federal level or gain support from GOP bosses. That lack of support held true for the local Progressive Party, too. Shortly after assuming control of city hall during the early months of 1912, the city's Progressive Party immediately reneged on its promise to build an inclusive government with the city's Black leaders. Although the city's newly elected reform mayor stated during the mayoral election that merit, not politics, would determine who would keep their municipal jobs, as early as mid-March 1912, reports surfaced that Black clerks with long-term experience were being replaced with inexperienced white Keystone Party supporters. The continued expulsion of Black people in municipal employment who gained their berth through the Republican organization, attempts by Progressives to eliminate Bass in the upcoming election, and their efforts to eliminate Black committeemen within the Seventh Ward led the *Tribune*'s editor to call the Keystone Party a "white man's party."[36]

White's campaign reveals much about African American urban political history in cities like Philadelphia during the early twentieth century.

Although he failed to secure the nomination, his campaign placed significant pressure on Penrose to protect limited examples of African American political power. The reelection of Bass, whose seat had been targeted by white reformers, offers such an example. By winning election in 1910, Bass not only gave Black people their first racial representative in the Pennsylvania House of Representatives; with Cleveland's Harry Clay Smith's loss in 1902, Bass became the only African American state legislator in the country. His election indirectly restored Black state-level representation nationally. Pressure from White's campaign and the gradual defection of Black voters to reformers indicates that the preservation of GOP political power, not racial liberalism, was the primary motive behind white Republican managers' modest support. Equally important, the failure of White's campaign to attract support from the GOP and the city's reform party reveals that, by spring of 1912, the industrialized urban North mirrored the racism in the South when it came to disenfranchising Black people by denying them any chance to win elective office on the federal level. Black Philadelphians did not achieve racial representation in Congress until the election of Democrat Robert N. C. Nix Sr. in 1958.[37]

The general election in November 1912 produced important outcomes that significantly shaped the trajectory of African American electoral politics, reform organizational politics, and partisan politics in Philadelphia until the early years of the civil rights movement during the Cold War era. On the local level, GOP bosses provided strong organizational support for the reelection of Bass against the local reform organization's white candidate. Bass won by a substantial margin. His reelection had been a rejection of reform democracy by Black voters in the Seventh Ward. It was also an indicator that flirtation with the local reform organization held serious consequences for Black political interests. It also showed that as long as reformers remained a threat to Republican power in the ward, the Black vote held the balance of power. During local elections in the fall of 1913, Black leaders in the Seventh Ward returned to the same balance of power strategy to retain racial representation in the common council after Democrats and reformers sought to eliminate the only Black member in city council.

The struggle for power between the African American community, Philadelphia's reform organization, and the Republican Party reveals how Black people effectively used the ballot to preserve access to the political arena and local institutions of self-governance at a time when political reform in the industrialized urban North acted as a variant of Southern disenfranchisement. No example symbolized this more than the racial exclusionary policies of the newly elected Progressive Democratic president, Woodrow Wilson, which gave Southern Democrats control of all branches of the federal government.

Shortly after his inauguration Wilson promptly directed his cabinet to reverse a long-standing policy of racial integration in the federal service. Some federal offices set up screens to separate white and Black workers. African Americans also experienced great difficulty securing high-level civil service positions, which some had held under previous Republican administrations. The following year, in response to Wilson's actions, a delegation of Black Progressives from the National Independent Political League led by William Monroe Trotter appeared at the White House to protest the president's new policy of segregation.[38]

By 1914, Philadelphia's African American community began to unify their power as a bloc vote in support of Penrose and the Republican Party. During a meeting in late January, Penrose turned to Black Philadelphians to support his reelection. Among those who met with Penrose was *Tribune* editor, Christopher Perry. Perry acknowledged Penrose's record as a staunch advocate in Washington when it came to supporting the political and economic interests of Pennsylvanians. This included Penrose's support to Judge Mayer Sulzberger and the Jewish American Committee's campaign against Russia's violent persecution of Jews. Perry asked the state's most powerful Republican leader why his voice had been silent in the halls of the U.S. Senate regarding the Constitutional interests of loyal Black Republicans in Pennsylvania and the nation. There is no evidence of a response to Perry's question. Two months later, during an evening rally at Varrick Temple, Penrose continued to pivot away from an accounting of his silence on Black political and civil rights. Instead, he spoke about valuable lessons from Pennsylvania's Emancipation Exposition of 1913, the historic relationship between the Republican Party and African Americans, and attempts by the Wilson administration and the Democratic Party to undo the GOP's historic legacy regarding Black Constitutional rights. Among the city's prominent Black antimachine advocates who spoke in favor of Penrose's reelection were Richard R. Wright Jr. and William A. Sinclair.[39]

Although Penrose did not directly seek to protect and promote Black political and civil rights, he and other Senate Republicans from the Northeast did indirectly support Black Constitutional rights when they blocked further attacks against the Fifteenth Amendment during the Sixty-First and Sixty-Second Congresses. They successfully defeated state's rights resolutions from Southern Democrat segregationists and Northern Progressive senators, like La Follette, of Wisconsin, that would have eliminated federal oversight of the Seventeenth Amendment and given exclusive control of senatorial elections to states. The decision by Northeast Republicans in the U.S. Senate to block Southern Democrats' and Northern Progressives' efforts to disenfranchise Black people was in no small measure motivated by GOP ambitions for future political fortune given the large and growing number of Black voters in the urban North. This was, in fact, the case with Penrose. However, it also reflected the attention that the Black vote commanded.[40]

Additionally, while Black independents and stalwarts did not receive the same outcome as Sulzberger and the Jewish American Committee, they were aware that Penrose opposed a Progressive-segregationist alliance in the Senate. This indicates their successful use of the vote to halt further attacks against Black suffrage regarding the direct election of U.S. senators. Essentially, by 1914, nihilistic attacks of Progressive political reformers and the racial exclusionary policies of the Wilson White House helped align the national political interests of Philadelphia's Black Progressives with the reelection of Penrose, the state's most powerful political boss.[41]

After Penrose's reelection, the city's Black political leaders focused their attention on the upcoming mayoral election and the elimination of the local reform party from power. No issue fueled their political activities more than the color line. In June 1915, Perry made the case that a Republican mayor would be more inclusive of the city's Black citizens. He also attacked those who used the color line. "We draw no color line on any one, but when one draws it upon us, in politics or any other place, we conceded his right to do it, when not restrained by law, but at the same time we reserve the right to draw it upon him."[42] According to the *Tribune*, Black citizens believed that the concept of good municipal government was one grounded in policies of racial inclusion rather than exclusion and that the politics of race could be used to achieve either. In a Republican administration, he emphasized, the city's Black citizens could expect fair consideration of their roles as taxpayers and voters. The call for reconciliation between the Black vote and the Republican Party was connected to a national strategy. Because of the 1916 presidential election, Perry and Penrose argued that the restoration of GOP control in city hall held national implications for both the Republican Party and African American political interests. "Senator Penrose points out also," Perry concluded, "the fact that unusual interests will attach to the municipal election in Philadelphia this year because of the Presidential election next year. Philadelphia should get in line to help drive the Democratic Party out of the White House and conduct of the affairs of the Nation."[43]

As the campaign for the city's new mayor moved toward the fall primary, tensions between the city's Black citizens and the reform administration shifted from protest to physical confrontation on Broad Street in the city's downtown section. In late September, the director for public safety and reform mayoral candidate, George D. Porter, led police in what the *Tribune* termed a "brutal attack" against unarmed African American men, women, and children. The repressive actions of the police had been a direct response to a peaceful protest march organized by the National Independent Political League. The march was in opposition to the film *Birth of a Nation* at the Forrest Theatre, located on Walnut Street. Given the utter absence of lawlessness on behalf of protesters, this evidence suggests that Porter's decision to deploy the police had been politically motivated rather than out of a need to restore law and order. Porter's decision also ran contrary to one of Blankenbug's key campaign promises to halt the use of police in local politics. For the city's African American voters, the clubbing of Black protesters was viewed as the final litmus test of racial exclusion and a symbol of what could be expected of the next reform administration.[44]

By the mayoral election of 1915, Black Philadelphians understood that new strategies for mobilization and institutions were necessary if they were to succeed in driving the reform party out of power. African American leaders from the Seventh Ward organized Black men and women political workers throughout the city. This marked the genesis of what would later be known as the United Republican Workers Association. What had been the Afro-American Congressional Committee in 1912 reemerged as the Colored Republican Central Committee during the 1915 mayoral election. They adopted as their motto, "Vigilance Is the Eternal Price of Liberty." Throughout the election, the committee campaigned in Black neighborhoods across the city citing the failures of reformers to bring an efficient business administration to the city, its unrelenting policies of racial exclusion, and the beating of women and children during the protest march. In a three-way contest during November 1915, Republicans recaptured city hall by an overwhelming majority. The African American effort to oust the reform party was more than a local victory. The segregationist policies of Wilson and the influence of Southern Democrats in national politics meant that Black people were shut out of the nation's political structure. During the post–World War I years, many African Americans faced increasing levels of racism as they struggled to hold onto their wartime jobs. Returning Black soldiers confronted joblessness and the irony of having fought for freedom abroad only to face the Ku Klux Klan, which, unlike its Southern beginning during Reconstruction, was based chiefly in the North and exerted significant political influence in all levels of U.S. politics from 1915 through 1925. Additionally, the political use of local, and at times national, law enforcement to disrupt Black protest politics in Philadelphia and other urban centers across the nation not only persisted throughout the long twentieth century, it has lasted beyond the first two decades of the twenty-first century. The unprovoked attack against African Americans during the protest of *Birth of a Nation* in Philadelphia reflects the roots of a larger, complex, and unresolved national pattern of white supremacy and racial violence, including extra-judicial racial repression, to Black political activism and Black social mobility.[45]

As northward migration, legal disenfranchisement, and acts of violent extralegal repression during the early decades of the twentieth century rendered more and more of the Black vote inconsequential in local, state, and national elections in the South, Black electoral and protest activism in Philadelphia reflected the growing significance of Northern urban industrial centers in the East, Midwest, and West as the most important fronts in the African American struggle for political recognition and civil rights from the early decades of the twentieth century through the post–World War II years of the modern civil rights movement. Equally significant, while Black settlement occurred across southern, western, and northern regions of the city between 1890 and the 1920s, the Seventh, Thirtieth, and Thirty-Sixth of the city wards not only reflected concentrated areas of Black settlement and political power, they also constituted critical sites of hope for racial, political, and civil integration as African Americans fought to maintain access to the gateway of electoral politics in the urban North.

NOTES

1. Robert Gregg, *Sparks from the Anvil of Oppression: Philadelphia's African American Methodists and Southern Migrants, 1890–1940* (Philadelphia: Temple University Press, 1993), 24, 25, 28; Vincent P. Franklin, *The Education of Black Philadelphia: The Social and Educational History of a Minority Community, 1900–1950* (Philadelphia: University of Pennsylvania Press, 1979), 12; Sadie Tanner Mossell, "The Standard of Living among One Hundred Negro Migrant Families in Philadelphia," *Annals of the American Academy of Political and Social Science* 98 Child Welfare (November 1921): 173–174; Kimberley L. Phillips, *Alabama North: African American Migrants, Community, and Working-Class Activism in Cleveland, 1915–45* (Urbana: University of Illinois Press, 1999), 16–17; Joe William Trotter Jr., "The Great Migration," *OAH Magazine of History* 17, no. 1, World War I (October 2002): 31; Joe William Trotter Jr., *Black Milwaukee: The Making of an Industrial Proletariat, 1915–45* (Urbana: University of Illinois Press, 1988), 8; Frederic Miller, "The Black Migration to Philadelphia: A 1924 Profile," *Pennsylvania Magazine of History and Biography* 108, no. 3 (July 1984): 317; James Wolfinger, "African American Migration," *The Encyclopedia of Greater Philadelphia*, accessed April 14, 2020, available at https://philadelphiaencyclopedia.org/archive/african-american-migration/.

2. C. L. Harris, "Race, Leadership, and the Local Machine: The Origins of the African American Struggle for Political Recognition and the Politics of Community Control, 1915–1968" (Ph.D. diss., University of Pennsylvania, 2013), 47–50; Roger Lane, *William Dorsey's Philadelphia and Ours: On the Past and Future of the Black City in America* (New York: Oxford University Press, 1991), 257–258.

3. This argument aligns with a growing body of literature that argues against "southern exceptionalism" within African American civil rights historiography. Monographs by W.E.B. Du Bois, *The Philadelphia Negro* (Philadelphia: University of Pennsylvania Press, 1899), 368, 383; Thomas J. Sugrue, *Sweet Land of Liberty: The Forgotten Struggle*

for Civil Rights in the North; Robert O. Self, *American Babylon: Race and Struggle in Postwar Oakland*, and Matthew J. Countryman, *Up South: Civil Rights and Black Power in Philadelphia* have all challenged the geographic primacy of the South in our understanding of the emergence of the African American civil rights movement after World War II. Similarly, Heather Cox Richardson, *West from Appomattox: The Reconstruction of America after the Civil War*; Hugh Davis, *"We Will Stand for Nothing Less": The African American Struggle for Equal Rights in the North during Reconstruction* (Ithaca, NY: Cornell University Press, 2011), pp. ix–xi; and Andrew Diemer, "Reconstructing Philadelphia: African Americans and Politics in the Post–Civil War North," *Pennsylvania Magazine of History and Biography* 133, no. 1 (January 2009) have called into question the role of the South in our understanding of African American activism and Reconstruction.

4. My argument on Black politics in the Progressive Era builds on the work of other scholars such as John Hope Franklin and Alfred A. Moss Jr., *From Slavery to Freedom: A History of African Americans*, 7th ed. (New York: McGraw-Hill, 1994), 311; and August Meier, *Negro Thought in America, 1880–1915* (Ann Arbor: University of Michigan, 1969), 188–189. Meier supports this argument. He states that the Progressive movement of 1912 provided an indication of the left of center swing on the Black vote. Allan H. Spear, *Black Chicago: The Making of a Negro Ghetto, 1880–1920* (Chicago: University of Chicago Press, 1967), 79. David M. Katzman, *Before the Ghetto: Black Detroit in the Nineteenth Century* (Urbana: University of Illinois Press, 1975), 204–210; Linda Gordon, SHGAPE Distinguished Historian Address, "If Progressives Were Advising Us Today, Should We Listen," *Journal of the Gilded Age and Progressive Era* 1, no. 2 (April 2002): 110–113; Modupe Labode, "'Defend Your Manhood and Womanhood Rights': The Birth of a Nation, Race, and the Politics of Respectability in Early Twentieth Century Denver, Colorado," *Pacific Historical Review* 84, no. 2 (May 2015): 164–165; Alain L. Locke, *The New Negro: Voices of the Harlem Renaissance* (New York: Touchstone Books, 1925), 10–11. On the ballot as uplift, Kevin K. Gaines represents the dominant study on the topic. See Gaines, *Uplifting the Race: Black Leadership, Politics, and Culture in the Twentieth Century* (Chapel Hill: University of North Carolina Press, 1996), xi–xv. On FDR and the New Deal, see Nancy J. Weiss, *Farewell to the Party of Lincoln: Black Politics in the Age of FDR* (Princeton, NJ: Princeton University Press, 1983), viii–ix. Weiss's book remains an important work in Black political realignment to the Democratic Party. However, the book focuses on the national story and overlooks the local.

5. Patricia A. Schechter, *Ida B. Wells-Barnett and American Reform, 1880–1930* (Chapel Hill: University of North Carolina Press, 2001), chapter 3; Lane, *William Dorsey's Philadelphia and Ours*, 204; Meier, *Negro Thought in America*, 21–23.

6. Lane, *William Dorsey's Philadelphia and Ours*, 210–212; Harry C. Silcox, "The Black 'Better Class' Political Dilemma: Philadelphia Prototype Isaiah C. Wears," *Pennsylvania Magazine of History and Biography* 113, no. 1 (January 1989), 57–58, 60, 62–63.

7. Lane, *William Dorsey's Philadelphia and Ours*, 197, 206, 213–215, 221, 222; Silcox, "Black 'Better Class' Dilemma," 62–64; Du Bois, *The Philadelphia Negro*, 372–384; Peter McCaffery, *When Bosses Ruled Philadelphia: The Emergence of the Republican Machine, 1867–1933* (University Park: Pennsylvania State University Press, 1993), 54–55, 73–74.

8. Lane, *William Dorsey's Philadelphia and Ours*, 197.

9. "Republicans Are Jubilant over the Election," *Philadelphia Inquirer*, November 4, 1909, 1–2; Lane, *William Dorsey's Philadelphia and Ours*, 119; Ira V. Brown, "Pennsylvania and the Rights of the Negro," *Pennsylvania History: A Journal of Mid-Atlantic Studies* 28, no. 1 (January 1961): 53–54; Hugh Davis, "The Pennsylvania Equal Rights League and the Northern Black Struggle for Legal Equality, 1864–1877," *Pennsylvania*

Magazine of History and Biography 126, no. 4 (October 2002): 631; Harry C. Silcox, *Philadelphia Politics from the Bottom Up: The Life of Irishman William McMullen, 1824–1901* (Philadelphia: Balch Institute, 1989), 77–82; Silcox, "Black 'Better Class' Dilemma," 49; Edward Price, "The Black Voting Rights Issue in Pennsylvania, 1780–1900," *Pennsylvania Magazine of History and Biography* 100, no. 3 (July 1976): 369–370. "Earl Foresees End of Clay Tyranny," *Philadelphia Inquirer*, September 23, 1911, 2; "Blankenburg Says Campaign Pledges Will Be Kept," November 9, 1911, 1–2; Julie Davidow, "A Political Challenge: Reformers, Republicans, and the Black Vote in 1890s Philadelphia," *Pennsylvania Legacies* 11, no. 2 (November 2011): 11. "Police Guilty of Kidnapping Reform Voters," *Philadelphia Inquirer*, December 9, 1910, 1; "Superior Court Hears Appeal of Policemen," *Philadelphia Inquirer*, October 21, 1911, 4. On the Progressive reform movement in the early twentieth century including police in politics, see William H. Issel, "Modernization in Philadelphia School Reform," *Pennsylvania Magazine of History and Biography* 94, no. 3 (1970): 378–381; Lloyd M. Abernethy, "Insurgency in Philadelphia in 1905," *Pennsylvania Magazine of History and Biography* 87, no. 1 (January 1963): 3, 6–11; McCaffery, *When Bosses Ruled Philadelphia*, 140–141; C. L. Harris, "Race, Leadership, and the Local Machine: The Origins of the African American Struggle for Political Recognition and the Politics of Community Control, 1915–1968" (Ph.D. diss., University of Pennsylvania, 2013), chapter 3; Arthur P. Dudden, "Lincoln Steffens' Philadelphia," *Pennsylvania History: A Journal of Mid-Atlantic Studies* 31, no. 4 (October 1964): 456–458; Abernethy, "Insurgency in Philadelphia in 1905," 3.

10. Davidow, "Political Challenge," 10; "Wm Penn Men Will Talk over Senatorship," *Philadelphia Inquirer*, April 22, 1910, 4; "5000 Colored Voters Applaud Candidate Tener," *Philadelphia Inquirer*, November 1, 1910, 2; Eric Ledell Smith, "Asking for Justice and Fair Play: African American State Legislators and Civil Rights in Early Twentieth-Century Philadelphia," *Pennsylvania History* 63, no. 2 (April 1996): 174.

11. "Republicans Jubilating," *Philadelphia Inquirer*, November 18, 1906, 18; "Philadelphians in Harmonious Caucus," *Philadelphia Inquirer*, April 29, 1908, 7; "West Philadelphia Rally," *Philadelphia Inquirer*, October 30, 1908, 2; "Colored Voters Applaud Candidate," *Philadelphia Inquirer*, October 30, 1908, 2; "Wm Penn Men Will Talk," *Philadelphia Inquirer*, October 30, 1908, 4; Smith, "Asking for Justice," 172–174; "Philadelphia Colored Voters: Attention!" *Philadelphia Tribune*, October 26, 1912, 1; Lane, *William Dorsey's Philadelphia and Ours*, 206, 214–215; Davidow, "Political Challenge," 8; Lucretia L. Blankenburg, *The Blankenburgs of Philadelphia* (Chicago: John C. Winston, 1929), 21.

12. "Philadelphia Sustains Republican Ticket by Substantial Majority," *Philadelphia Inquirer*, November 9, 1910, 2; "Tener by 25,000 in Pennsylvania," *New York Times*, November 9, 1910, 2; "Tener Elected by 33,000," November 10, 1910, 2; "Real Democrats Go on the Warpath in Pennsylvania," *New York Times*, March 12, 1911, SM7; "Tener by 25,000 in Pennsylvania," *New York Times*, November 8, 1910, 2; "Democrats Sweep Country; Win Congress, Many States," *New York Times*, November 9, 1910, 1; "Democrats Win the House by 60," *New York Times* November 10, 1910, 1.

13. Smith, "Asking for Justice," 175. Also see the editorial "Bass Amendment Defeated," *Pittsburgh Courier*, April 15, 1911, 4.

14. "State Police Sent to Coatesville," *New York Times*, August 15, 1911, 1; "National Capital," *Pittsburgh Courier*, June 10, 1911, 1; James Campbell, "'You Needn't Be Afraid Here You're in a Civilized Country': Region, Racial Violence, and Law Enforcement in Early Twentieth Century New Jersey, New York, and Pennsylvania," *Social History* 35, no. 3 (August 2010): 253–255.

15. Margaret Garb, *Freedom's Ballot: African American Political Struggles in Chicago from Abolition to the Great Migration* (Chicago: University of Chicago Press, 2014), 147, 149. I borrow from Garb's recent study of Chicago. Also see "Discrimination Laws Denounced by Minister: Rev. W.E. Williams Interprets Aim of Class Litigation," *Pittsburgh Courier*, November 11, 1911, 1; "Story of the Baptist Church," *Pittsburgh Courier*, September 16, 1911, 1; "Sinclair and NAACP Delegation Meet with Taft," *Pittsburgh Courier*, June 10, 1911, 1.

16. Samuel P. Hays, "The Politics of Reform in Municipal Government in the Progressive Era," *Pacific Northwest Quarterly* 55, no. 4 (October 1964): 161; Steve P. Erie, "Two Faces of Ethnic Power: Comparing the Irish and the Black Experiences," *Polity* 13, no. 2 (Winter 1980): 270, 273–275; Jerome Hodos, "The 1876 Centennial in Philadelphia: Elite Networks and Political Culture," in *Social Capital in the City: Community and Civic Life in Philadelphia*, ed. Richardson Dilworth (Philadelphia: Temple University Press, 2006), 27–28, 34–35, 37; "Blankenburg to Economize: Hopes to Save $1,000,000 a Year to Philadelphia by Cutting Off Jobs," *New York Times*, November 12, 1911, 13. The article emphasizes the fiscal context for political reform. For example, it shows that in 1910 the departments coming under the mayor the collective wages and salaries of nearly ten thousand employees was estimated at $3.5 million; "To Reform Philadelphia: Police Will Keep Out of Politics, Blankenburg Says When He's Mayor," *New York Times*, November 19, 1911, C10. For more on key issues behind reform politics during the mayoral election of 1911 see McCaffery, *When Bosses Ruled Philadelphia*, 180–184. For evidence on the plurality of support, including antiorganization support from African Americans for the Blankenburg reform agenda, see "Host of 25,000 March in Honor of Blankenburg," *Philadelphia Inquirer*, December 3, 1911, 6. For response of African Americans who supported the GOP organization see "Politics in the Quaker City: Election of New Mayor Starts Query among Afro-Americans," *Pittsburgh Courier*, December 2, 1911, 1.

17. Blankenburg, *Blankenburgs of Philadelphia*, 49–50; "Politics in the Quaker City," *Pittsburgh Courier*, December 2, 1911, 1; also see *Philadelphia Tribune*, "Colored Men Are to Receive a Square Deal," *Philadelphia Tribune*, October 18, 1919, 2. Cooper was first elected in 1907 and served until 1919. My research shows that, in 1911, Bass appears to have been the only African American serving in a state legislature within the country. The closest city for historical examination might have been Cleveland. See footnote 4 in Lloyd L. Sponholtz, "Harry Smith, Negro Suffrage and the Ohio Constitutional Convention: Black Frustration in the Progressive Era," *Phylon* (1960–), 35, no. 2 (2nd quar., 1974): 167. See Charlene Mires, "Race, Place, and the Pennsylvania Emancipation Exposition of 1913," *Pennsylvania Magazine of History and Biography* 128, no. 3 (July 2004): 257–278. The three cities North of the Mason Dixon line with the largest Black populations between 1900 and 1910 were Philadelphia, New York, and Chicago. Of these three, by 1911, only Philadelphia produced a Black city councilman and a Black state representative. I am challenging John Hope Franklin's framing on Black political regeneration during the period. He does not mention Philadelphia's accomplishments in the area of organized politics. Furthermore, he situates Chicago, in 1917, as the leading model. See John Hope Franklin and Moss, *From Slavery to Freedom*, 385. James Oliver Horton, "Urban Alliances: The Emergence of Race Based Populism in the Age of Jackson," in *The African American Urban Experience: Perspectives from the Colonial Period to the Present*, ed. Joe W. Trotter, Earl Lewis, and Tera W. Hunter (New York: Palgrave MacMillan, 2004), 28–30. For a better understanding on the relationship between the spirit of independence during the post-Revolution period and the hope for greater inter-

racial equality in Philadelphia and Pennsylvania, see Richard R. Wright Jr., *The Negro in Pennsylvania: A Study in Economic History* (LaVergne, TN: Kessinger, 2009), 22.

18. "Politics in the Quaker City: Election of New Mayor Starts Query among Afro-Americans," *Pittsburgh Courier*, December 2, 1911, 1; "Colored Men See Mayor," *Philadelphia Inquirer*, January 6, 1912, 11.

19. "Negro Problem Is Defined by Sociologist," *Pittsburgh Courier*, January 13, 1912, 1; "Discriminating Laws Denounced by Minister," *Pittsburgh Courier*, November 11, 1911, 1; W.E.B. Du Bois, *The Souls of Black Folk* (Oxford: Oxford University Press, 2008), 7-9; TuKufu ZuBeri, *Thicker than Blood: How Racial Statistics Lie* (Minneapolis: University of Minnesota Press, 2003), xvii.

20. "Second in Third Course of Lectures," *Philadelphia Tribune*, January 13, 1912, 1; on Black women activism during the long nineteenth century in the urban North, see Ira V. Brown, "Cradle of Feminism: The Philadelphia Female Anti-Slavery Society, 1833-1840," *Pennsylvania Magazine of History and Biography* 102, no. 2 (April 1978): 147-166; on Black women in the urban South, see Elsa Barkley-Brown, "Negotiating and Transforming the Public Sphere: African American Political Life in the Transformation from Slavery to Freedom," *Public Culture* 7 (1944): 107-110, 120; on Black women activism in the rural South see Steven Hahn, *A Nation under Our Feet: Black Political Struggles in the Rural South from Slavery to the Great Migration* (Cambridge, MA: Harvard University Press, 2003), 185, 214, 227.

21. "Negro Problem Is Defined by Sociologist," *Pittsburgh Courier*, January 13, 1912, 1; "Discriminating Laws Denounced By Minister," *Pittsburgh Courier*, November 11, 1911, 1; "Second In Third Course Of Lectures," *Philadelphia Tribune*, January 13, 1912, 1; V. P. Franklin, "The Voice of the Black Community: The Philadelphia Tribune, 1912-1941," *Pennsylvania History* 51, no. 4 (October 1984): 264; Kali N. Gross, *Colored Amazons: Crime, Violence, and Black Women in the City of Brotherly Love, 1880-1910* (Durham, NC: Duke University Press, 2006), 73-74, 101-102; Khalil Gibran Muhammad, *The Condemnation of Blackness: Race, Crime, and the Making of Modern Urban America* (Cambridge, MA: Harvard University Press, 2010), 15-18, 21, 22, 24, 28, 30, 35. On ANHS, see Tony Martin, "The Banneker Literary Institute of Philadelphia: African American Intellectual Activism before the War of the Slaveholder's Rebellion," *Journal of African American History* 87 (Summer 2002): 303-307, 311, 313, 318.

22. See V. Franklin, "Voice of the Black Community," 265. By Black liberals, independents, and Progressives, I mean someone whose ideas on racial reform were left of center and who used external pressure techniques to influence African American political culture and the national political structure. These individuals were more than likely nonpartisan, supported third parties, and were influenced by the civil rights protest tradition, or what Martin Kilson calls the Black communitarian model, engendered by W.E.B. Du Bois. See Martin Kilson, *Transformation of the African American Intelligentsia, 1880-2012* (Cambridge, MA: Harvard University Press, 2014), 86-91. I use the terms "Progressives" and "independents" interchangeably. By Black conservatives, partisans, organizational, or stalwarts, I mean those whose ideas about racial reform were shared by Black Progressives but whose methods differed. These individuals were more than likely Republicans who used traditional practices to change the party structure from within. By third-party democracy, I mean a political party other than the Democrats or Republicans. "Blankenburg to Aid Negroes in Philadelphia," *Pittsburgh Courier*, February 10, 1912, 1. Robert H. Weibe, *The Search for Order: 1877-1920* (New York: Hill and Wang, 1967), 167. There are two other studies on this period worth mentioning: Gabriel Kolko, *The Triumph of Conservatism* (New York: Free Press, 1963), 2-8;

Daniel T. Rogers, *Atlantic Crossings: Social Politics in a Progressive Age* (Cambridge, MA: Belknap Press of Harvard University, 2001), 64–65.

23. "Blankenburg to Aid Negroes in Philadelphia," *Pittsburgh Courier*, February 10, 1912, 1; Wilson Record, "Negro Intellectual Leadership in the National Association for the Advancement of Colored People: 1910-1940," *Phylon* (1940-1956), 17, no. 4 (4th quar., 1956): 377.; "Denounced Lynch Law," *Philadelphia Tribune*, February 24, 1912, 1.

24. "Denounced Lynch Law," *Philadelphia Tribune*, February 24, 1912, 1.

25. "Dr. William Sinclair Answers Criticism of Drs. Wm. A. Creditt and E.W. Moore," *Philadelphia Tribune*, March 2, 1912, 1.

26. "Dr. William Sinclair Answers Criticism of Drs. Wm. A. Creditt and E.W. Moore," *Philadelphia Tribune*, March 2, 1912, 1.

27. See Kevin K. Gaines, "From Slavery to Freedom: Uplift and the Decline of Black Politics," in *Uplifting the Race: Black Leadership, Politics, and Culture in the Twentieth Century* (Chapel Hill: North Carolina University Press, 1996); Spear, *Black Chicago*, 51. Charles Flint Kellogg, *NAACP: A History of the National Association for the Advancement of Colored People*, vol. 1: 1909–1920 (Baltimore: Johns Hopkins Press, 1967), 209–216; J. John Hope Franklin and Moss, *From Slavery to Freedom*, 312. For an additional discussion on violence in both sections, see Ray S. Baker, *Following the Color Line: American Negro Citizenship in the Progressive Era* (New York: Harper and Row, 1964). For targeted discussions on the North, see David A. Gerber, *Black Ohio and the Color Line, 1865–1930* (Urbana: University of Illinois Press, 1976); Frank U. Quillen, *The Color Line in Ohio: A History of Race Prejudice in a Typical Northern State* (Ann Arbor, MI: G. Wahr, 1913); William W. Giffin, *African Americans and the Color Line in Ohio, 1915–1930* (Columbus: Ohio State University Press, 2005). For more discussion on lynching, see Arthur Raper, *The Tragedy of Lynching* (Chapel Hill: University of North Carolina Press, 1933); Mary Frances Berry and John W. Blassingame, *Long Memory: The Black Experience in America* (New York: Oxford University Press, 1982); Schechter, *Ida B. Wells-Barnett and American Reform*. Also see Campbell, "'You Needn't Be Afraid Here,'" 253–255.

28. John Hope Franklin and Moss, *From Slavery to Freedom*, 312–317.

29. On Creditt's reputation, see *Philadelphia Tribune*, March 9, 1912. Creditt's thoughts on American Jews as a model for the African America struggle were published in the *Philadelphia Tribune*. See "Rev. William A. Creditt, D. D., Makes Strong Suggestions for the Race," *Philadelphia Tribune*, March 2, 1912. Creditt's views on American Jewish activism as a political model for social and political justice were picked up by the African American press in Pittsburgh. See "The Anti-Lynching Society's Influence: Work for Human Protection Receives Substantial Aid-Right Use of Ballot," *Pittsburgh Courier*, May 4, 1912.

30. Alan J. Ward, "Diplomacy: American Jews and Russia, 1901–1913," *Bulletin British Association for American Studies*, n.s., no. 9 (December 1964): 19.

31. On Black population statistics, see Campbell Gibson and Kay Jung, "Historical Census Statistics on Population Totals by Race, 1790 to 1990, and by Hispanic Origin, 1970 to 1990, for Large Cities and Other Urban Places in the United States," Population Division Working Paper No. 76, U.S. Census Bureau, Washington, DC, 2005, 94; T. Martin, "Banneker Literary Institute of Philadelphia," 304; Davidow, "Political Challenge," 8.

32. "Roosevelt Lead Gains: Wilson Follows Him in Keystone Party Post Card Canvass," *New York Times*, February 25, 1912, 4.

33. *Congressional Record*, 56th Congress, 2nd Session, vol. 34, pt. 2 (Washington DC: Government Printing Office, 1901), 1635, 1636, 1638. On White's response to the Wilmington race riot, see Glenda E. Gilmore, *Gender and Jim Crow: Women and the*

Politics of White Supremacy in North Carolina, 1896–1920 (Chapel Hill: University of North Carolina Press, 1996), 114–115. For a discussion on White's career as the nation's last Black congressman, see Gaines, *Uplifting the Race*, 20–21. For more information on White's career as a banker, see "The Marvelous Growth of the Peoples Saving Bank," *Philadelphia Tribune*, January 23, 1915, 1. For information on an ad placed for the Peoples Savings Bank see *Philadelphia Tribune*, June 22, 1912, 6. Also see Kenneth C. Martin, *The Historical Atlas of Political Parties in the United States, 1789–1989* (New York: MacMillan, 1989), 151.

34. "Announces His Candidacy for Congress," *Philadelphia Tribune*, March 30, 1912, 1; "He Has Heard the Battle Cry," *Chicago Defender*, April 20, 1912, 4. White also sought, unsuccessfully, a judicial appointment from Governor Tener in 1913. See "Citizens Petition Governor Tener to Name Lawyer White," *Philadelphia Tribune*, April 26, 1913, 1. On Bingham, see "Pencil Pusher Points," *Philadelphia Tribune*, April 13, 1912, 4.

35. "W. S. Vare Now in Congress," *The Washington Post*, May 8, 1912, 4.

36. For an account on Blankenburg's campaign statements, see "Just Gone," *The Philadelphia Tribune*, January 6, 1912, 1. For a discussion on the expulsion of Black officeholders and the framing of the Keystone Party as a "white man's party" and the linkages to the Roosevelt presidential candidacy, see "Just Gone," *The Philadelphia Tribune*, March 16, 1912, 1; "Just Gone," *The Philadelphia Tribune*, June 29, 1912, 1; "Just Gone," *The Philadelphia Tribune*, September 14, 1912, 1; "Just Gone," *The Philadelphia Tribune*, September 21, 1912, 1; "Just Gone," *The Philadelphia Tribune*, October 26, 1912, 1; "Just Gone," *The Philadelphia Tribune*, November 9, 1912, 1.

37. "Politics in the Quaker City," *The Pittsburgh Courier*, December 2, 1911, 1. For more on Black coalition politics with the GOP, see Percy E. Murray, "Harry C. Smith–Joseph B. Foraker Alliance: Coalition Politics in Ohio," *Journal of Negro History* 68, no. 2 (Spring 1983); "Hon. Harry W. Bass Soon to Visit Here," *The Pittsburgh Courier*, April 13, 1912, 1; "Mr. Bass Won His Spurs at the Legislature," *The Philadelphia Tribune*, January 28, 1913, 1.

38. Henry Chase, "Memorable Visitors: Classic White House Encounters," *American Visions*, (February–March 1995): 26–33.

39. "Senator Penrose," *The Philadelphia Tribune*, January 31, 1914, 4; "Rousing Meeting at Varrick Temple Monday Night: Large Audience Gives Senator Penrose an Enthusiastic Ovation and Reception," *The Philadelphia Tribune*, March 21, 1914, 1; "Protective League Formed to Look after Many Things," *The Philadelphia Tribune*, April 18, 1914, 1; "Negro Protection League of Penna in Two Large Meetings," *The Philadelphia Tribune*, May 2, 1914, 1; "League Holds Big Meeting," *The Philadelphia Tribune*, May 23, 1914, 5.

40. Howard W. Allen, Aage R. Clausen, and Jerome M. Clubb, "Political Reform and Negro Rights in the Senate, 1909–1915," *Journal of Southern History* 37, no. 2 (May 1971): 203–204.

41. "Penrose Scores Wilson Tariff," *The Philadelphia Tribune*, April 19, 1913, 1. For a discussion on Sinclair's meetings with Wilson on segregation, see "Colored Delegation to Meet President Wilson November First," *The Philadelphia Tribune*, November 1, 1913, 1; "President Rebukes Visitors," *The Philadelphia Tribune*, November 14, 1914, 8.

42. "We Should Have a Republican Mayor," *The Philadelphia Tribune*, June 5, 1915, 4.

43. "We Should Have a Republican Mayor," *The Philadelphia Tribune*, June 5, 1915, 4.

44. For insight on community mobilization over the film *Birth of a Nation*, see "Say Candidate for Judge Is Too Hot Headed," *The Philadelphia Tribune*, August 14, 1915, 1; "Citizens Organize to Fight the Infamous Photoplay," *The Philadelphia Tribune*, September 4, 1915, 1; "Judge Ferguson Ignorant of Temper of Our People: Citizens Hold Meeting

and Arrange to Proceed Against Infamous Films," *The Philadelphia Tribune*, September 11, 1915, 1. For a discussion on allegations of police abuse during the protest, see "Director Porter's Police Thugs Clubbed Defenseless Women and Children: Colored Voters Given Notice in Advance What They May Expect Should Director Porter Be Elected Mayor of Philadelphia," *The Philadelphia Tribune*, September 25, 1915, 1; "Well Known Republican Ward and Division Workers Organize," *The Philadelphia Tribune*, August 8, 1915, 1. On Black electoral strategy, see "Members of the Colored Republican Central Committee Actively Engaged in the Municipal Campaign just Close," *The Philadelphia Tribune*, November 6, 1915, 1. For a discussion on an alleged conspiracy between Porter and the film's promoters, see "How the Bluff Was Arranged to Fool Some People," *The Philadelphia Tribune*, October 2, 1915, 1; "Stirring Address Calling Thinking Men to Action for the Great Contest in November," *The Philadelphia Tribune*, October 3, 1915, 1.

45. "Thomas B. Smith Leads Ticket by over 77,832 Majority," *Philadelphia Tribune*, November 6, 1915, 15; Chad L. Williams, "Vanguards of the New Negro: African American Veterans and Post–World War I Racial Militancy," *The Journal of African American History* 92, no. 3 (Summer 2007): 347–370. On racial violence just before the turn of the century see David Zucchino, *Wilmington's Lie: The Murderous Coup of 1898 and the Rise of White Supremacy* (New York: Atlantic Monthly Press, 2020). For more on racial violence in Philadelphia and the East during the twentieth century, C. L. Harris, "Race, Leadership, and the Local Machine: The Origins of the African American Struggle for Political Recognition and the Politics of Community Control, 1915–1968" (Ph.D. diss., University of Pennsylvania, 2013), Chapter 3; Matthew J. Countryman, *Up South: Civil Rights and Black Power in Philadelphia* (Philadelphia: University of Pennsylvania Press, 2006); Komozi Woodard, *A Nation within a Nation: Amiri Baraka (LeRoi Jones) and Black Power Politics* (Chapel Hill: University of North Carolina Press, 1999). On racial violence and law enforcement during the twentieth century in the Midwest, see Simon Balto, *Occupied Territory: Policing Black Chicago from Red Summer to Black Power* (Chapel Hill: University of North Carolina Press, 2019); Charles L. Lumpkins, *American Pogrom: The East St. Louis Race Riot and Black Politics* (Athens: Ohio University Press, 2008); Thomas J. Sugrue, *Origins of the Urban Crisis: Race and Inequality in Postwar Detroit* (Princeton: Princeton University Press, 1996). In the West, see Robert O. Self, *American Babylon: Race and the Struggle for Postwar Oakland* (Princeton: Princeton University Press, 2003). In the South, see Edward Gonzalez-Tennant, *The Rosewood Massacre: An Archaeology and History of Intersectional Violence* (Gainesville: University Press of Florida, 2018); Tim Madigan, *The Burning: Massacre, Destruction, and the Tulsa Race Riot of 1921* (New York: Thomas Dunne Books/St. Martin's Press, 2001).

2

Building Black Philadelphia

DAVID A. CANTON

During the last week of October, just before the 1915 election in Philadelphia, Andrew F. Stevens Jr., a real estate agent and the president of the Colored Republican Central Committee, organized Black Republican political rallies across the city in support of Thomas B. Smith, Republican nominee for mayor, and the entire Republican ticket. The Black community was critical of Mayor Rudolph Blankenburg of the Keystone Party, who had promised to reform local politics, to no avail. According to the *Philadelphia Tribune*, it was time for Black Philadelphians not to be "silly enough to drink down all such false promises." Black political leaders, such as Richard A. Cooper, the only African American councilman in Philadelphia, Christopher Perry, founder of the *Philadelphia Tribune*, and Amos Scott, owner of the Scott Hotel and president of the Citizens Republican Club (CRC)— a social and political organization of Black male elites and "many white friends"—attended and spoke at the rallies. Both the Colored Republican Central Committee and the CRC were determined to get all Black men to vote the entire Republican ticket.[1]

Dissatisfied with the "utter failure of Blankenburg and of the duplicity of the Reform administration," Stevens also voiced his displeasure with George Porter, the former director of public safety and the mayoral candidate endorsed by the Franklin Party. Porter had "allowed his police officers to club our preachers and brutally assault our women while in front of the Forrest Theatre." That assault along with Stevens's rallies helped galvanize Black voters. On November 6, the front-page story of the *Philadelphia Tri-*

bune told readers that Thomas B. Smith won the election by 77,832 votes and argued "that the colored vote contributed largely toward the success attained." At a broader level, the Black vote that ensured Smith's victory came as a direct result of the Great Migration, new economic opportunities, and the work of a rising cadre of African American political leadership that included African American women.[2]

Early histories that chronicled Black politics in Philadelphia, during the first two decades of the twentieth century through the civil rights/Black Power era, focused on elite Black men who participated in a number of social and political organizations, such as the CRC. Black women have only recently moved to the center of these stories. The passage of the Nineteenth Amendment in 1920 gave Black women, such as Lena Trent Gordon, S. Willie Layton, and Maude Morrisette, who had already been important activists, the opportunity to be power players in the Republican Party. They formed local political groups, organized Black women voters, and obtained appointed positions in local government. Between 1915 and 1929, the rise of Black middle-class leadership and the increase of Black voters allowed the African American community to take advantage of white Republican Party division, and the Black vote emerged as a "balance of power vote" that led to more African Americans gaining city employment and political appointments. Despite the expanding Black vote, racial discrimination continued and when necessary white political elites often overlooked their differences to try to stymie Black political power.[3]

Between 1915 and 1920, half a million African Americans left the South and migrated north to obtain jobs and escape Southern white domestic terrorism. In addition to poor rural Southern Black migrants, many successful Black businessmen left the South to take advantage of expanding economic opportunities in the North. According to historian Robert Weems, by World War I, the urban Black community was a $15 billion consumer market that attracted Black and white capitalists. Similar to middle-class Germans who immigrated to the United States during the mid-nineteenth century, the Black middle class who migrated had the skills and resources to become successful in the North. These migrants found a small but robust Black community in Philadelphia, often referred to as the Old Philadelphians. Yet, despite their skills, Black Philadelphians encountered police brutality, longstanding segregation in housing, schools, and public accommodations, and what historian Carol Anderson refers to as white rage that intensified when the Black community demanded power, inclusion, and equality.[4]

The small core of Old Philadelphians, led by elite Black male Republicans during the late nineteenth century, had formed political organizations that represented their class and community interests, and these persisted into the twentieth century. In 1883, for example, Andrew F. Stevens Sr. founded the Citizens Republican Club (CRC), which quickly became known as "the most prosperous and successful political organization composed of colored men in the United States." The membership included the most prominent Black businessmen and professionals in Philadelphia, such as Amos C. Scott, president of the CRC (1908–1920) and owner of the Scott Hotel; A. I. Jones, owner of the Roadside Hotel; Andrew F. Stevens Jr., son of the CRC's founder, a real estate agent and part owner of Brown and Stevens Bank; John C. Asbury, attorney; and Christopher Perry, founder and owner of the *Philadelphia Tribune*. Scott and the CRC, early on, played a major role in successfully pushing Pennsylvania's Republican governor, Martin Grove Brumbaugh, for the appointment of African American attorney John W. Parks to a "special assignment" position in the Pennsylvania attorney general's office. A man with the ability to "deal with heads of the party in the city and the state," they claimed, merited a robust salary of $5,000 per year and a $15 per diem.[5]

Black attorneys and newspapers played a central role in Philadelphia's Black politics. Every major city with a large African American population had a coterie of Black lawyers and an influential Black newspaper such as Chicago's *Defender* and Pittsburgh's *Courier*. In 1919, Philadelphia had nineteen Black lawyers and the *Tribune* praised their work in its pages. Christopher Perry founded the *Philadelphia Tribune* in 1884 and hired G. Grant Williams as the city editor in 1903. The two men guided the *Tribune* into becoming one of the most influential African American newspapers in the country. Williams had been a barber in Hartford, Connecticut, and worked as a correspondent for the *Tribune*. From 1903 to 1922, Williams wrote witty and critical essays and articles on racism in Philadelphia, and he castigated Black and white politicians who failed to protect Black voters and provide them with city jobs. Perry told Williams that he was "in politics and too busy to bother with the paper," so Perry allowed Williams to run the paper like he owned it.[6]

Williams also served as president and manager of the Academy of Music, which sponsored plays and held "Emancipation Exercises" that included a performance from noted contralto Marian Anderson. Williams's professions provided him with the financial independence that allowed him to write scathing critiques of the political class. His op-eds and the expanding power of the Black vote helped African American leaders hold white politicians accountable and demand more patronage on the city and state level. One year into Mayor Smith's administration, Williams wasted no time in criticizing the mayor. In a *Tribune* op-ed titled "The Disgrace of Mayor Smith," Williams wrote that Smith's motto in South Philadelphia was "look out for the boys ... thugs, pimps and loafers" who prevent "decent men" from obtaining jobs in the local government. In addition, "The lawgiver sees no disgrace clubbing citizens, permitting police to terrorize those whom they are paid to protect." Williams was upset that Smith took a photo with Thomas Hayden, a Black police officer, who allowed the "thugs, pimps, and loafers" to do their work. To Williams, Smith's head "contain[ed] saw-dust, with hair on top." Many Black leaders were disappointed with Smith's administration, as he failed to increase Black representation in city jobs and end racial discrimination.[7]

The Black community had celebrated its limited political victory, but racial and ethnic tensions grew. Many African Americans supported Black-owned businesses, but many continued to shop at white- and Jewish-owned establishments. South Street was a popular shopping area in South Philadelphia where one could find Philadelphians from all backgrounds in the markets. The *Philadelphia Tribune* reported about the growing tensions between Black customers and some Jewish store owners. In one emblematic story, a Black woman had purchased some fish and gave the store owner a quarter, but the Jewish store owner replied in a loud voice, "No, you did not and if you don't pay me I will have you arrested." The woman retorted, "Mr. Jew you are at liberty to have me arrested if you wish and I have enough money to pay my way out. So if you do not give me my quarter I am prepared to die and go to hell and take you with me for my 25 cents." The store owner "returned her quarter and she gave him a final lecture and left." Some Jewish Philadelphians supported the NAACP and socialized with W.E.B. Du Bois, but others certainly did not.[8]

After the Great Migration, Black leaders in Philadelphia recognized African American economic power and decided to boycott South Street business owners who disrespected Black consumers. Such campaigns foreshadowed the better-known "Don't Buy Where You Can't Work" movement of the 1930s. After numerous encounters with Black customers, an organization of businessmen called the South Street Business Association (SSBA) asked the city to remove the only African American police officer from South Street. Isaac Deutsch, president of the SSBA, said it was best "for both races that the colored police was removed" because the black police officer's presence was "unbecoming." Deutsch said, "The colored people who crowd that thoroughfare would have more respect for the authority of a white man" and insisted "racial prejudice had nothing to do with the recent removal of the colored patrolman on South Street." After the SSBA's request, G. Grant Williams organized an "indignation meeting" at O'Neil Hall where seven hundred African Americans attended to "voice their protest against the SSBA" and support the "Stay off South Street" campaign. Scott, Stevens from CRC, and Williams led the meeting. "If it is lawful for them to remove our patrolmen because of their color," Williams told the audience, "it is just as lawful for us to find some other place to spend our money," and J. M. Easton, pastor of Varick AME Church, told the five hundred members of his church "not to make any purchases from the white merchants on South Street."[9]

During the boycott, a reporter from the *Tribune* interviewed several South Street merchants. "All this rumpus is only a tempest in a teapot," said one merchant. "It will soon blow over. I am not a bit disturbed." He claimed he knew "the colored folks" well. "One minute they are mad with you, the next minute they are your friend." Another SSBA merchant viewed Black people as a group of emotional children who got upset when they were discriminated against. These comments demonstrated the deep tensions that existed between some Jewish merchants and Black customers on South Street.[10]

At the same time, a comment more indicative of positive relations came from a merchant who belonged to the West End Association, another organization of South Street business owners, who said African Americans were "their best customers" and their members had nothing to do with the SSBA boycott. The threat of a boycott demonstrated the growing political and economic power of the Black community, but some SSBA merchants refused to take the boycott seriously, which alarmed some South Street business owners who feared financial losses. Williams believed that SSBA had removed the Black patrolman because a number of SSBA members had "short changed colored people, gave them rotten meats, and when they protested they would call in a policeman." According to Williams, "the colored police would not stand for their cheating," and this is why the SSBA wanted all-white police officers.[11]

The members wrote a resolution that stated the community's resentment of the wholesale discrimination practiced by Director of Public Safety William Wilson and the SSBA. They intended to send their resolution to Mayor Smith and every Black church and social and fraternal organization in the city. The attendees passed the resolution and the committee agreed to have the next meeting at Mother Bethel AME Church. During that meeting, they declared that "women should be heard." Black women did the majority of the shopping on South Street and had encountered racism from some SSBA members. Mother Bethel AME hosted the second meeting, and it "was so crowded that an over flow meeting was held downstairs," demonstrating Black women's political activism, which made an even bigger difference in 1920 when they obtained the right to vote.[12]

The SSBA's views were a local manifestation of a much more virulent racism growing in the United States. The second Ku Klux Klan, which began in 1915, spread throughout the nation (by the 1920s, the state of Indiana had the most KKK members in the United States) and counted white elected officials as members. The same year, the film *Birth of a Nation* premiered and was the first film shown in the White House. Enthralled by the film's racist interpretation of Reconstruction, President Woodrow Wilson, who had a Ph.D. in history, said, "It's like writing history with lightning. My only regret is that it is all so terribly true." The following year, Wilson resegregated the White House and promoted racial segregation in federal employment. The KKK, Woodrow Wilson, *Birth of a Nation*, and many more manifestations of the nation's racism provided the context for white racial violence that occurred throughout the United States. While the Great Migration provided African Americans with an opportunity to leave Southern terrorism, many Black migrants encountered racist violence in Northern cities, including police brutality and white resistance to African Americans moving into white neighborhoods.[13]

From 1866 to 1943, there were some forty-five race riots in the United States. White mobs attacked Black people for voting, lynched Black men for alleged sexual assaults of white women, assaulted World War I veterans refusing to obey Jim Crow laws, and confronted working- and middle-class Black people moving into white neighborhoods. During each riot, more African Americans were killed than white people. Despite that fact, law enforcement sided with white mobs and ordered Black men to turn over their guns. The majority of these riots occurred in the South, but racial violence, like racism and segregation, was an American problem. The North had several infamous race riots. One of the earliest and most prominent occurred in Springfield, Illinois, in 1908, and it led to the creation of the NAACP. Perhaps the worst Northern race riot took place in Chicago, Illinois, in 1919, in the season known as "Red Summer." Not as well known, but still calamitous for the Black population, was the riot that struck Philadelphia in 1918.[14]

Prior to the Great Migration, the majority of Black Philadelphians had lived in the Seventh Ward, but a growing number of middle-class African Americans had started to purchase homes in all-white neighborhoods. The growth of the city's Black population exacerbated Philadelphia's racially charged housing problems. By the end of the 1910s, the Black population in Philadelphia stood at 134,000, a 58 percent increase over the previous decade, with the majority arriving between 1915 and 1920. When Black migrants arrived in Philadelphia, they found a housing shortage and white real estate agents and residents who prohibited African Americans from moving into white neighborhoods.

Local organizations such as the National Urban League warned white officials about the emerging housing crisis. But the city, rather than construct new housing or repeal racial segregation laws, forced African Americans to address the housing crisis on their own terms, either by crowding into small row houses or, if they had money, buying their own homes. During the summer of 1918, more African Americans started to purchase homes in all-white neighborhoods. That is when the riot began. The leading student of Philadelphia's race riot, V. P. Franklin, recounted how the violence began on July 26, 1918, when a white mob attacked the home of Ms. Adella Bond, who worked for the municipal court. Bond was one of many middle-class African Americans who had the resources to purchase a home in an all-white neighborhood. A white person threw a rock through her window, and Bond responded by firing her revolver and calling the police.[15]

For the next three days, a race riot enveloped the city. There were shootings between white people and Black people, and the city called on "The Home Defense Reserves," a group of white citizens, to support the police due to the shortage of white men deployed overseas to fight in World War I. On the last day of the violence, two white police officers arrested and murdered an African American man named Riley Bullock, who they claimed tried to escape on their way to jail. Angered by the violence, the *Tribune*'s G. Grant Williams wrote an op-ed titled "Dixie Methods in Philadelphia" in which he told Black Philadelphians to "favor peace . . . but when they tread upon your rights, fight them to the bitter end." To combat racial violence, protect Black citizens, and obtain civil rights, a group of African Americans founded the Colored Protective Association, which helped protect Black Philadelphians and worked to improve race relations for years to come. The *Tribune* regularly reported on instances of white violence against Black homeowners in the decades after the 1918 riot, but the next major race rebellion did not occur in Philadelphia until 1964. Many Black leaders knew self-defense was a necessity for protecting African American homeowners.[16]

The expanding Black middle class allowed Black real estate agents to sell homes to African Americans in all-white neighborhoods. Although Black real estate agents such as Andrew Stevens Jr. tried to meet the needs of African Americans, white mob violence was rampant in Philadelphia and the local police failed to protect African Americans. At times, men like Stevens became so angry they decided they had to protect their clients. The month after the infamous race riot, Martin Cowdery and his family, who the *Tribune* described as "one of Philadelphia's oldest and most respected families of color," purchased a home at 3849 North Sixteenth Street. Joseph Sternberger, a resident on that block, warned Cowdery "not to move in under threat of mob violence." In mid-August, Stevens informed city hall that Cowdery was moving in on September 1, even if there was a threat. Moreover, Stevens informed the white officials that "he had two automatic guns and he intended to spend the night at the home of his client the date he moved in and if there was any mob violence there will be some other troubles that might call the coroner and undertaker into service." On move-in day, Stevens brought his two guns and "20 men of color as special guards, well-armed and stationed in good positions to pick off the rioters." True to his word,

Stevens and his armed men ensured that a white mob did not attack his client's family.¹⁷

In spite of Stevens's efforts, white Philadelphians continued to "oppose the sale of real estate to colored people in white residential sections." C. E. Wright, president of the West Philadelphia Business Man's Association, asked the police to remove African Americans from apartments they rented from white landlords. Stevens sent Wright's name to city hall and said, "If he causes any trouble [and] gets hurt, he can blame himself." The city's director of public safety declared he could not tell landlords to whom to sell or rent their property. An insurance agent named W. Rote would not let the Cowdery matter rest, telling Stevens, "The presence of colored people carried a depreciation in the valuation of real estate . . . this was why whites objected to a Stevens client moving in." That rationale still does not "warrant threats of mob violence," Stevens replied, and he warned Rote that if his "crowd goes over the authority . . . of the police" and injures Cowdery, African Americans "will come to you and Mr. Sternberger and blow your families to _____." Stevens, an upper-middle-class African American leader, turned to violent language to make it clear that African Americans were going to defend themselves from white terrorism.¹⁸

With violent opposition to housing desegregation a flash point of racial oppression in Philadelphia, political leaders made efforts to address racial discrimination in the state. In April 1915, Representative Abram Stein from Pittsburgh introduced a civil rights bill in the Pennsylvania House of Representatives. The Pennsylvania Legislature had passed an equal rights bill in 1887, but it had no teeth and was not enforced. Stein's equal rights bill prohibited discrimination in "hotels, entertainment venues, and public conveyances," and any individual who violated the law faced a "maximum penalty of five hundred dollars." Stein's bill passed in the House, but, in spite of the efforts of Black Republicans, it failed in the State Senate.¹⁹

The inability to pass the Stein bill resulted in a contentious debate between CRC members and J. Max Barber, a dentist and member of the newly formed Philadelphia Chapter of the NAACP. The local NAACP, which was founded in 1913, was critical of Scott's inability to get Stein's equal rights bill passed. President Elwood Heacock and Secretary Isadore Martin praised the work of the NAACP's Executive Committee on behalf of Stein's equal rights bill, but they believed the bill did not pass "on the account of disloyal members of the race, and the ingratitude and treachery of those who pretended to be our friends." The House watered down the bill, making it "an insult to the race and absolutely worthless." The two believed the NAACP was the only organization that could provide a "square deal for all men," and "it is only by agitation, by asking for what one wants . . . we shall ever get what we want." Barber stated, "The rum seller (Scott), as a political leader among us must go." Scott seemed, in Barber's estimation, more interested in selling "the best liquor in Philadelphia" at his hotel than in representing the race. John Asbury, a Black lawyer and member of CRC, responded to Barber's harsh criticism of Scott. Asbury viewed Scott's pragmatism as the key to becoming a great leader, and he believed that the best strategy was to "accept the bill in its amended form or get nothing and go down in ignominious defeat." Barber was known to refer to himself as an outsider, not born in Philadelphia, and his critique of the CRC's tactics was indicative of the NAACP and the contestation of the approach Black leadership should take. While agitation remained largely outside the activities of the CRC, the expanding Black electorate forced the Republican Party to at least take up the equal rights bill in Pennsylvania.[20]

Despite the disappointments of the Smith administration and the civil rights bill, Black voters remained optimistic for the upcoming 1919 and 1920 elections. G. Grant Williams encouraged Black voters to "keep a solid front," because "they will be the balance of power . . . and be a more important factor to the Republican Party than ever before." In 1919, Black voters supported J. Hampton Moore as Republican candidate for mayor, and they believed it was time to elect Amos Scott as Philadelphia's first Black magistrate. Scott was not the first such candidate—Aaron Mossell ran for that office in 1900 and lost—but Black voters believed they could win if they received just enough white support. G. Edward Dickerson, a Black attorney, also put his name on the ballot for municipal judge.

During the early twentieth century, urban politics was dominated by a local political machine consisting of formal and informal elected officials, institutions, and networks. In Philadelphia, the Vare machine, run by William S. and Edward Vare, dominated local politics. In order to win local elections, Black candidates needed support from the Vare machine, but this group refused to support Scott and Dickerson, and both men lost in the September primary. Many African Americans were nonetheless confident about the significance of their vote and believed that 1920 offered an excellent opportunity to elect two Black men to the state Legislature. The elections of 1920 also saw Black women voters emerge as a major factor in Philadelphia politics.[21]

In the presidential election year of 1920, political leaders recognized the shifting demographics in the nation. The *Tribune* told its readers that a half million African Americans had relocated to Northern and Western cities. With eight states and thirteen industrial cities seeing a rising African American population, the paper argued that the nation could see "unexpected results in this presidential election," saying many campaign managers were concerned about the "women vote," "shifting soldier vote," "labor shift," and "negro voter from the South" who is "naturally Republican." All of those categories contained Black voters. In 1920, the Industrial Board of the state of Pennsylvania asked R. R. Wright Jr., editor of the *Christian Recorder* and president of the Colored Protective Association, to study the migration of Southern African Americans to Philadelphia. According to Wright, there were 134,000 African Americans in Philadelphia, a 30 percent increase from the last census, but Black Philadelphians continued to face the sting of racism and segregation under the Republican Party.[22]

The Republican Party so dominated Philadelphia politics that, from 1884 to 1952, the GOP only lost one mayoral election. Some white Republicans supported Black Republican candidates, but that cross-racial support was the exception in Philadelphia. In his essay "Fearless Writer Assails Conditions in Philadelphia," Williams highlighted the impact of racism and segregation in Philadelphia. Across the city, African Americans were "denied admission in many public places such as Horn and Hardart's and Reading Terminal," and restaurants posted signs that said "Colored Customers Not Wanted Here." Black elected officials were not protected from racial discrimination. In March 1921, newly elected State Senator John Asbury and some white colleagues attended the opening of the Stanley Theatre in downtown Philadelphia. Asbury, the only Black person in the group, gave his ticket to the usher, who seated him in a separate section. Asbury argued, "I am a member of the State Legislature and we all have seats together," to which the usher responded, "That's all right sir, your seat is this way," and directed Asbury to sit in the last row of the gallery. Philadelphia was a one-party city, but Williams informed Black voters there were "two Republican factions of this city at war with each other . . . and the Black voter can mobilize to select a Republican candidate who best represents their interests."[23]

In 1920, Black women voters emerged as an important constituent for Black elected officials and the Republican Party. African Americans had the opportunity to elect two Black state representatives from the predominantly Black Seventh and Thirtieth Wards. With the passage of the Nineteenth Amendment, the *Tribune* told its readers that suffragist Carrie Chapman Catt, speaking on behalf of the women voters of the world, argued that "1.5 million women in 29 states have the right to vote in the next Presidential election." By supporting local Black politicians, Black women voters could force white Republicans to appoint more African Americans to high-level positions. African American men had created social and political organizations to organize Black male voters for some time, but, in 1920, the *Tribune* found thirty-five thousand Black women voters in Philadelphia and a cadre of emerging Black women leaders who registered and organized them.[24]

After the passage of the Nineteenth Amendment, Black women wasted no time getting registered and joining the Republican Party. In 1920, the *Philadelphia Tribune* published a number of articles praising Black women's commitment to voting. The front page of the September 4 edition of the paper noted the "1st Colored Woman in City Assessed Before Registration," and, two weeks later, voter registration began and at "almost every registration district women took the lead." "Unlike many men," the *Tribune* added, "they took advantage of the first day and qualified." Black women voters' issues were "child labor, high cost of living . . . education [and] Democratic Rule in Haiti." Because American politics is gendered, the *Tribune* argued Black women's political issues were "naturally" associated with children, family, and home. "Their innate interests in the home" encouraged women to advocate for laws that create "the best possible home life" for their families. Black women were concerned with American imperialism in Haiti, but this journalist focused on their concern about children and their families. Most Black men relegated Black women's political interests to the family, but the Black community needed Black women's votes, and, in due time, these women leaders obtained gendered leadership positions, such as director of welfare agencies.[25]

Throughout the 1920s, in spite of gendered ideas, Black women voters contributed to growing Black political power in Philadelphia. By the 1920s, Black women voters in Northern cities allowed more Black men and women to obtain city and statewide political positions. As the Black population increased, the time was ripe for African Americans to elect Black state representatives. In 1920, J. Hampton Moore was the Republican candidate for mayor and Asbury and Stevens emerged as the two leading candidates for the state Legislature. During the campaign, Black women organized rallies of Black women voters for Black and white candidates. Following the election, the Republican Party rewarded these Black women with leadership positions, and their goal was to get Black women to the polls in the future.[26]

The Republican ticket won the 1920 elections, and a number of women emerged as leaders in the Republican Party: S. Willie Layton, chair of Colored Women of Philadelphia County; Margaret Corbett, leader of Black women voters in the Thirtieth Ward; Maude Morrisette, clerk of the municipal court; and Lena Trent Gordon, special investigator of Public Welfare. The *Philadelphia Tribune* published Layton's letter that congratulated the role Black women played in the growing "pluralities" of the Republican Party. Layton said the nation was "tired of Bossism and Wilsonism." By bossism, she meant the Vare machine not rewarding Black voters with the appropriate patronage for their support and not addressing racial discrimination. Wilsonism highlighted the president's resegregation of the federal government and screening of *Birth of a Nation*. Layton believed in the "old time religion of Republican rule" and despised "democratic rule [that promoted] class against class" and resulted in "race intolerance and bolshevism." During the election, she visited a number of polling stations in Philadelphia where she saw "husbands and wives entering polling places . . . as if they were going to church." She believed Black women voters were responsible for Republican victories and argued that the "minds of men against women voting must now be wiped out." With significant credit belonging to Black women voters, Andrew Stevens Jr. and John Asbury both won landslide victories that made them state representatives from Philadelphia. Their first order of business was the passage of a new equal rights bill.[27]

On February 1, 1921, the equal rights bill, generally referred to as the Asbury bill, began making its way through the state Legislature. The bill prohibited segregation in public accommodations, such as hotels, theaters, and public amusements, and violators of the law faced a $500 fine and thirty days in jail. Two weeks later, the CRC and Allied Racial Welfare Committee, an organization that represented twenty "race organizations," cosponsored a meeting in Philadelphia at the Dunbar Theatre in support of Asbury's bill. Speakers included Asbury, Stevens, and labor leaders A. Philip Randolph and Chandler Owens, editors of *The Messenger* who the *Tribune* referred to as "men of intelligence and forceful orators." In April, Stevens gave a brilliant speech in Coatesville, the site of one of Pennsylvania's most gruesome lynchings. He told his audience, "To think of a state having to pass a bill to give people the right to eat when hungry and to sleep when tired. Aliens come here with instruments of destruction in their hands and are permitted to do what they like, yet the negro is denied the simple rights of citizenship."[28]

As the bill started to gain momentum, Representative John R. Tyson, originally from Montgomery, Alabama, criticized the legislation, saying small businesses had the right to decide whom to serve. State Senator Cadwallader Barr asked to move the bill from the Law and Order Committee to the Judiciary Committee. Lobbyists from the hotel and theater industries pressured state senators not to support the bill. According to Smith, Barr interpreted the "civil rights bill as requests for favors from a special interest group rather than the legitimate demand of citizens." Asbury, a successful businessman, and Stevens, a University of Pennsylvania graduate, were part of Du Bois's "Talented Tenth," whose civil rights activities represented their class and community interests. Yet, many white state legislators viewed the Black elite as a "special interest group," defined as people who had graduated from college or held upper-class Black occupations such as barbers and caterers. To many of these white politicians, Black elites actually desired "social equality," which translated to Black men desiring sexual relationships with white women.[29]

White elites used the sexually charged "social equality" racist myth to reinforce the Black male beast racist stereotype and to justify Jim Crow, segregation, and lynching. In truth, most African American men had no desire to marry white women or socialize with white people. Moreover, Senator Barr insisted that the Asbury bill did not represent African American "citizens," in other words, the masses of Black folks who, Barr believed, without asking any African Americans, were content with racial discrimination. Barr's anti–equal rights bill rhetoric resembled the rhetoric of Southern segregationists during the later civil rights movement. Although the Senate voted 39–9 against the Asbury bill, all of the senators who represented Black voters in Philadelphia supported the bill. Black voters clearly did not have enough leverage in the state to force white politicians to strengthen equal rights in Pennsylvania.[30]

During the summer of 1921, the Black community started to prepare for the November elections and Black women readied themselves to play an important role. The most important names on the ballot were Amos Scott for magistrate and G. Edward Dickerson for municipal judge. In July, G. Grant Williams found that African Americans continued to complain about their lack of representation in city government. If a ward has a Black majority, he argued, "we should be our own bosses." With Black political power limited, local government and the police allowed "men of color [to run] bawdy houses, gambling joints and speak easies" in the Black community. In August, African American councilman Charles Hall fought to get "colored women admitted to membership in the Republican City Committee" along with their "white sisters." Philadelphia had eight state senatorial districts and each selected two women representatives. Districts that contained large African American wards selected Black women as their Republican City Committee members, such as Bertha Perry, wife of the *Philadelphia Tribune*'s Christopher Perry; Lena Trent Gordon of the Seventh District; Evelyn Robinson from the Sixth District that contained "a thousand colored women and 5,000 colored men"; and Margaret Corbett of the Second District.[31]

In September, a number of Black women organized political rallies across the city in support of Amos Scott. Lena Trent Gordon organized a rally in North Philadelphia, Evelyn Robinson held a rally at the YMCA that nine hundred people attended, and Margaret Corbett "aroused the whole of the central part of the city . . . so nothing can prevent a tremendous vote for the colored candidates." African American voters supported Scott and Dickerson in their races as well as Layton to serve as a delegate to the state constitutional convention. In spite of Black support, Mayor Moore and Senator Boies Penrose refused to endorse any African American candidates and treated Black women voters with contempt. Penrose and Moore were members of the Voters League, an organization that did not support a "single reputable colored candidate for public office . . . and ignored and insulted" Black leaders who tried to make a case for African American candidates. In addition, Bessie Altemus, a white woman and member of the Women's Auxiliary to the City Committee "refused to select a single colored woman from any district" for her organization. Although African Americans were building a political power base in the city, they found the political establishment committed to resisting Black political progress.[32]

Although Penrose killed the Asbury bill in April and Moore and the Voters League did not endorse any Black candidates, W. Freeland Kendrick gave Black voters hope. Kendrick, who was running for reelection as receiver of taxes (and would be the next mayor in 1924), was very popular with Black voters because of "his fair treatment of colored men serving under him in the City Tax Office." Black voters believed in meritocracy in city government. A person who is "sufficiently qualified," wrote the *Tribune*, "should get the position and no matter their race." During his tenure as receiver of taxes, Kendrick hired African Americans in the positions of "two Deputy Delinquent Tax Collectors, seven senior clerks and two janitors." Evelyn Robinson claimed a vote for Kendrick will "guarantee a continuation of Negro representation." The evening before the primary, two thousand Black voters attended meetings across the city, and Scott won the primary due to the "solidarity of the colored vote [including] colored women [who] did their share, [the] equal of men voters."

In spite of warnings to support Scott, reporters found that some "white ward and division leaders refused to obey orders to support Scott and after the election white Republican leaders met and discussed why they did not vote for Scott." Scott won with a sixty-thousand-vote majority because Councilman Charles B. Hall, who served as chairman of the Campaign Committee of the Republican City Executive Committee, encouraged Black women voters. Hall divided white Republican leaders who had opposed Scott, and he allowed women to join the Republican City Committee. During the summer of 1921, Layton, Robinson, Gordon, and others were instrumental in getting the Black women's vote. A week after the election, the *Tribune* recognized Layton, Corbett, and Morrisette as "women prominent in the Political and Social life of the city [who] assisted the race for the accomplishment of greater things in public life."[33]

In spite of the Vare machine's corruption and obvious racism, the majority of African American Republicans remained loyal to the Republican bosses, but a new generation of Black activists pushed for greater rights. To most African Americans, the Republicans were far better than the moribund Democrats. Black voters helped elect Kendrick, and, unlike previous mayors, he appointed numerous Black men to city jobs. Many Black leaders insisted, however, that they remained underrepresented in city employment and applied pressure to Kendrick and the Republican Party to provide more patronage.

Philadelphia in the 1920s had a growing number of young Black leaders, such as attorney Raymond Pace Alexander, who was born and raised in Philadelphia and graduated from the University of Pennsylvania and Harvard Law School. Alexander represented a younger cadre of Black lawyers who challenged the Republican Party to increase Black representation in city government and was joined in his activism by his wife, Sadie Tanner Mossell Alexander. Born to the old Black elite of Philadelphia, she graduated with a BA and in 1921 received her Ph.D. in economics from the University of Pennsylvania. Although she was only the second Black woman to obtain a Ph.D. in the nation, the racism and sexism of the day denied her the opportunity to teach at a university. Sadie Alexander instead obtained her law degree in 1927 from her alma mater and became the first Black woman to practice law in Pennsylvania. These younger Black leaders demanded more city jobs from the Vare machine, sued over racial discrimination, protested racial segregation in public schools, and challenged older Black politicians such as Amos Scott. Some in this vanguard became independent Republicans.[34]

Three months into Kendrick's first term, an interracial committee sent a letter to the mayor insisting African Americans have equal opportunity employment in the city's police and fire departments, clerical work, and executive positions. In addition, qualified Black city workers who had obtained jobs in past administrations were routinely overlooked for promotion. African Americans continued to use the rhetoric of meritocracy, knowing full well that the reason for not obtaining jobs and promotions was racism. "The impartial promotion of all who merit regardless of race and color, would be a policy of justice," the letter read. Many articles in the *Tribune* echoed this language, asserting the need for "fair treatment and fair play" but finding "American politics is about power and not justice." Black political and economic advance would only come with Black community empowerment and political success.[35]

During the summer of 1926, Philadelphia hosted the Sesqui-Centennial International Exposition celebrating the 150th anniversary of the United States. Event organizers expected a quarter of a million African Americans to visit the city. Mayor Kendrick served as the president of the African American exhibition committee, and he appointed former state representative John Asbury as chair and Rev. Charles Tindley as vice chair to lead "the committee to represent the colored people in the Sesqui-Centennial Celebration." In August, Isadore Martin, president of the Philadelphia Chapter of the NAACP, and Julian St. George White, secretary of the organization, sent a letter to Kendrick to find out if appointing Asbury and Tindley indicated that he had in mind "a segregated committee for a segregated people in a segregated building." Two days later, Kendrick responded that he had "no thoughts of segregation in connection" with African Americans and as mayor it "was his duty to serve with justice and equity."[36]

In February 1926, the Associated Negro Press reported that the city gave the African American exhibition committee $25,000. According to the press, the city of Philadelphia had appropriated $5 million for the exhibition. A. P. Dabney, a Black journalist from Ohio, sent a letter to Pennsylvania's U.S. Senator George Pepper about the exhibition's funding. Dabney was astonished that Mr. Asbury only requested $25,000 for the African American exhibition, and the white members of the committee considered this "amount too large" and the "expansive and expensive budget" presented by Asbury was the reason why white committee members kept African Americans from planning the arrangements. Dabney said the government should provide $1 million because the "Sesqui Centennial is not a local county fair" and "is one story in which we demand a chapter." Kendrick increased membership on the committee in charge of Negro activities to twenty-five members, including such people as Mrs. S. Willie Layton, Maude Morrisette, and younger leaders such as attorneys E. Washington Rhodes and Henry P. Cheatham. But the lack of funding of the Black exhibition created contempt among many Black Republicans.[37]

The exhibition opened on Memorial Day and lasted through the summer. On opening day, five thousand to six thousand African Americans "largely of the laboring classes" attended the exhibition. Local officials such as African American state representative Samuel Hart were in attendance and labor leader A. Philip Randolph, editor of the *Messenger*, was an invited speaker, although white organizers intentionally omitted his name from the program. In addition, the exhibits that covered the American military omitted the role of Black soldiers. In his speech, Randolph told the crowd that the role of "Negro labor is the backbone of this country's boasted supremacy." "Negro culture," he contended, was present in the Americas and had "preceded Columbus in the discovery of America." The majority of African Americans in attendance were working-class and unskilled laborers who supported Randolph's Brotherhood of Sleeping Car Porters Union, but the Black elite who had supplied the members of the sesquicentennial committee were few and far between. In spite of the Black committee's work, Black middle-class leaders believed their input was ignored and that was the reason for their low attendance on opening day.[38]

While events at the sesquicentennial highlighted the marginalization of Black Philadelphians, at the same time, the *Tribune* emphasized what African Americans contributed to the city. The July 3 edition of the paper ran a front-page story that highlighted Black buying power and provided statistics about the African American occupational structure. The *Philadelphia Tribune* published this issue during the exposition to demonstrate Black progress and contributions to the development of Philadelphia. In 1926, there were 165,000 African Americans in Philadelphia who deposited $25 million in local banks, and, the *Tribune* told its readers, "they spend 75 million dollars annually, 1.4 million dollars weekly, and $205,479 per day." The average weekly wage for Black men, the paper continued, was $25 and for Black women $16. The city held a total of 53,000 unskilled and 22,000 skilled Black workers and 674 professionals, doctors, lawyers, teachers, and preachers. Yet, in spite of this growing population and economic strength, there were only 200 political appointees.[39]

Regardless of the economic development of Black Philadelphia, the Vare machine and other Republican officials continued to disappoint Black voters. District Attorney Charles Fox, for example, refused to hire an African American assistant district attorney, but, when asked, he stated he was color-blind and selected his "assistants because of their capabilities and the manner in which they will fit" into his office. Belying such claims, he appointed inexperienced younger white assistants over seasoned African Americans. The Vare machine supported Jim Crow schools, and when pressed about segregated police and fire departments, officials claimed, "No Negro has been able to pass the examination for promotion." The Vare organization maneuvered to remove Asbury from the state Legislature for sponsoring his equal rights bill and promoted Samuel Hart and William Fuller instead because the Vares believed they could be controlled.[40]

African Americans had been growing in their political power since the Great Migration, but they clearly did not yet have enough clout to force the Vare machine to share power or provide more leadership positions. A frustrated *Tribune* in April 1926 presented a hypothetical scenario of how the Black vote could finally defeat the Vare machine. In most elections, the Vare organization received approximately two hundred thousand votes. Independents cast one hundred thousand ballots, as did approximately seventy-five thousand to one hundred thousand African Americans. According to the *Tribune*'s analysis, if Vare lost the Black vote and it were added to the one hundred thousand independents, then those two camps "will beat Vare by a 50,000 majority." Given this cold calculation, "There is not any need for colored organization men bowing and pleading with Mr. Vare."[41]

With this article, the *Tribune* demonstrated a growing independent voice that had always existed in at least limited form among Black Republicans in Philadelphia. In May 1918, for example, the "independent Republican Club" had sponsored a "Red Hot Anti Vare Meeting" in the Twenty-Sixth Ward, the former home to Ed and William Vare. Attorney G. Edward Dickerson attended the meeting and gave a speech that "called the Vares every hard name he could think of." In 1921, Black men and women Republicans in the Thirtieth Ward met because they were not "entirely satisfied with political conditions in their ward." They did not "want to destroy the Republican party" but wanted to ensure that both "Black and white" Republicans provided

African Americans with "all the privileges and rights accorded other groups in the party." The Thirtieth Ward was a predominantly Black district that was dissatisfied with ward leader Billy McCoach, who gave "all the best jobs to his white henchmen" and was "an ingrate to the loyal Black voters." McCoach, the protesters asserted, believed "the colored voters are too ignorant to use their votes to displace him." The anti-McCoach sentiment continued the following year, as Black voters in the Thirtieth Ward told the press that they "disapprove of his attitude toward colored people." In addition, Black "organization" men and women discussed demanding a member on both the board of education and the city council and a doctor at Philadelphia General Hospital. This independence movement was a response to the Vare machine not passing the Asbury equal rights bill and also failing to provide Black voters with fair representation in city government.[42]

Such growing independence fit in with the development of the "New Negro." After World War I, the increased Black population in urban communities fueled the growth of a class of Black college graduates, business owners, professionals, and businesspeople who collectively called themselves the New Negro.

New Negroes were men and women who believed the way to racial uplift lay through challenging Jim Crow and defending African American rights. Alain Locke, the Black philosopher and first African American to receive a Rhodes scholarship, wrote the anthology *The New Negro* in 1925, which served as the intellectual and cultural text of the Harlem Renaissance and the larger New Negro movement. Harlem was often referred to as the Black Mecca of the New Negro, but one could find New Negroes throughout the country. Many were from the Caribbean and migrated to the United States, such as Marcus Garvey who founded the Universal Negro Improvement Association, and Cyrill Briggs who established the African Blood Brotherhood, a radical organization that provided a race and class analysis of the Black experience. Every major city contained a population of New Negroes who fought for civil rights and were committed to developing and supporting Black-owned institutions. The New Negro was associated with the cultural ferment of the Harlem Renaissance, but men and women of this movement also developed political and economic critiques and initiatives that invigorated Black businesses and politics.[43]

Philadelphia's New Negro generation consisted of lawyers, businesspeople, ministers, and doctors. Advertising in the *Philadelphia Tribune* demonstrated the New Negro spirit, highlighting Black-owned businesses such as banks, funeral homes, and hotels. It also included announcements for Black baseball teams and performances in Black-owned venues. Taking pride in the flowering of Black economic development, the *Tribune* dedicated the entire first page of a January 1926 edition to documenting the amount of

African American wealth and occupational diversity in the city. New Negro attorneys emerged to challenge the Republican Party on a national and local level. The new generation of local Black lawyers comprised the Alexanders, E. Washington Rhodes, and others, who also contributed to the growing movement for political independence. In 1925, Black attorneys in Philadelphia formed the John Mercer Langston Club, an organization that critiqued old guard Black lawyers such as John Asbury as well as the Vare machine that took the Black vote for granted, promoted unqualified white city employees, and failed to hire and promote qualified Black candidates.[44]

By the mid-1920s, the generational divide was evident in the CRC. The majority of members remained loyal Republicans, but they saw some national Black leaders start to leave the Republican Party. In the 1924 presidential election, most CRC members voted for the GOP, but a number of Black leaders, such as Howard University professor Kelly Miller, supported Democratic candidate John Davis or Progressive Party candidate Robert La Follette. The CRC organizational election that year had such a huge voter turnout that "many were forced to stand in line," and the election was "centered around two factions, the independent element and the regulars." The independents did not want to abandon the Republican Party; they just demanded more respect and patronage. The regulars were pragmatists and insisted on recognition of the end results and the progress that Black voters had accomplished. The "regulars" consisted of Amos Scott, John Asbury, and Ed Henry, and they voted for Dr. Thomas C. Coates, a prominent doctor, as president of the CRC. The independent candidate was Julian St. George White, secretary of the local NAACP. Former CRC president Scott had organized the regulars and the *Tribune* reported that "the grand old man played his best politics and that allowed Dr. Coates a 247 vote victory." The CRC avoided an independent takeover and the regulars remained loyal to the Vare machine, but they continued to apply pressure and, by the Great Depression, they began to secure a steady increase in the number of higher-level Black appointments.[45]

In 1926, Congressman William S. Vare ran for the U.S. Senate against George Pepper, and, during that election, Raymond Pace Alexander emerged as a leading voice of a younger generation of leaders who placed demands on the Vare machine. During the first week of May, Alexander sent a letter to Vare demanding that he "give recognition to the trained Negro" and appoint an African American to a prominent position by May 18, or he would vote against him. Black leaders particularly wanted Vare to appoint a Black lawyer to serve as assistant U.S. attorney. Councilman Charles Hall supported Asbury for the position, and attorneys Alexander, Dickerson, and Robert Nix Sr. removed their names from the list so Asbury could win. Vare still refused to appoint Asbury. Despite the outcome, the *Tribune* applauded these men who "put their race above their personal feelings." The following week, Alexander sent another letter, or what the *Tribune* referred to as an ultimatum, to Vare. Senator George Pepper, in an effort to secure the Black vote, had just helped secure for E. Washington Rhodes, attorney and editor of the *Philadelphia Tribune*, the first assistant U.S. district attorney position for an African American in Philadelphia's history. Edgar Roster of the *Tribune* wrote that Pepper "completely knocked the Vares off their feet . . . when he appointed Rhodes to a position of honor and trust." Alexander hoped Pepper's move coupled with Black political pressure would force Vare to appoint another Black candidate. Alexander stated African Americans were "anxious to know what the Organization will do to meet the challenge" and that he had "voted the Republican organization ticket since he was old enough to vote," but if Vare did not make an appointment he would leave the organization. Vare did not budge.[46]

In March 1926, Rhodes sent a letter asking for the racial views of the three white Republican candidates, Senator Pepper, Congressman Vare, and Governor Gifford Pinchot. Pepper was the only one to respond. Pepper stated he did not believe in segregation in public schools, and he supported the Dyer Anti Lynching Bill. He also believed "qualified Negroes should receive such appointments that pay between three and ten thousand dollars," and he supported the Reconstruction amendments. In April and May, Pepper purchased full-page ads in the *Philadelphia Tribune* that encouraged African Americans to register to vote. "The Vare Gang is organized," the ads read, "but it does not represent the true Republican strength of Philadelphia." In bold capital letters, the ads reminded readers, "REGISTRATION DAY—APRIL 14 . . . one must be a registered Republican to vote in the April 14th primary." The third, in bold letters, said "VAREISM," a "down-town political boss to grab control of the Republican Party of Pennsylvania." Pepper and the Black community were the true Republicans standing "against ballot stuffers." As Black support for Pepper grew, the *Tribune* reported that Vare responded by distributing "thousands of free newspapers that contain his propaganda," but he still "refused to say how he stands on the Dyer Anti Lynching bill." In spite of Pepper's efforts to rally Black support, the Vare machine was too strong. Vare won the primary and the subsequent Senate race, although he was never seated due to corruption and fraud.[47]

Through the remainder of the 1920s, the Vare machine continued to control many local elections, and the residents of the Thirtieth Ward continued to voice their frustrations with their lack of representation. In March 1928, Mayor Harry Mackey appointed three African Americans as assistant city solicitors: attorney and president of the CRC John Sparks, attorney Sadie Tanner Mossell Alexander, and attorney G. Edward Dickerson. Two weeks later, John Asbury, president of the Active Workers Republican Club, was sworn in as the first Black assistant district attorney in Philadelphia with a $3,500 annual salary. But, in the Thirtieth Ward, white political leaders who controlled the divisions continued to get high salaries and the district attorney refused to appoint "colored men to any position" in the area. This was despite the fact that the Thirtieth Ward had Black supermajority divisions, such as "the Fifth with 437 Black and only 26 white voters" and a "$232,920 annual payroll." The voters in the Thirtieth Ward made their views clear in the press: "Black Majority in the Thirtieth Ward 84 Percent. Should have 80 percent of the patronage."[48] (See Fig. 2.1.)

Although Black voters in Chicago and Harlem began to move to the Democratic Party in the late 1920s, the majority of Black Philadelphians remained in the Republican Party. In 1928, Raymond Pace Alexander served as a member of the Executive Committee of the Colored Workers Division, a group of African Americans who supported Republican presidential candidate Herbert Hoover. The *Tribune* argued that across the country Black Americans had the opportunity to send three African American men to Congress. According to the paper, the "Harlem Negro is locally a Democrat" but in New York City the Republican Party still "nominated a Negro for congress." Black politics was beginning to shift in 1928, when Hoover won

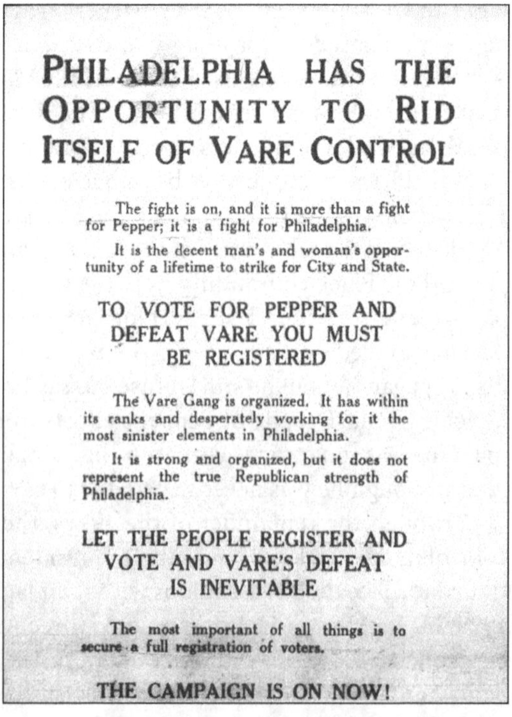

Figure 2.1 Republican senator George Pepper's political campaign ad encouraging African Americans to register and vote to defeat the "sinister elements" of the "Vare Gang."

> **PHILADELPHIA HAS THE OPPORTUNITY TO RID ITSELF OF VARE CONTROL**
>
> The fight is on, and it is more than a fight for Pepper; it is a fight for Philadelphia.
>
> It is the decent man's and woman's opportunity of a lifetime to strike for City and State.
>
> **TO VOTE FOR PEPPER AND DEFEAT VARE YOU MUST BE REGISTERED**
>
> The Vare Gang is organized. It has within its ranks and desperately working for it the most sinister elements in Philadelphia.
>
> It is strong and organized, but it does not represent the true Republican strength of Philadelphia.
>
> **LET THE PEOPLE REGISTER AND VOTE AND VARE'S DEFEAT IS INEVITABLE**
>
> The most important of all things is to secure a full registration of voters.
>
> **THE CAMPAIGN IS ON NOW!**

the election, and African Americans understood that "whether he [the African American] gets anything for it will depend on . . . 'the courage of the Negroes.'" While Hoover and the Republican Party were victorious, Black Democrats in Chicago elected Oscar De Priest to Congress and Chicago emerged as the Black Mecca in urban politics.[49]

In 1929, Philadelphia had the third largest Black population in the United States but did not approach the number of Black judges and state representatives in New York and did not have a congressman like Chicago. Condemning the situation, E. Washington Rhodes published a front-page article, "Real Political Power Found Among Negroes of Wide Awake Chicago," where he praised their "political power and patronage" and explained how the "Chicago Negro" was the model of Black political leadership. Philadelphia, however, remained committed to the Republican Party. In June 1929, the First African Baptist Church invited prominent Black Republican speakers such as Perry Howard, an attorney from Mississippi and former special assistant to the attorney general; R. R. Wright, president of Citizens and Southern Bank in Philadelphia; and Alexander. Alexander encouraged African Americans in Philadelphia to support Black banks in order to take advantage of their economic power. Howard told the crowd that "Negroes of Philadelphia could send a representative to Congress were they organized and worked together." Rhodes and Howard were convinced the lack of organization was the primary reason that Black Philadelphians had not elected a Black congressman. In spite of the Democratic gains in Chicago and New York, Black Philadelphians remained loyal to the party of Lincoln. They had learned to flex their political muscle on occasion, but not often enough to break free from the GOP.[50]

With Black Philadelphia remaining loyal to the GOP, the Republican organization published an ad in the *Tribune* for the upcoming September 1929 primary, in which four white male candidates were running for city controller, register of wills, city treasurer, and coroner. The ad made clear the amount of patronage the "Regular Republican Organization" had given to Black voters. The ad tallied the wages of Black city workers and reminded voters to vote for their candidates: "More Than a Million and a Half Dollars Worth of Reasons Why Colored Voters Should Support the Organization Ticket." The highest-paid Black city employee was a municipal judge who made $5,000 per year and the lowest was a "female cleaner" in city council chambers making $900 per year. The Vare organization let Black voters know they provided massive employment for Black voters and would continue to do so in exchange for their support. The organization won the election with Black votes, but this was one of the last times Republicans so strongly retained the African American vote.[51] (See Fig. 2.2.)

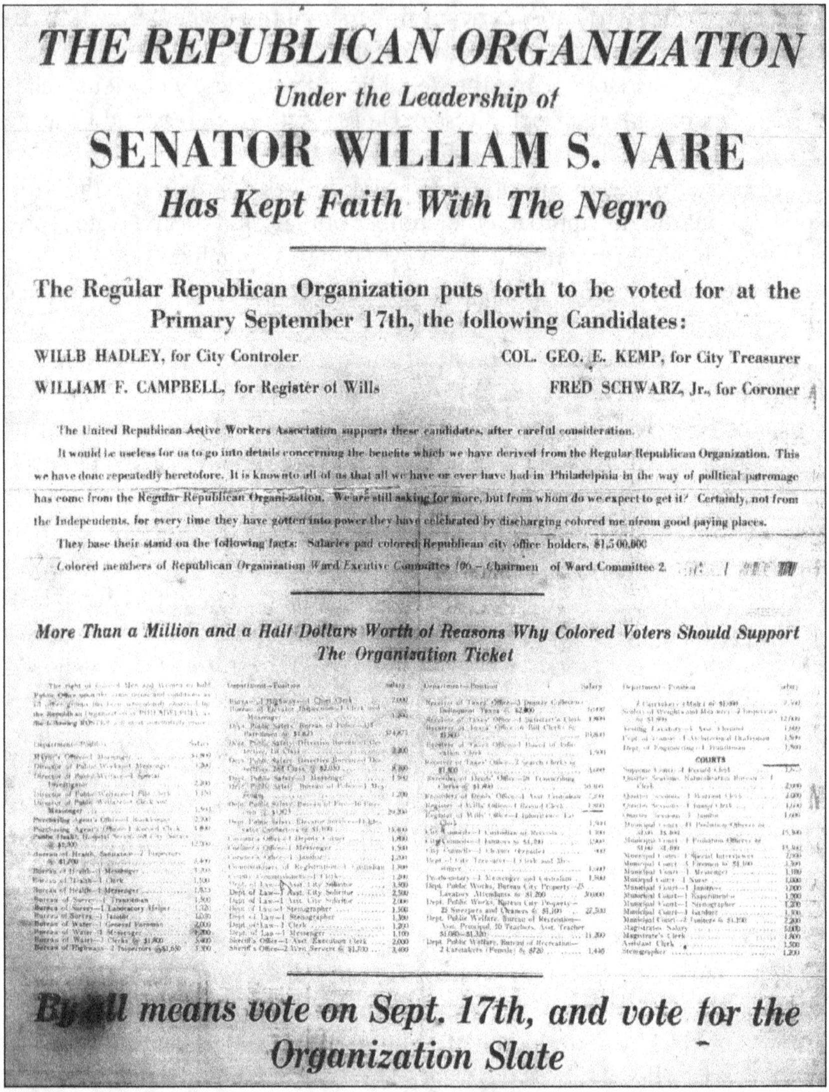

THE REPUBLICAN ORGANIZATION

Under the Leadership of

SENATOR WILLIAM S. VARE

Has Kept Faith With The Negro

The Regular Republican Organization puts forth to be voted for at the Primary September 17th, the following Candidates:

WILLB HADLEY, for City Controler

COL. GEO. E. KEMP, for City Treasurer

WILLIAM F. CAMPBELL, for Register of Wills

FRED SCHWARZ, Jr., for Coroner

The United Republican Active Workers Association supports these candidates, after careful consideration.

It would be useless for us to go into details concerning the benefits which we have derived from the Regular Republican Organization. This we have done repeatedly heretofore. It is knownto all of us that all we have or ever have had in Philadelphia in the way of political patronage has come from the Regular Republican Organization. We are still asking for more, but from whom do we expect to get it? Certainly, not from the Independents, for every time they have gotten into power they have celebrated by discharging colored me nfrom good paying places.

They base their stand on the following facts: Salaries paid colored Republican city office holders, $1,500,000

Colored members of Republican Organization Ward Excutive Committes 106 – Chairmen of Ward Committee 2.

More Than a Million and a Half Dollars Worth of Reasons Why Colored Voters Should Support The Organization Ticket

COURTS

By all means vote on Sept. 17th, and vote for the Organization Slate

Figure 2.2 Senator William S. Vare's Republican organization requesting Black voters' support for their Republican candidates for the September primary. There were $1.5 million "worth of reasons" why Black voters must support the Republican organization.

In 1932, Franklin Roosevelt's Democratic Party coalition of labor, women, and African Americans began to emerge in Philadelphia. Despite this fact, the Democratic Party would need another two decades to take over the city. Black voters in Chicago showed that they were much further along in this shift when they elected Oscar De Priest as the first Black congressman since

Reconstruction. African Americans did not really shift to Roosevelt until 1936, and it was not until 1958 that Robert Nix Sr. became Philadelphia's first Black Democratic congressman.

From 1915 to 1929, Black electoral politics mainly consisted of bloc voting and patronage. The increase of Black voters and a movement toward independence, or, at least, voting for the anti-Vare Republican candidate, forced the Vare machine to increase the number of Black political appointments and city workers. There was a clear quid pro quo in urban politics and all participants understood the rules of the game. African American professionals desired positions in government worthy of their education, and working-class Black workers desired jobs in local government with a chance for promotion. Chicago emerged as the ideal for Black politics because strict racial segregation produced a powerful Black base on the South Side. But Philadelphia consisted of three separate Black communities, north, west, and south, which made it difficult to elect a Black representative to Congress. In February 1926, the *Philadelphia Tribune* discussed the expansion of the Black population in North Philadelphia, which had "grown from four small streets to Forty-Eight City blocks . . . and 35,000 African Americans lived in that part of the city." There were also decent-sized Black communities in South and West Philadelphia. Some Black leaders blamed African American egos and infighting for the inability to elect a Black congressman. But, in reality, the white Republican Party leadership, especially the Vares, was racist and understood politics as being based on power, not justice, equity, and democracy. From 1915 to 1929, the Pennsylvania Senate did not pass any equal rights bill because Black people did not have the political power and white institutions and businesses were committed to a racist, segregated system. In spite of racism and segregation, by the Great Depression, Black men and women in the GOP had developed a committed group of leaders who registered Black voters and tried to hold the Republican Party accountable to the political needs of the Black community. They had also developed enough independence to listen when the Democratic Party of Franklin Roosevelt came calling.[52]

NOTES

1. "Big Republican Rallies Were Held in the Various Wards Throughout this Vast City," *Philadelphia Tribune*, October 30, 1915, 1; "Thomas B. Smith Leads Ticket by over 77,832 Majority: Sweeps City Carrying All Except Five Wards," *Philadelphia Tribune*, November 6, 1915, 1.

2. "Director Porter's Police Clubbed Defenseless Women and Children," *Philadelphia Tribune*, September 25, 1915, 1; *Philadelphia Tribune*, October 30, 1915.

3. James Wolfinger, *Philadelphia Divided: Race and Politics in the City of Brotherly Love* (Chapel Hill: University of North Carolina Press, 2007); David A. Canton, *Raymond Pace Alexander: A New Negro Lawyer Fights for Civil Rights in Philadelphia* (Jackson: University Press of Mississippi, 2010); Matthew J. Countryman, *Up South: Civil Rights and Black Power in Philadelphia* (Philadelphia: University of Pennsylvania Press, 2006); Charles Hardy III, "Race and Opportunity: Black Philadelphia during the Era of the Great Migration, 1916–1930" (Ph.D. diss., Temple University Press, 1989); Eugene Hartfield, "The Impact of the New Deal on Black Politics in Pennsylvania, 1928–1936" (Ph.D. diss., University of North Carolina, 1979); James E. Miller, "The Negro in Pennsylvania Politics: With Special Emphasis on the Years between 1927 and 1940" (Ph.D. diss., University of Pennsylvania, 1945); W.E.B. Du Bois, *The Philadelphia Negro: A Social Study* (Philadelphia: University of Pennsylvania Press, 1899).

4. Robert Weems Jr., *Desegregating the Dollar: African American Consumerism in the Twentieth Century* (New York: Oxford University Press, 1998); Robert Gregg, *Sparks from the Anvil of Oppression: Philadelphia's African American Methodists and Southern Migrants, 1890–1940* (Philadelphia: Temple University Press, 1993); Julie Winch, *Philadelphia's Black Elite: Activism, Accommodation and the Struggle for Autonomy, 1787–1848* (Philadelphia: Temple University Press, 1988); Willard B. Gatewood, *Aristocrats of Color: The Black Elite, 1880–1920* (Bloomington: Indiana University Press, 1990); Roger Lane, *William Dorsey's Philadelphia and Ours: On the Past and Future of the Black City in America* (New York: Oxford University Press, 1991); Carol Anderson, *White Rage: The Unspoken Truth of Our Racial Divide* (New York: Bloomsbury, 2016); V. P. Franklin, *The Education of Black Philadelphia: The Social and Educational History of a Minority Community* (Philadelphia: University of Pennsylvania Press, 1979); Richard Rothstein, *The Color of Law: A Forgotten History of How Our Government Segregated America* (New York: Liveright, 2017).

5. "Founder's Day Fitly Observed at Citizens' Club," *Philadelphia Tribune*, May 29, 1920, 1; "One of Our Astute Lawyers Given a Snug Berth in Harrisburg," *Philadelphia Tribune*, November 11, 1916, 1.

6. "Colored Lawyers Have Made Good in Philadelphia," *Philadelphia Tribune*, October 25, 1919, 1; "Sixteen Years on the Staff of the Tribune," *Philadelphia Tribune*, December 20, 1919, 1; V. P. Franklin, "Voice of the Black Community: The Philadelphia Tribune, 1912–1941," *Pennsylvania History* 51, no. 4 (October 1984): 261–264.

7. G. Grant Williams, "The Disgrace of Mayor Smith," *Philadelphia Tribune*, November 3, 1917, 1.

8. "Plan on Foot to Boycott South Street Stores," *Philadelphia Tribune*, July 1, 1916,1; Cheryl Greenberg, *Troubling the Waters: Black-Jewish Relations in the American Century* (Princeton, NJ: Princeton University Press, 2006).

9. "Colored Citizens Boycott White South St. Stores," *Philadelphia Tribune*, July 8, 1916, 1.

10. "Colored Citizens Boycott White South St. Stores," *Philadelphia Tribune*, July 8, 1916, 1.

11. "Colored Citizens Boycott White South St. Stores," *Philadelphia Tribune*, July 8, 1916, 1.

12. "Colored Citizens Boycott White South St. Stores," *Philadelphia Tribune*, July 8, 1916; "Business Man from the South Association," *Philadelphia Tribune*, July 15, 1916, 1.

13. Linda Gordon, *The Second Coming of the Ku Klux Klan: The KKK of the 1920s and the American Political Tradition* (New York: Liveright, 2018); Eric S. Yellin, *Racism*

in the Nation's Service: Government Workers and the Color Line in Woodrow Wilson's America (Chapel Hill: University of North Carolina Press, 2016).

14. David Zucchino, *Wilmington's Lie: The Murderous Coup of 1898 and the Rise of White Supremacy* (New York: Atlantic Monthly, 2020); Alfred L. Brophy, *Reconstructing the Dreamland: The Tulsa Race Riot of 1921, Race, Reparations, and Reconciliation* (New York: Oxford University Press, 2003); Robert V. Haynes, *A Night of Violence: The Houston Riot of 1917* (Baton Rouge: Louisiana State University Press, 1976); Mark Robert Schneider, *We Return Fighting: The Civil Rights Movement in the Jazz Age* (Boston: Northeastern University Press, 2001); David F. Krugler, *1919, The Year of Racial Violence: How African Americans Fought Back* (Cambridge: Cambridge University Press, 2015); V. P. Franklin, "The Philadelphia Race Riot of 1918," *Pennsylvania Magazine of History and Biography* 99 (July 1975): 336–350.

15. V. P. Franklin, "The Philadelphia Race Riot of 1918," *Pennsylvania Magazine of History and Biography* 99 (July 1975): 336–350.

16. Willams, "Dixie Methods in Philadelphia," *Philadelphia Tribune*, August 12, 1918.

17. "Police Superintendent Protects Our Citizens," *Philadelphia Tribune*, September 14, 1918, 1.

18. *Philadelphia Tribune*, September 14, 1918.

19. "The Stein Bill, Making It Unlawful to Refuse to Give Accommodations, Passes the House," *Philadelphia Tribune*, April 17, 1915, 1.

20. *Philadelphia Tribune*, June 2, 1915; *Philadelphia Tribune*, June 5, 1915.

21. "Thousands of Citizens Have Endorsed The Candidacy of Amos. M. Scott for Magistrate," *Philadelphia Tribune*, July 19, 1919, 1; "Wonderful Chance to Make the Colored Vote a Potent Factor in Coming Election in Philadelphia," *Philadelphia Tribune*, September 13, 1919, 1.

22. "Migration of Colored Voters Is Very Puzzling," *Philadelphia Tribune*, September 11, 1920, 1; Williams, "Fearless Writer Assails Conditions in Philadelphia," *Philadelphia Tribune*, February 26, 1921, 1.

23. G. Grant Williams, "Stanley Theater Regrets Insult to Hon. J.C. Asbury," *Philadelphia Tribune*, March 12, 1921, 1; Williams, "Fearless Writer," *Philadelphia Tribune*, February 26, 1921.

24. "Colored Lawyers Made Good in Philadelphia," *Philadelphia Tribune*, October 25, 1919, 1; "The Vare and Penrose Factions Bury the Hatchet," *Philadelphia Tribune*, June 18, 1921, 1.

25. "Colored Voters to Honor Harding on September 22," *Philadelphia Tribune*, September 18, 1920, 1.

26. "John C. Asbury Endorsed by Thirtieth Ward," *Philadelphia Tribune*, April 17, 1920; Rosalyn Terborg-Penn, *African American Women in the Struggle for the Vote 1850–1920* (Bloomington: Indiana University Press, 1998); Martha S. Jones, *Vanguard: How Black Women Broke Barriers, Won the Vote, and Insisted on Equality for All* (New York: Basic Books, 2020).

27. "Colored Woman First of Her Sex to Vote in Philadelphia," *Philadelphia Tribune*, November 6, 1920, 1; Eric Ledell Smith, "Asking for Justice and Fair Play: African American State Legislators and Civil Rights in Early Twentieth-Century Philadelphia," *Pennsylvania History* 63, no. 2 (April 1996): 185.

28. Old Timer, "Full Text of the Equal Rights Bill Gets Another Hearing," *Philadelphia Tribune*, February 19, 1921, 1; "Asbury's Equal Rights Bill Gets Another Hearing," *Philadelphia Tribune*, April 16, 1921, 1

29. Old Timer, "Theater and Hotel Interests Strive to Defeat Equal Rights Bill," *Philadelphia Tribune*, April 9, 1921; Smith, "Asking for Justice," 193.

30. Smith, "Asking for Justice." 191.

31. "Big Race Leaders Endorse Mr. Scott for Magistrate," *Philadelphia Tribune*, July 16, 1921, 1; "Colored Women Will Function in City Committee," *Philadelphia Tribune*, August 4, 1921.

32. "Colored Women Line Up for Scott and Dickerson," *Philadelphia Tribune*, September 17, 1921; "Colored Women Now Great Factors in Local Politics," *Philadelphia Tribune*, September 24, 1921.

33. "Amos Scott Wins by over 60,000 Majority," *Philadelphia Tribune*, November 12, 1921; "Hall In Charge of Scott's Campaign for Magistrate," *Philadelphia Tribune*, November 5, 1921, 1.

34. Canton, *Raymond Pace Alexander*; Kenneth Mack, *Representing the Race: The Creation of the Civil Rights Lawyer* (Cambridge, MA: Harvard University Press, 2012); Nina Banks, ed., *Democracy, Race, and Justice: The Speeches and Writings of Sadie T.M. Alexander* (New Haven: Yale University Press, 2021).

35. "Inter-Racial Committee Puts Problem Squarely Before Mayor Kendrick," *Philadelphia Tribune*, March 1, 1924, 1.

36. "Mayor Kendrick Says There Will Be No Segregation," *Philadelphia Tribune*, August 22, 1925, 1.

37. "Chairman Asbury Makes Statement on Exposition," *Philadelphia Tribune*, February 27, 1926, 1.

38. "Sesqui-Centennial Opening Attended by Thousands of Visitors to Quaker City," *Philadelphia Tribune*, June 5, 1926, 1. The World's Columbian Exposition in Chicago in 1893, often referred to as the White City, has received instructive racial analysis. See Christopher Robert Reed, *"All the World Is Here!" The Black Presence at White City* (Bloomington: Indiana University Press, 2000).

39. "A Tremendous Buying Power: Philadelphia Negroes Spend $205,479 Daily," *Philadelphia Tribune*, July 3, 1926.

40. "Fox Refuses to Appoint a Negro as an Assistant," *Philadelphia Tribune*, February 13, 1926.

41. "Colored Vote Can Win Any Election in State," *Philadelphia Tribune*, April 17, 1926.

42. "Fox Refuses to Appoint a Negro as an Assistant," *Philadelphia Tribune*, February 13, 1926; "Colored Vote Can Win Any Election in State," *Philadelphia Tribune*, April 17, 1926; "Independent Citizens of Wards West of the Schuykill Organized in Interest of John B. Taylor," Philadelphia Tribune, May 18, 1918; "Thirtieth Ward Will Fight Its Ward Leader," *Philadelphia Tribune*, June 15, 1921.

43. David Levering Lewis, *When Harlem Was in Vogue* (New York: Oxford University Press, 1979); Kevin K. Gaines, *Uplifting the Race: Black Leadership, Politics, and Culture in the Twentieth Century* (Chapel Hill: University of North Carolina Press, 1996); Winston James, *Holding Aloft the Banner of Ethiopia: Caribbean Radicalism in Early Twentieth-Century America* (New York: Verso, 1998); Minkah Makalani, *In the Cause of Freedom: Radical Black Internationalism from Harlem to London, 1917–1939* (Chapel Hill: University of North Carolina Press, 2011); Treva B. Lindsey, *Colored No More: Reinventing Black Womanhood in Washington D.C.* (Urbana: University of Illinois Press, 2017).

44. Canton, *Raymond Pace Alexander*, 27–29; J. Clay Smith Jr., *Emancipation: The Making of the Black Lawyer, 1844–1944* (Philadelphia: University of Pennsylvania Press, 1993).

45. "Citizens Club Elects Dr. Coates as Its President," *Philadelphia Tribune*, December 15, 1924; "Fight Fails to Develop: Citizens Republican," *Philadelphia Tribune*, September 13, 1924.

46. "Increasing Independent Sentiment Threatens to Nullify 'Gang' Influence," *Philadelphia Tribune*, May 1, 1926; "Vare Gets Ultimatum from Colored Lawyer: Must Give Recognition Before May 18th," *Philadelphia Tribune*, May 8, 1926.

47. "Senator Peppers Answers Questionnaire of Tribune: Others Fail to Reply," *Philadelphia Tribune*, April 10, 1926; "John Asbury Kicked Out of Legislature Because of Equal Rights Bill," *Philadelphia Tribune*, May 15, 1926.

48. *Philadelphia Tribune*, February 7, 1928; Edgar Roster, "City Solicitor to Have Three Colored Aides," *Philadelphia Tribune*, March 1, 1928; "Asbury Sworn Into Office Without Show," *Philadelphia Tribune*, March 15, 1928, 1.

49. "Negro Vote Most Important Says Chairman Work: Work Will Depend on Their Loyalty," *Philadelphia Tribune*, September 6, 1928, 1.

50. E. Washington Rhodes, "Real Political Power Found among Negroes of Wide Awake Chicago," *Philadelphia Tribune*, May 25, 1929; "Perry Howard Says Negroes Can Send Representative to Congress from Philadelphia," *Philadelphia Tribune*, June 27, 1929, 1.

51. "Negro Voters Prove Loyal to Vare Organization in Overwhelming 'Gang' Win," *Philadelphia Tribune*, September 19, 1929, 1.

52. "Colored Population Shifts to Northern Party of City," *Philadelphia Tribune*, February 6, 1926; St. Claire Drake and Horace Cayton, *Black Metropolis: A Study of Negro Life in a Northern City* (New York: Harper and Row, 1945); Andrew J. Diamond, *Chicago on the Make: Power and Influence in a Modern City* (Berkeley: University of California Press, 2017).

3

The Great Depression and World War II

STANLEY KEITH ARNOLD

Philadelphia's Black political environment underwent a dramatic realignment in the critical years between the beginning of the Great Depression and the conclusion of World War II. The developments within the Black community played an important role in the political realignment of the city's municipal government and contributed to Democratic victories on both the state and national levels. In addition to this shift in the Democratic Party, this period also witnessed an upsurge in radical activism in the city's African American community. Black disenchantment with the Republican Party was fueled by the economic devastation of the Great Depression and the emergence of New Deal policies.

In the late 1920s, Philadelphia was one of the nation's most important manufacturing centers. In contrast to cities like Detroit and Pittsburgh, Philadelphia's booming industrial sector was not dependent on a single industry. Rather, the Quaker City's diverse manufacturing environment gave it the moniker "Workshop of the World." The city produced most of the nation's locomotives, commercial ships, hats, and industrial saws. Companies such as Sun Oil, Baldwin Locomotive Company, and Cramp's Shipyard provided employment for tens of thousands of workers. With the onset of the Great Depression, however, the decline in consumer and commercial demand devastated the city's economy. By 1933, regional manufacturing output declined by 45 percent, factory payrolls dropped by 60 percent, and retail sales fell by 40 percent. The construction industry experienced an 84 percent drop. The city's financial institutions were also decimated by the economic crisis. Hundreds of building and loan associations failed, and one-third of the city's eighty-nine banks closed their doors. Tens of thousands became homeless and shantytowns known as "Hoovervilles" sprung up across the city.[1]

Prior to the Depression, the city's Black community endured an unemployment rate higher than the white population. Although Black migrants had found work in the city's bustling industrial defense sector during World War I, these jobs disappeared after the conflict ended. As a result, Black employment in manufacturing declined. By 1927, only 6.1 percent of the city's Black workers were employed in manufacturing, and 20 percent worked as waiters, cleaners, chauffeurs, and janitors. Most were employed as laborers. Black women fared worse, with 52 percent employed as domestics. Black workers occupied the lowest rungs of the economic ladder and were thus more vulnerable when the Depression unfolded. By 1933, Black unemployment reached 50 percent. In a report sanctioned by the federal government, New Deal official Lorena Hickok described "two negresses, mother and daughter who walked eight miles every day to earn, by doing a little cleaning and washing, a little money to pay forward to their rent." The women told Hickok that they earned 10 cents an hour for their labor. In addition to enduring massive rates of joblessness, the Depression had a devastating impact on Black homeowners. In 1930, African Americans owned more homes in Philadelphia than in any other Northern city. The city's housing stock was dominated by single-family row houses, which offered greater opportunity for homeownership. The stability of Black financial institutions like the Berean Savings Bank contributed to this development, as did the exodus of middle-class white people to outlying city neighborhoods and suburbs. However, while within a few years of the crash many Black homeowners were in danger of foreclosure, the most vulnerable were renters. The majority of Black Philadelphians rented their dwellings, and, by 1932, half of them faced eviction. Black Philadelphia faced its greatest crisis since the era of slavery.[2]

Although Black Philadelphians had been stalwart supporters of the Republican Party since the aftermath of the Civil War, neither they nor anyone else impacted by the economic crisis could expect substantial relief. The local GOP machine had achieved national infamy for its malfeasance. In the early twentieth century, the muckraking journalist Lincoln Steffens described Philadelphia as "corrupt and contented." As the Depression deepened, the city's Republicans supported Hoover's laissez-faire approach to the economy. Their long dominance of the city's political environment had seriously weakened the local Democratic Party. The Democrats' finances were so insolvent that the Republicans secretly paid the rent on their headquarters.³

With neither party addressing the crisis, some Philadelphians believed that radical solutions were needed. The City of Brotherly Love had a strong tradition of militant organizing. Prior to World War I, Benjamin Fletcher, an African American member of the Industrial Workers of the World, led a successful strike of the city's longshoremen. Fletcher's major accomplishment was his ability to unify workers across racial and ethnic lines. However, Fletcher and other Industrial Workers of the World leaders were victims of Woodrow Wilson's red scare and imprisoned. Wilson's campaign and the post–World War I conservative reaction diminished but did not destroy radicalism in the Quaker City. As the Depression deepened, the Communist Party became increasingly active in addressing the concerns of the most desperate victims of the economic catastrophe. Like their counterparts across the nation, Philadelphia's Communists contributed to the formation of unemployed councils. In November 1931, the city's unemployment councils selected Martha Jeffries, an African American widow and mother, to represent them at a congressional hearing in Washington, DC. Communists and their supporters also engaged in direct action to press for their demands. In February 1932, hundreds of Communists and their allies protested the lack of government action at city hall. The demonstrators were attacked by police, who arrested and injured dozens.⁴

The inability and unwillingness of the Republicans to confront the crisis created an opportunity for Philadelphia's Democrats. The resurgence of the local Democratic establishment was spearheaded by John B. "Handsome Jack" Kelly, one of the city's most successful contractors and a former Olympic sculling champion, and Anne Brancato, a local South Philadelphia activist who in 1932 became the first woman elected to the Pennsylvania General Assembly. Joseph Guffey, a member of the Democratic National Committee from Western Pennsylvania, also assisted Philadelphia's beleaguered Democrats. Guffey helped Franklin Delano Roosevelt secure his nomination and wanted to deliver Pennsylvania to the Democrats.⁵

As the city's Democrats capitalized on their candidate's promise of a "New Deal" for the American people, it was unclear if Black Philadelphians would support Roosevelt. Local Republicans depended on the allegiance of African Americans, who were rewarded with low-ranking patronage jobs. While many Black Philadelphians accepted this norm, some newcomers were willing to challenge the status quo. One such newcomer was Marshall Shepard Sr. The son of former slaves, the North Carolina–born Shepard was a graduate of Samuel Slater Normal School, now Winston-Salem State University, and earned his Doctor of Divinity at Virginia Union University. Like millions of African Americans during this period, Shepard migrated north.

In the 1920s, he served as assistant pastor of Harlem's Abyssinian Baptist Church, working under the direction of the famed Reverend Adam Clayton Powell Sr. While in Harlem, Shepard found an African American community challenging racism through art, music, and political expression. The young reverend accepted an offer to pastor West Philadelphia's growing Mt. Olivet Baptist Church. Although Mt. Olivet encountered financial difficulties during the Depression, Shepard mobilized the congregation to save the church. In this way, he drew on the historical Black tradition of mutual aid. However, Shepard and other Black leaders realized that the community needed something greater than mutual aid. He argued that Black people needed more representation within the GOP. Shepard and several of his colleagues journeyed to the Atlantic City, New Jersey, summer home of William Vare, one of the stalwarts of the Philadelphia GOP machine. Shepard and the delegation asked Vare to put a Black candidate on the ticket for the next municipal election. When rebuffed by Vare, Shepard returned to Philadelphia, joined the Democratic Party, and allowed his church to serve as one of the local headquarters for Roosevelt's presidential campaign.[6]

Shepard was not alone in his support for the slowly resurgent local Democratic Party. Like Shepard, Crystal Dreda Bird was a migrant from the Upper South. Born in Maryland, she was raised in Boston and taught in the New York City public schools, eventually earning a bachelor's degree from Teachers College, Columbia University. In the 1920s, Bird served as the YWCA field secretary for African American girls and lectured on African American culture for the American Friends Service Committee, the activist arm of the Religious Society of Friends (Quakers). In 1931, she married Arthur Huff Fauset, an anthropologist and principal of the all-Black Singerly School. Fauset hailed from the old Philadelphia Black elite; his half-sister was the famous Harlem Renaissance author Jessie Redmon Fauset. As a result of this union, Crystal Bird gained access to the small yet influential Black upper class of Philadelphia. Shortly after arriving in Philadelphia, Bird was recruited to work at the fledgling Institute of Race Relations at nearby Swarthmore College. More importantly, she worked to register Black voters, specifically Black women.[7]

An increasing number of prominent Black Philadelphians expressed interest in the Democratic Party. Arbertha White was a well-known small business owner from North Philadelphia. In the 1920s, White formed the North Philadelphia Welfare League, which established a soup kitchen and provided other services for poor Black Philadelphians. By 1931, her organization was suffering from a lack of donations, and White shifted her political allegiance to the Democratic Party. White became the first African American woman to run for the Pennsylvania state legislature, and, although she was defeated in the primary, her candidacy inspired Black Philadelphians.

In addition, Allied Roosevelt Clubs emerged in the city's Black neighborhoods. The clubs were the brainchild of J. Max Barber, founder of the *Philadelphia Independent* newspaper. Barber established his paper to counter the Republican-leaning *Philadelphia Tribune*, the city's leading Black news outlet.[8] (See Fig. 3.1.)

The effort to gain Black support for Roosevelt's campaign ran into opposition. The Republican establishment utilized prominent Black GOP officials to diminish Democratic hopes. E. Washington Rhodes, the editor of the *Philadelphia Tribune*, became the principal Black spokesman for the GOP machine. Born in South Carolina, Rhodes was educated in Pennsylvania at Lincoln University and Temple University School of Law. In the early 1920s, President Calvin Coolidge appointed Rhodes to serve as the assistant U.S. attorney for the Eastern District of Pennsylvania. In addition to criticizing the Communists, Rhodes warned Black voters that Roosevelt and his running mate, Texan John Nance Garner, were an uncertain and

Figure 3.1 By the late 1930s, African Americans were assuming more prominent roles in Philadelphia's Democratic Party. *Top row (left to right):* State Representative Samuel D. Holmes, Attorney Austin Norris, and State Representative Marshall Shepard Sr. *Bottom row (left to right):* Magistrate Joseph Rainey Jr., Governor George Earle, and State Representative Crystal Bird Fauset. (Photo ca. 1939–1940.)

potentially dangerous element. Despite Democratic efforts, the city's Black population gave their support to incumbent president Herbert Hoover. The Republican candidate won 73 percent of the African American electorate in Philadelphia, a crucial element in winning Pennsylvania. While the local GOP campaigned to dissuade Black voters from switching their allegiance, Philadelphia was not alone. Black voters in Chicago and Detroit threw their support behind Hoover. In contrast, Black voters in New York City voted for Roosevelt. They were familiar with Roosevelt's progressive policies when he served as governor of the Empire State and believed that he could lead the country out of the economic crisis.[9]

In Philadelphia, however, the GOP's grasp on power was by no means absolute. Although Hoover won the city, it was only by 70,766 votes. In a city dominated by the Republicans since the Civil War, this indicated a weakening of their power. The GOP's reputation was not helped by the policies and statements of Mayor J. Hampton Moore. In response to concerns about the Depression, Moore declared, "No one is starving in Philadelphia" and refused to address the city's deteriorating housing stock, claiming "Philadelphia is too proud to have slums." Moore's refusal to confront the crisis, coupled with increasing protests and the introduction of New Deal policies such as the bank holiday, contributed to a resurgence of the Democratic Party. In addition, the Democrats had registered over 179,000 new voters, many of whom were Black. Black Democrats had contributed to this upsurge in interest and hoped that these new voters would heed the words of *Pittsburgh Courier* editor, Robert L. Vann, who urged Black people to turn "Lincoln's picture to the wall" and embrace the Democrats.[10]

The 1934 elections included congressional and state races. Democratic leaders such as Guffey and Kelly argued that these elections constituted a mandate on Roosevelt's New Deal. On the state level, George Earle was elected governor, the first Democrat in forty years to occupy the highest office in the state. Although he faced a divided legislature, Earle forged close ties with Roosevelt and embarked on his own "Little New Deal." The new legislature included Marshall Shepard who was elected to represent West Philadelphia in the state House of Representatives. Shepard became the first African American Democrat to serve in the legislature. The freshman legislator delivered patronage jobs, much as the GOP had done. More importantly, he sponsored progressive legislation. Shepard cooperated with another freshman representative, Hobson Reynolds, on the passage of the 1935 Pennsylvania Equal Rights Law, which guaranteed access to restaurants and hotels. Like Shepard, Reynolds was a native of North Carolina who migrated to escape Jim Crow segregation. Educated as a mortician, Reynolds established a successful business in Philadelphia and became active in Republican Party politics in the late 1920s. Despite this victory, Reynolds was frustrated by his party's lack of interest in civil rights, and he ran as a Democrat in 1938. Later, he returned to Philadelphia and the doddering GOP to serve as city magistrate.[11]

While equal access to public accommodations was important, Black Philadelphians remained preoccupied with their economic survival. Within two years of Roosevelt's inauguration, jobs programs, such as the Civil Works Administration and its successor, the more comprehensive Works Progress Administration (WPA), began to have an impact on the Philadelphia region. However, these programs faced opposition from the city's GOP leadership. Republicans believed that the involvement of the federal government in local economic matters would challenge their power. As a result, thousands of unemployed Philadelphians commuted to the suburbs to work on New Deal projects.[12]

Philadelphia's resurgent Democratic Party attempted to capitalize on Roosevelt's growing popularity. The 1935 mayoral election presented an opportunity to win city hall. The Democrats nominated John B. Kelly, and the Republicans selected City Controller S. Davis Wilson who had competed against Kelly in the primary as a Democrat. The campaign was a bitter one, with Wilson employing anti-Semitic rhetoric against his Democratic rival. Kelly's campaign had reached out to Italians, Jews, and African Americans. Wilson managed to win the election, but only by forty-five thousand votes. Kelly won nearly 47 percent of the vote, an encouraging sign for Democrats. However, 56 percent of African Americans supported Wilson, indicating that the Democrats needed to cultivate more support among the city's Black voters. As mayor, S. Davis Wilson began to embrace some aspects of the New Deal. Although he had railed against "out of control" federal spending during the mayoral election, he managed to secure forty thousand WPA jobs for his constituents.[13]

By the beginning of 1936, the New Deal had started to lift the nation from its economic malaise. Philadelphia's African Americans held cautious optimism and were increasingly supportive of the New Deal, although many of Roosevelt's programs were administered by local politicians who engaged in discriminatory practices. Even the most popular of the New Deal programs, the Civilian Conservation Corps, established segregated camps in all states except Vermont and Wisconsin. Yet, Black people were aware that some aspects of their economic situation had improved. In addition to an uptick in Black employment rates, legislation such as the Wagner National Labor Relations Act (1935) and the Social Security Act (1934) convinced many that the New Deal was not a temporary measure. In particular, the Wagner Act, which protected the rights of workers who wanted to join labor unions, had special relevance for Black Philadelphians. Often employed as strikebreakers, an increasing number joined labor unions. Workers at companies such as the Budd Company, Westinghouse Turbine, and Atwater Kent Radio established unions. Although craft unions continued to exclude Black workers the newly formed Congress of Industrial Organizations (CIO) opened its doors to Black members. In contrast to American Federation of Labor (AFL) craft unions, the CIO's goal was to unionize semi-skilled and unskilled workers by industry.[14]

In terms of race, the most progressive union to emerge was Philadelphia's Municipal Workers Union (MWU). This new organization mainly comprised garbage handlers, the majority of whom were African American and first- and second-generation immigrants from Italy and Ireland. In addition to enduring long hours and low pay, these workers faced extremely dangerous and unhealthy conditions. In the spring of 1937, they affiliated with the Teamsters and promptly went on strike. Although the strike was settled and the union was recognized, the city limited the union's power. In the aftermath of the strike, the workers formed the MWU and elected Thomas McCann, a Black truck driver, as president. The MWU expanded its membership and initiated several militant strikes over the next decade that were bolstered by significant support from the Black community.[15]

The popularity of New Deal programs and legislation reinforced Roosevelt's reelection chances. For the Democratic Party, winning Pennsylvania was crucial. For this reason, the Democratic National Committee held its convention in the Quaker City. In an attempt to highlight the role of African Americans within the party, the Democratic National Committee invited Marshall Shepard to deliver the invocation. Shepard became the first African American to be accorded this honor. Not all members of the Democratic delegation approved of this symbolic gesture. As Shepard began to speak, Senator Ellison "Cotton Ed" Smith of South Carolina stormed out of the convention and declared his opposition to a party that he believed no longer embraced white supremacy. In response to Smith, Shepard said, "it was just a sign the good brother needs more prayer." Smith's action demonstrated that, although the Southern Democrats embraced the New Deal, acceptance of Black people as political colleagues was by no means certain. Until the 1960s, the segregationist wing of the Democratic Party continued to resist civil rights legislation.[16]

In November 1936, Franklin Delano Roosevelt won his second term as president in a landslide. The work of Shepard, Fauset, and others contributed to Roosevelt winning 62 percent of the city's Black vote. Irish Americans, Italian Americans, and Jewish Americans also turned out for Roosevelt, thus creating the potential for a local New Deal coalition. However, Black Philadelphians faced specific problems. The Depression had placed an added strain on the city's housing stock. Both the decline in new construction and the increase in evictions had contributed to a rise in overcrowding.

This crisis had a disproportionate impact on African Americans, most of whom lived in substandard housing. On December 19, 1936, a bandbox tenement house collapsed in South Philadelphia. Seven people, including four children, were killed. All the victims were African American, and the tragedy galvanized the community. Shepard argued that with both state legislative chambers in the hands of Democrats, housing safety should be a priority. Crystal Bird Fauset called for immediate action. In a *Philadelphia Independent* editorial, she argued, "Once sensing a situation, we must not wait on others to meet the need, whether they be officials or other (black) people. We must pitch in and compel action." While Wilson responded to the tragedy by hiring more housing inspectors, an increasing number of African Americans believed that direct action was needed.[17]

Neighbors of the victims rallied to provide housing and other means of support. Within six months of the disaster, these activists formed the Tenants League of Philadelphia. The new organization argued for stronger enforcement of the 1915 housing code and an end to segregated housing. In contrast to the quiet persuasion used by earlier reformers, the Tenants League employed street protests and rent strikes. The new mood of militancy around housing issues energized the Black community. By early 1938, there were a dozen tenants' rights committees across the city.[18]

In addition to housing, Black activists protested against economic inequality. Philadelphia's activists were inspired by the work of a new civil rights coalition with a strong local connection. In 1935, African American professors, teachers, and social workers met at Howard University and called for the creation of a movement that would agitate for an end to racial discrimination, especially in labor. The first meeting of the National Negro Congress (NNC) took place in Chicago in February 1936 and included eight hundred attendees representing over five hundred organizations. The goal of this new coalition was to engage "the broadest numbers of Negro organizations that are willing to join in the fight for the rights of Negroes." Arthur Huff Fauset was elected to lead the Philadelphia chapter of the NNC and later became the national vice president of the coalition. Fauset employed a multifaceted approach. Under his leadership, NNC activists initiated "Don't Buy Where You Can't Work" protests in North and West Philadelphia. These demonstrations targeted retail establishments that refused to hire Black people yet welcomed their dollars. Huff Fauset also cultivated the support of local and state politicians. In 1937, he convinced the NNC to hold its national convention in Philadelphia. In addition to attracting activists from around the nation, the conference featured speakers such as Mayor Wilson and Lieutenant Governor Thomas Kennedy. The most important speaker was A. Philip Randolph, the nation's most important civil rights leader. Randolph was the driving force behind the creation of the Brotherhood of

Sleeping Car Porters, an African American labor union that had won significant concessions from the Pullman company. The participation of Randolph exemplified the NNC's commitment to seeking racial equality in labor.[19]

Like her husband, Crystal Bird Fauset was heavily invested in the success of the NNC. However, she argued that it was important to influence public policy from within the political system. In 1938, she began to campaign for a seat in the Pennsylvania House of Representatives. Bird Fauset utilized the telephone to contact voters, an innovative strategy at the time. In contrast to other candidates, Bird Fauset made direct appeals to female voters. In November 1938, she became the first Black woman elected to a state legislature anywhere in the United States. Bird Fauset won in a district that was 66 percent white, an encouraging sign to many progressive activists. Although deeply involved in civil rights, Bird Fauset declared that "my interest is in no way limited to my race . . . it is universal."[20]

While Bird Fauset's victory was a cause for celebration for Philadelphia's Democrats, the national picture was increasingly cloudy. Roosevelt's attempt to place his judicial allies on the Supreme Court by enlarging the number of justices affected his popularity. In addition, an economic downturn known as the Roosevelt Recession of 1937–1938 led some to believe the New Deal had run its course. In December 1937, a coalition of conservative Democrats and Republicans issued a manifesto critical of the New Deal. Although the Democrats managed to hold onto power in both chambers, their majorities had been considerably reduced.[21]

State and local politics reflected the conservative resurgence. Republicans regained control of the governor's office and both houses of the state legislature. Although the GOP repealed some of Earle's "Little New Deal" programs, most remained intact. Despite their concern over government involvement in the economy, Republicans privately acknowledged that the majority of Pennsylvanians still needed New Deal programs. On the local level, Republicans accused Democrats of embracing Communism and continued to criticize the New Deal. In the late 1930s, jobs programs such as the WPA faced criticism from conservatives, and the agency endured an increasingly precarious existence. Despite the criticism, the WPA contributed to the upgrade of the nation's infrastructure. In the Philadelphia area, the agency provided funding for a rail link across the Delaware River Bridge (now the Benjamin Franklin Bridge). In addition, the WPA assisted in a major renovation of city hall and built stations and shelters in Wissahickon Park. These projects provided needed jobs for the region's Black workers. In addition to building public works, the WPA also sponsored arts and cultural programs, providing employment for artists, musicians, writers, and actors. In Philadelphia, the WPA-funded Fine Print Workshop cultivated the talents of African American artists such as Claude Clark, Raymond

Steth, and Dox Thrash. The work of these artists portrayed African Americans in a positive light. Yet, it was not clear how long the WPA or other programs would last.[22]

As the Democrats pondered their next move, tension increased across Europe and Asia. In East Asia, the Japanese had launched a full-scale war against China in 1937. Chinese Communists and Nationalists, who had been embroiled in a civil war since 1927, agreed to cooperate to defeat Japan. Some American policy makers argued that Japan had designs on Southeast Asia, including the American territory of the Philippines. In Europe, Adolf Hitler's occupation of neighboring Austria and Czechoslovakia went unchecked by the international community. Emboldened by this inaction, Germany invaded Poland in September 1939. In response, Britain and France declared war on Germany. While World War II raged on, Americans remained divided over the question of involvement. The defeat of France, in 1940, and the continual bombardment of Great Britain led Roosevelt to initiate a massive increase in defense spending.[23]

While Roosevelt's New Deal had contributed to economic revival, unemployment in Philadelphia still stood at 17 percent. The unemployment rate among the city's African American workers was nearly 30 percent. Black voters in Philadelphia and across the nation were increasingly frustrated by the Democratic Party. In addition to high unemployment rates, Southern Democrats controlled leadership positions in Congress and blocked any meaningful civil rights proposals. The Republican candidate, Wendell Willkie, argued for a federal anti-lynching bill and voiced his support for the integration of the armed forces. Willkie's relatively progressive civil rights plank won him considerable support in the African American community. Two of the country's leading Black newspapers, the *Baltimore Afro-American* and the *Pittsburgh Courier* endorsed Willkie. Despite many people's misgivings about the Democrats, Roosevelt once again won Philadelphia's Black vote, this time with 68 percent of the ballots. Substantial support from the city's Black voters contributed to the Democrats retaking the state legislature. However, Black Philadelphians were increasingly concerned about the lack of job opportunities. On November 16, 1940, thousands of African Americans protested against racial discrimination in the local defense industry. This demonstration indicated that despite strong support for the New Deal, many Black people were concerned that they would be excluded from this growing economic sector.[24]

Defense spending rejuvenated the local economy. Philadelphia had been a shipbuilding center since the colonial era, and the shipyards were among the first industries to benefit from the federal government's largesse. In 1939, there were only a few thousand workers at the Philadelphia Naval Shipyard, but, by the war's end, fifty-eight thousand workers were employed at the sprawling facility. Other shipyards, including Cramp's in the Kensington section, the New York Shipbuilding Company across the river in Camden, and the Sun Shipyard in nearby Chester, increased production. In addition to ships, the Frankford Arsenal hired twenty thousand workers to produce small arms and ammunition. The Baldwin Locomotive Company manufactured railroad equipment for the military, and the Budd Company of Northeast Philadelphia produced armored cars and tanks. Long a center of textile manufacturing, Philadelphia produced uniforms and tents. In 1940, the region received 11 percent of federal defense spending, and, by early 1941, manufacturing rates had returned to pre-Depression levels.[25]

The expanding and lucrative defense sector was rife with racial discrimination. Black people viewed the defense industry as both a way to demonstrate their patriotism and an opportunity to secure a measure of economic stability. Civil rights leaders such as A. Philip Randolph and NAACP secretary Walter White urged Roosevelt to end racial discrimination in defense industries. Randolph increasingly believed that direct action would be the most effective means of pressuring the administration. He called for a massive march on Washington, DC. Anxious to forestall this demonstration, Roosevelt met with Randolph and White. On June 19, 1941, Roosevelt issued Executive Order No. 8802, which maintained: "There shall be no discrimination in the employment of workers in the defense industry and in government because of race, creed, color or national origin." Executive Order No. 8802 was the first presidential directive on race since Reconstruction. To ensure enforcement of the directive, the federal government established the FEPC. Satisfied with Roosevelt's efforts, Randolph and his colleagues postponed the march indefinitely. While Executive Order No. 8802 did not bring an end to racial discrimination in the defense industry, the order established a means through which grievances could be adjudicated and clearly identified that racism was a central problem in the labor sector. Most importantly, Randolph's proposed march indicated that the threat of direct action could transform policy.[26]

As discussions on defense employment ensued, Crystal Bird Fauset left the legislature to become the assistant director of recreation and education for the WPA in Pennsylvania. In her brief legislative career, Bird Fauset had introduced nine bills and three amendments focusing on public health, public relief, housing, and working women. While her WPA position was an important one, federal officials believed her talents would be better utilized in the defense sector. In 1941, Bird Fauset, with the assistance of First Lady Eleanor Roosevelt, was hired by the Office of Civil Defense to serve as assistant director and race relations coordinator, where her role consisted of investigating racial discrimination in United Services Organizations facilities, the armed forces, and the defense industry. Federal officials were concerned that Black support for the war effort could decline; therefore, it was advantageous to place someone as prominent and effective as Bird Fauset in such a position. By this time, neither she nor her husband were involved with the NNC, which had split over ideological differences in 1940. Many local members of the NNC remained interested in civil rights and direct action. During the war, Philadelphia provided an opportunity to test these strategies and to challenge the racial status quo.[27]

Integration of the defense sector was not the only issue on the minds of Black Philadelphians. In 1942, Carolyn Davenport Moore became branch secretary of the local NAACP. The Philadelphia branch had been criticized for its conservatism, elitism, and lack of militancy. Moore expressed interest in transforming the branch into a grassroots organization that would adopt a more militant tone. The dynamic Moore hoped to capitalize on was the nationwide "Double V" campaign, popularized by the civil rights community. The slogan Double V referred to victory against the Axis powers as well as victory against racial discrimination at home. Under Moore's leadership, the NAACP targeted the Philadelphia Transportation Company (PTC) and its union, the Philadelphia Rapid Transit Employees Union (PRTEU). Black people held only menial positions at the transit company, so the NAACP argued that Black workers needed to be upgraded. Although the FEPC ordered the company and the union to cease their discriminatory practices by late 1943, they refused. In the spring of 1944, the War Manpower Commission issued new guidelines for the PTC. Eight Black workers were designated to be trained as trolley operators. On August 1, the PRTEU ordered its members to strike, halting public transportation in the nation's third largest city. Most defense workers depended on the PTC to commute to their jobs. Thus, the strike affected the production of critical war matériel.[28]

Racial tensions rose, and many Philadelphians feared an outbreak of deadly violence like Detroit had suffered in 1943. In contrast to Detroit and other cities where wartime violence had occurred, activists mobilized to forestall any danger. In addition to the NAACP, Fellowship House, an interracial civil rights organization with roots in the city's Quaker community, played a prominent role. Activists from Fellowship House (known as the Young Peoples' Interracial Fellowship prior to 1941) had protested with the NNC in "Don't Buy Where You Can't Work" demonstrations. During the strike, they quelled rumors by distributing leaflets in racially tense neighborhoods. Arthur Huff Fauset also sprang into action. The former NNC leader had attempted to join the army in 1942 but was rebuffed for his "radical leanings." In response to the crisis, Huff Fauset utilized his organizing skills to mobilize the United People's Action Committee, which provided working-class support for the NAACP and other civil rights organizations.[29]

The hate strike did not last long. Alarmed at the disruption of defense production, the army dispatched five thousand troops to take control of the mass transit system. Four strike leaders were arrested, and striking workers were informed they would be fired and lose their draft deferments. The strikers returned, the Black trainees resumed their training, and, by August 17, the military returned control to the PTC. Later that year, the CIO-affiliated Transport Workers Union replaced the PRTEU as the bargaining unit for PTC employees.[30]

Civil rights activists hailed the end of the strike as a major victory. Although often critical of Roosevelt, Huff Fauset credited his actions. The civil rights leader also praised the CIO and called for a permanent FEPC. Black workers were allowed to operate streetcars, and the peaceful resolution of the strike demonstrated that large-scale racial violence could be averted. The city's civil rights community placed pressure on law enforcement, city hall, and the media, and their timely efforts were crucial in preventing a race riot. However, Republicans criticized the federal government's role in ending the strike. Using racist appeals, the GOP argued that Black people were emboldened by this victory and would "take over" white neighborhoods and destroy the city. The Democrats worried that white ethnic working-class voters would shift their allegiance to the GOP in the November election. Although Roosevelt won his fourth presidential election, his margin in Pennsylvania was less than one hundred thousand votes. Black people gave Roosevelt 68 percent of their vote, thus solidifying their role in his increasingly fragile New Deal coalition. Demographic changes in the city contributed to Democratic Party success. The African American population of Philadelphia rose by 126,000 during and immediately after World War II. The new migrants affirmed their loyalty to the Democrats, identifying the party with Roosevelt's New Deal and the CIO. They did not associate the Democrats with Southern segregationists or the AFL.[31]

While the Black electorate was safely in the Democratic camp by the end of 1944, a leadership void had developed. Marshall Shepard declined to run in the 1938 election but was returned to office in the election of 1940. After the conclusion of his two-year term, Roosevelt appointed the West Philadelphia minister to the recorder of deeds position in Washington, DC, where he stayed until the late 1940s. In 1951, Shepard returned to electoral politics when he was elected commissioner of records in Philadelphia. In the 1930s, the prominent civil rights attorney Raymond Pace Alexander had campaigned for the Democrats. However, in 1940, he left the Democratic Party, citing their indifference to civil rights. In 1947, Alexander returned to the Democrats and became an active supporter of Truman. He advised Charles Hamilton Houston on the *Brown* case and later won election to the Court of Commons Pleas in 1959. Perhaps the most surprising defection to the GOP was Crystal Bird Fauset. In 1944, Bird Fauset announced her departure from the Democratic Party. She had attempted to secure a position with the Democratic National Committee but was rebuffed. Like Alexander, the unwillingness of the Democrats to push for civil rights legislation was also a factor. She attended the Republican National Convention and appeared on the podium with candidate Dewey. Although she became involved with international affairs through the Philadelphia World Affairs Council, traveling to India, West Africa, and the Middle East, she did not return to electoral politics. She was ostracized by the Democrats and sidelined by the Republicans. Bird Fauset's experience demonstrated the perils of changing allegiance in a politically charged time.[32]

The orientation of Black Democrats presented a problem. Although there was a growing number of party activists such as Willa Moss and Robert N. C. Nix, longtime Thirty-Second Ward committeeman who served briefly as special assistant attorney general under the Earle governorship, there were no Black Democrats in the nineteen-member city council. Despite their slowly declining political fortunes, the Republicans still retained control of city hall. The lack of local Black politicians meant the growing Democratic constituency had no direct way to articulate their concerns, and an increasing number of African Americans were anxious about the postwar world.[33]

The immediate aftermath of World War I had witnessed race riots, unemployment, and labor strikes. The bitter memory of this unsettled period was fresh among many Philadelphians, both Black and white. Although victory was not certain, by 1945, the Allies were winning the war in Asia and Europe. As a result, there was less need for war matériel and layoffs began. The shipyards were the first industries affected by the cutbacks, and both the Philadelphia Naval Shipyard and Sun Shipyard scaled back operations. Tens of thousands were laid off. These layoffs had a disproportionate impact on African American workers, many of whom were employed at these sprawling facilities on the Delaware River. In addition, workers at textile firms and manufacturers such as Baldwin and Budd also experienced massive layoffs. By August 1945, every defense contractor had discharged workers. Although manufacturing in Philadelphia continued after the war, an increasing number of these industries relocated to the suburbs or the South.[34]

In this uncertain time, civil rights activists began to campaign for permanent fair employment legislation. For most white Americans, the FEPC was a wartime emergency measure, while African Americans envisioned it as the cornerstone of a new paradigm in race relations. In Philadelphia, the Fellowship Commission launched "FEPC Emergency Week." The coalition circulated over one hundred thousand leaflets and placed advertisements in major newspapers. The campaign for a permanent FEPC was spearheaded by the Council on Equal Job Opportunity. Founded in 1943 by Fellowship House member Frederick Brill, the purpose of this agency was "to establish and protect the right and opportunity of all persons to seek, obtain and hold gainful employment without discrimination on account of race, creed, color, national origin or ancestry." The Council on Equal Job Opportunity pledged to engage in educational work and lobby political leaders.[35]

In addition to concerns over employment, Philadelphia's wartime population increase created a housing shortage. The shortage was exacerbated by racial segregation. During the war, the Philadelphia Housing Association established separate housing projects for Black people and white people, although "experimental" integrated developments were pioneered in 1944. The postwar period presented new challenges for Philadelphia. Encouraged by the GI Bill, returning veterans wanted homes, as did families whose housing choices had been limited by years of Depression and war. The Housing Association of the Delaware Valley, a housing reform agency, estimated that twenty thousand veterans needed homes. For African Americans, the Federal Housing Association's segregation policies known as redlining, curtailed possibilities for integration. Since most children attended neighborhood schools, the public school system reflected the city's segregation.[36]

Despite the transition to Harry S. Truman after the death of Roosevelt in May 1945, Republicans still controlled the city hall and state government. Republican governor Edward Martin became the state's most vocal opponent of the FEPC. Although Martin stated his belief in equal opportunity, he criticized the FEPC as an expensive extension of federal power. For Martin and his supporters, the New Deal was a precursor to socialism. Martin's opposition to the FEPC, coupled with his inaction during the transit strike, convinced African Americans that the governor was openly hostile to their needs. Thus, the best hope for an FEPC would be a city ordinance.[37]

By the end of World War II, it was clear that Black Philadelphians faced an uncertain future. Any hope that Black workers would acquire well-paying employment in the city's industrial sector was gone. Despite the wartime rhetoric of interracial unity, Black Philadelphians continued to face discrimination in housing, education, and labor. With reactionary Republicans in control of city hall and Harrisburg, Black Philadelphians could expect no help from the political sector.[38]

However, encouraging signs appeared on the horizon. The city's Democratic Party underwent a change of leadership during World War II. In the early days of the New Deal, a small group of reformers within the city's Democratic Party urged their colleagues to focus on the corruption in city hall. Emboldened by Democratic victories and Republican graft and inefficiency, they set their sights on ending the GOP's stranglehold on local political power. The most important of these reformers were Joseph Sill Clark and Richardson Dilworth. Both were Ivy League–educated attorneys who sought to build a coalition that could bring an end to decades of Republican misrule. After their return from military service, Clark and Dilworth began their campaign to take city hall.[39]

Democrats needed to build a strong local coalition to confront the GOP machine. The city's growing Black population was increasingly aligned with the Democrats. In addition, the Philadelphia branch of the NAACP had grown substantially during World War II. Thanks to the efforts of Moore and others, the Philadelphia branch had grown into one of the largest and most active in the nation. A small yet growing number of African Americans worked on Democratic neighborhood committees. With the NAACP and their own coterie of activists, the Democrats could mobilize a significant number of supporters. Yet, leadership was firmly in the hands of a white male elite, and, if the Democrats wanted to take city hall, they had to recognize and nominate promising Black candidates.[40]

From 1932 to 1945, the political allegiance of Black Philadelphians shifted. Although considerable numbers continued to vote Republican in local elections, Black Philadelphians believed the Democratic Party represented their best hope for a just and equal society. Despite the power of the Southern segregationist wing, New Deal programs and the FEPC had convinced most of the city's African American electorate to support the Democratic Party. With the 1947 mayoral election on the horizon and a host of postwar uncertainties, however, the strength of that support remained an open question.

NOTES

1. Stanley Arnold, *Building the Beloved Community: Philadelphia's Interracial Civil Rights Organizations and Race Relations, 1930–1970* (Jackson: University Press of Mississippi, 2014), 73–74; "Closed for Business: The Story of Bankers Trust Company during the Great Depression," Historical Society of Pennsylvania, Philadelphia, accessed March 14, 2019, available at https://hsp.org/history-online/digital-history-projects/closed-for-business-the-story-of-bankers-trust-company-during-the-great-depression; Roger D. Simon, "Great Depression," *The Encyclopedia of Greater Philadelphia* (Camden, NJ: Mid-Atlantic Regional Center for the Humanities, Rutgers University, 2013), accessed March 15, 2019, available at https://philadelphiaencyclopedia.org/archive/great-depression/.

2. Arnold, *Building the Beloved Community*, 74; Simon, "Great Depression"; John Bauman, Thomas H. Coode, and Lorena Hickok, "A New Dealer Tours Eastern Pennsylvania," *Pennsylvania Magazine of History and Biography* 104, no. 4 (January 1980).

3. Kenneth J. Heineman, "A Tale of Two Cities: Pittsburgh, Philadelphia and the Elusive Quest for a New Deal Majority in the Keystone State," *Pennsylvania Magazine of History and Biography* 132, no. 4 (October 2008): 313–320.

4. Simon, "Great Depression"; Mary Eleanor Triece, *On the Picket Lines: Strategies of Working Class Women in the Depression* (Champaign: University of Illinois Press, 2007).

5. Heineman, "A Tale of Two Cities," 317–322.

6. Arnold, *Building the Beloved Community*, 115; "Marshall L. Shepard: Historical Biographies," Pennsylvania House of Representatives 2017, available at https://www.house.state.pa.us/; James Reichley, *The Art of Government* (New York: Fund for the Republic, 1959), 69.

7. Philip Clark, "Lifting the Curtain: Crystal Bird Fauset," American Friends Service Committee, March 2010, accessed March 25, 2019, available at www.afsc.org.

8. Jennifer Reed Fry, "'Our Girls Can Match 'Em Every Time': The Political Activities of African American Women in Philadelphia, 1912-1941" (Ph.D. diss., Temple University), 189-190.

9. Arnold, *Building the Beloved Community*, 76-77; Heineman, "A Tale of Two Cities," 320-322; Charles Pete Banner-Haley, "The Philadelphia Tribune and the Persistence of Black Republicanism during the Great Depression," *Journal of Mid Atlantic Studies* 65, no. 2 (1998): 190-202.

10. Simon, "Great Depression"; Fry, "'Our Girls Can Match 'Em,'" 191-195.

11. Shepard and Reynolds, "Historical Biographies"; Richard C. Keller, "Pennsylvania's Little New Deal," *Pennsylvania History: A Journal of Mid Atlantic Studies* 29, no. 4 (October 1962): 398-406.

12. Simon, "Great Depression."

13. Simon, "Great Depression"; Heineman, "A Tale of Two Cities," 327-329.

14. Simon, "Great Depression"; Benjamin Alexander, *The New Deal's Forest Army: How the Civilian Conservation Corps Worked* (Baltimore, MD: Johns Hopkins University Press, 2018), 125-127; Steve Valocchi, "The Racial Basis of Capitalism and the State and the Impact of the New Deal on African Americans," *Social Problems* 14, no. 3 (August 1994): 347-362.

15. Francis Ryan, *AFSCME'S Philadelphia Story: Municipal Workers and Urban Power in the Twentieth Century* (Philadelphia: Temple University Press, 2011), 45-64.

16. Shepard, "Historical Biographies."

17. Heineman, "A Tale of Two Cities," 328-329; Marcus Anthony Hunter, *Black Citymakers: How the Philadelphia Negro Changed Urban America* (Oxford: Oxford University Press, 2013), 93-103.

18. Arnold, *Building the Beloved Community*, 75-76.

19. James Wolfinger, *Philadelphia Divided: Race and Politics in the City of Brotherly Love* (Chapel Hill: University of North Carolina Press, 2007), 75-77; Arnold, *Building the Beloved Community*, 76.

20. Fry, "'Our Girls Can Match 'Em,'" 237-240.

21. Heineman, "A Tale of Two Cities," 329-333.

22. Simon, "Great Depression"; Wolfinger, *Philadelphia Divided*, 75-82; Patrick Glennon, "Black Artists in Philly Flourished during the Great Depression," February 2018, available at www.inquirer.com.

23. David Kennedy, *Freedom from Fear: The American People in Depression and War, 1929-1945* (Oxford: Oxford University Press, 1999).

24. Fry, "'Our Girls Can Match 'Em,'" 251-260.

25. Herbert Ershkowitz, "World War II," available at https://philadelphiaencyclopedia.org/.

26. Arnold, *Building the Beloved Community*, 116.

27. Fry, "'Our Girls Can Match 'Em,'" 235-245.

28. Wolfinger, *Philadelphia Divided*, 144-159; Arnold, *Building the Beloved Community*, 117-118.

29. Arnold, *Building the Beloved Community*, 118.

30. Arnold, *Building the Beloved Community*, 118.

31. Arnold, *Building the Beloved Community*, 118–119; Heineman, "A Tale of Two Cities," 337; Wolfinger, *Philadelphia Divided*, 168–173.

32. Shepard, "Historical Biographies"; Fry, "'Our Girls Can Match 'Em,'" 245–250.

33. Fry, "'Our Girls Can Match 'Em,'" 260–272.

34. H. Ershkowitz, "World War II."

35. Arnold, *Building the Beloved Community*, 119.

36. Arnold, *Building the Beloved Community*, 83.

37. Wolfinger, *Philadelphia Divided*, 223–230.

38. Arnold, *Building the Beloved Community*, 120–121.

39. Terry Madonna and John Morrison McLarnon III, "Reform in Philadelphia: Joseph S. Clark, Richardson Dilworth and the Women Who Made Reform Possible," *Pennsylvania Magazine of History and Biography* 127, no. 1 (2003): 57–70.

40. Wolfinger, *Philadelphia Divided*, 206–208.

4

Postwar Philadelphia

ABIGAIL PERKISS

When Joseph Clark entered city hall on January 7, 1952, he did so as the first mayor under Philadelphia's new Home Rule Charter. The charter called for an end to racial and religious discrimination in hiring practices and was the first in the country to provide for the creation of a commission on human relations, tasked specifically with ameliorating racial intolerance in this new postwar city. The Philadelphia Commission on Human Relations, replacing the city's FEPC established three years earlier, allocated additional resources and staff to overhaul discriminatory policies in the city, once so destructive that, in 1927, they prompted W.E.B. Du Bois to remark, "[Philadelphia] is the best place to discuss race relations because there is more race prejudice here than any other city in the United States."[1]

The new commission on human relations came at a time when the nation was grappling with the legacy of a global conflict through which activists had linked Fascism abroad with racism at home. Out of that crisis emerged a philosophy of racial justice that brought together the moral impulse of individual persuasion with a sense of governmental responsibility to create policies that fostered access and opportunity across racial lines. The 1944 publication of Gunnar Myrdal's *An American Dilemma* laid bare a fundamental disconnect between the American Dream and the reality of race relations in the United States. This dissonance, the Swedish economist wrote, between the historical ideals of the nation and the contemporary realities of racial prejudice had created a pervasive moral angst in the country. To redeem the soul of the nation, then, liberals needed to work to reshape the hearts and minds of the American public. The solution to racial inequity in the United States, Myrdal argued, rested not in a dramatic reconfiguration of the political and economic systems but in a commitment to individual change grounded in the historic ideals of American democracy. And the commission's new director, George Schermer, aligned himself with that notion of postwar liberalism. Schermer, a recent transplant to Philadelphia who brought with him a strong record at the Detroit Housing Commission, sought to create a multiracial commission built on the beliefs that racial segregation threatened to undermine development in the city and that the way forward was a racially inclusive society.[2]

A decade earlier, Philadelphia had experienced a sharp increase in its Black population, as men, women, and children relocated from the American South in search of New Deal and wartime economic opportunities. The so-called Second Great Migration brought more than 125,000 people of color to the city between 1940 and 1950, nearly 50,000 between 1941 and 1943 alone. The vast majority settled in North Philadelphia. During that same two-year period, wartime restrictions on residential construction meant that the city saw the development of only twenty-four thousand new homes, creating an acute housing shortage. These problems persisted after the war. Though production restarted quickly, the market could not keep up with demand. In 1946, sixty-five thousand Philadelphia families were living communally in units designed for single-family occupancy. The city's vacancy rate hovered between 0.5 and 1 percent, nearly nonexistent.[3]

At the same time, with expanded job opportunities and the emerging postwar legal reforms, members of a new African American middle class began to push outward, seeking to escape the overcrowded streets of North Philadelphia. The rapid demographic shifts generated anxieties for white homeowners, who believed that both their property values and their ways of life were being jeopardized by the in-migration of prospective Black buyers. In Philadelphia, Detroit, Brooklyn, Chicago, Boston, and other urban centers across the nation, fears of these African American families moving into previously all-white enclaves created intense hostility. White blue-collar homeowners felt particularly at risk. They had the means to purchase a home and root themselves in their chosen neighborhoods, but they were ill-equipped to absorb the financial loss of diminishing property values. Thinking they had to protect their most valuable asset—their homes—many of these families waged campaigns of violence and intimidation against Black buyers.[4]

On Philadelphia's North Thirteenth Street, for instance, Luther and Juanita Green experienced a violent reprisal after moving onto the block. One white neighbor grabbed Mrs. Green on the street and threatened her. Others threw full paint cans through their front windows and fired shots into their home as the Greens entertained friends. Sympathetic neighbors looked away, fearful that befriending or advocating for the Greens might compromise their own safety.[5]

Stepping into the role of mayor amid this growing residential turmoil, Clark, the first Democrat to hold the office in six decades, had his work cut out for him in addressing the needs of a changing city. The creation of the human relations commission evidenced a fundamental shift in the power structure of a city with a deep history of racist policies and practices. To bring such reform to fruition, Clark needed to build a coalition of highly regarded and well-positioned local and national leaders in race relations who could work with him to implement the liberal reforms on which he ran. In his first year, he brought on Robert Callaghan, Francis Coyle, Nathan Edelstein, Elizabeth Fetter, James Jones, Albert Nesbitt, Lawrence Smith, Leon Sunstein Sr., and Sadie Tanner Mossell Alexander as commissioners.[6]

Alexander, the first Black woman to serve on a presidential commission—President Harry Truman's Committee on Civil Rights—and her husband, Judge Raymond Pace Alexander, had been a force for racial change in Philadelphia since the early 1920s. From a young age, both believed in the power of the law to effect positive change in race relations in the city. On one of their early dates, when both were students at the University of Pennsylvania, the pair joined two friends for a movie at the downtown Shubert Theatre. When they tried to enter, the theater's manager told the couples that their seats had been double-booked and that they would be unable to see the show. Clearly angered, the foursome spoke among themselves in Spanish and French, presumably discussing the situation and offering sharp invectives against the indignity. The manager, surprised by the exchange among the four students, proclaimed, "Why, they are not Niggers!" and permitted them into the show. Nearly fifty years after the incident, Sadie recalled them pledging, "If we ever become lawyers, we are going to break this thing—segregation and discrimination. And, yes—we are going to open up those restaurants, too. You just wait! Just wait!"[7]

They held firm to that promise. Raymond earned his JD in 1923, the only African American student in his class at Harvard Law School. Sadie soon followed suit. After earning her Ph.D. from the University of Pennsylvania in 1921 (the second Black woman in the United States ever to earn such a distinction), she entered Penn's law school two years later and completed her degree in 1927 as the first African American woman both to graduate from the school and to be admitted to the Pennsylvania bar. The pair teamed up in private practice and, from the early days of their careers, waged legal battles on behalf of disenfranchised African Americans across the city. They pushed courts to remove segregation ordinances in hotels, restaurants, lunch counters, and theaters throughout Philadelphia and across Pennsylvania. In 1939, following a long campaign, they convinced the state to pass a new statewide equal rights law. They demonstrated, held marches, and organized rallies in an effort to erode the de facto segregation that existed across the urban North. Their goal, Judge Alexander later recalled, was "to make Philadelphia and Pennsylvania a city and state where black people could enjoy the fundamental freedoms guaranteed to them in our federal Bill of Rights."[8]

Raymond and Sadie Alexander epitomized the postwar liberal turn in how the city—and the nation—approached reforming race relations. They were members of a powerful coalition of middle-class white people and professional African Americans who saw desegregation as the central goal of civil rights progress and that counted its victories in the erosion of barriers in employment, education, and housing. This breed of coalition politics complemented well the goals of Mayor Clark and the commission on human relations, which sought to provide redress for individual cases of discrimination and open up the city to a growing cohort of middle-class African Americans. (See Fig. 4.1.)

One of the early campaigns of the commission on human relations came in response to the proliferation of housing disputes that emerged as the city's residential landscape was redrawn. Adopting a case-by-case approach to neighborhood stabilization, the commission intervened in individual conflicts, seeking to open up housing opportunities to Black buyers and ameliorate flare-ups of attendant violence. Between 1954 and 1956, twenty-eight previously all-white neighborhoods saw Black home buyers moving in. And, during the first year, the commission on human relations received reports of twenty-eight instances of vandalism targeted at either those Black home buyers or the white residents selling to them. By fostering relationships with local community groups in transitioning areas and making a moral appeal to white liberals, the commission believed it could reduce such tensions. As historian Matthew Countryman writes, "By the end of 1955, the commission believed that the Neighborhood Stabilization Program had succeeded in averting panic selling and unethical real estate practices in many areas experiencing racial change. The following year, the CHR received not a single report of vandalism or violence directed at black move-ins." It seemed as though their efforts were working.[9]

Just as such reform came from the offices of city hall, so, too, did individual communities come together to respond to the threats of volatility and transition, drawing on the same postwar Myrdalian vision of racial justice

Figure 4.1 Raymond Pace and Sadie T. M. Alexander appeared in the *Philadelphia Evening Bulletin*, March 9, 1950.

to persuade homeowners to welcome prospective Black buyers seeking entry into previously all-white spaces. In the northwest corner of the city, nestled between Germantown to the south and Chestnut Hill to the north, the community of West Mount Airy became a nationwide model for this experiment in integrated living.[10]

Historically, the city's northwest Germantown borough had served as a bucolic getaway for Philadelphia's elite. Even after the 1854 Consolidation Act incorporated the region into Philadelphia County and placed it under the authority of the Philadelphia municipal government, the high cost of living and relative geographic separation allowed the region to maintain its exclusivity through high prices and racially restrictive covenants. In the late 1800s, members of the city's Black elite—those who could afford to purchase homes in the affluent area—began moving in, gradually opening up the region to upwardly mobile African Americans who were just as invested as their white neighbors in maintaining the historical economic and social standing of the community. With these shifts, the earlier contractual restrictions gave way to a de facto class-based exclusivity that persisted through much of the twentieth century.

Early on, many of the region's white residents expressed concerns about the influx of new Black homeowners. In 1950, more than 90 percent of West Mount Airy's 18,462 residents were white. Reflecting attitudes in urban areas throughout the country, neighborhood homeowners feared that African American buyers would diminish their property values, that neighborhood institutions would crumble, and that crime rates would spike. Blockbusting real estate agents inflamed these fears, forecasting mass home sales, communal instability, and sharp declines in real estate values.[11]

Many West Mount Airy residents, though, steeped in the language of postwar liberalism that had precipitated reforms in the public sphere, saw the possibility of something different. Rejecting the idea that racial transition necessarily created neighborhood decline, these white homeowners, including the commission on human relations director George Schermer himself, worked to uphold what they viewed as the cultural and fiscal values of the community, while welcoming the new Black families.[12]

The neighborhood's unique geographic, cultural, economic, and political circumstances created the material conditions for the possibility of integrated living. Mount Airy's diverse housing stock and robust parks and green spaces made many resistant to flight, aware that it would be difficult to replicate the region's distinct landscape in other areas of the city and the surrounding suburbs. Furthermore, the neighborhood was home to a critical mass of high-achieving white residents—lawyers and musicians, physicians and business owners, entrepreneurs and public servants, activists and judges—who had experienced interracial connections in their professional lives and may have been more open to such relations in the residential sphere. Finally, Mount Airy residents were financially stable. Though the region's housing diversity meant that homeowners spanned the middle-class spectrum, overwhelmingly, they were economically secure and, therefore, risking less during the unpredictable period of transition than the blue-collar homeowners of many of the rapidly shifting communities that resisted transition, in part out of a fear of the property devaluation that so often came with neighborhood volatility.[13]

In the early 1950s, Mount Airy community leaders joined—and later became the engine for—a small but important national movement whose members sought to recast discussions about race and residential space. At times collaboratively and more often in isolated silos across the Northeast and Midwest, neighborhood groups channeled the lessons from public integration efforts to shift the narrative of white flight and reclaim control over their blocks, creating a model of interracial residential stability. These integrationist leaders guided residents through the complicated process of racial transition. At first, the community grounded their efforts in the belief that, with individual moral persuasion—social gatherings, public-facing promotional efforts, and case-by-case troubleshooting—organizers could successfully coax their neighbors into working toward integration. As they moved forward, though, activists worked to bring their emotional pleas with the growing governmental push toward racial liberalism in public and professional worlds. By the end of the decade, through this fusion of moral appeal with a concerted interventionist effort toward legal and economic changes, integrationist communities created a reform movement predicated on a strategy of grassroots moral liberalism that relied on both individual persuasion and structural change.

Within a decade, West Mount Airy was home to a cohort of African American city leaders. The commission on human relations's Sadie Alexander and Judge Raymond Pace Alexander owned a home on the 700 block of Westview Street. William Coleman, who would later serve as secretary of transportation under Presidents Nixon and Ford, lived on the 500 block of West Hortter Street. Joseph Coleman, Philadelphia's first Black city council president, lived in the area, as did Rev. Leon Sullivan, whose efforts funded the development of North Philadelphia's Progress Plaza, the nation's first Black-owned shopping district. All of them were drawn to the community for its reputation for consensus politics and integrated living. In these postwar decades, civil rights progress was founded on this idea of integration—an antidote to segregation and a material goal around which African Americans and white liberals could come together in the pursuit of justice.[14]

But support for that approach was not universal. By the early 1960s, some Black Philadelphians began pushing back on integration as the consensus vision of civil rights in America. To a growing collection of African Americans, interracial collaboration was a flawed but well-intentioned movement for racial justice, born out of a particular historical moment that prioritized class-blind inclusion and equality of opportunity but fell short of a full reorientation of the nation's racial hierarchy. The goal of integration, these voices charged, subverted efforts to reorient the material conditions of American society and had the effect of dismantling a distinctive Black American culture and identity. As historian Robin D. G. Kelly writes, for some, the goal of integration had become "a means of creating racial harmony without a fundamental transformation of the social and economic order. In most white liberal circles . . . the goal was to produce fully assimilated black people devoted to the American dream. Sharing power was rarely part of the equation."[15]

In Philadelphia and other Northern cities, movements for Black Power and intraracial pride had been central to the civil rights agenda since the early 1950s. The Muslim Brotherhood, the Citizens Committee against Juvenile Delinquency and Its Causes, the Nation of Islam, and others emerged to challenge the sluggish pace of reform that had come to define the liberal fight for racial justice. By the decade's end, even the Philadelphia branch of the NAACP, a national organization historically seen as a moderating force focused around change for the African American elite, had begun to shift its focus away from city hall. Fearful of losing its legitimacy in the fight for racial progress, the organization embarked on a campaign to work directly with the city's Black neighborhoods.[16]

In 1963, Black Philadelphians elected Cecil Bassett Moore as the new local NAACP president. Moore, the son of a respected local doctor in Yukon, West Virginia, began to develop a racial consciousness at an early age. As a child, Moore's light-skinned father was threatened by the Ku Klux Klan, whose members charged the senior Moore with miscegenation. Though he was ultimately able to prove to the Klan's satisfaction that he and his wife were both in fact African American, the experience shaped the younger Moore's experience of race long into adulthood.[17]

Moore graduated from the Bluefield State Teachers College, a historically Black institution that cultivated in its students the notion of a cohesive national African American community. Though far removed from the Black cultural renaissance of Northern cities, as a student, Moore likely met such Black leaders as Langston Hughes, Duke Ellington, John Hope Franklin, Dizzy Gillespie, and Joe Louis. When he became a parent, he told his children stories of taking classes with Carter G. Woodson, founder of Negro History Week. Even as Moore dedicated his career to advocating for the Black poor—even as he, himself, struggled to pay his way through college—he navigated the world from a position of relative privilege, rooted in his education among the nation's African American elite.[18]

When he moved to Philadelphia, Moore was caught off guard by the racial politics he encountered there. Having grown up in West Virginia, he was accustomed to the de jure system of Jim Crow segregation. He believed that he would find something different in the Northeast, and he was disenchanted by the intolerance that pervaded the city. African Americans faced systemic discrimination in housing, employment, and education. Though not legally recognized, this new breed of segregation that Moore encountered in Philadelphia felt no less dangerous to the budding lawyer.

In 1960, as Moore rose to prominence, 535,000 African Americans lived in Philadelphia, nearly 27 percent of the city's total population, up from 13 percent two decades earlier. Though many Black families had moved to the city's outer edges, nearly one-third still lived in North Philadelphia, considered the city's Black ghetto. These Black residents had been alienated from the city's power structure. With the lowest rates of education and employment in the city, limited access to medical care, and substandard housing, many felt voiceless at the same time that expectations for inclusion were rising with the spread of civil rights activism around the nation. In 1964,

Andrew G. Freeman, president of the National Urban League, called the city a "racial tinderbox." Philadelphia's high unemployment rate and pervasive poor housing conditions created the environment for a racial explosion, Freeman warned. "Consigned to street corners," he said, "the young Negro is building up a store of frustration and resentment."[19]

When Cecil B. Moore became president of the city's NAACP, he pledged to empower the residents of North Philadelphia, those, he said, who had been excluded from the commission on human relations's efforts to assuage racial tensions within the city's power structure. In this way, Moore's 1963 rise to power unmasked the limitations of the integrationist reformers who had occupied city hall for the previous decade. The new leader promised to rebuild the idea of racial justice, to move past the victories of Black professionals gaining token advances and to cultivate a broad-based campaign geared toward addressing the material needs of the Black masses.[20]

Though Moore's critiques were far-reaching, he reserved particular rebuke for the Black residents of Mount Airy, those he said had turned their backs on the realities facing the majority of the city's Black population. Of Freeman's reference to Philadelphia as a "racial tinderbox," Moore said, "[Freeman] was asremote [sic] in his thoughts from the true situation as it exists in Philadelphia as he was when he made the observation in Louisville, Kentucky, and upon his return to Philadelphia the distance was just as great, for he had no identification, contact, or rapport with the masses he purports to speak about during the eighteen months he lived in . . . Mount Airy."[21]

Moore also held up his own decision to remain in North Philadelphia both as a symbol of his commitment to the community and as emblematic of his very identity as a Black man. "I'd be lost if I had to move up to Mount Airy," he said, "where I'd have to be so damned respectable I couldn't stand on a street corner on Friday night. The Negro is always on the corner on Friday or Saturday nights. That's where you go to talk." Perhaps ironically, the Moore family had bought their home from the Alexanders when the couple left North Philadelphia for West Mount Airy. Their block, 1700 West Jefferson Street, had earned the moniker "Strivers Row" during and after World War II, for its reputation as an elite enclave within North Philadelphia. In 1965, the *Philadelphia Tribune* reported that most of those residents of Jefferson had moved to Mount Airy, West Oak Lane, Germantown, Chestnut Hill, and other communities on the edges of the city. For many, Moore's commitment to the block signaled a profound shift in responsive leadership.[22]

Moore's presidency exposed these tensions among the city's African American residents. Though, privately, Moore socialized with members of Philadelphia's Black elite, publicly he routinely clashed with local and national leadership, fueling debates about the legitimacy of their reform efforts and notions of Black identity throughout the city. In moving the fight for racial justice to the streets of North Philadelphia, Moore empowered those who had felt marginalized by the city's power structure and drew support away from the consensus liberalism that had defined Philadelphia's racial agenda. Moreover, in attacking the legitimacy of integrationist leaders, in casting them as sellouts to their race and charging them with abandoning their heritage, he forced them to defend their very Blackness.[23]

In this campaign, Moore drew West Mount Airy as the ideological dividing line in the city's fight for civil rights. He cast African Americans moving to the northwest Philadelphia neighborhood as symbols of the complicity with the white establishment Moore so frequently condemned. "I run a grassroots group, not a cocktail-party, tea-sipping, fashion-show-attending group of exhibitionists," Moore said of Mount Airy's Black professionals. "That's the difference. Those things divide the Negro, separate him into classes. I want nothing to divide the Negro; I want a one-class Negro community. Your so-called middle-class Negro is a 'professional Negro' who doesn't come into contact with the masses." In Moore's Philadelphia, the neighborhood's Black residents had not only abandoned the Black masses when they moved there; they had relinquished their claims to Blackness. In this way, Moore used these rhetorical turns to shift the balance of power and position himself at the center of the city's fight for racial justice.[24]

Moore's ideas aligned with a nationwide turn in civil rights activism, a movement away from a vision of justice that prioritized the equality of opportunity and bans on discrimination and toward a more radicalized—and Black-led—effort grounded in street protests and consumer boycotts. The NAACP leader welcomed this more militant turn and the leaders who supported it, noting, in 1964, that "there's always room for more in the civil rights struggle. So, we welcome Malcolm X into the field." During his tenure, he led protests to integrate the city's construction unions, to fight against discrimination in employment, and to desegregate schools.[25]

This shift in both strategy and ideology is perhaps best exemplified by Moore's efforts to integrate Girard College, a boarding school for orphaned boys in North Philadelphia. In 1953, when he served as a member of the city council, Raymond Alexander introduced a resolution to desegregate the school, which had opened its doors in 1883 in a community that, by the 1950s, was populated overwhelmingly by African Americans. Alexander filed suit in Orphans' Court on behalf of six African American boys who had been denied admission to Girard. The case ultimately reached the U.S. Supreme Court, where the majority held in favor of the Black applicants. Though the school itself was private, the court ruled, its oversight by the board of city trusts required that it abide by federal law. By refusing to admit Black students, therefore, the college was in violation of the Fourteenth

Amendment. Rather than integrating, Girard College responded by replacing the public board with privately appointed trustees, effectively removing the need for constitutional compliance.[26]

The efforts to integrate stalled for nearly a decade, until, in 1965, Cecil Moore began a coordinated public campaign for desegregation. Eschewing the courts as a battleground, Moore instead took to the streets. On May 1, twenty protesters showed up to the gates of the college. In the following months, the campaign grew. By summer, it had gained the attention of national civil rights leaders; Martin Luther King Jr., James Farmer, and Roy Wilkins joined the picket line. In December, the state of Pennsylvania filed suit to force the school to comply. Moore briefly called off the picket, but, as the case moved through the federal court system, he and his followers reaffirmed their commitment to street protests. More than two years later, and fifteen years after Alexander's initial filing, Girard College opened its doors to Black students on May 20, 1968.[27] (See Fig. 4.2.)

Figure 4.2 Philadelphia NAACP president Cecil B. Moore (*center*, with cigar) speaks with Stanley E. Branche (*left*, glasses), executive secretary of the Chester, Pennsylvania, branch of the NAACP, and the Reverend Henry Nichols (*right*, white straw hat), vice president of the Philadelphia School Board, before a 1967 rally at Fifteenth and South Streets.

Moore's strategy in integrating Girard College was reflective of his larger vision for racial justice. In his Philadelphia, liberal Black reformers, Moore's daughter Cecily Banks later recalled of her father's views, "were seen as not paying attention to what was going on for the black poor. It was a matter of concern for our own people, not trying to fit into a 'white world.'" In this calculation, race was based not on self-identification or lineage but, rather, on a person's commitment to a larger Black community. Moore saw those who furthered that mission as Black; he deemed those who did not as sellouts, "warmed-over part-time Negroes," and "refugees from the Negro race." Viewed through this lens, Moore charged Mount Airy's Black residents as race traitors: "the Negro middle-class . . . subsist[ing] on the blood of the 'brother down under,' the brothers they are supposed to be leading." They had fled for the material comforts that the middle-class white world afforded; they had abandoned their roots. Moore's attacks came on two levels. First, he censured their financial status; second, he critiqued their commitment to a racially integrated community.[28]

Generally, Moore's biggest targets chose not to speak publicly against the NAACP president, believing that doing so would compromise the image of a coalition effort toward change. In 1963, for instance, Raymond Alexander wrote to James Klash, editorial director of WDAS, the city's premiere African American radio station, "[Moore's] charges do not merit an answer and we cannot lower ourselves to his position to answer scurrilous attacks made without a semblance of truth." The following spring, Leon Sullivan issued a plea for unity at an NAACP rally at the city's Zion Baptist Church.[29]

In 1963, the *Philadelphia Tribune* reported that many of the city's Black civic leaders offered "no comment" to questions on whether they agreed with Cecil Moore's demands that the mayor appoint five African Americans to top city posts. "Philadelphia Negro 'leaders' had a bad case of 'clam-up-itis' this week," wrote staff reporter Chris Perry, "an ailment which renders its victims virtually speechless." According to Perry, there were indications that many did not approve of Moore's remarks, but few were willing to speak on the record. Out of more than thirty prominent Black Philadelphians interviewed, reported the paper, more than half issued "no comment" and the rest either voiced support or expressed only minor disagreement. Perry speculated that some of this reticence stemmed from Moore's response to those he deemed "Uncle Toms," often holding NAACP picket lines around their houses and publicly denouncing them.[30]

Occasionally, Black leaders did speak out against Moore's censure. In 1964, Henry Nichols launched a campaign to challenge Moore's NAACP branch presidency, describing himself as a "militant moderate leader," an alternative to Moore's more confrontational personality. In rebuke, Moore condemned Nichols as one of the "big Negro power structure . . . divisive 'Uncle Tom' hatchet boys." The reverend of the James Memorial Church responded with charges that Moore was pitting African Americans against each other, dividing the city's Black residents into factions that hampered change for the community as a whole. Apparently, Black Philadelphians were not convinced. Nichols lost his bid for president.[31]

Though the Alexanders tried to minimize their public condemnation of Moore, at times the couple did speak out in response to the NAACP president's attacks on their racial allegiance. As the *Philadelphia Tribune* reported in 1963, "Ending a long silence in the face of continued attacks from the NAACP and CORE, Mrs. Sadie T. M. Alexander, chairman of the Commission on Human Relations and wife of Raymond Pace Alexander, came to her own defense Thursday with a statement in rebuttal of charges that she is a part-time Negro." Alexander elected to respond to Moore by tracing her hundred-year family history of racial activism, including her own work on Truman's Committee on Civil Rights and efforts to dismantle the color line across Pennsylvania. "I do not intend to be dragged into any personal vendetta with Mr. Cecil Moore," she said, "[but] my contribution to democracy in the US is recorded and cannot be diminished by irresponsible accusations." That Alexander grounded her racial identity in activism, rather than bloodline, geography, or economics, was significant. Playing on Moore's own equation of racial authenticity with racial allegiance, she used her history of justice work to connect herself to the African American populace.[32]

Raymond Alexander, too, rarely sought to link himself to the city's Black community through lineage. It was not until 1969 that he made public his family history of slavery, as he wrote to Dr. Clifton H. Johnson, director of the Amistad Research Center and Race Relations Chair at Fisk University, "I am the grandson of slaves on both my mother's and father's side. . . . May I not have blood in my veins of one of those first twenty African slaves who were brought to Virginia, the birthplace of my progenitors." He wrote that he had not released his slave heritage because there had been no occasion to do so. It was only in beginning to construct his own autobiography that he thought to include his background. He saw no value in linking his roots of bondage with an affirmation of his Black identity. Rather, it was his activism that legitimized his racial authenticity, which connected him to the larger Black community.[33]

Alexander, here, seemed to want to minimize the dissonance between the postwar liberal approach to civil rights progress and the emerging radical turn. Whereas Moore and his cadre saw the trickle-down strategy of expanding opportunity as failing to effect meaningful change, in linking his activism to his claim to Blackness, Alexander sought to draw connections across ideologies of change. The evocation of this big tent approach not only elided the sharp lines drawn by Moore; it envisioned an expansive strain of Black politics in Philadelphia and legitimized a multivariate strategy of justice.

At times, public media outlets spoke out to defend the Alexanders against Moore's charges. In an on-air editorial broadcast in 1963, Philadelphia radio's WDAS said that while the station had supported Moore throughout his first six months in office, it could no longer sit by in the face of the leader's vitriolic attacks. "As president of the NAACP in Philadelphia," the report said, "Moore has brought to the fore many of the racial ills besetting the Quaker City and has, in this instance, been the right man at the right time.... But this does not, in our opinion, grant him the right to attack the race relations record of Mrs. Alexander.... We must remind Mr. Moore that down through the years, prior to his appearance on the local scene, Mrs. Alexander, and many others like her, were waging an unrelenting war against bias and bigotry—not in a spectacular fashion, perhaps, but a war nonetheless—and suffered along with the rest of the Philadelphia Negroes."[34]

At the same time that the deejay told Moore that his election did not give him license to speak on behalf of the entire African American community, he sought to remind the Black leader that he and Alexander were working toward the same goals. "We are all in this together," the editorial concluded. "Mr. Moore, Mrs. Alexander, and every one of us, Negro and white who demand justice for all men. We cannot afford to let personalities or personal feuds slow our march to our ultimate goal of equal jobs for all." As the radio host indicated, the Alexanders, Nichols, and other Black liberal leaders believed that they were as authentically Black as the residents of Moore's North Philadelphia. It was a disservice to the pursuit of racial justice, they charged, to limit the African American community politically, economically, or spatially.[35]

These public clashes between Moore and the Alexanders spoke to broader tensions in Philadelphia's Black political structure. Though Moore's leadership proved short lived—his more militant tactics, combined with a flamboyant personality and routine charges of anti-Semitism, often drew the ire of the NAACP's white membership and national leadership, and, by 1966, Moore was effectively run out of office—his rise to power laid bare for many the failure of liberalism to create meaningful economic changes for African Americans throughout the city. In the years to follow, Philadelphia's Black leadership worked to redefine their priorities and reconcile the push for socioeconomic transformation with the fight for inclusion in the city's power structure.[36]

NOTES

1. Matthew Countryman, *Up South: Civil Rights and Black Power in Philadelphia* (Philadelphia: University of Pennsylvania Press, 2006), 59–61; W.E.B. Du Bois, as quoted in James Wolfinger, *Philadelphia Divided: Race and Politics in the City of Brotherly Love* (Chapel Hill: University of North Carolina Press, 2007), 11.

2. For more on the link between Fascism abroad and racism at home, see Gary Gerstle, "The Protean Character of American Liberalism," *American Historical Review* 99, no. 4 (October 1994); Neil McMillen, ed., *Remaking Dixie: The Impact of World War II on the American South* (Jackson: University Press of Mississippi, 2007); David Southern, *Gunnar Myrdal and Black-White Relations: The Use and Abuse of "An American Dilemma," 1944–1969* (Baton Rouge: Louisiana State University Press, 1994). For more on Gunnar Myrdal, see Myrdal, *An American Dilemma: The Negro Problem and Modern Democracy* (New York: Harper and Row, 1944); Southern, *Gunnar Myrdal and Black-White Relations*; William Barber, *Gunnar Myrdal: An Intellectual Biography* (New York: Palgrave MacMillan, 2007); Gerstle, "Protean Character of American Liberalism"; McMillen, *Remaking Dixie*; Walter A. Jackson, *Gunnar Myrdal and America's Conscience: Social Engineering and Racial Liberalism, 1938–1987* (Chapel Hill: University of North Carolina Press, 1990). "George Schermer, Biography," prepared by Gracia M. Hardacre, May 7, 1982, George Schermer Manuscripts Collection, Amistad Archives, New Orleans, LA; Abigail Perkiss, *Making Good Neighbors: Civil Rights, Liberalism, and Integration in Postwar Philadelphia* (Ithaca, NY: Cornell University Press, 2014).

3. With this influx of new residents, the city's African American population grew from almost 251,000 to 376,000. Because the number of white people remained relatively stagnant—at 1.7 million—the percentage of Black residents rose from 13 percent of the city's overall population to 18 percent. Countryman, *Up South*, 14; W. Benjamin Piggot, "The 'Problem' of the Black Middle Class: Morris Milgram's Concord Park and Residential Integration in Philadelphia's Postwar Suburbs," *Pennsylvania Magazine of History and Biography* 132, no. 2 (2008), citing "Housing Facts and Figures—Philadelphia, 1948," Philadelphia Housing Authority, July 1948, 1, box A–622, accession 152.1, Philadelphia City Archives.

4. For reference, see, e.g., Thomas Sugrue, *The Origins of the Urban Crisis: Race and Inequality in Postwar Detroit* (Princeton, NJ: Princeton University Press, 1996); Jonathan Rieder, *Canarsie: The Jews and Italians of Brooklyn against Liberalism* (Cambridge, MA: Harvard University Press, 1987); Arnold Hirsch, *Making the Second Ghetto: Race and Housing in Chicago 1940–1960* (New York: Cambridge University Press, 1983).

5. Wolfinger, *Philadelphia Divided*, 85.

6. Philadelphia Commission on Human Relations, "Our History," City of Philadelphia, accessed December 14, 2021, https://www.phila.gov/departments/philadelphia-commission-on-human-relations/about/our-history/.

7. *Philadelphia Bulletin*, January 24, 1965, Sadie Tanner Mossell Alexander Papers, box 1, folder 6, University of Pennsylvania Archives, as cited in David A. Canton, *Raymond Pace Alexander: A New Negro Lawyer Fights for Civil Rights in Philadelphia* (Jackson: University Press of Mississippi, 2010), vii.

8. Letter from Raymond Pace Alexander to Dr. Clifton H. Johnson (director, Amistad Research Center and Race Relations Department, Fisk University), 1969, box 89, folder 19, accession 374, Raymond Alexander Pace Papers, University of Pennsylvania Archives, Philadelphia, PA.

9. Countryman, *Up South*, 72.

10. Though Philadelphia is home to the neighborhoods of both East Mount Airy and West Mount Airy, for the purposes of this chapter, *Mount Airy* and *West Mount Airy* are used interchangeably, as community leaders, residents, and journalists are quoted as using them as such. Though these early efforts toward integrating living took place in West Mount Airy, by the mid-1960s, a similar campaign emerged on the east side of Germantown Avenue, the geographic dividing line between the two neighborhoods. The East Mount Airy campaign was less recognized nationally and, ultimately, had different results: eventual transition and the creation of a stable largely Black middle-class community. For reference, see Barbara Ferman, Theresa Singleton, and Don DeMarco, "West Mount Airy, Philadelphia," *Cityscape* 4, no. 2 (1998): 29–59 ; Sheryll Cashin, *The Failures of Integration: How Race and Class Are Undermining the American Dream* (New York: Public Affairs, 2005); Murray Friedman, *Philadelphia Jewish Life, 1940–2000* (Philadelphia: Temple University Press, 2003); Jack Guttenberg, "Racial Integration and Home Prices: The Case of West Mount Airy," *Wharton Quarterly* (Spring 1970); Leonard Heumann, "The Definition and Analysis of Stable Racial Integration: The Case of West Mount Airy, Philadelphia" (Ph.D. diss., University of Pennsylvania, 1973); Perkiss, *Making Good Neighbors*; Juliet Saltman, *A Fragile Movement: The Struggle for Neighborhood Stabilization* (Westport, CT: Praeger Press, 1990); Juliet Saltman, *Open Housing: Dynamics of a Social Movement* (Westport, CT: Praeger Press, 1978); Juliet Sternberg, "Can We Talk about Race? The Racial Discourse of Activists in a Racially 'Integrated' Neighborhood" (Ph.D. diss., Rutgers University, 1996); William G. Grigsby and Chester Rapkin, *The Demand for Housing in Racially Mixed Areas* (Berkeley: University of California Press, 1960); Brian F. Leaf, "Breaking the Barrier: The Success of Racial Integration in the Philadelphia Community of Mount Airy, 1950–1975" (Senior honors thesis, University of Pennsylvania, 1995); Thomas Sugrue, *Sweet Land of Liberty: The Forgotten Struggle for Civil Rights in the North* (New York: Random House, 2008).

11. Outside of the neighborhood's Sharpnack section, an eighteenth-century industrial village made up of densely populated two-story stucco homes for domestic workers, 98.6 percent of the residents were white. U.S. Bureau of the Census, *Census of the United States, Philadelphia SMSA* (Washington, DC: Government Printing Office, 1950), as cited in Leaf, "Breaking the Barrier," 10; Memorandum, "History of Church Community Relations Council," n.d., box 20, accession 737, West Mount Airy Neighbors Paper, Manuscripts Collection, Urban Archives, Philadelphia, PA; Meeting Report, Joint Meeting between the West Mount Airy Neighbors Association and the Church Community Relations Council, March 27, 1954, West Mount Airy folder, American Friends Service Committee Archives, Philadelphia, PA.

12. For an extended history of integration in Mount Airy, see Perkiss, *Making Good Neighbors*.

13. Heumann, "Definition and Analysis of Racial Stable Integration," 22. Though Heumann's statistics come from a 1973 survey of the neighborhood, he points out that less than 10 percent of the housing stock resulted from postwar development. Only seven completely new blocks were built between 1951 and 1973, most of which were constructed as high-quality one-of-a-kind projects prior to 1954 or after 1964. Thus, the overall physical landscape of the neighborhood changed little once integration began. Mrs. Hiram MacIntosh, *An Incomplete History of West Mount Airy*, n.d., box 2, folder 40, accession 274, WMAN, Urban Archives, Philadelphia, PA; Gladys Thompson Norton, interview by Vida Carson, 1993, audio recording, WMAN Oral History Project, Germantown Historical Society, Philadelphia, PA; Frank Harvey Jr., interview by Patricia

Henning, 1993, audio recording, WMAN Oral History Project, Germantown Historical Society, Philadelphia, PA; Jim Foster, "Germantown 'Monopoly Has a Parallel History,'" *Germantown Courier*, November 24, 2011; Bernice Schermer, interview by Marjorie Kopeland, 1993, written transcription, WMAN Oral History Project, Germantown Historical Society, Philadelphia, PA; Steve Sacks, interview by author, February 17, 2011, written transcription, Philadelphia, PA; Suzette Parmley, "The Day That Hollywood Glamour Came to West Mount Airy," *Philadelphia Inquirer*, May 16, 1998.

14. "Mount Airy, Philadelphia," *U.S. News and World Report*, July 22, 1991; "Historic Marker in Mount Airy Honors Sadie Alexander," *Mount Airy Times Express*, May 26, 1993; "Mount Airy Hailed for Racial Stability," *Philadelphia Inquirer*, May 4, 1967; Joseph Coleman, interview by Szabi Zee, 1993, written transcription, Germantown Historical Society, Philadelphia, PA.

15. Robin D. G. Kelley, "Integration: What's Left?" *The Nation*, December 3, 1998. See also Judith Stein, "History of an Idea," *The Nation*, December 14, 1998; Eric Foner and Randall Kennedy, "Reclaiming Integration," *The Nation*, December 4, 1998; Matthew Johnson, *The Origins of Diversity: Managing Race at the University of Michigan, 1963–2006* (Ph.D. diss., Temple University, 2011); Bruce Schulman, *The Seventies: The Great Shift in American Culture, Society, and Politics* (Boston: De Cape, 2002).

16. Countryman, *Up South*, 84–92; Manning Marable, *Race, Reform, and Rebellion: The Second Reconstruction of Black America, 1945–2006*, 3rd ed. (Jackson, University Press of Mississippi, 2006); Robin D. G. Kelly, *Race Rebels: Culture, Politics, and the Black Working Class* (New York: Free Press, 1996); Charles Flint Kellogg, *NAACP: A History of the National Association for the Advancement of Colored People* (Baltimore, MD: Johns Hopkins University Press, 1967).

17. Cecily Banks, interview by author, September 21, 2009, Philadelphia, PA.

18. Cecily Banks, interview by author, September 21, 2009, Philadelphia, PA; Mildred O'Neill, "Councilman Cecil Moore Dies," *Baltimore Afro-American*, February 24, 1979; C. Stuart McGegee, "Bluefield State History," Bluefield State College Archive Collection, accessed November 1, 2009, available at http://www.bluefieldstate.edu/Archives/Archives/History.html; Cecily Banks and Alexis Moore Bruton, interview by author, September 21, 2009, Philadelphia, PA. As scholar Gerald L. Early writes, "Moore's entire history places him within W.E.B. Du Bois's 'talented tenth.'" Early, *This Is Where I Came In: Black America in the 1960s* (Lincoln: University of Nebraska Press, 2003), 89.

19. Countryman, *Up South*, 14; Early, *This Is Where I Came In*, 81–82; Arthur Willis, *Cecil's City: A History of Blacks in Philadelphia 1638–1979* (New York: Carlton, 1989); "Judge Alexander Denies Phila. 'A Racial Tinderbox,' Refutes Claims by Urban League Head That City Is Headed for Explosion," *Philadelphia Tribune*, August 8, 1964.

20. Cecily Banks and Alexis Moore Bruton, interview by author, September 21, 2009, Philadelphia, PA.

21. Press Release from Moore, August 10, 1964, NAACP Records, Part III: Branch Files, Philadelphia, 1956–65, box C137, folder 5, Library of Congress Archives, Washington, DC.

22. "Pennsylvania: The Goddam Boss," *TIME*, September 11, 1964. As Countryman writes, "Moore rooted his claim to racial authenticity and identity with the majority of the city's blacks in his decision to keep his family in North Philadelphia" (*Up South*, 165); "Top Negroes Resided in North Philly," *Philadelphia Tribune*, June 20, 1965.

23. Cecily Banks and Alexis Moore Bruton, interview by author, September 21, 2009, Philadelphia, PA.

24. "Pennsylvania: The Goddam Boss," *TIME*, September 11, 1964.

25. Clayborne Carson, *Malcolm X: The FBI File* (New York: Skyhorse, 1991), 37.

26. Pennsylvania v. Board of Trusts, 353 U.S. 230 (1957); Canton, *Raymond Pace Alexander*, 128–137.

27. Countryman, *Up South*, 170–174.

28. Cecily Banks, interview by author, September 21, 2009, Philadelphia, PA; Orrin Evans, "Moore Says His Three Critics Are 'Part-Time Negroes,'" *Philadelphia Bulletin*, April 20, 1967; C. Eric Lincoln, "The Negro Middle-Class Dream," *New York Times*, October 25, 1964.

29. Countryman, *Up South*, 165; Chris Perry, "Negro Leaders Mum on Newest Cecil Moore Demands," *Philadelphia Tribune*, November 12, 1963; letter from Raymond Pace Alexander to Mr. James Klash, June 18, 1963, box 89, folder 19, accession 374, WDAS, Raymond Pace Alexander Papers, University of Pennsylvania Archives, Philadelphia, PA; Mark Lloyd, "Re: Raymond Pace Alexander (RPA) Papers," personal email, December 18, 2009. Alexander's general silence may also be attributed to his professional status; as a judge for the Court of Common Pleas, Alexander was forbidden from making political statements. According to archivist Mark Frazier Lloyd, an expert on the Alexander papers, "It may be that he viewed the West Mount Airy Neighbors Association as a group which was actively involved in working to influence the political authorities in Philadelphia. To the best of my knowledge, [Alexander] . . . did not . . . express himself about [his experience] with the integration of West Mount Airy." Lloyd, "Re: Raymond Pace Alexander (RPA) Papers."

30. Perry, "Negro Leaders Mum."

31. Countryman, *Up South*, 165–167.

32. "Sadie Alexander, Austin Norris, Deny Moore's 'Part-Time Negro' Rap," *Philadelphia Tribune*, June 8, 1963.

33. Letter from Raymond Pace Alexander to Dr. Clifton H. Johnson.

34. Station Break: WDAS Radio Editorial, June 14, 1963, box 89, folder 19, accession 374, Raymond Alexander Pace Papers, University of Pennsylvania Archives, Philadelphia, PA,

35. Station Break: WDAS Radio Editorial, June 14, 1963.

36. G. A. Wilson, "Other Look at Him: Cecil Moore Takes a Look at 'His City,'" *Pennsylvania Guardian*, June 7, 1963; Joseph Lelyveld, "Militant Ex-Marine Leads Philadelphia Negroes," *New York Times*, September 2, 1964; "NAACP Tries Its Own," *Philadelphia Evening Bulletin*, December 5, 1964; Owen Evans, "NAACP Votes to Fight Split: Moore Supporters Say They'll Resist National Policy," *Philadelphia Bulletin*, December 5, 1965; Letter to Roy Wilkins from G. A. Wilson, with *Guardian* clippings, June 10, 1963, box C137, folder 3, NAACP Records, Part III: Branch Files, Philadelphia, 1956–65, Library of Congress Archives, Washington, DC; Complaint against Cecil B. Moore, filed to the National Board from Viola Allen, Alphonso Deal, Dolores Tucker, Ethel Barnett, Senora Gratton, and James Smith, June 10, 1963, box C137, folder 5, NAACP Records, Part III: Branch Files, Philadelphia, 1956–65, Library of Congress Archives, Washington, DC.

5

The 1960s and Expanding Ideas of Black Rights

CLEM HARRIS

By the mid-1960s, the combination of Black migration, discrimination in labor and housing markets, industrial flight, poverty, hypersegregation, and white exodus, all of which led to the economic and social underdevelopment of Black working-class communities like North Central Philadelphia, overdevelopment of the city's suburbs, and an erosion of Philadelphia's tax base, signaled something far worse than the failure of civil rights liberalism to address these issues. These changes overshadowed the fact that by the arrival of the postindustrial era the city's political structure was changing. Philadelphia's political landscape went from a two-party system to, essentially, a single-party machine structure led by white ward-based Democratic Party regulars who dominated city hall, the city council, and the state capitol in Harrisburg. Three key factors explain the rise and growth of the Democratic machine. First, despite the surge of reformist energy during the postwar years that eliminated nearly seven decades of dominance under the Republican machine, the 1950s coalition of progressive middle- to upper-middle-class white people along with trade unionists, Black civil rights activists, and white row house regular Democrats, which resembled the New Deal coalition, dissolved due to factionalism. Second, as a result of reapportionment and gerrymandering, white Democratic machine leaders were able to solidify their influence over the city's wards and exerted tremendous authority over the largest segment of Black voters, thereby controlling the balance of power. Third, the tactic of redrawing political boundaries entrenched the power of white-dominated political organizations that determined the nomination and election of Black candidates. This process virtually eliminated the ability of African American political leaders to develop Black political organizations within the party, and it severely marginalized the ability of Black elected leaders to negotiate policy for hard-hit Black working-class communities. Equally important, before the emergence of the Black Political Forum (BPF) and the independent Black political movement by the end of the decade, this complex transformation triggered the rise of both hypermasculine Black Nationalist leaders such as Cecil B. Moore and efforts to establish community control in predominantly Black wards.[1]

One of several important indications that the city's political structure was changing occurred in early February 1957, when Earl Chudoff officially announced his decision to leave the Fourth Congressional District seat he had occupied since 1948. For African Americans, Chudoff's decision meant that for the first time since the congressional run of George H. White in 1912, Black Philadelphians had a real chance of receiving racial representation in Congress. Located mostly in North Central Philadelphia, the city's Fourth Congressional District contained the most densely populated area of Black voters throughout the city. The following year, the *Tribune* echoed this point after the Democrats announced their intention to slate Robert N. C. Nix Sr. to fill the seat in the May 20 special election. But, if the selection of Nix represented a strong indication of transformation regarding the political aspirations of Black people in Philadelphia, and indirectly African Americans across the state, for higher office, it was also an indicator of how Black political pressure drove broader transformation within the Democratic Party. The Fourth Congressional District contained mostly registered Democrats. And, although Chudoff had successfully withstood challenges from Black GOP candidates, the Democrats knew that the failure to slate a highly regarded Black candidate from a predominantly Black congressional district in the nation's third-largest city would likely result in shifting a majority of more than eighty thousand Black voters within the district to the GOP. In addition to increasing levels of direct political pressure from Black people in both major parties for recognition in higher elective offices, the fact that no Black person had ever been elected to Congress from Pennsylvania could no longer be ignored. In this respect, Chudoff's decision not only provided an opportunity for Black people to fulfill a long-held political aspiration; it also provided the Democratic Party with a crucial opening to preserve its commanding lead over the GOP regarding the Black vote.[2]

The slating of Nix had been primarily engineered by the Democratic City Committee (DCC) chairman and congressman William "Bill" Green. His selection reveals that two critical observations were unfolding during the period. First, by 1958, mounting tensions between liberal reformers and regular Democrats were expanding. Second, by the 1958 electoral cycle, leaders of the city's reform movement were not only rapidly losing power among Black people within the Democratic Party; they were losing control of the party hierarchy itself. Nix, a graduate of the University of Pennsylvania Law School who was one of the city's most well-known defense attorneys, advocate for civil rights, and former GOP operative, became a Democrat in 1937. By the early 1950s, he had gained a citywide reputation as one of the Democratic Party's most important operatives when it came to steering the Black vote to Democrats. By 1958, Nix had chaired a string of successful victories for Democrats that included the "Good Government" campaign in 1953, the 1954 election of the first Democratic governor since the New Deal, and, in 1955, the reelection of a second reform administration with Richardson Dilworth, who succeeded Joseph Clark. Nix's impressive résumé also included the election of Rev. Marshall L. Shepard Sr. as councilman-at-large and the reelection of Raymond Pace Alexander to city council, both African American. After gaining the party's nomination, Nix underscored his shift from the postwar coalition toward an alliance with machine leadership when he declared, "It [the selection of a Black candidate] is certainly what I would expect of the Democratic Party because I have complete confidence in its progressive leadership under Cong. William Green."[3] Many Black Philadelphians from the Fourth Congressional District in both parties were enthusiastic in their support of Nix Sr. "It is altogether proper that the vast and increasing Negro population in the Fourth Congressional district be represented in Congress by one of their own race," Alexander said. "This means at long last the nearly 700,000 Negro people in Pennsylvania have a voice." Dr. William H. Gray Jr., pastor of the Bright Hope Baptist Church, prominent Black civic leader, and longtime GOP supporter, stated, "I want to commend the leadership of the Democratic Party for seeing fit to endorse a qualified Negro as its candidate to carry the Party's banners in the coming election." Cecil B. Moore added, "I'm glad. I offer my congratulations. I'm sure he will be a very worthy opponent."[4]

While many hailed the selection of Nix, his candidacy and the slating process drew sharp criticism from numerous African American religious and civic leaders. Some pointed out that Nix had been a lifelong resident and former ward leader of West Philadelphia's Forty-Fourth Ward, which was not a part of the Fourth Congressional District. Only during the nomination process did he provide an address in the official district that he hoped to represent. Nix's nomination also marked a change in the Democratic Party's slating policy. Green broke from his party's precedent of allowing the slating process to be determined among ward executive committees. Instead, Green centralized control of candidate selection within the city committee, which was located downtown. Nix's selection also reopened factional disputes between reformers and stalwarts. Beginning with the ouster of James Finnegan, the former DCC chair who embraced reform, and the rise of Green as the new chair of the city committee in February 1953, reformers were perpetually locked in ongoing battles against stalwarts. At the center of these struggles were attempts by stalwarts to roll back civil service protections on the city's vast reservoir of jobs in an effort to expand and control the patronage system. For example, in 1953, reformers and stalwarts clashed over Mayor Clark's decision to hire technocrats from outside the city, like Kirk R. Petshek, a Harvard-trained economist who had previously served as director of postwar economic aid to Yugoslavia. Petshek came to Philadelphia to serve in the newly created position of city economist in the city's Commerce Department. In 1954, Clark and Green clashed again. This time it was over whether the Democratic Party should endorse Donald C. Rubel, a liberal Republican, for a vacancy in the city council, over GOP hopeful John T. Murphy, who many Democratic stalwarts supported. A year later, the clash repeated when Clark, with the backing of labor leaders from the local International Ladies Garment Workers Union, tried to have the union's secretary Joseph Schwartz, who also chaired the local Americans for Democratic Action chapter, placed on the councilmanic ticket. Green and other stalwarts flatly refused.[5]

On the issue of patronage, many working-class, rank-and-file Black people in the Democratic Party sided with the organization. Part of their reasoning grew from the growing importance of public sector employment and a shift of manufacturing jobs to the suburbs and Sunbelt states. Notwithstanding the economic opportunity African Americans gained from being able to compete with white people for municipal jobs as a result of the antibias clause and independent civil service commission, by the late 1950s, complexities engendered from these structural transformations severely undermined the ability of reformers to hold the Black vote. Equally significant, as the Black population grew and the white population declined from an exodus of white middle-class families to the suburbs, independents and stalwarts in the Democratic Party as well as the GOP became increasingly dependent on Black votes in segregated African American communities. For example, by 1959, the Black vote in the Fourth Congressional District increased from 80,000 to 97,559. During the same year, in the Fifth Councilmanic District, whose wards made up a significant part of the Fourth Congressional District, Black voters outnumbered white voters by nearly 53,000. This dynamic was not only a crucial factor for understanding how the very reforms that helped promote fairness in city employment became interpreted as prohibitive to Black economic progress toward the end of the decade; it was also the most important dynamic for understanding the downfall of the reform faction's influence in Black institutional politics during the period.[6]

By 1955, Green's power had increased over the city's largest rank-and-file Black Democratic organization. The reasons were twofold. First, many African Americans in the party had become alienated from participation in public sector employment by the antispoils system of the new city charter. Second, Black people were also deeply aggrieved by the policies of Clark to hire experts from outside the city. An example of this issue on the state level can be seen from the observations of Black drivers who wondered why they never saw Black people working on the Pennsylvania Turnpike as they traveled. An unnamed driver stated, "I rode from Philadelphia to Harrisburg and didn't even see a colored truck driver. The only brown face I saw over that stretch of 101 miles was my own windshield mirror."[7] Another driver stated, "I didn't even see anybody who was sunburned. I got a little scared about whether I should be driving on the Pike."[8] In the summer of 1955, after his appointment as chairman of the Pennsylvania Turnpike Commission by Democratic governor George Leader, Green publicly stated that he was convinced the state's African American citizens deserved better recognition in the matter of jobs than had been received in the past twenty years. A second example of the spoils issue on the local level can be gleaned from the statement of a white West Philadelphia Democrat, Councilman Sam Rose. Rose was an organizational loyalist and reputed expert on Black political interests. He had recommended Nix to Green. Unlike the earlier days when the reform influence was strong, Rose believed Black people were prepared to reject reformers during the 1958 election cycle. On the issues of control and patronage, he stated, "We have the jobs today, we have the control."[9]

By mid-March, tensions between reformers and regular Democrats erupted when the Citizens Committee of the Fourth Congressional District selected Harvey N. Schmidt, an African American attorney, civic leader, and independent Democrat of the Twenty-Fourth Ward, to oppose Nix in the May 20 special election. The committee was an ad hoc organization backed by white reformers such as Clark, Dilworth, Councilman Henry Sawyer, the Congress of Industrial Organizations Political Action Committee (CIO-PAC), dissident Democratic committeemen from the Forty-Seventh Ward, labor groups, and the local Americans for Democratic Action chapter. A few days later, the Citizens Committee targeted Herbert Arlene, the African American Democratic leader of the Forty-Seventh Ward, when they announced their support for the reelection of Jesse Shields, an African American and incumbent Democratic state representative from the Tenth Legislative District (i.e., the Twenty-Ninth and Forty-Seventh Wards). Shields had become disaffected by the growth of the Democratic organization's power in the Forty-Seventh Ward. By May, the battle between reformers and regular Democrats for the Black vote intensified when Rev. H. J. Trapp, African American pastor of the Thankful Baptist Church, agreed to chair Schmidt's campaign committee. Two weeks later, the political stakes increased when Councilman-at-Large Marshall Shepard sided with reformers by publicly endorsing Schmidt's candidacy. The support of Trapp and Shepard, two of the most popular and powerful Black leaders in North Philadelphia and West Philadelphia clearly indicated the importance of the enormous Black vote in the Fourth Congressional District. It also indicated the strong intentions of reformers to compete with regular ward politicians for the support of rank-and-file Black Democrats and independent Black voters. In addition to being a pastor, Trapp was president of the Baptist Ministers Conference, which carried influence with nearly twenty thousand voters, and he led the Committee for the Prevention of Juvenile Delinquencies and Its Causes, a citywide nonpartisan civic organization developed by Rev. Leon Sullivan of North Philadelphia's Zion Baptist Church. In accepting his new role, Trapp told supporters, "I shall use every influence necessary to assure the election of Harvey N. Schmidt to Congress on May 20, 1958. Not only because of his qualifications and demonstrated interests in the welfare of the people of the Fourth Congressional District, but also because it is important that the people of our district reaffirm their inherent right to select qualified leadership existing in our neighborhood. We shall win this election," he concluded, "because the cause justifies the effort."[10]

Trapp overstated the moral justification for Schmidt's campaign. He was correct to point out that Schmidt's candidacy represented a strong desire by Black voters of the Fourth Congressional District to choose someone from within their district rather than have an interloper forced on them. However, there was virtually no credible difference within the candidate selection process conducted by either the Democratic machine or reformers in the Citizens Committee. The meeting orchestrated by independents resulting in Schmidt's endorsement did not reflect the voices of members from key Black wards. Black electors from these wards had not been informed that a slate was being formulated, and, as a result, the meeting was not only poorly attended; it dismissed the same democratic process reformers accused the machine of dismissing when they slated Nix.[11]

As the factional fight within the Democratic Party grew, GOP forces in the Fourth Congressional District hoped to benefit from the intraparty war. In early February, on the recommendation of Hobson Reynolds, the African American GOP leader of the Forty-Seventh Ward, Republicans endorsed Cecil B. Moore as their candidate. After his discharge from the U.S. Marines in 1947, Moore moved to North Central Philadelphia and wasted little time developing deep ties to the district's poor and working-class Black residents. In 1954, he graduated from Temple Law School and, in the same year, became a member of the Pennsylvania Bar. After building a successful law practice as a defense attorney, he joined arguably the most exclusive Black social organization in North Philadelphia, the Pyramid Club, and took his place among the area's Black elite. He was a member of the local NAACP and a leading advocate in the fight against the proliferation of "taprooms," neighborhood institutions that sold alcohol and contributed to the delinquency of Black children. Tradition informed his role as a committeeman in the Forty-Seventh Ward. Consistent with a long history of independent Black politics in the city that stretched back well before the New Deal era, along with a combative style he acquired while in the U.S. Marine Corps, Moore was not only an independent activist politician; he was competent, charismatic, and outspoken. He once stated, "I was determined when I got back [from World War II combat] that what rights I didn't have I was going to take, using every weapon in the arsenal of democracy. After nine years in the Marine Corps, I don't intend to take another order from any son of a bitch that walks."[12] He believed, like Congressman Adam Clayton Powell Jr., who became Moore's political ally and friend during the presidential election of 1956, that organizational interests played second to the interests of the race. Also similar to Powell, Moore believed that partisan fights over African American interests were best fought publicly rather than behind closed doors. Moore used his position as vice chairman of the Citizens for Eisenhower reelection campaign, in 1956, to articulate this view in repeated attacks against the power Southern Democrats held over national civil rights policy. And, in a letter in 1957, Moore attacked Roy Wilkins for what he called the NAACP leader's willingness to side with Democrats and accept a weak civil rights bill. "Your statement," Moore wrote, "reflects such a vacillatory, conciliatory state of mind that you have aligned yourself with the Senate vote of Eastland, Russell, Thurmond et al."[13] (See Fig. 5.1.)

By May 21, 1958, polling results showed that Black voters of the Fourth Congressional District overwhelmingly elected Nix over Schmidt and Moore as the state's first African American member to the U.S. Congress. Nix received one of the highest votes ever polled by an organization candidate in a Democratic primary. On May 20, he tallied 16,895 votes to win the nomination over Schmidt, who received 8,277 votes. In the special election against his GOP rival, Nix received 14,097 to the 7,350 polled by Moore. With regard to Moore, although he had been a long-term resident and an important populist symbol of Black poor and working-class interests in the district, it was a seemingly impossible task to overcome the vast registration advantage Democrats had over Republicans. Additionally, as time went on, it had become evident that the GOP did not place the full financial weight of their party behind Moore. Historically, the election of Nix was only the sixth time that an African American had been elected to Congress nationwide

Figure 5.1 Cecil B. Moore employed a more activist approach and won widespread support in Philadelphia's Black community.

since the Gilded Age. In addition to Powell from New York, Nix would now join William L. Dawson from Chicago and Charles C. Diggs Jr. from Detroit. His election resolved a key question as to where the loyalty of the city's most powerful Black Democratic rank-and-file organization resided. Since 1951, independents had not lost an election, and they managed to resist all attempts to undo the reform agenda. Because of the enormous wealth and strong propaganda of independent forces backing Schmidt, it was widely held that Nix would not win. Compared to the thousands of dollars from reformers, Green and the Democratic organization provided only $60 to Nix's campaign. In all seven wards of the Fourth Congressional District, Black voters overwhelmingly defeated every Black candidate backed by reformers. During the victory celebration at DCC headquarters, a jubilant Green stood with his arms wrapped around Nix's shoulders and stated, "Congressman Nix, your victory means as much to me as my own victory in the 5th Congressional District."[14] Green's adulation was not overstated. The landslide election of Nix meant that the city's largest Black Democratic voting bloc had emphatically shifted the balance of power to the organization. It also signaled the beginning of an important transformation in Black politics that soon would have negative long-term consequences. The resounding defeat of reformers simultaneously reduced the leverage of the Black vote in the Fourth Congressional District. This was largely due to the fact that it significantly reduced the degree of strong intraparty competition. It also eliminated the ability of Black independents within the Democratic Party to challenge machine Democrats on issues regarding racial reform, especially in elective and appointive positions. And it eliminated an important space for independent voices during the formulation of party rules in various Democratic ward executive committees throughout the Fourth Congressional District. Finally, the tension between reformers and regular Democrats, complicated by the Black movement for independent politics during the 1970s, remains one of the most powerful dynamics in the party to this day.[15] (See Fig. 5.2.)

For those Black independents who stood with reformers, it was now a question of political survival. No one knew this better than Alexander, the longtime independent Black liberal from North Philadelphia. After his re-election in 1955, Alexander moved steadily toward the organization and throughout the congressional campaign he publicly praised Nix. Following the special election, he stated that the decision by insurgent Democrats like Councilman-at-Large Rev. Marshall L. Shepard Sr. to oppose the organization effectively ended their political careers. Alexander had not been entirely incorrect. For example, while Shepard Sr. was able to effectively hold his seat on the city council until 1965, it was the last office he held. In contrast, Alexander had been initially promised the support of the Democratic Party when Chudoff stepped down. Rather than challenge the party's choice, Alexander's loyalty to the organization paid off when, after Nix secured a second term during the general election against Moore in November 1958, Alexander, in January 1959, became the first African American appointed to the city's highest court of record—the Court of Common Pleas—by Governor George Leader.[16]

Figure 5.2 Robert N. C. Nix Sr. helped lead the political transformation of Philadelphia when he won election to Congress in 1958.

The appointment of Alexander was an important political victory for Black Philadelphians. Since the Progressive Era, African Americans fought to break Jim Crow barriers that prevented a member of their race from being seated on the city's highest court. Notwithstanding the importance of Alexander's appointment, it was far from the degree of equitable racial representation African Americans deserved. Black people constituted approximately one-fourth of the city's total population in 1960. Based on their percentage of the city's total population and the total of thirty judges in the Court of Common Pleas, Black people deserved approximately eight seats on Philadelphia's highest court. By 1967, the disparity under Democrats had not much improved. By then, Black people had achieved three seats on the Court of Common Pleas, despite the fact that their numbers rose and constituted one-third of the total population. During the same year of Alexander's appointment, Green and the organization supported Black liberals in the attack against racially restrictive real estate practices with the introduction of fair housing legislation. The bill, which was eventually signed in 1961 by Democratic governor David Lawrence, represented a collaborative effort between the Pennsylvania Equal Rights Council, NAACP, Fellowship Commission, and Black people elected to the Pennsylvania House of Representatives from Philadelphia, such as Susie Monroe. However, after the introduction of fair housing legislation, Black people not only found it increasingly difficult to secure the machine's support for civil rights legislation; they were gradually shut out of policy-making posts in the Democratic Party and key positions within the municipal government.[17]

A principal reason behind the reduction in Black electoral power lay in yet another shift in the city's political structure. Although the congressional election of 1958 effectively established organizational Democrats as the dominant power, it did not eliminate reformers from the Democratic coalition. After reconciliation, Dilworth and Green turned to the mayoral election of 1959. In the fall of the same year, Dilworth, having gained particularly large returns in Philadelphia's Black wards, carried the city in a virtual landslide. The Democrats also gained support among wards that contained some of the most prominent liberal white households in the city and picked up strong support among working-class white people in the city's lower socioeconomic wards. The mayoral election marked a zenith for Democratic candidates, the strength of Green, and the organization. The landslide victory over the GOP shifted the city's political structure from a strong two-party system to essentially a strong one-party system with a weak opposition party in the GOP. With one notable exception, the election of Arlen Specter as district attorney in 1965, between 1959 and 1967, the GOP was consistently shut out of executive power in the city's top three elective offices.[18]

Republicans found it increasingly difficult to compete in part because by the end of the 1960s, African Americans, who constituted the city's largest minority voting bloc, were overwhelmingly registered with the Democratic Party. Also, the spatial and racial foundations of the GOP were moving away from the city's Black wards to mostly white wards and suburbs. By the late 1970s, the racial composition of the city's GOP base had become increasingly working-class to lower-middle-class white ethnics. These changes reflected a rightward shift of Philadelphia's GOP organization away from liberalism toward a national conservative movement that began during the mid-1960s and later defined much of the country's Republican electoral landscape by the late 1970s. The transition to single-party democracy also had a reductive effect on Black electoral power. First, the plurality from all socioeconomic levels, ethnic groups, independents, and machine supporters meant that, while the Black vote was a significant part of the Democratic majority in 1959, it was not critical to the outcome. Second, the GOP had begun to write off the Black vote after the 1958 congressional election. In 1959, Republicans in the State Senate blocked passage of a fair housing bill. During the 1960 presidential election, Moore publicly acknowledged the unwillingness of Republicans to strongly compete for the Black vote when he accused the GOP of warming up to lily-white people in the segregationist South. Despite having resisted the repeated urging by Democrats to switch his registration, it was the progressive abandonment of the Black vote by Philadelphia's Republican Party that finally led Moore to switch his registration to the Democrats in the fall of 1961. For Dorothy Anderson, a political reporter for the *Tribune*, the outcome of the 1959 mayoral election reflected a low point for democracy in the city. Shortly after the November general election, she wrote, "THERE MUST BE A STRONG TWO-PARTY SYSTEM HERE unless you want the evident corruptions in City Hall to grow until they reach the proportions of the last days of the old Republican Regime."[19]

Concurrent with the political transformations that hit Philadelphia and its metropolitan region during the postindustrial period, a new generation of Black community protest leaders surfaced. These leaders explicitly based themselves in the city's Black working-class neighborhoods rather than the offices of liberal reform organizations located in Center City. As historian Matthew Countryman has rightly argued, these neighborhood-based leaders did not openly question civil rights liberalism's faith in the legal protection of individual liberty and interracial coalitions as the keys to eradicating racial injustice. They instead questioned the exclusive focus on legislative means and the sole reliance on professional middle-class leadership. These critics of civil rights liberalism believed leadership was too narrowly focused on the successful outcome of abstract legal rights and willfully ignored pressing issues like urban blight, juvenile delinquency, and police brutality that were equally significant to residents of Black working-class neighborhoods. They also blamed the Black middle class for not fulfilling its responsibilities to less fortunate members of the community. Inspired by the emergence of Dr. Martin Luther King Jr. and the Southern civil rights movement and later the rise of Malcolm X and Black Nationalism, this new generation of Black activists and organizations concluded that only mass mobilization of working-class Black Philadelphians could successfully achieve genuine racial progress.[20]

In the 1950s, among the most prominent of this group located in North Philadelphia was Rev. Leon Sullivan of Zion Baptist Church, who also founded the Opportunities Industrial Center. Also, despite a series of attacks against the Black left, which either silenced or relegated Black radicalism to the margins of African American political culture during the anticommunist period, by the end of the 1950s, the most prominent voices of Black Nationalism in the city were ministers, most notably Malcolm X, and members of the Nation of Islam. During the early to mid-1960s, an additional wave of leaders and organizations arose in Black Philadelphia, the most prominent of which were the Congress of Racial Equality, under the leadership of Louis Smith; Max Stanford, founder of the Revolutionary Action movement; and John Churchville, a former field secretary with the Student Nonviolent Coordinating Committee (SNCC) and founder of a small storefront organization called the Freedom Library. By the fall of 1965, Churchville, along with others such as Walter Palmer, Edward Robinson, and Father Paul Washington, an Episcopal Priest, founded an all-Black political organization called the Black People's Unity Movement. Drawing on Malcolm X's call for an "all Afro-American people organization to henceforth unite so that the welfare and well-being of our people will be reassured,"[21] the Black People's Unity Movement embodied a vision of movement politics based on the principles of Black Nationalism, an ideology that calls for racial unity, Black consciousness, and community control over key political, social, and economic institutions operating within predominately African American communities. In 1965, SNCC, under the leadership of Fred Meely, a longtime member of the organization's Mississippi staff, also established a beachhead in the city.[22]

The postindustrial period also witnessed the ascension of Black Philadelphia's "New Messiah," Moore, to the presidency of the local NAACP, as arguably the city's most efficacious militant protest leader. Moore's elevation as president symbolized a rejection of Black middle-class liberal leadership. The dominant scholarly treatment on Moore has focused on his role as a protest leader. Yet, Moore was more than a protest leader. He was the only African American political leader in postindustrial Philadelphia to exert consistent influence in Black electoral and protest politics. Moore called for an independent Black third party as a strategy for reallocating political power to the city's Black working class. This effort to develop an independent Black electoral politics prefigured the model used by Black Power advocates in Philadelphia during the 1970s.[23]

By the beginning of the 1964 primaries, the principles of Black Nationalism were at the center of a major debate regarding the slating process for elective office with the biggest argument taking place in North Philadelphia. In mid-February, five independent Black candidates announced their intentions to seek endorsements from the Democratic Party and civil rights organizations. Their campaigns were a critique of "candidates hand-picked by the political machines" of the Democrats and Republicans as well as a critique of postwar liberalism. Furthermore, they represented an emerging call for "race pride" and grassroots Black political leadership. The call for a form of Black politics rooted in race pride, or racial unity, was a core principle of Black Nationalism. It was consistent with the political philosophy of "community control" espoused principally by Malcolm X, who argued that Black people should control the political, social, and economic institutions within their communities. Four of the five machine candidates opposed by Black independents were African American. The white candidate was Charles R. Weiner, a Jewish resident of the largely white Wynnefield section of the Fifty-Second Ward and Democratic incumbent for the Seventh State Senatorial District, which covered much of West Philadelphia. The most prominent among Weiner's challengers was Rev. Marshall Lorenzo Shepard, Jr., an assistant pastor of the Mt. Olivet Tabernacle Baptist Church and son of Councilman-at-Large Marshall L. Shepard Sr. The younger Shepard, who took aim at Weiner, hoped to become Pennsylvania's first independently elected Black state senator. On the front page of the *Tribune*'s February 15 edition, they referred to the all-Black slate as a "Third Party." The architect behind the all-Black slate was Cecil B. Moore.[24]

During the same week of Shepard's announcement, Moore initiated a bruising attack against Kathryn Woodard, an African American civic leader and publisher of the *Philadelphia Independent*. In response to Woodard's charges that the civil rights leader was both a dictator and the person who drew up the list of Black candidates, Moore declared that Woodard's motives were a threat to race pride. By invoking race pride, Moore aligned his political attack against Woodard within the Black Nationalist tradition. He stated, "It is rather obvious that she sought to prepare her readers for her forthcoming endorsement of a white candidate (Charles R. Weiner) in a senatorial district (the 7th) where the Negro voting strength is more than three to one." Although denying any direct role in creating the slate, Moore articulated the NAACP's political objective when he stated, "The NAACP is seeking to advance the cause of Negro leadership, and will support those Negro candidates who will give strong and intelligent leadership."[25]

Despite the fact that nearly 70 percent of voters in the Seventh Senatorial District were Black, the "race pride" platform of Moore and other Black Nationalists failed. But failure of the Black independent slate did not translate into a reduction of Moore's popularity. After a fatal riot in North Central Philadelphia during the late summer of 1964, Moore achieved national acclaim as a populist Black Nationalist leader when, in response to a question from a reporter for *Time* magazine, he declared, "I am the goddamn boss."[26]

In February 1965, Moore was overwhelmingly reelected as president of the local NAACP, and by May he launched an epic battle when he led working-class Black Philadelphians, including youths, the middle-aged, and gang members, in a series of campaigns that finally brought an end to anti-Black racial barriers at Girard College in 1968. After 1965, Moore once again turned to a strategy designed to reallocate electoral power to independent Black candidates during the 1966 Democratic primary. As a result of a decline in the city's total population, Philadelphia had gone from six to five congressional seats. Adoption of a new congressional reapportionment plan by Democrats in 1966 meant that Philadelphia had a new ward structure that accommodated a reduction in congressional strength. For Black Philadelphians, changes to the political boundaries and designations of preexisting districts meant the dissolution of the Fourth Congressional District and with it the state's most powerful Black voting bloc. What emerged was the new Second Congressional District, which diluted Black voting strength by integrating the old district with predominantly white middle-class areas that strongly supported the Democratic Party. By disaggregating Black voting strength, the Democratic organization preserved its advantage over the Republican Party, Black independent forces, and, by extension, its hegemony over African American electoral power.

In February of the same year, some hoped that the new ward realignments would help elect Pennsylvania's first independent Black state senator. Moore announced the NAACP's intentions to fight in order to ensure that independent Black candidates were slated for state senatorial seats in predominantly Black districts like the Second, Third, and Seventh. In March, Moore became an independent candidate for the Democratic Party's endorsement against Nix for the Second Congressional District. Even though Moore succeeded in getting his name on the ballot by the end of the primary, Nix received overwhelming support for the Democratic nomination. Additionally, although Black voters delivered significant political support to Milton Shapp, a white industrialist and independent Democratic gubernatorial candidate who later became Pennsylvania's first Jewish governor in 1971, every Black independent state senatorial candidate was defeated. Results from the 1966 primaries reveal that the new reapportionment plan had indeed served to further entrench the Democratic organization's power over the Black vote. During the fall of 1967, Moore once again faced defeat when his Freedom Rights Party lost handily in a bid to unseat Democratic mayor James Tate. It would be his final attempt to redirect electoral power to Black grassroots leaders.[27]

Despite two critical judicial victories achieved by civil rights activists and liberal reformers in *Wesberry v. Sanders*, which extended the maxim "one-voter, one vote" to all congressional districts, and *Reynolds v. Sims*, which required reapportionment of all state and federal legislative districts on a decennial basis, the 1966 reapportionment plan had not violated either of these rulings. Nor had the plan violated the Civil Rights Act of 1964, which eliminated the effects of legalized Jim Crow in public life, and Sections Two and Five of the Voting Rights Act of 1965. The Democrats' reapportionment plan reflected a form of racial gerrymandering explicitly designed to fracture the Black voting power of a single African American district while simultaneously protecting the city and state's first African American congressional representative, who was also an extension of the organization's power. Additionally, while Black congressional representation could not be denied, white party elites like Green could control the Black vote by ensuring the reelection of Nix. A more egregious form of racial gerrymandering had been standard practice in Black and Latino communities in the Bedford-Stuyvesant area of Brooklyn, New York. In 1966, civil rights activists and liberal reformers challenged New York's congressional reapportionment plan, which sought to separate the Black community into five districts. Plaintiffs charged this was a violation of the Constitution because the plan ensured no Black person could be elected to Congress. In 1967, a federal district court ruled in favor of the plaintiffs. As historian J. Morgan Kousser indicates, redistricting is a strategic game in which areas containing people with certain racia or ethnic identities and political proclivities are rearranged to benefit a particular outcome. Hence, given the intentionality of redistricting by partisan bodies, every plan will be a gerrymander in some sense because it will look to benefit one group and not another.[28]

The effects of reapportionment remain underexplored in studies of the urban Black freedom struggle during the latter half of the twentieth and early decades of the twenty-first centuries. And while the Democrats' congressional reapportionment plan of 1966 was inarguably the most important structural factor for understanding how white political bosses maintained control of the Black vote after 1958, it was not the sole factor for understanding why Black independents under Moore failed in 1966 and 1967. Three critical shifts in the city's political structure and the national political landscape point to weaknesses in the Black organizational structure and a volatile white electorate. First, during these two years, the strategies of Black Nationalists like Moore were encouraged by increases in the city's African American population and the reignition of an intraparty war between reformers and stalwarts in the Democratic Party.

Second, they were also indirectly aided by the regeneration of the local GOP organization under Arlen Specter. And, after electing Governor Lawrence in 1958, the Democrats lost the state capitol to Republicans in 1963 and 1967. Democrats would not regain control of Harrisburg until 1971. These changes foretold a broader national rejection of Democratic liberalism that would ultimately play out with the election of Nixon and GOP conservatives during the presidential election of 1968. However, while this appears to have weakened the power of the city's Democratic organization and aided Black Nationalists' aspirations for a place on the ballot, it was highly probable that, in addition to weaknesses in the political infrastructure of Black independents, their efforts may have been weakened by the popularity of urban federalism (i.e., the War on Poverty and the Model Cities Programs). This indicates that Moore's Black Nationalist politics may have suffered from competition with other Black activists within the city whose form of populism was slightly less radical and whose focus on community action fused together elements of civil rights and Black Power and who emphasized the importance of local politics for Black liberation and the poor. At the center of this populism was the argument that urban policy must be controlled by the "people" within the community—not elected representatives or the political machine. This form of populism also focused on community action strategies that included self-help and urban policies supported by the U.S. Office of Economic Opportunity War on Poverty Program and, later, the U.S. Department of Housing and Urban Development Model Cities Program. Both placed an emphasis on a form of political engineering called "maximum feasible participation" when it came to the incorporation of poor indigenous groups in the decision-making process regarding the administration of programs that directly impacted their lives. Additionally, Moore's brand of Black Nationalist electoral politics in Philadelphia, including the independent Black third-party initiative, never posed a real threat to the Democratic machine. During the 1967 mayoral election, Moore vigorously denounced James Tate as he campaigned solely in Black neighborhoods throughout the city. The final tabulations after the polls closed on November 7 revealed that Moore had finished in last place with 6,675 votes, a number significantly below the 9,018 votes received by Leonard M. Smalls, a relatively unknown Black mayoral candidate who represented the Consumer Party. Moore had garnered less than 1 percent of the vote. The broader implications of his poor performance meant that his Freedom Rights Party was not viable for the 1968 electoral cycle. To make the ballot for 1968, Moore needed to attract at least 2 percent of the vote.

Finally, Moore's brand of Black Nationalism was a critical factor that led to the rise of Frank L. Rizzo as police commissioner under a Democratic administration in 1967 and the emergence of a form of conservative populism rooted in what historian Timothy Lombardo calls white ethnic blue-collar identity throughout communities in South and Northeast Philadelphia. This brand of conservative populism later propelled Rizzo from police commissioner to mayor from 1971 to 1979. The rise of Rizzo from police commissioner to two-term mayor as well as the wave of white conservatism that supported him were part of a broader national conservative movement in postindustrial urban America that grew from reactions to Black activism in the nation's cities, urban disorder, and fear of social, political, and economic displacement by urban liberalism, particularly the restricting of urban space, and the liberal agenda of President Lyndon B. Johnson's administration.[29]

Notwithstanding these barriers as well as the hypermasculine leadership style Moore used that excluded Black women as independent candidates for elective office, the goal and strategies of Moore and other Black Nationalists to reallocate electoral power to an all-Black independent neighborhood-based leadership structure are nonetheless important to African American urban political history during the late twentieth century. These efforts connected Moore and other Black Nationalists to struggles for political recognition and local power that shaped racial politics in the city during the Progressive Era and New Deal period. Efforts by those like Moore ultimately became the foundation on which the rise of Philadelphia Black Power electoral politics later emerged during the 1970s under the successful efforts of independent Black political organizations like the BPF.

By 1968, the failure of Moore's efforts to reallocate electoral power to independent neighborhood-based Black political leaders triggered a series of transitions in the city's Black leadership structure. Not only had he failed to wrest power away from the Democratic Party in the 1967 mayoral election; during the same year, the national office of the NAACP proposed to break up the Philadelphia branch into five smaller offices, essentially eliminating its power as a citywide Black institution. Moore was also deposed from his role as president and effectively kicked out of the civil rights organization by its national executive secretary, Roy Wilkins. And, although Moore would eventually emerge as president of the Black Independent Alliance in 1968, it was evident that changes in the city's Black leadership structure meant that the responsibility for redirecting electoral power to African American grassroots leaders was no longer his to bear alone. Equally important, the shift toward Black independent politics Moore ignited in the 1960s helped propel African American independent politics in the city during the post–civil rights era and fueled the quest for a Black mayor.[30]

NOTES

1. Carolyn Adams, David Bartelt, David Elesh, Ira Goldstein, Nancy Kleniewski, and William Yancy, *Philadelphia: Neighborhoods, Division, and Conflict in a Postindustrial City* (Philadelphia: Temple University Press, 1991), 125–134; Francis Ryan, *AFSCME'S Philadelphia Story: Municipal Workers and Urban Power in the Twentieth Century* (Philadelphia: Temple University Press, 2011), 113–120; also Francis Ryan, *The Memoirs of Wendell W. Young III: A Life in Philadelphia Labor and Politics* (Philadelphia: Temple University Press, 2019), 28–34; Matthew J. Countryman, *Up South: Civil Rights and Black Power in Philadelphia* (Philadelphia: University of Pennsylvania Press, 2006), 180–201, 307–322. For more on the failure of liberalism in Philadelphia during the deindustrialization era, see Guian A. McKee, *The Problem of Jobs: Liberalism, Race, and Deindustrialization in Philadelphia* (Chicago: University of Chicago Press, 2008).

2. "Congressman Chudoff May Step Down to Run for Judgeship," *Philadelphia Tribune*, February 5, 1957, 3; "Blast Cops at Council Hearing: Demos Slate Nix for Congress," *Philadelphia Tribune*, January 18, 1958, 1, 3; "Bob Nix or Cecil Moore Will Be Elected to Congress Today," *Philadelphia Tribune*, May 20, 1958, 1, 3. See C. L. Harris, "Race, Leadership, and the Local Machine: The Origins of the African American Struggle for Political Recognition and the Politics of Community Control, 1915–1968" (Ph.D. diss., University of Pennsylvania, 2013), chapter 2, for more on White's campaign for Pennsylvania's First Congressional District. Only the Twenty-Fourth Ward was not in North Philadelphia. "Congressman Chudoff May Run for Judgeship," 3; "Blast Cops at Council Hearing," 1, 3; "Bob Nix or Cecil Moore," 1, 3. Also see chapter 2 of dissertation for more on White's campaign for Pennsylvania's First Congressional District. James Reichley, *The Art of Government* (New York: Fund for the Republic, 1959), 45–46.

3. "Blast Cops at Council Hearing: Demos Slate Nix for Congress," *The Philadelphia Tribune*, January 18, 1958, 1, 3.

4. "Blast Cops at Council Hearing," 1, 3. "People in Both Parties Hail Slating of Bob Nix," *Philadelphia Tribune*, January 18, 1958, 1, 16.

5. On the spoils, change in leadership, slating, Nix address, and battle over city council, see "People in Both Parties Hail Slating of Bob Nix," *Philadelphia Tribune*, January 18, 1958, 1, 16, Reichley, *Art of Government*, 46, 47, 65–68; McKee, *Problem of Jobs*, 24–25; "Philadelphia Democrats Elect," *New York Times*, February 17, 1953, 17; "See Clark Moves as Visionary," *Philadelphia Tribune*, February 21, 1953, 9; "Fight Republicans Not Each Other, Democrats Told," *Philadelphia Tribune*, March 14, 1953, 2; "Dems Split Is Seen as Certainty," *Philadelphia Tribune*, April 7, 1953, 9; "What's with Politics," *Philadelphia Tribune*, October 31, 1953, 9; "What's with Politics," *Philadelphia Tribune*, October 23, 1954, 9; Charles A. Ekstrom, "The Electoral Politics of Reform and Machine: The Political Behavior of Philadelphia's 'Black' Wards, 1943–1969," in *Black Politics in Philadelphia*, ed. Miriam Ershkowitz and Joseph Zikmund (New York: Basic Books, 1973), 97–98. On Finnegan, see "Outstanding Philadelphians," *Philadelphia Tribune*, November 20, 1954, 5; "Strictly Politics," *Philadelphia Tribune*, April 1, 1958, 9. It should

be noted that attempts to constrain the union by Green were based on the fact that unions were proreform and competed for control of municipal jobs. See Ryan, *AFSCME'S Philadelphia Story*, 1–8, 74. On the intraparty fight, see Harris, "Race, Leadership, and the Local Machine," 460, 464.

6. On the issue of voter registration by reformers and stalwarts in both parties, from 1952 to 1959, see speech from Mayor Joseph Clark et al., "Register and Vote," June 22, 1955, 1–8. Official Memorandum from Mrs. B. Landreth to Wayne Barr on the subject of Clark et al., speech, July 14, 1955, 1–2, box A-498, folder 48, Mayor Joseph Clark Papers, Philadelphia City Archive. "The Political Arena," *Philadelphia Tribune*, June 28, 1955, 9; "The Political Arena," *Philadelphia Tribune*, August 27, 1955, 9; "The Political Arena," *Philadelphia Tribune*, February 21, 1956, 9; "GOP, Democrats Battling for Negro Vote," *Philadelphia Tribune*, September 4, 1956, 7; "Negro Democrats Campaign Headquarters at Broad, Lombard: Nix, Jones Heading Vote Drive; Rallies Set for All Areas," *Philadelphia Tribune*, October 9, 1956, 3. For a broader perspective, see Morley Cassidy's article "Most Explosive Race Problem in North," *Human Events Magazine*, reprinted in the *Tribune* as a public service. See "Most Explosive Race Problem in North," *Philadelphia Tribune*, February 18, 1958, 1, 9; and "Most Explosive Race Problem in North," *Philadelphia Tribune*, February 22, 1958, 1, 5. For more on city efforts in 1958–1959, see "Registration Drive Now On; Goal 300,000 by Sept. 15th," *Philadelphia Tribune*, July 26, 1958, 1–2; "Negro Voting Registration Here Increased 49,216 since 1950," *Philadelphia Tribune*, February 7, 1959, 1–2; "97,559 Negroes Registered in 4th Congressional Dist.," *Philadelphia Tribune*, February 10, 1959, 1–2; "Can Double Negro Registration in Many of City's Big Wards," *Philadelphia Tribune*, February 14, 1959, 3; "5th Councilmanic Negro Vote Outnumbers White by 52,928," *Philadelphia Tribune*, February 17, 1959, 1–2.

7. "The Political Arena," *Philadelphia Tribune*, July 16, 1955, 9.

8. "The Political Arena," *Philadelphia Tribune*, July 16, 1955, 9.

9. "The Political Arena," *Philadelphia Tribune*, June 14, 1955, 9; "The Political Arena," *Philadelphia Tribune*, July 16, 1955, 9; and Reichley, *Art of Government*, 71–72.

10. "Major Parties Name Candidates after Considerable Bickering: Independents on Both Sides Hoping for Upset Victories," *Philadelphia Tribune*, March 11, 1958, 3; "GOP Cong. Candidate Says He Is a Negro," *Philadelphia Tribune*, March 8, 1958, 1, 3; "Strictly Politics," *Philadelphia Tribune*, March 15, 1958, 11; "Shields-Arlen Battle for Legislative Post," *Philadelphia Tribune*, April 8, 1958, 2; "Strictly Politics," *Philadelphia Tribune*, April 19, 1958, 11; "Red-Hot Primary Battle Sizzling in 47th Ward: 32 Committeemen Supporting Nix and Arlene in Big Fight," *Philadelphia Tribune*, May 10, 1958, 2; "Delinquency Committee Names Rev. H.J. Trapp," *Philadelphia Tribune*, December 25, 1954, 2; quotes from "Rev. Trapp Heads Schmidt for Congress Committee," *Philadelphia Tribune*, April 29, 1958, 17; "Shepard Endorses Harvey Schmidt," *Philadelphia Tribune*, May 17, 1958, 2; "Moore and Schmidt Overwhelmed by Nix, Pennsylvania's First Negro Congressman," *Philadelphia Tribune*, May 24, 1958, 1, 8.

11. "Major Parties Name Candidates," 3; "Strictly Politics," *Philadelphia Tribune*, March 15, 1958, 11.

12. Wikipedia, s.v. "Cecil B. Moore," last modified December 30, 2021, 14:13, http://en.wikipedia.org/wiki/Cecil_B._Moore.

13. "Strictly Politics," *Philadelphia Tribune*, January 25, 1958, 11; "Strictly Politics," *Philadelphia Tribune*, January 28, 1958, 9; "Women in Politics: Sgt. Annette Sledge Addresses Local NCNW," *Philadelphia Tribune*, February 11, 1958, 7; "Strictly Politics," *Philadelphia Tribune*, March 15, 1958, 11; "Strictly Politics," *Philadelphia Tribune*, April 12, 1958, 11; "Women in Politics," *Philadelphia Tribune*, May 13, 1958, 7; "Col-

lege Heads Seeking Funds," *Philadelphia Tribune*, November 7, 1961, 8; "Jack Saunders Says," *Philadelphia Tribune*, July 16, 1968, 6; "Combat Marine Named for OCS; Precedent Set," *Philadelphia Tribune*, February 2, 1946, 1, 22; "Credit Murder Trial Success to WWII Brushes with Death as Marine Combatist," *Philadelphia Tribune*, April 18, 1962, 11; "College Heads Seeking Funds," 8; "Community Club Seeking Recreation Center Funds," *Philadelphia Tribune*, March 26, 1955, 3; "Successful Law Student Takes the Oath," *Philadelphia Tribune*, June 29, 1954, 9; "Race First, Party Second, Powell Says," *Philadelphia Tribune*, October 30, 1956, 8; "Eisenhower Backers Plan Uptown Office," *Philadelphia Tribune*, October 2, 1956, 7; "Citizens for Eisenhower Keep Organization Intact," *Philadelphia Tribune*, January 19, 1957, 8; for quote on Wilkins, see "Cecil Moore, Roy Wilkins in Running 'Rights' Feud," *Philadelphia Tribune*, August 27, 1957, 16; for quote on war experience, see Moore bio on Wikipedia, available at http://en.wikipedia.org/wiki/Cecil_B._Moore, accessed on 06/24/2019. Moore embodied traits that were used by many prolific Black activist/political leaders such as Arthur Huff Fauset, Raymond P. Alexander, Crystal Bird Fauset, Joseph Rainey, Hobson Reynolds, Sadie Alexander, Edward Henry, Marshall Shepard, G. Edward Dickerson, and Eugene Rhodes. Of the ten, only Dickerson, Rhodes, Shepard, and Henry were not from North Philadelphia. On Moore and Powell, see *Philadelphia Tribune*, "Powell's Switch to Ike Hailed by GOP Backers," October 16, 1956, 13; "Hundreds Attend GOP 30th Ward Tea," October 23, 1956, 6.

14. "Moore and Schmidt Overwhelmed by Nix, Pennsylvania's First Negro Congressman," *The Philadelphia Tribune*, May 24, 1958, 8.

15. "Bob Nix or Cecil Moore," 1, 3; "Moore and Schmidt Overwhelmed by Nix," 1, 8; "Strictly Politics," *Philadelphia Tribune*, May 24, 1958, 11; "A Man Who Says He Loves God Whom He Has Not Seen and Hates His Brother Is a Liar—The Bible," *Philadelphia Tribune*, May 27, 1958, 4; "Strictly Politics," *Philadelphia Tribune*, May 27, 1958, 9; "Cecil Moore vs. Nix—Trouble; Moore vs. Judge—More Trouble," *Philadelphia Tribune*, May 27, 1958, 2; "Strictly Politics," *Philadelphia Tribune*, July 22, 1958, 9; "Moore Hits Muddleheads Aiding Dems," *Philadelphia Tribune*, October 25, 1958, 10; "Beaten Cecil B. Moore Thanks Backers at Trinity AME Rally," *Philadelphia Tribune*, November 8, 1958, 11; "Strictly Politics," *Philadelphia Tribune*, November 11, 1958, 5. Polling results, see "Moore and Schmidt Overwhelmed by Nix," 8. On the registration advantage, see William J. McKenna, "The Negro Vote in Philadelphia Elections," in *Black Politics in Philadelphia*, ed. Miriam Ershkowitz and Joseph Zikmund (New York: Basic Books, 1973), 74–80. Adams, Bartelt, Elesh, Goldstein, Kleniewski, and Yancy, *Philadelphia*, 126.

16. Reichley, *Art of Government*, 70–71; "What Does Future Hold for Shepard?" *Philadelphia Tribune*, May 24, 1958, 1, 14; "Will Dems Dump Rev. Shepard," *Philadelphia Tribune*, November 15, 1958, 1–2; "West Philly Negroes Make Politics Pay Off," *Philadelphia Tribune*, August 24, 1965, 20; "Congressman Chudoff May Run for Judgeship," 3; "Alexander for Judge," *Philadelphia Tribune*, August 12, 1958, 4; "Great Progress Made by Negroes in Many Fields during 1958," *Philadelphia Tribune*, January 3, 1959, 8; "Judge Raymond Pace Alexander," *Philadelphia Tribune*, January 6, 1959, 4; "I Love a Parade," *Philadelphia Tribune*, January 10, 1958, 9. For more on Alexander, see David A. Canton, *Raymond Pace Alexander: A New Negro Lawyer Fights for Civil Rights in Philadelphia* (Jackson: University Press of Mississippi, 2010).

17. McKenna, "Negro Vote in Philadelphia Elections," 81; and "Jack Saunders Says," *Philadelphia Tribune*, August 19, 1967, 6. Alexander was joined by Thomas M. Reed and Robert N. C. Nix Jr. Countryman, *Up South*, 28; the Fellowship Commission was a coalition of liberal organizations established in October 1941 to work against racial and

religious bigotry. Countryman, *Up South*, 92–95; "Support Housing Bill," *Philadelphia Tribune*, March 3, 1959, 4; "Both Parties Pledge Support to State Fair Housing Law," *Philadelphia Tribune*, August 4, 1959, 12; "GOP Should Act," *Philadelphia Tribune*, August 11, 1959, 4. The only exceptions were Nix's efforts on national civil rights legislation and postal patronage. Nix was also elected leader of the Thirty-Second Ward, in 1958, a position he held throughout his tenure as a member of Congress.

18. Reichley, *Art of Government*, 46–48; Ekstrom, "Electoral Politics of Reform and Machine," 98. I am challenging an interpretation of Philadelphia's Black politics put forth by John Hadley Strange. While Strange focuses on the period between 1963 and 1966, his analysis of Black electoral power during the period prior to 1963 not only fails to take into consideration the 1958 congressional election but also ascribes total power to white political bosses. He fails to see the power of the Black vote in shaping the outcome of the 1958 congressional race and how that race determined key transformations in the city's political structure. The fact that Black people did not determine who was slated does not explain historical precedent nor the additional political stakes nor does it translate into the type of reductions in power he analyzed until after shifts in the city's political structure eliminated strong competition for the Black vote and, subsequently, reduced the leverage of Black electoral power. See John Hadley Strange, "Blacks and Philadelphia Politics: 1963–1966," in *Black Politics in Philadelphia*, ed. Miriam Ershkowitz and Joseph Zikmund (New York: Basic Books, 1973), 110. Reichley, *Art of Government*, 46–48; Ekstrom, "Electoral Politics of Reform and Machine," 98.

19. In 1967, of the city's registered voters, 562,166 were Democrats and 373,994 were Republican, and, according to the County Board of Elections, there were 264,459 registered Black voters. By 1969, that number increased to 280,000, the vast majority of whom were registered Democrats. See Jack Saunders Says, *Philadelphia Tribune*, May 23, 1967, 6; Women in Politics, *Philadelphia Tribune*, November 4, 1967, 12; Jack Saunders Says, *Philadelphia Tribune*, March 4, 1969, 6; Timothy J. Lombardo, *Blue-Collar Conservatism: Frank Rizzo's Philadelphia and Populist Politics* (Philadelphia: University of Pennsylvania Press, 2018), 6–7. On 1959 victory, see McKenna, "Negro Vote in Philadelphia Elections," 80, 83; Ekstrom, "Electoral Politics of Reform and Machine," 98, 101. On the reductive effects of a single party, see "Strictly Politics," *Philadelphia Tribune*, November 10, 1959, 5; "Ward Leaders Have Climbed to Great Power on Backs of Negroes," *Philadelphia Tribune*, May 24, 1960, 4; "Negroes Bypassed in City Hall for Bread-and-Meat Positions," *Philadelphia Tribune*, May 9, 1961, 9. On fair housing, see Countryman, *Up South*, 92–95; "Strictly Politics," *Philadelphia Tribune*, September 15, 1959, 5; "On the Town," *Philadelphia Tribune*, September 22, 1959, 5; "Pa. Senate Says 'Damn the Public,'" *Philadelphia Tribune*, September 26, 1959, 4. On GOP abandoning the Black vote, see James Wolfinger, *Philadelphia Divided: Race and Politics in the City of Brotherly Love* (Chapel Hill: University of North Carolina Press, 2007), 4–6, 177–248; "Strictly Politics," *Philadelphia Tribune*, December 1, 1959, 5; "Republican Chairman Calls Charges False," *Philadelphia Tribune*, November 24, 1959, 16; "Hit Absentee Politicians," *Philadelphia Tribune*, April 5, 1960, 3; Moore on the GOP and the South No title, *Philadelphia Tribune*, July 26, 1960, 16; "Failure to Woo the Negro Vote Costly to GOP's," *Philadelphia Tribune*, January 14, 1961, 2; "Negro GOPs Rap Party Selections in Primaries," *Philadelphia Tribune*, May 16, 1961, 1, 19; "Negroes Forgotten as GOPers Hit Democrat Foes," *Philadelphia Tribune*, September 26, 1961, 1. On Moore's switch to the Democrats, "Strictly Politics," *Philadelphia Tribune*, January 20, 1959, 5; "Atty. Cecil Moore Bolts to Democrats," *Philadelphia Tribune*, October 17, 1961, 1–2; "No Comment from GOP on Moore's Switch to Dems," *Philadelphia Tribune*, October 24, 1961, 4.

On patronage advantage, see comments from former GOP mayoral candidate Thacher Longstreth in "Local Republicans to Play the Waiting Game," *Philadelphia Tribune*, June 4, 1960, 4; Leah Wright-Rigueur, *The Loneliness of the Black Republican* (Princeton, NJ: Princeton University Press, 2015), 28, 30, 33, 35–37, 48–49.

20. Countryman, *Up South*, 83. Police brutality was an extremely important issue to Black Philadelphia. "End Police Brutality," *Philadelphia Tribune*, August 4, 1956, 8; "Inspector Selfridge Promises Probe in Police Brutality Case," *Philadelphia Tribune*, January 28, 1958, 1; "Detective Sgt. Hits Freeing of Assault Suspect," *Philadelphia Tribune*, September 27, 1960, 1, 12; "Pace Quickens as 1960 NAACP Elections Near: Call Made for New Leadership by Cecil Moore," *Philadelphia Tribune*, December 10, 1960, 1, 14; "Clique Controls Local NAACP, Cecil Moore Charges: Policy Stagnant Says Candidate for Presidency Raps Inactivity in Housing, Police Brutality, and Schools," *Philadelphia Tribune*, December 4, 1962, 4; "Police Brutality, School Bias to Be Targets," *Philadelphia Tribune*, December 15, 1962, 1, 12.

21. Countryman, *Up South*, 83–119, 122, 180–220.

22. Countryman, *Up South*, 83–119, 122, 180–220.

23. See Countryman's (*Up South*) analysis on civil rights and Black Power in Philadelphia. The principal difference between our respective studies is that, whereas the former has sought to explain the outside dynamics of protest politics, I have sought to analyze the inside game of Black electoral politics. For sources on reference of Moore as the "New Messiah" and the import of his leadership model for racial justice in postwar Black Philadelphia, see "Plumbers, 'New Messiah' in Tiff," *Philadelphia Tribune*, May 18, 1963, 1–2; "Heavyweights, Bob Nix, Cecil Moore Square Off," *Philadelphia Tribune*, July 23, 1963, 1, 4; "Jack Saunders Says," *Philadelphia Tribune*, July 16, 1968, 6; "Peyton's Place: Cecil Moore," *Philadelphia Tribune*, September 17, 1968, 6; "Jack Saunders Says," *Philadelphia Tribune*, September 21, 1968, 6; "Peyton's Place," *Philadelphia Tribune*, March 19, 1968, 6; "Jack Saunders Says," *Philadelphia Tribune*, December 14, 1968, 8.

24. "Nix and Weiner Face Threat; 3rd Party Is Formed," *Philadelphia Tribune*, February 15, 1964, 1, 20; "Cecil Moore Seeks Motives of 'Inde' Owner," *Philadelphia Tribune*, February 15, 1964, 3; Strange, "Blacks and Philadelphia Politics," 112–113. For more on the ideology of race pride and location of Wynnefield, see "Emotion Doesn't Win Elections, Five Losing Candidates Find," *Philadelphia Tribune*, May 9, 1964, 6; "Emotion Doesn't Win Elections, Five Losing Candidates Find," *Philadelphia Tribune*, May 5, 1964, 5; for Shepard Jr.'s response, see "Political Analyst Jack Saunders Is Guilty of Falsifying, Distorting Facts," *Philadelphia Tribune*, May 19, 1964, 7.

25. "Cecil Moore Seeks Motives of 'Inde' Owner," *Philadelphia Tribune*, February 15, 1964, 3.

26. For more on the 1964 primary, see "See Political 'Davids' with No Chance vs. 'Goliaths' in Next Tuesday's Primary," *Philadelphia Tribune*, April 25, 1964, 2; "Rights Leaders Urge Large Primary Turn Out," *Philadelphia Tribune*, April 28, 1964, 1–2; "Independents Dealt Crushing Blow by Democratic Machine Candidates," *Philadelphia Tribune*, May 2, 1964, 2; "Militant Ex-Marine Leads Philadelphia Negroes," *New York Times*, September 2, 1964, 23; "Jack Saunders Says," *Philadelphia Tribune*, July 16, 1968, 6; "Peyton's Place," *Philadelphia Tribune*, September 17, 1968, 6; Countryman, *Up South*, 164–165.

27. On reelection to the NAACP, see "Moore Wins 2215–474," *Philadelphia Tribune*, February 9, 1965, 1–2; "Cecil Moore's Mandate from the Masses," *Philadelphia Tribune*, February 9, 1965, 6. On Girard College, see Countryman, *Up South*, 168–179, "Jack Saunders Says," *Philadelphia Tribune*, July 16, 1968, 6; "Peyton's Place: Cecil Moore," *Philadelphia Tribune*, September 17, 1968, 6. Pennsylvania went from thirty to twenty-seven

congressional seats. On congressional reapportionment, see "Census Figures Drop Will Not Bother Nix," *Philadelphia Tribune*, May 28, 1960, 1, 14; "Summary Randy Dixon Views the News," *Philadelphia Tribune*, February 3, 1962, 1, 11; "The Political Arena: After Ward Revision, Watch for First Negro State Senator," *Philadelphia Tribune*, April 20, 1965, 6. On impact to Black Philadelphia, see "Negroes File for State Senate Posts," *Philadelphia Tribune*, February 15, 1966, 1–2; "Core Hits New Vote Boundaries: Say Measure Prevents Negroes from Electing Own Congressmen," *Philadelphia Tribune*, March 8, 1966, 1–2; "Boom Moore for Bob Nix's Congress Seat: Three Already Filed for 2nd District Post," *Philadelphia Tribune*, March 22, 1966, 1, 5; "OK Cecil Moore for Congress: Gets on Ballot vs. Nix after 11th Hour Fight," *Philadelphia Tribune*, April 2, 1966, 1–2; "Moore Says He Beat Nix to Punch in Legal Fight to Keep on Ballot in Congressional Race," *Philadelphia Tribune*, April 9, 1966, 1–2. Herbert Arlene, the Black machine candidate, was the only exception. For results on primaries, see "Shapp Wins, Independents Lose," *Philadelphia Tribune*, May 21, 1966, 1–2; "Moore Forms Negro Party for Politics," *Philadelphia Tribune*, February 21, 1967, 3; "Peyton's Place: Negro History," *Philadelphia Tribune*, February 28, 1967, 6; "All-Negro Parties Blasted by Treasurer of NAACP: Philly NAACP Head Running for Mayor on Negro Ticket," *Philadelphia Tribune*, April 1, 1967, 5; "Dick Gregory Soundly Beaten in Chicago Mayor Vote," *Philadelphia Tribune*, April 8, 1967, 5; "Final Returns Show Cecil Moore Finished Last in Race for Mayor," *Philadelphia Tribune*, December 9, 1967, 28.

28. George Derek Musgrove, *Rumor, Repression, and Racial Politics: How the Harassment of Black Elected Officials Shaped Post-Civil Rights America* (Athens: University of Georgia Press, 2012), 15; William L. Van Deburg, *New Day in Babylon: The Black Power Movement and American Culture, 1965–1975* (Chicago: University of Chicago Press, 1992), 124–125; Julie Gallagher, "Waging 'The Good Fight': The Political Career of Shirley Chisholm, 1953–1982," *Journal of African American History* 92, no. 3 (Summer 2007), 399–400; J. Morgan Kousser, *Colorblind Injustice: Minority Voting Rights and the Undoing of the Second Reconstruction* (Chapel Hill: University of North Carolina Press, 1999), 75, 374.

29. Musgrove, *Rumor, Repression, and Racial Politics*, 15; Countryman, *Up South*, 296–322; Jeffrey L. Pressman and Aaron Wildavsky, *Implementation: The Oakland Project* (Berkeley: University of California Press, 1984), 1–6; Ira Katznelson, *City Trenches: Urban Politics and the Patterns of Class in the United States* (Chicago: University of Chicago Press, 1981), 110–111; Robert O. Self, *American Babylon: Race and the Struggle for Postwar Oakland* (Princeton, NJ: Princeton University Press, 2003), 179–214, 217–242; Thomas J. Sugrue, *Sweet Land of Liberty: The Forgotten Struggle for Civil Rights in the Urban North* (New York: Random House, 2008), 368–369; "Final Returns Show Cecil Moore Finished Last in Race for Mayor," *Philadelphia Tribune*, December 9, 1967, 28; "The Inquiring Reporter-Photographer," August 22 and October 10, 1967, 8, 6; Lombardo, *Blue-Collar Conservatism*, 1–16; Self, *American Babylon*, 260–290; Julian E. Zelizer, *The Fierce Urgency of Now: Lyndon Johnson, Congress, and the Battle for the Great Society* (New York: Penguin, 2015), 247–261; Lisa McGirr, *Suburban Warriors: The Origins of the New American Right* (Princeton, NJ: Princeton University Press, 2001), 187–197; Matthew D. Lassiter, *The Silent Majority: Suburban Politics in the Sunbelt South* (Princeton, NJ: Princeton University Press, 2006), 121–147; Kevin M. Kruse, *White Flight: Atlanta and the Making of Modern Conservatism* (Princeton, NJ: Princeton University Press, 2005), 105–130, 234–240.

30. Moore knew he could not win, but he wanted to severely weaken Democratic mayor James Tate. See "Jack Saunders Says," *Philadelphia Tribune*, July 1, 1967, 8.

6

African American Politics in Frank Rizzo's Philadelphia

TIMOTHY J. LOMBARDO

In late September 1978, Mayor Frank Rizzo made an appearance before an all-white neighborhood association in predominantly white Northeast Philadelphia. The embattled two-term Democrat was nearing the end of his mayoral tenure, but he was not about to go quietly. He had spent the past few months making a series of controversial statements, including that liberals wanted to destroy white neighborhoods by introducing unwanted public housing projects and that he planned to become a national spokesman for "white ethnic rights" when his mayoralty ended. By the time he appeared in Northeast Philadelphia, he and his supporters had successfully lobbied to get an amendment to the city's Home Rule Charter placed on the ballot in the upcoming November election. The proposed amendment would allow Rizzo to run for a third term as mayor. Rizzo told his audience that local and national Black leaders were asking Philadelphia's African American residents to "vote black" against charter change. Turning to his own campaign, Rizzo said "I'm going to say to the people of this city, 'Vote White,' and the black people who think like me, and there are a lot of them . . ." The crowd erupted into applause before Rizzo could finish his sentence.[1]

The phrase "vote white" resounded throughout the city and mobilized Philadelphia's Black voters. The charter change amendment became a referendum on Frank Rizzo. While allies and foes rallied supporters, Philadelphians voted nearly two to one to reject the charter change. In a deeply segregated city, Rizzo's amendment only managed to carry all-white wards in South and Northeast Philadelphia. African American voter turnout was the highest in the city's electoral history.[2]

The defeat of Rizzo's charter change amendment showed the collective muscle of Philadelphia's Black electorate, but it would be a mistake to view it as a singular rebuke of an exceptionally racist campaign. It was also the first major success in a decade-long effort to build a new Black-led coalition capable of remaking city politics. Rizzo's mayoralty was an undeniable setback for African American leaders seeking to transfer the still vulnerable gains of the civil rights era into local political power, but organizing in opposition to Rizzo offered an opportunity to rebuild and remake Black politics in Philadelphia. By engaging the Rizzo machine and putting its leader at the center of a broader campaign for urban power, local Black activists awakened an African American community whose power was not proportionate to their population, what many called "a sleeping giant." When African Americans proved to be the decisive factor in the defeat of the charter change amendment, the *Philadelphia Tribune* declared, "The Sleeping Giant Awakens and Votes."[3]

Frank Rizzo had long provided a basis for African American oppositional organizing. He was easily one of the most controversial figures in the city's history. Before serving as mayor in the 1970s, Rizzo was commissioner of the Philadelphia Police Department in the late 1960s. As Philadelphia's top cop, Rizzo gained a national reputation for his get-tough policing and the heavy-handed tactics of his police force, especially when dealing with civil rights and Black Power protesters. When he won his first campaign for mayor in 1971, Rizzo represented a rebuke of an urban reform liberalism that had shaped Philadelphia politics since the 1940s, when reform Democrats Joseph Clark and his mayoral successor Richardson Dilworth wrested control of city hall from a long-corrupt Republican machine. Clark and Dilworth also put civil rights policy making at the center of their efforts to deliver "good government." Rizzo's mayoral campaign promised to protect segregated white blue-collar neighborhoods and offered a clear sign that Philadelphia's reform era had ended. Black empowerment in the 1970s arose within this context, in a city undergoing a transitional period in its political culture.

The emergence of a new era of Black political empowerment also took place against the backdrop of a number of other crucial economic and political developments, both nationally and locally. On a national level, despite its robust civil rights movement and African American leadership, Philadelphia lagged behind other cities when it came to electing Black politicians.

In 1967, Cleveland elected Mayor Carl Stokes, Gary, Indiana, elected Mayor Richard Hatcher, and Washington, DC, elected Walter Washington as its chief executive. In the 1970s, several others joined their ranks as the first Black mayors of other major American cities, including Newark's Kenneth Gibson, Detroit's Coleman Young, and Atlanta's Maynard Jackson. Yet, while majority Black enclaves in North and West Philadelphia began electing city council members and sending representatives to the state legislature, the mayor's office proved elusive until the 1980s. Many Black Philadelphians openly wondered why a city with such a large African American population had yet to reach that plateau. Indeed, the *Philadelphia Tribune* ran regular columns and editorials asking when the City of Brotherly Love would reach the same milestone. Part of the answer, they knew, lay in the city's white Democratic power structure. Challenging an established party machine became a key part of African American political advancement and an explicit goal for African American political leaders in the 1970s.[4]

Another reason Philadelphia was slow to elect a Black mayor was due to city leaders' successes in staving off the ill effects of deindustrialization. The city had managed to weather deindustrialization better than a number of other cities throughout the country, notably by using massive city-led and funded industrial relocation plans that shifted significant levels of manufacturing from run-down facilities in decaying parts of North Philadelphia to newly opened facilities in less-developed parts of Northeast Philadelphia. Because Northeast Philadelphia was geographically disconnected from the inner city and almost exclusively open to white residents, industrial relocation and disinvestment in Black communities encouraged working- and middle-class white people to stay in the city while rust belt cities like Detroit, Cleveland, and Gary succumbed to white flight. Nevertheless, the economic trends that afflicted industrial cities finally hit Philadelphia in the 1970s. Manufacturing job loss accelerated and construction work—a pillar of Philadelphia's working-class economy as recently as the 1960s, when federal spending on highways and urban renewal poured into the city—dried up in the sagging economy. Shifts in the city's industrial economy accelerated white flight. Where earlier efforts to promote Black politicians were stymied by the Democratic Party's reliance on white blue-collar voters, the loss of this population offered African American politicians a new opportunity.[5]

While African Americans had made significant gains in the reform era and Black leaders had the ear of city hall—some received top administrative posts—they never led what had been a predominantly white patrician municipal reform movement. Rizzo offered the opportunity to forge an alliance between progressives and veterans of the civil rights and Black Power movements with the aim of limiting the damage of the Rizzo administration and rebuilding a new coalition for the city's future. Rizzo's racist reputation served as an organizing tool. African Americans engaged his reputation on three main fronts: in law enforcement politics and reform, in the fight for low-income housing, and in a sustained effort to win local elective offices. By engaging law enforcement, housing, and electoral politics over the course of the late 1960s and 1970s, African American political and community leaders, journalists, and activists remade not only Black politics in Philadelphia but the city's political culture as well.

Throughout the fall of 1967, civil rights and Black Power activists held a series of rallies at predominantly African American schools. Local activists organized Black students and held workshops on Black pride, Black history, and Afrocentrism. They also promoted the third-party mayoral campaign of Cecil B. Moore, the fiery lawyer and longtime president of the local NAACP. Frank Rizzo monitored the school rallies. Having recently received the appointment to acting commissioner of the Philadelphia Police Department, Rizzo was seeking to make his promotion permanent. Not content with the sort of administrative duties that accompanied the commissionership, Rizzo seemed eager to confront the student activists.[6]

The largest of these confrontations took place on November 17, 1967. Around thirty-five hundred students from at least twelve predominantly African American high schools converged on the board of education administration building in Center City, Philadelphia. Many chanted Black Power slogans as representatives of the city's chapter of the Congress of Racial Equality distributed leaflets calling for community control of Black public schools. Demonstration leaders also demanded more Black teachers, the inclusion of African American history in the school curriculum, and permission to wear traditional African clothing. Superintendent Mark Shedd and board of education president Richardson Dilworth—the former reform-era mayor—agreed to meet with student leaders and even promised to implement several of their demands. Yet, as the school board officials worked toward a speedy end of the demonstration, Rizzo responded to a report that the protest was "getting out of hand." Witnesses claimed they heard Rizzo say, "Get their black asses!" before leading a charge of nightstick-wielding police into a throng of students. The police left fifteen of the young protesters hospitalized. Critics later called the events outside the board of education building a "police riot."[7]

African American community leaders voted to boycott public schools and white merchants until Mayor James H. J. Tate removed Rizzo from his position. The North Philadelphia–based North City Congress (NCC) released a report comparing the demonstration at the board of education to several days of unrest that had occurred a year earlier when the first Black family attempted to move into an all-white section of Kensington. Comparing media reports of both incidents, the NCC argued that the police were "much more restrained and polite" when dealing with white mobs and "did not feel called upon to use such extreme force." The NCC further detailed that the Kensington rioters were more lawless and provocative than the students at the board of education. Like many others, the NCC placed responsibility for the violent end to the school board demonstration squarely at the feet of Frank Rizzo.[8]

The melee at the board of education building spurred African American anger, but it was hardly the first time Rizzo's reputation as a racist enforcer of law and order came to light. Black residents complained about ill-treatment shortly after Rizzo received his first command post in West Philadelphia. In 1965, when Cecil B. Moore led a series of demonstrations to integrate Girard College—an all-white boarding school for orphaned boys in the heart of all-Black North Philadelphia—he engaged in near-daily confrontations with then deputy commissioner Rizzo who commanded the police response. Publicity surrounding Moore's clashes with Rizzo led a group of Black clergymen to send Mayor Tate a memorandum reporting on "widespread negro feeling that Deputy Commissioner Frank Rizzo hates negroes." The following year, in 1966, acting commissioner Rizzo responded to growing civil rights militancy by orchestrating a series of raids on the local chapter of SNCC. When Rizzo accused SNCC of planning an attack on police and plotting to dynamite Independence Hall, he drew the ire of the national organization. SNCC chairman Stokely Carmichael came to Philadelphia specifically to denounce "racist Rizzo." By the time of the school board demonstration in late November 1967, large segments of Philadelphia's African American population had already come to see Rizzo as a symbol of racist policing. Nevertheless, due to support from white Philadelphia, Mayor Tate officially retained Rizzo as police commissioner less than a month later, on December 21, 1967.[9]

Civil rights and Black Power activists viewed confrontations with Rizzo as part of a deeper strain between African American communities and the Philadelphia police. Black communities had long complained about discriminatory treatment, and improving police-community relations had been a centerpiece of civil rights activism in the city. Yet, at the same time, African American neighborhoods bore the brunt of rising crime in the previous two decades. Rising rates of major and minor crimes, drug use and trafficking, and urban gangs all afflicted Philadelphia's African American neighborhoods. Recognizing the twin problems of being overpoliced and underprotected, Black clergy were particularly concerned about the effect crime had on their congregations. At first, many were willing to work with Commissioner Rizzo. The Reverend Thomas S. Logan of West Philadelphia's Calvary Episcopal Church wrote Rizzo in April 1968 to tell him how clergy walked the streets on Saturday nights to deter crime. "I hope and pray that you will give due credit to the Negro leadership in helping to keep calmness within our city," wrote Logan. Praising Rizzo for the job he had done so far, Logan implored the commissioner to work to maintain good relations between the police department and African American communities. Similarly, North Philadelphia's NCC brokered a truce between rival gangs and started a police-community relations training program. But Rizzo refused to cooperate or share credit for crime reduction. Instead of fostering better police-community relations, Rizzo favored the kind of get-tough policing that had become a hallmark of law-and-order politics nationwide. African American communities shared concerns about crime, drugs, and gangs, but community organizations and leaders desired a solution that addressed the problem without criminalizing the entire community. Indeed, the rise of white law-and-order politics was accompanied by an equally important desire for law and justice in African American communities.[10]

Complementing the concerns about crime in Black communities that formed one arm of African Americans' pursuit of law and justice was a similarly pressing concern about police brutality. Where some initially hoped that Rizzo would respond to their concerns about crime and underprotection, they worried about his commitment to addressing overpolicing. While Rizzo never outright condoned police brutality, he frequently excused clear examples of police abuse as the actions of a few bad officers. Worse, he often dismissed charges of police brutality as the overreaction or imagination of civil rights organizations. He also made it clear that he did not support official investigations into allegations of misconduct. From 1958 to 1966, Philadelphia had a municipal agency tasked with investigating police misconduct and providing civilian oversight of the police. The first agency of its kind in the United States, the Police Advisory Board was the centerpiece of a police administration that aimed to maintain good police-community relations until political pressure and backlash from the Fraternal Order of Police forced it to cease operations. Frank Rizzo's appointment to commissioner was a death knell to the Police Advisory Board. A brief African American–led effort to revive the agency in 1969 failed. Rizzo's recalcitrance directly led to a more militant response to police brutality. The Black Panther Party, the Revolutionary Action Movement, the Council of Organizations on Philadelphia Police Accountability and Responsibility, among others, all formed or gained strength in response to Rizzo's administration of the police department.[11]

Despite the growth of his Black detractors, Frank Rizzo always enjoyed pockets of support within the African American community. Some Black clergyman continued to view his get-tough policing as an antidote to urban crime. While the *Philadelphia Tribune* eventually became one of Rizzo's biggest critics, the city's premier African American newspaper first took a cautious approach to the new police commissioner. "The new Commissioner deserves and should have the complete cooperation of all citizens so that law and order will prevail," the *Tribune* editorial page stated upon reporting on Rizzo's promotion, before adding that "He has the obligation to assure all citizens, regardless of race, creed, color, or political affiliation, equal treatment under the law." As for Rizzo himself, when faced with accusations of bias or racism, he frequently claimed that he had promoted more African Americans within the police department than his predecessors. As a result, Black police officers remained especially defensive of Rizzo.[12]

For most African Americans, however, Rizzo's insensitivity to the problem of police brutality spoke to their larger concerns about his racial animus. His racist reputation remained strong on the eve of his first mayoral run. Early in 1971, the *Philadelphia Tribune* conducted a poll showing an overwhelming majority feared a Rizzo mayoralty. One woman flatly compared Philadelphia in 1971 to "Germany just before Hitler took over." Many recognized that Rizzo's rise represented a threat to still vulnerable civil rights gains they had earned in the previous two decades. When Rizzo officially resigned as police commissioner and announced his run for the Democratic nomination for mayor as the self-proclaimed "toughest cop in America," he did little to reassure Black voters that he took their concerns about police brutality seriously.[13]

Yet, a few Black political leaders thought Rizzo's racist reputation would spur more African Americans to register and vote. That reasoning, in part, convinced West Philadelphia attorney and State Representative Hardy Williams to challenge Rizzo for the Democratic nomination. Williams's candidacy stemmed from the efforts of the Black Political Forum (BPF), an organization that formed in the late-1960s with the goal of breaking the Democratic machine's control of local politics by electing Black politicians who would be accountable to Black communities. Importantly, the BPF was committed to running Black politicians within the Democratic Party, rather than running third-party candidates or working from outside the system. Williams was one of the first to achieve success using this strategy when he won election as leader of West Philadelphia's Third Ward Democratic Committee in 1968. Two years later, Williams challenged and defeated the white Democratic machine-backed candidate for West Philadelphia's 191st Legislative District and went on to win the general election to the state House of Representatives. Williams and the BPF viewed his early victories as evidence that their strategy was working. Making a run for the mayor's office not only became a priority in the quest for Black empowerment; it seemed to be the next step in the BPF's overall effort to wrest control from the white Democratic machine.[14]

Standing in their way was Frank Rizzo, who secured the endorsement of the Democratic City Committee (DCC) and the loyalty of Philadelphia's white blue-collar voters, and William Green III, who sought the nomination from the party's liberal reform wing. A second-generation Philadelphia Democrat, Green received endorsements from Joseph Clark, Richardson Dilworth, and other stalwarts of the reform era, but, without the backing of the Democratic power structure, he had little chance of defeating Rizzo. Neither did Hardy Williams. His candidacy was the most serious run for mayor by a Black politician in the city's history, and he believed he could spur Black voter registration and participation, but he was a clear underdog. In fact, unsubstantiated rumors accused the Rizzo campaign of funding Williams in order to draw Black voters away from Green. Williams denied the accusations and continued predicting a victory deep into the primary. But Williams's optimism was not enough to overcome Rizzo's popularity among white voters or Green's ties to the liberal establishment. He lost fourteen out of sixteen primarily African American wards to Green. *Philadelphia Tribune* columnist Pamala Haynes called Williams's loss a major setback toward the goal of a Black mayor. Yet, his protest campaign against the Democratic machine still advanced the overall goal of Black political empowerment in Philadelphia by making inroads in the Democratic Party. Like the effort to achieve law and justice in the face of the politics of law and order, Williams's campaign helped redirect and remake Black politics by laying the groundwork necessary to present a real challenge to Rizzo and the DCC.[15] (See Fig. 6.1.)

Without a candidate in the general election, most African Americans turned to alternatives. When the president of the Philadelphia Chamber of Commerce, and self-proclaimed "Main Line WASP," W. Thacher Longstreth captured the Republican nomination, he vowed to capitalize on anti-Rizzo sentiment among African Americans and liberals. He campaigned hard in predominantly Black wards and won the endorsement of the *Philadelphia Tribune*. His appeal to Black voters made the election close. Despite a driving rain, voter turnout was the city's highest since the 1930s. The results upset traditional voter demographics, as all but one of the city's majority Black wards went to the Republican. But Rizzo swept every white working- and middle-class ward in the city, beating Longstreth by a count of 394,067 to 345,912. Yet, in a sign that the political setback would not permanently hamper the goal of Black political power, the NAACP planned to picket Rizzo's inauguration. Highlighting the strategy Black activists employed throughout his mayoralty, the NAACP protested to "remind Mr. Rizzo and his supporters that we won't forgive or forget how he rose to become Mayor and how Rizzo during his police days disrespected the rights and aspirations of black people."[16]

Figure 6.1 Hardy Williams campaigning for mayor, 1971.

The NAACP was not alone. Other Black activists sought to put Rizzo's racist reputation front and center in their effort to secure quality low-income housing for people of color. The availability of low-income housing had long been a central concern of African American civic leaders. For decades—especially since the 1950s, when city planners initiated an urban renewal program that disproportionately displaced poor African Americans—the struggle for adequate low-income housing had occupied a central place in African American politics. In the 1960s, the housing movement closely aligned with the civil rights movement. In addition to desegregating urban and suburban neighborhoods, their foremost aim was the construction of new public housing in areas that had not already succumbed to urban blight. That aim ran headlong into Frank Rizzo's mayoral aspirations. As he campaigned for mayor, residents of the small river ward neighborhood of Whitman in South Philadelphia began picketing the construction of the planned Whitman Park housing project. Whitman was a predominantly white ethnic working-class community. It was precisely the kind of community that Rizzo targeted in the election, so he made a campaign promise to not allow public housing in any neighborhood that objected to it.[17]

When outgoing Mayor Tate aided Rizzo by halting construction on Whitman Park, fair housing and tenants' rights activists put the effort to restart the project at the center of a broader effort to secure low-income housing throughout the city. More than that, they determined that the most effective strategy toward ensuring the construction and rehabilitation of public housing was to attack Rizzo's long record of hostility toward civil rights. By invoking Rizzo's racist reputation and charging his administration with violating civil rights law, housing activists were able to build on the strategy first outlined by his law enforcement critics. They also added another side to the emerging Black-led political coalition. The most important part of this emerging coalition was led by Black women.

Philadelphia's housing movement underwent a significant transformation in the late 1960s. Since the Progressive Era, the predominantly white middle-class Philadelphia Housing Association had been at the forefront of the city's housing reform movement. The organization only rarely addressed housing segregation, until being pressured by low-income women of color in the 1960s. In response to these complaints, the housing association merged with the Fair Housing Council of the Delaware Valley, an organization that worked to integrate suburban housing. Together, they formed the Housing Association of the Delaware Valley (HADV), an organization committed to the twin goals of open housing and public housing reform throughout the Philadelphia region. In addition to the merger, new leadership shifted the HADV's direction when African American housing activist Shirley Dennis became its director in 1969. Dennis applied her experience with the Black Power movement's battles for neighborhood services and jobs to housing reform and advocacy. Tying the problems of poverty and inadequate housing to racism and inequality, Dennis made the HADV more action oriented and race conscious. She also put the HADV at the forefront of the fight to restart construction on Whitman Park. When two bills in the Pennsylvania state house sought to give communities the right to decide on public housing site selection, Dennis led a campaign to resist a "neighborhood veto" of public housing. She blamed the state effort on "backlash resulting from community opposition to the proposed public housing in the Whitman area." Additionally, when Whitman residents began protesting the project's construction, Dennis issued a statement condemning the "racial innuendos that are constantly used to deprive people of decent housing."[18]

Black women's central role in advocating for equitable housing policies was reinforced by the Residents Advisory Board (RAB), a women-led tenants' organization working for better living conditions within existing public housing complexes. When the fight over Whitman Park erupted, the RAB joined the HADV's efforts. Along with Dennis, longtime tenants' rights organizer and early supporter of the BPF Rosetta Wiley became one of the main forces behind the effort to restart construction on Whitman Park. Dennis and Wiley understood that their effort to restart construction on Whitman Park was bigger than the case of one public housing complex in South Philadelphia. Its implications were citywide. Together, they contextualized their advocacy for low-income housing in the broader movement for racial equality. In 1971, the RAB wrote to the *Philadelphia Tribune* to argue that the "Whitman Park controversy demonstrates a tragic and on-going situation of inequality that exists in this country." The efforts to stop the project represented a depressing pattern, they said. "It is a deep tragedy of our times when public resentment and hate can be utilized to halt such a small step towards alleviation of unbearable housing shortages," they continued. "And that these intolerant and (racist) motivations can result in a paralysis of the judicial system so one citizen can deny a home to his fellow citizen dramatized a shameful decay of the conscience of this country." The RAB was even blunter in a similar letter to the *Tribune*. "Poor people—blacks, whites, and Puerto Ricans are citizens," they announced. "They are people who like all citizens received the promise of the federal government for safe and decent homes as a basic and undeniable human right." The RAB further condemned the "intolerant and (racist) motivations" that delayed the goal of equal housing for all.[19]

By combining welfare rights with the larger pursuit of racial equality, the RAB illustrated how the struggles against poverty and for civil rights were one and the same. Just as importantly, by taking on Rizzo's crusade against public housing and framing it within the broader battle for housing and welfare rights, Black women in the HADV and RAB imbued their efforts with larger political import. Their movement became an essential part of the demand for Black equality and self-determination that revived African American politics in Philadelphia during the 1970s.

Rizzo helped shape that revival. Prior to his election, the RAB had entered into a cooperative relationship with the Philadelphia Housing Authority, ensuring that the RAB was a participant in its modernization program. The RAB was instrumental in drawing attention to the poor conditions in several existing public housing complexes and securing federal funds to improve them. Yet, after Rizzo took office, new Philadelphia Housing Authority director Gilbert Stein eliminated tenant participation in its policy making and ended the cooperative relationship with the RAB.[20]

Viewing the move as a direct attack on tenant rights and public housing writ large, the RAB and HADV recruited other housing activists to join their efforts. Rosetta Wiley's North Philadelphia Tenant Union responded by calling hostility to public housing a "hastily contrived and poorly disguised mask for rank racism." A newly formed Citizens Committee for Tenants Rights (CCTR) also organized to resist the Rizzo administration's efforts to roll back protections for residents of public housing. The CCTR was headed by W. Wilson Goode, a West Philadelphia community leader and one of the founders of the BPF. Declaring that the "Philadelphia Black community has long been concerned with the conditions existent in Philadelphia public housing," Goode and the CCTR argued that poor conditions in the city's public housing projects emanated from "socially insensitive and racist attitudes" helped by administrators in Rizzo's Philadelphia Housing Authority. They further called the end of policies that gave public housing tenants a voice in the housing authority "part of the political strategy of a number of northern White politicians to decimate the political strength of northern Black urbanites and to create new political coalitions based on 'law and order' or white fears of so-called 'Black militancy.'" The CCTR concluded that "Philadelphia Mayor, Frank Rizzo, is, of course, the High Priest of such strategies."[21]

Following the lead of the RAB, HADV, and others, Goode and the CCTR came to the conclusion that attempting to control public housing tenants was an attempt to curtail Black political power. The argument fit within the broader goals of the BPF, whose leaders, like Goode, explicitly linked their efforts to end the white Democratic machine's control of the electorate to Black community control over their neighborhoods and the institutions that served them. In this way, Rizzo galvanized housing activists in ways that reinforced the BPF's efforts to remake Black politics in Philadelphia. He also confirmed their fears when his administration filed a lawsuit to halt construction on Whitman Park in December 1972.[22]

Housing and tenants' rights activists believed the battle for Whitman Park represented more than the fate of one housing project. Refusing to confront Rizzo might jeopardize the broader effort for equal opportunity and political empowerment. Shortly after construction ended, the RAB filed a federal suit against the Rizzo administration for violating antidiscrimination housing laws. By charging the Rizzo administration with violating equal opportunity housing laws and forcing the court to consider Whitman Park as a civil rights case, the RAB directly invoked the racist reputation that civil rights leaders had charged against Rizzo since he was police commissioner. But they also maintained that the effort was bigger than Rizzo or this one housing project. "The continuation of this policy, which would be implicit in any settlement other than getting Whitman Park built," wrote the RAB's lawyer, "subverts any present or future effort toward integrating low-income in the City." The argument struck a chord with the larger African American community. Increasingly, higher profile organizations threw their weight behind the efforts to restart Whitman Park. Both the local NAACP and the Urban League joined the effort because they feared a Rizzo victory would embolden other white neighborhoods and further jeopardize Black political power. Black women in organizations like the HADV and

RAB had long linked fair and low-income housing to civil rights in Philadelphia. In the Rizzo era their efforts also made it a core component of Black political empowerment.²³ (See Fig. 6.2.)

While public housing emerged as a key avenue for challenging the Rizzo administration, other African Americans sought urban power through elected office. Black civic leaders first made strides in state and city council elections. Following Hardy Williams's election to the state legislature, for instance, Cecil B. Moore won election to the city council in 1976 and served in the chamber until his death in 1979. Each election of local Black politicians or appointments in white mayoral administrations advanced Black political empowerment. Yet, since the founding of the BPF, the effort to run Black candidates that would be responsive to Black needs and wrest control away from white Democratic Party leaders became more pronounced. Following Williams's failed campaign in 1971, the mayor's office became the highest goal among Black political leadership.²⁴

The timing seemed ripe. After a first term that included not only Rizzo's effort to halt public housing but also a series of high-profile gaffes and controversies—including a series of embarrassing media appearances and serious allegations over the misappropriation of public funds—the mayor ap-

Figure 6.2 Residents Advisory Board members Shirley Dennis (*right*) and Nellie Reynolds (*left*) are joined by Charles Bowser at a press conference on the Whitman Park controversy, 1976.

peared vulnerable. Plans to challenge Rizzo for the Democratic primary were underway well ahead of the 1975 election, and several high-level white Democrats refused to back his reelection. When Rizzo's 1971 primary opponent, William Green III, declined to run, white Democrats turned to Louis Hill, a well-connected lawyer and stepson of former reform mayor Richardson Dilworth. Inspired by Williams, two African Americans also emerged as political challengers. Executive director of the Black Economic Development Conference, Muhammad Kenyatta, and president of the Philadelphia Urban Coalition, Charles Bowser, both eyed the Democratic nomination. Both also agreed that it would take an African American candidate to defeat Rizzo. While Kenyatta primarily appealed to the more militant elements of the African American community, Bowser appealed to both militants and moderates. His long record in city government also offered potential appeal among white liberals. Bowser soon emerged as the most likely Black candidate in the primary race against Rizzo.[25]

In addition to his work in the Urban Coalition, Bowser had a well-known legal career and had served as deputy mayor under James Tate. He was the highest-ranking African American in municipal government in the 1960s and a prominent civic leader into the 1970s. Like most influential African Americans, Bowser was a critic of Frank Rizzo. In 1974, he formed a committee to explore a run at the Democratic nomination and "Bowser for Mayor" clubs opened in West Philadelphia. Explaining the purpose of one club, founder Rev. Lorenzo Shepard echoed the long-held motivations of the BPF by saying that he hoped to bring the political issues facing African Americans to their neighborhoods. Still, despite his qualifications and long record, Bowser knew winning over the DCC would be difficult. Party leader and Rizzo rival Peter Camiel privately admitted to Bowser that the DCC would not support a Black candidate. Instead, they backed Louis Hill. Bowser declared Hill "unacceptable," but he decided not to challenge him for the Democratic nomination. Instead, Bowser announced a third-party bid on the ticket of his newly formed Philadelphia Party. Despite running counter to the BPF's strategy to work within the Democratic Party, Bowser staffed his campaign with BPF veterans like Wilson Goode. By the time Rizzo defeated Louis Hill and Muhammad Kenyatta in the Democratic primary, Bowser emerged as a top contender among African Americans and white liberals.[26]

Bowser's mayoral run marked an important step in the larger pursuit of a new political coalition founded on the principle of Black political empowerment. In addition to running on his experience and record of public service, he also put anti-Rizzo sentiment at the center of his campaign. He earned endorsements from white business leaders and liberals in the Philadelphia chapter of Americans for Democratic Action. The BPF, the *Philadelphia Tribune*, and African American political leaders throughout the country endorsed him enthusiastically. In 1975, however, their enthusiasm was not enough. Although Bowser came in second in a three-way race—the city's moribund Republican Party launched a weak attempt at matching Rizzo's white ethnic politics with the candidacy of city councilman Thomas Foglietta—he only received 138,783 votes to Rizzo's 321,513. But the crushing loss did come with a silver lining. Bowser earned 100,000 more votes than Hardy Williams in 1971. His campaign tapped into the movement for Black political empowerment and began forging the alliances with white progressives that would eventually remake Philadelphia politics.[27]

It also laid the groundwork for the next major challenge to the Rizzo administration. The year following his electoral loss, Bowser and the Philadelphia Party spearheaded an effort to remove Rizzo from office. During his reelection bid, Rizzo promised not to raise the city wage tax. But facing the fiscal shortfalls that afflicted most deindustrializing cities in the 1970s, Rizzo proposed the largest wage tax in the city's history. Bowser helped initiate a recall drive ostensibly over the broken promise. Yet, there was more at stake. When Bowser issued a statement announcing the recall effort, the city wage tax was only one reason among many. He also listed fifteen "serious grievances" that justified removal, including fiscal irresponsibility, abuse of public office, misuse of federal funds, the closing of Philadelphia General Hospital, several charges of using the police department to attack political enemies, and "refusing to utilize available funds to build low income housing in support of racists opposition to that housing." Comparing Rizzo to both King George III and Attila the Hun, Bowser claimed his effort was nothing short of an attempt to "save Philadelphia by the recall of Frank L. Rizzo." Needing 145,000 signatures to put the recall on the ballot, the Citizens Committee to Recall Rizzo collected 211,190 by the July 1976 deadline. Much to the Citizens Committee's dismay, Rizzo loyalists in the city commissioners' office negated 115,818 signatures. With little recourse, the recall drive collapsed. Nevertheless, for leaders like Bowser, the effort reinforced important alliances with white progressives and maintained the African American–led effort to use anti-Rizzo politics to spur Black political empowerment.[28]

At the same time, the results of Bowser's third-party mayoral run and the recall drive exposed what seemed to many a surprising development: Rizzo did better in African American wards in 1975 than he did in 1971. Indeed, African American anti-Rizzo politics never negated the fact that some African Americans continued to support the mayor. That was especially true among Black police officers and their families. When, for example, *Philadelphia Daily News* columnist Chuck Stone wrote a scathing indictment of Rizzo's insensitivity to African Americans, he received a torrent of letters from Black officers defending the mayor.[29]

One of Rizzo's earliest supporters was Alphonso Deal. A decorated police officer, Deal had joined the police department in 1954 after serving as a member of the military police during World War II. Soon after joining the police force, Deal began a career-long effort to increase Black representation within the Philadelphia police. He helped found the Guardian Civic League, an African American policemen's association dedicated to establishing and maintaining better relationships between Black communities and the police. In the late 1960s, Deal and the Guardian Civic League led a delegation of Black officers honoring Rizzo's promotion to commissioner. Rizzo even appointed Deal to serve as an expert councillor to the police department in Fayette, Mississippi, where Deal modernized the city's police department. Yet, Deal's increasing civil rights activism led him to break with Rizzo. Long involved with the city's NAACP, he eventually became president of the organization's North Philadelphia branch. By the 1970s, Deal was publicly feuding with the majority white Fraternal Order of Police over fresh allegations of police brutality. Once one of Rizzo's African American supporters, Deal joined other civil rights activists in blaming the mayor for condoning police misconduct.[30]

In 1977, the *Philadelphia Inquirer* published a scathing indictment of the police department, including accusations of widespread corruption and police brutality. The *Inquirer*'s reporting only confirmed what law enforcement reform advocates had been arguing for decades. The Coalition Against Police Abuses (CAPA) followed the *Inquirer* story with a lengthy statement naming specific officers that had histories of abuse but no formal reprimand from the police department. They charged the city with sanctioning a system of police misconduct. "By tolerating the conduct of these officers," the CAPA concluded, "Police Commissioner Joseph O'Neil and Mayor Rizzo show that in actuality they condone such acts of unwarranted violence on the part of Philadelphia police officers. This gives a green light to every police officer to further abuse the citizens of our city. They know that whatever they do they will get away with." By dismissing the argument that police brutality was only the work of a few bad cops and holding Rizzo responsible for misconduct, CAPA and other organizations again invoked Rizzo's racist reputation as the cause of inaction on the problem of police misconduct. Joining CAPA, Alphonso Deal used his position as both a police officer and a civil rights leader to hold Rizzo and the police department accountable.[31]

With the issue of police brutality forcefully thrown back into the limelight, the three main issues reshaping African American politics in Frank Rizzo's Philadelphia—law enforcement and police brutality, low-income housing, and the pursuit of elective office—converged in the late 1970s. Indeed, 1978, the same year Rizzo attempted to change the city charter, saw these issues come together and forge the final mobilization of the city's new political coalition. First, a series of confrontations between the Philadelphia police and the obscure Black Nationalist and back-to-nature collective known as MOVE hastened concerns about police brutality in the wake of the *Inquirer*'s explosive report.

Although small and loosely organized, MOVE quickly earned notoriety for their unconventional lifestyles and militant protest tactics. By the late 1970s, most MOVE members lived in a single home in West Philadelphia's Powelton Village neighborhood. Journalists reported that they advocated the abolition of modern technologies and amenities like indoor heat, manufactured soap, and waste disposal. They were also vehement in their beliefs, at times calling themselves "violent revolutionaries" and almost always making heavy use of profanity as a protest strategy. Complaints from Powelton Village neighbors led to the police putting MOVE under constant surveillance. After a series of small clashes with the police, Rizzo ordered a blockade of MOVE headquarters to starve the organization into leaving West Philadelphia. It wore on for nearly a year. As a result, an organization whose unconventional lifestyle and militant politics garnered little sympathy with the broader public appeared as the latest victim of overpolicing African Americans in Frank Rizzo's Philadelphia. Those accusations worsened in August 1978, when Rizzo ordered the police to remove MOVE from their home. On the morning of August 8, 1978, a police raid ended only after they unloaded several hundred rounds of ammunition into the MOVE house and one officer lay dead. When MOVE members desperately tried to escape, the police captured Delbert Orr Africa. Forcing him to the ground in full view of gathered crowds and the press, police officers repeatedly kicked Africa's midsection as he lay with outstretched arms and a rifle pressed against his head.[32]

Within days, organizers led marches and rallies in support of MOVE and against police brutality. At the forefront was Alphonso Deal. "Whether or not we agree with Delbert Africa is not the issue," Deal said at a city hall demonstration. Demanding the immediate dismissal of the officers responsible, Deal exclaimed, "As long as I have breath in my body, I will not stand by and watch anyone abuse someone on the street." The police confrontation with MOVE spurred Deal and other anti–police brutality activists into further action. Believing a systemic problem required a systemic solution, Deal helped make the MOVE conflict a larger part of Black politics in the late 1970s. By linking the raid on an otherwise unsympathetic organization to the broader history of Frank Rizzo's racist policing, Deal effectively engaged the strategy that had spurred anti-Rizzo forces since the 1960s and helped push Black political empowerment.[33] (See Fig. 6.3.)

Figure 6.3 Alphonso Deal (*center*) leads a press conference on police brutality, 1977.

Meanwhile, the controversy over Whitman Park returned to the Black community. In late 1977, federal judge Raymond Broderick ruled against the Rizzo administration. RAB lawyers had relied on ample evidence and testimonies highlighting how the Rizzo administration's public housing policies reinforced segregated housing in Philadelphia. Broderick ruled that the Rizzo administration had violated federal antidiscrimination law, and he ordered construction on Whitman Park to recommence immediately. Housing and civil rights activists hailed the decision. The *Philadelphia Tribune* called the decision a "major victory for minorities," while one letter writer plainly called it a "victory over racism."[34]

The decision enraged Frank Rizzo and white opponents of Whitman Park. Both contributed to years of delays, as the Rizzo administration slowed the process with a series of appeals and area residents again took to the streets to protest construction. With the end of his mayoralty in sight, Rizzo used the controversy to rile up his supporters. Shortly after the U.S. Supreme Court refused to hear an appeal to stop construction again, Rizzo held a meeting with Whitman area residents. He assured them that he would keep fighting on their behalf and told them that "liberals want to destroy" white ethnic neighborhoods like Whitman. He further argued that they had a right to "neighborhood purity" and encouraged them to "join hands" with other white ethnics. After a tirade against programs that gave "special privileges" to African Americans and other people of color, he closed his speech by saying he planned to become "a national spokesman" for "white ethnic rights" when his mayoral term expired.[35]

To reaffirm why African American leaders had put the Whitman Park issue at the center of their politics in the 1970s, the *Philadelphia Tribune* reported on Rizzo's remarks extensively. *Philadelphia Daily News* columnist Chuck Stone responded with a three-part series on "An Authentic American Racist: Frank Rizzo, 1978." By the end of the 1970s, activist T. Milton Street—who had earlier waged a squatting campaign against the Rizzo administration's inaction on the twin problems of quality low-income housing and abandonment in North Philadelphia—organized a series of confrontational marches in the Whitman neighborhood. His largest took place on April 4, 1979, the eleventh anniversary of Dr. Martin Luther King's assassination. Like others before him, Street linked the availability of public housing to the broader struggle for racial equality in Frank Rizzo's Philadelphia. As the Rizzo administration continued to drag its feet, Charles Bowser called for another march on Whitman. He compared the efforts to stop construction to "George Wallace standing at the school house door." Each of these efforts engaged the now decade-long strategy of invoking Frank Rizzo's racist reputation in an effort to rally African Americans and redirect Black politics.[36]

While the controversy over Whitman Park reignited the Black political response to Rizzo's housing policies and the MOVE raid raised the specter of unpunished police misconduct, Rizzo began reevaluating his political career. African Americans overwhelmingly disapproved of Rizzo's actions, but he received an outpouring of support from white working- and middle-class Philadelphians both for the announcement that he would lead a movement for white ethnic rights and for his handling of the MOVE situation. That support convinced him to embark on his plan to change the city charter. It was only one month after the police raid on MOVE headquarters that Rizzo traveled to Northeast Philadelphia to campaign for his charter change amendment and told his audience to "Vote White" in favor of it.[37]

The phrase "vote white" seemed to confirm all of the charges anti-Rizzo activists had levied against him since he was police commissioner. Yet, when asked if he would have any Black support in the effort to change the city charter, Rizzo quipped that he knew he had "two Black supporters who believed in everything he said." Motioning to Tony Fullwood and James Turner, Rizzo's two African American bodyguards, the mayor scored a laugh at his own reputation for alienating Black voters. African Americans did not find it as amusing. The *Philadelphia Tribune* published an anonymous open letter to Fullwood and Turner asking them to speak out against their boss because Rizzo "believes that the Blacks of this city do not deserve better housing, education, job opportunities, health care and that the Blacks are the scum of the earth." Indeed, all of the forces that had put Rizzo's racist reputation at the forefront of their efforts to secure low-income housing, to combat police brutality, or to elect African American public officials coalesced in their opposition to the charter change amendment. Black voters responded mightily. The *Tribune*'s Jim Davis wrote that "Philadelphia voters KOed" the charter change amendment "with the finesse of the Ali shuffle and the power of a Joe Louis left hook, leaving Mayor Frank L. Rizzo and his 'vote white' philosophy down for the 14-month count." The lion's share of that victory, Davis concluded, belonged to Philadelphia's Black voters.[38]

The failure of the charter change amendment meant more than a short-term victory over Frank Rizzo. As it was the culmination of a decade-long fight to strategically put Rizzo's racist reputation at the center of a broader movement toward Black empowerment, it also signaled something bigger: the arrival of a new political coalition that would be Black-led and responsive to African American concerns. As the *Philadelphia Tribune* editorialized, "The rumblings and echoes of bigotry and racism espoused by Mayor Rizzo in his bid for life tenure as mayor have once again awakened the Black Sleeping Giant." The massive Black voter turnout in 1978—the largest in the city's history to that point—showed the power of the city's Black electorate.[39]

While African Americans rightfully celebrated their first victory over Frank Rizzo, full success was not immediate. Rizzo's defeat once again raised the old question of when Philadelphia would elect its first Black mayor. African Americans believed the time was right, as editorials and letters to the editor filled the *Tribune* with announcements that the time had come. Indeed, the record-breaking number of Black voters who turned out to ensure the defeat of Rizzo's charter change amendment led many community members to rally around the idea of a Black mayor. That ultimate goal, however, proved disappointing, as Charles Bowser ran another failed campaign in 1979. Instead, Rizzo's old white liberal opponent William Green III won the mayoral election.[40]

That setback, however, should not overshadow some very real successes that resulted from the rise of Black political empowerment in the 1970s. While Green was a throwback to the reform Democrats who remade Philadelphia politics in the post–World War II era, he was far more indebted to Black voters than any of his predecessors. As a result, Green was responsive to African Americans and championed two of the most significant issues that Black activists promoted in the previous decade. First, he promised a direct repudiation of Rizzo's law enforcement regime. When Green took office in 1980, he immediately sought reforms to curb police abuses and address the problem of police brutality. A new report from the U.S. Civil Rights Commission confirmed the arguments about misconduct and malpractice that antipolice brutality activists had waged for decades. Green promised a reinstitution of a civilian review process and a reduction in police personnel. Not only that but when white police officer John Ziegler shot and killed the unarmed Black teenager William Howard Green for an alleged robbery, the mayor responded to protests organized by Milton Street and his brother John to prosecute Ziegler to the full extent of the law. As if to signal that this was no longer Frank Rizzo's Philadelphia, the mayor issued new guidelines for the use of deadly force. Just as importantly, he declared that "police misconduct will not be tolerated" as he dismissed Officer Ziegler and announced that he would be charged with the murder of William Howard Green.[41]

In addition to law enforcement reform, Mayor Green also sought a reversal of Rizzo's housing policies, especially on Whitman Park. Federal courts had already ruled that construction must recommence, but Rizzo and his allies spent the remainder of his mayoralty causing delays. Green put an end to the obstruction and oversaw the final construction of the housing project. The Whitman community felt so betrayed by Green that they hung a large sign across the street from the construction site reading, "The Boy Blunder Bill Green and the U.S. Govt. Bring Yous [sic] Whitman Park: A 10 Million Dollar Housing Failure." Nevertheless, construction continued and Whitman Park finally opened in October 1982. The final arrangement led to a compromise that allowed Whitman residents to have a say in the composition of the project's occupants, but the housing, tenants' rights, and political leaders that had long worked for the completion of Whitman Park cheered their victory with its opening.[42]

Despite these triumphs, the movement for Black political empowerment seemed unfulfilled. The goal of the mayor's office had yet to be met, and Mayor Green's overtures to law and justice and housing equality failed to satisfy that aim. So, when Green announced in late 1982 that he would not seek a second term, African American leaders saw an opportunity to finally reach that long-held goal. Their hopes fell to Green's managing director, a founder of the BPF and ally to the housing movement, W. Wilson Goode. Since his start as a West Philadelphia community organizer, Goode had worked to push Black political advancement through grassroots efforts. Because of his community leadership and administrative experience, Goode received an appointment to the state Public Utilities Commission under Governor Milton Shapp. By the time Green announced that he would not seek a second mayoral term, Goode had earned a reputation as an effective administrator. He was easily the best candidate to achieve the milestone other major American cities began surpassing in the 1960s. Goode accomplished that breakthrough in 1983, when he became Philadelphia's first

Black mayor. As if to add another layer of significance to his historic victory, Goode first defeated a resurgent Frank Rizzo in the Democratic primary before winning the general election.[43]

Goode's victory was the final culmination of the new political coalition that had organized in opposition to Frank Rizzo's racist reputation throughout the late 1960s and 1970s. It was forged through the determination to counter Police Commissioner Rizzo's aggressive policing and inattention to the problem of police brutality. It matured through the housing and tenants' rights movement's struggle to secure low-income housing for people of color in spite of Mayor Rizzo's housing policies. It coalesced around the efforts to place Black elected officials in positions of local power so that they would be responsive to the needs and desires of Philadelphia's Black communities. Each of those efforts were hard-fought and came at great expense. Victory was too often Pyrrhic. Black political empowerment coincided with broader shifts in Philadelphia's deindustrializing economy. Black leaders like Goode inherited a new era in America's urban history, one that came with massive disruptions to big city economies and social structures. Nevertheless, the coalition that formed in the 1970s did usher in a new era of Black-led politics in Philadelphia. As Goode said of Black politics in 1972, "Black priorities have moved from integration in the 1950s through the riots of the 1960s and civil rights movement to control of institutions in the 1970s." Taking control of institutions and changing Philadelphia politics meant overcoming many obstacles, not the least of which was Frank Rizzo. But, in that obstacle came opportunity, because over the course of Rizzo's controversial and combative career in law enforcement and politics, African Americans effectively used his racist reputation to awaken a sleeping giant.[44]

NOTES

1. "Rizzo: 'Vote White,' Charter Change," *Philadelphia Evening Bulletin*, September 22, 1978, *Philadelphia Bulletin* Clippings Collection, Special Collections Research Center, Temple University Libraries, Philadelphia, PA (hereafter PBCC); "Next? Neighborhood Lobbyist," *Philadelphia Evening Bulletin*, March 16, 1978, PBCC; "Rizzo Urges Whites to 'Join Hands,'" *Philadelphia Evening Bulletin*, March 17, 1978, PBCC; Sandra Featherman, *Jews, Blacks and Ethnics: The 1978 "Vote White" Charter Campaign in Philadelphia* (New York: American Jewish Committee, 1979); S. A. Paolantonio, *Rizzo: The Last Big Man in Big City America*, 10th Anniversary ed. (Philadelphia: Camino Books, 2003), 229.

2. "Wake Up! Take Part in Elections," *Philadelphia Tribune*, May 16, 1978; "The People Will Not Soon Forget," *Philadelphia Tribune*, September 29, 1978; Paolantonio, *Rizzo*, 229; Featherman, *Jews, Blacks and Ethnics*.

3. "The Sleeping Giant Awakens and Votes," *Philadelphia Tribune*, November 10, 1978; "The City of Brotherly Love: The Sleeping Giant v. the White Crusader," *Encore American and Worldwide News*, November 20, 1978, box 1, folder 14, National Association for the Advancement of Colored People, Philadelphia Branch Records, URB

6, Special Collections Research Center, Temple University Libraries, Philadelphia, PA (hereafter SCRC).

4. "How Soon Will Philadelphia Elect a Negro Mayor," *Philadelphia Tribune*, June 15, 1968; Roland Black, "Black Candidates Everywhere But Phila.," *Philadelphia Tribune*, May 6, 1969; Pamala Haynes, "Why Is Phila. So Politically Retarded," *Philadelphia Tribune*, October 28, 1969; Len Lear, "Is There a Black Mayor in Philadelphia's Future," *Philadelphia Tribune*, July 18, 1970.

5. Timothy J. Lombardo, *Blue-Collar Conservatism: Frank Rizzo's Philadelphia and Populist Politics* (Philadelphia: University of Pennsylvania Press, 2018); Guian A. McKee, *The Problem of Jobs: Liberalism, Race, and Deindustrialization in Philadelphia* (Chicago: University of Chicago Press, 2008); Guian A. McKee, "'I've Never Dealt with a Government Agency Before': Philadelphia's Somerset Knitting Mills Project, the Local State, and the Missed Opportunity of Urban Renewal," *Journal of Urban History* 35 (2009): 387–409.

6. Matthew J. Countryman, *Up South: Civil Rights and Black Power in Philadelphia* (Philadelphia: University of Pennsylvania Press, 2006), 223–225.

7. Countryman, *Up South*, 223–225; "Black Schools Unite," flier, 1967 and "Attention Brothers and Sisters," flier, 1967, box 140, folder 15, Richardson Dilworth Papers, Collection 3112, Historical Society of Pennsylvania, Philadelphia; "Aide Says Shedd Backs Most Negro Demands," *Philadelphia Evening Bulletin*, November 24, 1967, PBCC; "Dr. Shedd Sets 'Reason' as Goal in Race Relations," *Philadelphia Evening Bulletin*, November 26, 1967, PBCC.

8. Paolantonio, *Rizzo*, 93–94; North City Congress, "The Double Standard: A Comparison of Police Action in the Kensington Riots, October 1966, and the School Board Demonstration, November 1967," November 29, 1967, box 5, folder "Student Demonstration at Administrative Building," Citizens Committee on Public Education Papers, SCRC.

9. William White Jr., Confidential Memorandum, August 18, 1965, box A-4491, folder "War on Crime," Mayor's Correspondence and Files, Administration of James H. J. Tate, Record Group 60-2.5, City of Philadelphia, Department of Records, City Archives, Philadelphia City Archives, Philadelphia, PA (Tate Papers); "SNCC Director Assails Rizzo as a 'Racist,'" *Philadelphia Evening Bulletin*, August 30, 1966, PBCC; Paolantonio, *Rizzo*, 94.

10. Thomas S. Logan to Frank Rizzo, April 15, 1968, box A-4596, folder "Comm. Frank Rizzo," Tate Papers; North City Congress, Police-Community Relations Program, Summary Final Report, April 8, 1968, box 635, folder 7, General Pamphlet Collection, Special Collections Research Center, Temple University Libraries, Philadelphia, PA; Countryman, *Up South*, 285. On the overpolicing and underprotecting of African American communities in urban America, see Simon Balto, *Occupied Territory: Policing Black Chicago from Red Summer to Black Power* (Chapel Hill: University of North Carolina Press, 2019), 1–13.

11. "Rizzo Asserts U.S. Official Talks Hogwash," *Philadelphia Evening Bulletin*, June 18, 1969, PBCC; "Rizzo Charges Plot against All Police," *Philadelphia Evening Bulletin*, September 1, 1970, PBCC; Lombardo, *Blue-Collar Conservatism*, 68–76, 140–141; Eric C. Schneider, Christopher Agee, and Themis Chronopoulos, "Dirty Work: Police and Community Relations in the Limits of Liberalism in Postwar Philadelphia," *Journal of Urban History*, May 1, 2017, available at https://doi.org/10.1177/0096144217705497; Countryman, *Up South*, 284–294.

12. "Commissioner Rizzo Faces Challenge of Keeping Order with a Just Hand," *Philadelphia Tribune*, May 20, 1967; "Many Black Policemen Promoted under His Command, Rizzo Says," *Philadelphia Tribune*, December 26, 1970.

13. "Majority Quizzed Do Not Want Rizzo to Be City's Next Mayor," *Philadelphia Tribune*, February 6, 1971; Countryman, *Up South*, 295–317.

14. Mark Briklin, "Black Political Convention Planners See Rizzo's Candidacy as Good Omen," *Philadelphia Tribune*, February 6, 1971; Countryman, *Up South*, 310–312.

15. Pamala Haynes, "Hardy Williams' Real Intentions Subject of Crystal Ball Gazing," *Philadelphia Tribune*, February 9, 1971; Pamala Haynes, "Rizzo's Big Victory: How, Why and What It Means," May 22, 1971.

16. Pamala Haynes and Ruth Rovner, "Thacher Longstreth Banking on Black Vote to Beat Rizzo," *Philadelphia Tribune*, May 22, 1971; "Our Choice for Mayor Is Thacher Longstreth," *Philadelphia Tribune*, October 30, 1971; "Crossover Vote Likely in Central City," *Philadelphia Evening Bulletin*, October 20, 1971, PBCC; Paolantonio, *Rizzo*, 121–122; Phillip H. Savage to Friends for Dignity, December 23, 1971, box 24, folder 4, Jewish Labor Committee Records, SCRC.

17. Timothy J. Lombardo, "The Battle of Whitman Park: Race, Class, and Public Housing in Philadelphia, 1956–1982," *Journal of Social History* 47, no. 2 (Winter 2013): 401–428; John Bauman, *Public Housing, Race, and Renewal: Urban Planning in Philadelphia, 1920–1970* (Philadelphia: Temple University Press, 1987); "Protests Halt Whitman Park Housing Work," *Philadelphia Evening Bulletin*, March 23, 1971, PBCC; "PHA Refuses to End Job at Whitman Park," *Philadelphia Evening Bulletin*, April 7, 1971, PBCC; "Builder Agrees to Halt Job at Whitman Park," *Philadelphia Evening Bulletin*, April 30, 1971, PBCC.

18. Bauman, *Public Housing, Race, and Renewal*, 205–206; Shirley Dennis and Joseph Miller to All Pennsylvania State Representatives, June 9, 1971, HADV; "Mrs. Dennis Presses for Fair Housing," *Philadelphia Evening Bulletin*, April 3, 1969, PBCC; "New Chief Sees Housing Unit as 'Advocate,'" *Philadelphia Evening Bulletin*, October 2, 1971, PBCC.

19. Residents Advisory Board, "Whitman Pk. Issue," *Philadelphia Tribune*, June 26, 1971; "14,000 Families Now on Housing Authority Waiting List for Homes," Statement of the Resident Advisory Board, *Philadelphia Tribune*, June 26, 1971.

20. Memorandum from Charles W. Bowser to James H. J. Tate, December 2, 1970, Rizzo Files; Testimony by Cushing N. Dolbeare before Commission to Investigate Public Housing, December 12, 1973, HADV records.

21. North Philadelphia Tenant Union, *Speak Out* Community Bulletin, n.d., box A-3532, folder "Whitman Park (2)," Mayor's Correspondence and Files, Administration of Frank L. Rizzo, Record Group 60-2.6, Philadelphia City Archives, Philadelphia, Pennsylvania (hereafter Rizzo Papers); Memorandum from the Citizens Committee for Tenants Rights to All Philadelphia Media, December 5, 1972, box A-3531, folder "Philadelphia Housing Authority," Rizzo Papers.

22. Countryman, *Up South*, 308–309; "Opponents Are Apparent Victors in Whitman Park Housing Battle," *Philadelphia Inquirer*, June 29, 1972, PBCC; "Whitman Fight Won, but the Debts Remain," *Philadelphia Daily News*, March 23, 1973, PBCC.

23. "Rizzo Public Housing Policy Is on Trial," *Philadelphia Inquirer*, November 10, 1975, PBCC; "City Prevents Good Housing, Aide Charges," *Philadelphia Evening Bulletin*, May 27, 1976, PBCC; Resident Advisory Board v. Rizzo, No. 71-1575 (E.D. Pa., 1976); Jonathon Stein to Arthur Lefco, April 30, 1975, box 1, folder "Krusen, Evans, and Byrne,"

accession 332, Whitman Council Records, SCRC; "Group Wants Whitman Park Built," *Philadelphia Tribune*, December 14, 1976; "Whitman Park Wins Some Support," *Philadelphia Evening Bulletin*, December 12, 1976, PBCC; "Group Demands Start of Project," *Philadelphia Daily News*, December 13, 1976, PBCC.

24. Countryman, *Up South*, 322–324.

25. Paul A. Bennet, "Kenyatta and Bowser Agree, 'Dems Need a Black to Beat Rizzo,'" *Philadelphia Tribune*, February 1, 1975; Countryman, *Up South*, 322–329; Paolantonio, *Rizzo*, 180–181.

26. Paul A. Bennet, "'Bowser for Mayor Club' Opens in W. Philadelphia," *Philadelphia Tribune*, December 14, 1974; Paolantonio, *Rizzo*, 180; Paul A. Bennet, "Bowser Labels Hill 'Unacceptable' as Candidate for Mayor," *Philadelphia Tribune*, February 4, 1975.

27. Harry Amana, "Clark Says Bowser Backed by City's Top Businessmen," *Philadelphia Tribune*, June 24, 1975; "ADA Endorses Charles W. Bowser for Mayor," *Philadelphia Tribune*, August 2, 1975; "Charles Bowser for Mayor," *Philadelphia Tribune*, October 21, 1975; Countryman, *Up South*, 322–323.

28. Statement of Charles Bowser, 1976, box 1B, folder "Public Release Rizzo Recall," Citizen's Committee to Recall Rizzo Records, SCRC; Paolantonio, *Rizzo*, 208–211.

29. Chuck Stone, "Rizzo's Anti-Black Image," *Philadelphia Daily News*, November 28, 1972; Sergeant James Holley to Editor of the Daily News, November 29, 1972, box A-3535, folder: Newspapers—Daily News, Rizzo Papers; Detective Theodore Scurry to Chuck Stone, no date, box A-3535, folder: Newspapers—Daily News, Rizzo Papers; Earl Grey Roberts, Jr. to Chuck Stone, November 29, 1972, box A-3535, folder: Newspapers—Daily News, Rizzo Papers; Zack Clayton to Chuck Stone, November 29, 1972, box A-3535, folder: Newspapers—Daily News, Rizzo Papers; Lt. Edward P. Harrell to Rolfe Neill, December 1, 1972, box A-3535, folder: Newspapers—Daily News, Rizzo Papers; Ted Jordon to Chuck Stone, December 1, 1972, box A-3535, folder: Newspapers—Daily News, Rizzo Papers.

30. Alphonso Deal Biographical Information, PBCC; "Deal Denounces Guardian Civic League for Backing Rizzo's Re-Election Bid," *Philadelphia Tribune*, April 22, 1975; Michael von Moschzisker, "2 Worlds of Al Deal: Policeman, Militant," *Philadelphia Evening Bulletin*, August 15, 1968, PBCC; "Negro Policemen Protest FOP Chief's Political Stand," *Philadelphia Evening Bulletin*, September 4, 1968, PBCC.

31. Statement of the Coalition Against Police Abuses, July 11, 1977, box A-5218, folder "Police Brutality," Rizzo Papers; Paolantonio, *Rizzo*, 218–219.

32. Claude Lewis, "MOVE Stirs Anger," *Philadelphia Evening Bulletin*, October 25, 1974; John T. Gillespie, "MOVE Rejects 'Modern Life-Style,'" *Philadelphia Evening Bulletin*, April 8, 1975, PBCC. On MOVE, see John Anderson and Hilary Hevenor, *Burning Down the House: MOVE and the Tragedy of Philadelphia* (New York: W. W. Norton, 1987); David Runkel, "Siege Is Eyed to Starve Out Move," *Philadelphia Evening Bulletin*, July 11, 1977, PBCC; "The MOVE Impasse: $1M Dilemma," *Philadelphia Daily News*, February 17, 1978, PBCC; Robert J. Terry, "MOVE Supporters Rally in W. Phila.," *Philadelphia Inquirer*, July 10, 1977, PBCC; "Protesters Liken to Hitler," *Philadelphia Evening Bulletin*, March 17, 1978; "Siege Ended as Predicted: With Blood, Controversy," *PEB*, August 9, 1978, PBCC.

33. "Cop Calls for Firing of Police," *Philadelphia Daily News*, August 18, 1978, PBCC.

34. Resident Advisory Board v. Rizzo, Exhibit 195, Report of Professor Yale Rabin: "The Whitman Park Townhouse Public Housing Project and Its Relationship to Black Population and the Housing Policies of Government Agencies," 1976, box 6, folder 16, Community Legal Services Records, Special Collections Research Center, Temple Uni-

versity Libraries, Philadelphia, PA; "City Vows to Fight Integrated Housing," *Philadelphia Evening Bulletin*, November 9, 1976, PBCC; "From Politics to Judiciary, Swirl Surrounds Broderick," *Philadelphia Evening Bulletin*, November 10, 1976, PBCC; "Whitman Decision Is Major Victory for Minorities, Low-Income People," *Philadelphia Tribune*, September 3, 1977; "Victory Over Racism," *Philadelphia Tribune*, September 20, 1977.

35. "Next? Neighborhood Lobbyist"; "Rizzo Urges Whites to 'Join Hands.'"

36. "Rizzo Turning Back the Clock with 'Protect the Whites' Edict," *Philadelphia Tribune*, March 21, 1978; Maurice F. White, "List of Mayor Rizzo Critics Grows, Grows," *Philadelphia Tribune*, March 25, 1978; "Rizzo's Remarks Shock Musician Stevie Wonder," *Philadelphia Tribune*, March 28, 1978; Chuck Stone, "Yesterday's Collapse of White and Black Leadership," *Philadelphia Daily News*, March 23, 1978, PBCC; Chuck Stone, "Kerner + 10: 2 White Americas, 2 Black Americas," *Philadelphia Daily News*, March 24, 1978, PBCC; Chuck Stone, "Inequality of the Races: From Gobineau to Rizzo," *Philadelphia Daily News*, March 28, 1978, PBCC; Chuck Stone, "Honoring King: Selma to Whitman," *Philadelphia Daily News*, January 10, 1980, PBCC.

37. "Rizzo's Mail Backs Him Up," *Philadelphia Evening Bulletin*, April 3, 1978, PBCC.

38. "Rizzo's Bodyguards," *Philadelphia Tribune*, October 10, 1978; Jim Davis, "Black Anti-Charter Change Forces Victorious in Spite of Hassles," November 10, 1978.

39. "Sleeping Giant Awakens and Votes."

40. "Ready for Black Mayor," *Philadelphia Tribune*, December 8, 1978; "Philadelphia: Is It Ready to Elect a Black Mayor?" *Philadelphia Tribune*, December 26, 1978; Paolantonio, *Rizzo*, 231.

41. "Green Appeals for Calm," *Philadelphia Evening Bulletin*, August 26, 1980, PBCC; Fawn Vrazo and Randolph Smith, "Cop Kills Youth after Car Chase," *Philadelphia Evening Bulletin*, August 25, 1980, PBCC; "Youth's Slaying Protested," *Philadelphia Evening Bulletin*, August 26, 1980, PBCC.

42. Joe Davidson, "Whitman Project Started," *Philadelphia Evening Bulletin*, March 18, 1980, PBCC; William J. Storm and Joe Reichwien, "Whitman Park Foes Express Their Anger with Blaring Music," *Philadelphia Evening Bulletin*, November 9, 1980, PBCC; "Old Accepts New: A Housing 'Project' Wins Respect in S. Phila.," *Philadelphia Inquirer*, November 23, 1984.

43. Countryman, *Up South*, 322–327; "Why Wilson Goode Won," *Philadelphia Inquirer*, May 19, 1983.

44. Goode quoted in Countryman, *Up South*, 307.

7

Taking Political Power

ALYSSA RIBEIRO

As the closing decades of the twentieth century dawned, Black electoral strength in Philadelphia reached its height. Drawing on decades of activism and painstaking coalition building, Black officials finally took formal control of city politics and institutions in the early 1980s. These were significant victories, but they came with nearly insurmountable challenges. The Urban League's 1983 *State of Black Philadelphia* report opened by proclaiming that saying "blacks and other minorities are in a state of crisis is an understatement." To start with, Black officials inherited the established trends of a declining population, fiscal crisis, and aging infrastructure. Budgets for public services were woefully inadequate even as the demand for those services continued to grow; these dynamics were especially visible in the public schools and public transit. Philadelphians continued to worry about crime and hostile relations with the police, while they also confronted public health crises due to the spread of crack cocaine and the AIDS virus. Meanwhile, many residents staunchly opposed any tax hikes. An atmosphere of recurring cuts took hold. The financial situation aggravated an existing tension: now that Black politicians headed "the establishment," how would they balance the demands of the city's traditional stakeholders against those of their grassroots base? Overall, even as Black representation in the city took huge strides forward, austerity severely limited the efforts of Black residents and policy makers to enact comprehensive change.[1]

Despite its large Black population, nearly 40 percent of a city of 1.68 million by the early 1980s, Philadelphia lagged behind many major American cities in electing a Black mayor. The larger presence of white suburban areas within city limits (particularly in the Northeast), as well as the local Democratic machine's rightward lean, enabled white residents to continue their hold on city politics. In this atmosphere, the burgeoning Puerto Rican population and liberal whites represented crucial allies for most Black candidates and activists. Coalition politics that bridged racial lines pushed Black candidates over the threshold and into power.[2]

Philadelphia's coalitions have usually been framed in terms of Black and white, with little attention to the pivotal role that the Latino population played in this era. Puerto Ricans began migrating to Philadelphia in substantial numbers during the 1950s, taking jobs in agriculture, food processing, domestic work, and manufacturing. This population growth coincided with the continuing arrival of African Americans from the Southeastern United States. Most Puerto Rican migrants initially concentrated in enclaves in North Philadelphia neighborhoods such as Spring Garden and Ludlow; over time, they moved northward and established a business corridor called the "Golden Block" along North Fifth Street. They were few in number compared to the Black population, representing perhaps 5 percent of the city's population in 1980. But, by virtue of their citizenship, geographic concentration, and shared socioeconomic circumstances, Puerto Ricans were attractive potential allies for their Black neighbors. Initially, much of the earlier generation remained relatively conservative and hoped to access white privilege from their racially ambiguous position. But, throughout the 1970s, Puerto Ricans began to vote in larger numbers for more progressive candidates and issues, ultimately shifting the political trajectory of the city.[3]

Multiracial political coalitions drew strength from community support networks that grew and matured through prolonged organizing. Concerns about housing and police, in particular, fueled a formidable grassroots movement that built cooperation across the city through large umbrella organizations like Tenant Action Group and the Council of Organizations on Police Accountability and Responsibility. Community groups such as Association of Community Organizations for Reform Now (ACORN), Kensington Joint Action Council, and Inner-City Organizing Network led squatting campaigns to place poor families in houses owned by the government, while others coordinated rent strikes and pressured city regulators. Activists pushed for police reform by testifying to abuses, demanding media attention, and launching class action lawsuits.[4]

As a result, fractures in Philadelphia's white political rule appeared in electoral politics throughout the 1970s. Multiracial coalitions backed unsuccessful Black mayoral candidates Hardy Williams in 1971 and Charles Bowser, in 1975 and 1979. Bowser's campaigns, backed by the independent

Philadelphia Party, built an alternative political infrastructure outside of the traditional Democratic machine that aided future campaigns.

Moreover, public aversion to Frank Rizzo's mayoral administration, widely perceived as corrupt and racist, surged in the Rizzo recall and charter change campaigns of the late 1970s. Many of the same residents active with groups like the Tenant Action Group, the Council of Organizations on Police Accountability and Responsibility, and countless community organizations rallied around these efforts. Those forces coalesced to mark the political realignment of the city's Puerto Rican population into a more progressive voting bloc and the simultaneous strengthening of ties between Black and liberal white voters. As of the early 1980s, these and other efforts had, as the historian Andrew Feffer has pointed out, "removed a racist mayor from office, helped change the political composition of city government, and . . . laid a durable foundation in city institutions and in the city's left political culture on which opposition to Reaganism could be maintained into the early 1990s." Such strong activist voices placed significant pressure on policy makers already challenged by other dynamics.[5]

Many Black residents were disheartened that the city elected yet another white mayor, William Green, in 1979. But Green's administration staffing and priorities foreshadowed the ascendancy of formal Black political control. During the campaign, both Green and his Republican opponent David Marston pledged to appoint a Black managing director, who would be the second most powerful policy maker in the city. This indicated that both parties realized the critical power Black voters held. Yet, Black votes were not enough on their own; those of Puerto Ricans and liberal whites were critical to winning elections. Groups like the Black United Front, along with dozens of neighborhood organizations, therefore emphasized Black-brown unity more than ever. At the Black Political Convention in January 1979, a human rights agenda emerged that stressed the similar needs of Black and Puerto Rican residents on nearly every page. Philadelphia's second Puerto Rican Political Convention, held in 1980, similarly sought to "specifically address itself to Blacks and Puerto Ricans working more closely together to solve some of their common problems." A 1979 Green mayoral campaign document titled, "A Historic Commitment of Conscience to the People of Philadelphia," repeatedly mentioned the linked and overlapping interests of Black and Puerto Rican residents. The willingness of so many Black voters to support Green rather than the independent Black candidate Lucien Blackwell—without concern about being accused of "selling out"—was to some a significant indication of strong coalitions across racial lines. The promised Black managing director, W. Wilson Goode, became Green's obvious successor.[6]

Observers hailed Goode's performance as city manager during an administration that faced a large deficit and a recession. In that role, he cut expenses and shored up city finances by laying off nearly one thousand police and firefighters and cutting other positions for a payroll savings of over $5 million. He also curbed regular expenses by eliminating credit cards for public agencies and downsizing the city motor pool. Despite his ninety-five-hour workweeks, Goode's efforts to attack infrastructure problems such as poor housing found less success due to the sheer scale of need. The tension that Goode faced between reducing government spending to appease elites and redirecting badly needed resources to marginalized communities followed him into the mayor's office.[7]

Goode's political journey was emblematic of a historical moment in which seasoned activists continued their efforts from elected office. A sharecropper's son, Goode had built skills and established networks through involvement in Great Society–era antipoverty programs. He served as head of the Philadelphia Council on Community Development, where housing issues became his specialty. He was an elder in his church. Even more, his experience as city manager and head of the Pennsylvania Utilities Commission gave him credibility as a technocrat adept at strategic planning. Thus Goode seemed a near-perfect candidate. He had support on the streets of Black Philadelphia and working relationships with both agitators and policy makers. Goode's reputation as "an intelligent, forceful, yet mainstream, spokesman for community betterment" had risen steadily during the previous decade. In other words, his approach to urban issues was sufficiently moderate to garner the support of the business community and many white voters. That very moderation came to disappoint some of his Black base.[8]

When Goode ran for mayor in 1983, his campaign promises reflected the support of a broad multiracial coalition that included "prominent civic, business, and community leaders—blacks, white[s], and Hispanics." Goode still had to survive a primary challenge from Frank Rizzo, who hoped to secure a third, nonsequential mayoral term. During the primary campaign, Goode could not depend on the traditional Democratic Party machinery due to its support for Rizzo and, instead, drew heavily on Black church congregations and neighborhood organizations. Of eleven field offices, the campaign placed one in a Puerto Rican neighborhood, two in predominantly white neighborhoods, and the remaining nine in predominantly Black or integrated neighborhoods.[9]

The Goode campaign focused on voter engagement. Increasing the proportion of Black voter registration as well as turnout on Election Day by just a few points, in addition to securing around 20 percent of the white vote, could provide the margin of victory that had eluded Black mayoral candidates in the past. This strategy was successful. In the six-month period between November 1982 and May 1983, Democratic voter registration surged by 29 percent overall. Black Democratic registration rose by 35 percent, or 103,000 voters. And Democratic registrants identifying as "Other," who would have been predominantly Puerto Rican with some Asian Americans mixed in, increased an impressive 59 percent, or about 9,500 voters. Altogether over 200,000 additional voters either registered for the first time, renewed a lapsed registration, or switched their party affiliation. Democratic turnout for both the primary and the general election exceeded 60 percent. This municipal contest essentially drew participation akin to a presidential election. Goode comfortably won the mayoralty with 55 percent of the popular vote, fortified by 75 percent support among Latino voters (the vast majority of whom were Puerto Rican) and a whopping 98 percent support among Black voters.[10]

Once in office, Goode's administration staffing and his relationships with city council members continued to appeal to not only Black residents but also Puerto Ricans, white liberals, and many women. On city council, Lucien Blackwell and Joe Coleman, both well-established advocates for Black communities, were Goode's strongest allies. Goode appointed Angel Ortiz, who had just lost a city council race, as commissioner of records, making him the highest-ranking Puerto Rican city official up to that point.[11]

Women had long formed the backbone of community organizations across the city. By the 1980s, female grassroots leaders could increasingly appeal to the growing number of women in elected and appointed offices, some of whom came from the very same neighborhoods. Shirley Hamilton, Goode's chief of staff, wielded unprecedented political influence for a Black woman in Philadelphia. Journalist Mike Mallowe described her as "a matriarch of estimable power and consequence" who effectively served as a gatekeeper for all but Goode's closest associates. In the school system, Dr. Constance E. Clayton, a native of North Philadelphia who herself had attended public schools, became superintendent in 1982. Black women in Philadelphia outnumbered Black men by more than sixty thousand in 1980, lending greater urgency to their particular concerns.[12]

The Goode administration's reliance on existing social networks in the Black community provided more opportunities for Black business and professional advancement, creating "a new, vibrant, black commercial establishment in the making." Similarly, Black labor leaders had unprecedented access to the mayor's office, even as Goode took an increasingly hard line in contract negotiations with public employees. Among the larger Black population, Goode maintained broad support but faced criticism of his management style, staffing decisions, relationship with the media, and seeming arrogance.[13]

Goode's initial election roughly coincided with the ascendancy of other seasoned community activists, both Black and Puerto Rican, into political office. In addition to increasing electoral strength, Black candidates benefited from other circumstances clearing the way. ABSCAM, an FBI operation that indicted public officials for accepting bribes, epitomized some federal officials' growing concern over corruption in local government. The sting operation took down several Philadelphia politicians, including three city council members (George X. Schwartz, Louis Johanson, and Harry P. Jannotti) and two congressmen (Raymond Lederer and Michael "Ozzie" Myers), in 1981. The scandal further roiled the political waters, opening up more space for new faces and handing control of city council to a coalition of liberal Black and white politicians. And the deaths of sitting city council members Cecil B. Moore in February 1979, John C. Anderson in October 1983, and Al Pearlman in June 1984 created additional openings. Finally, James Tayoun resigned his council seat in early 1984 to run for Congress. Altogether, these additional council openings led to four white male officeholders being replaced by two Black women, one Black man, and one Puerto Rican man.[14]

City council became more representative of the city's demographics in terms of female, Black, and Latino representation. Composed of seventeen seats total, the body combined ten district-based seats with seven at-large openings (two of which were reserved for Republicans as the minority party). From 1976 forward, there was a minimum of five Black city council members serving at any given moment. And while some Black members had previously been elected as Republicans, all were Democrats by the 1980s. Angel Ortiz, previously active with Community Legal Services and Puerto Rican community organizations, gained a city council seat by special election in 1984 and served several consecutive terms. John Street took Cecil B. Moore's seat in 1979 and remained a fixture in the body until resigning two decades later to run for mayor.

As city council diversified, it increased spending on neighborhood services in acknowledgment of activists' long-standing demands. Lucien Blackwell, in particular, steadfastly advocated for poor and homeless constituents. The presence of more progressive Black politicians in positions of power also eased the path for gay rights in the form of an antidiscrimination ordinance. When gay activists likened discrimination on the basis of sexual orientation to racial bias in the mid-1970s, most policy makers rejected the analogy. In 1982, the Philadelphia Gay and Lesbian Task Force tried once more, again linking gay rights to civil rights. By this time, the support of Joseph Coleman as city council president and W. Wilson Goode as city manager enabled the bill's passage. Another affirmative vote came from Black councilman John C. Anderson, who was later publicly recognized as a pioneering gay politician.[15]

Districting that reflected sharp residential segregation had long assured some level of Black representation in the Pennsylvania legislature, but by the 1980s the delegation was generally more progressive. Milton Street (John's brother), veteran of campaigns on behalf of street vendors and homesteaders claiming vacant housing, was elected to the state house in 1978. Even as an elected official, Street led dramatic protests inside city council chambers. After ascending to the state senate in 1980, Street disappointed and confounded many by defecting to the Republican caucus in order to gain political power. Roxanne Jones, renowned for her work on welfare rights, challenged Street and took his state senate seat in 1984. Chaka Fattah, whose mother Falaka Fattah founded the West Philadelphia gang violence reduction center House of Umoja, was meanwhile elected to the state house in 1982. Already sitting in the legislature were figures such as David P. Richardson, who started out as a youth organizer and was first elected in 1973.[16]

The MOVE bombing (discussed in more detail below) made Goode's reelection in 1987 anything but a foregone conclusion. Goode ultimately won a second mayoral term, while, once again, facing Frank Rizzo, who had rebranded himself as a Republican. Yet, Goode remained far more subject to criticism throughout his second term; his constituents felt his administration was big on strategic plans but short on action. Many were left disappointed that the tenure of Philadelphia's first Black mayor was not more radical.

Though Goode had initially maintained good relationships with Puerto Rican leaders, by 1989, many felt that the administration had neglected Latino issues. All sixteen members of the mayor's Commission on Puerto Rican/Latino Affairs resigned, criticizing the lack of Latino appointees in the higher echelons of city government. Israel Colon, then chief of staff to Councilman Angel Ortiz, attributed this in part to Goode's "aloof" nature. But he also noted that Puerto Rican leaders could have been more assertive immediately after the election, rather than assuming that "a bridge would be built overnight."[17]

Despite impressive growth in the number and stature of Black officeholders, it was difficult to govern in an environment where entrenched political machine members still wielded considerable power, memories were long, and personal rivalries deep. Joe Certaine, a Black appointee in the Goode administration, explained, "There's nothing like politics here. If you can work Philly, you can work El Salvador or Afghanistan. There are the same kind of land mines and hand grenades all over." Incremental progress meant a lot in such a fraught environment. As Black policy makers, activists, and their constituents chipped away at deeply entrenched barriers, a gradual but decisive transition took place. Journalist Mike Mallowe's assessment for *Philadelphia Magazine* at the end of 1985 reveals the sense of broader possibility that some felt at the time. In Mallowe's eyes, Goode had "done exactly what the first black mayor of Philadelphia could have been expected to do—changed forever the power structure of the city and the people who dominate it." Mallowe was perhaps too optimistic, underestimating the ways in which Black politicians would continue to be pulled in multiple and conflicting directions.[18]

Major challenges beset Black policy makers and their constituents from the outset. And, to make matters worse, they faced those challenges with limited resources. The federal government began to shift its attention and money away from cities during the 1970s, and relationships with Harrisburg over funding issues had long been tense. Traditional sources of local revenue such as sales and property taxes were insufficient to cover growing costs, but demand for services was as strong as ever.

In the wake of successful tax-limitation referendums in California and Massachusetts, prospects for increasing property tax revenue were dim by the late 1970s and early 1980s. White residents, in particular, listed taxes as one of their top concerns at this time. Though many would acknowledge that the city needed money, they resisted making any personal sacrifices to produce the funds. As businesses and households relocated to the suburbs and beyond, Philadelphia lost tax dollars. Meanwhile, the number of abandoned residential properties that yielded no tax revenue for the city continued to increase. Indeed, the city often had to spend money to board up these properties or tear them down completely. Resourceful residents converted some of the resulting vacant lots into urban gardens, which had many local benefits but did not create tax revenue. The city reassessed property values in a bid to climb out of the hole, but policy makers were wary of increasing property tax rates at the same time.[19]

Philadelphia had the nation's first local income tax, instituted way back in the 1930s. This tax applied not only to city residents but also to people who worked in the city but lived outside its borders. Responding to a huge deficit in 1975, the Rizzo administration raised both property taxes and payroll taxes. Public anger at these rate increases helped fuel an unsuccessful attempt to recall the mayor. Businesses were particularly critical of the wage tax; they claimed the extra burden discouraged employers and residents from locating in the city and instead encouraged suburban growth. What had been a 1 percent wage tax rate in 1945 had by 1981 risen to a little over 4 percent. Under the Green administration, a promise of "responsible budgeting" led to a small wage tax increase accompanied by public employee wage cuts and frozen service levels. This mixed approach was unpopular with many residents, but it reassured the city's business elite. City council rejected the Goode administration's attempt to raise the wage tax further in 1990.[20]

In some corners of the city, long-standing racial animus peaked with the election of a Black mayor, leading to an outright secession movement. Portions of the predominantly white suburban Northeast launched a campaign to separate entirely from Philadelphia and become a separate county. These residents argued that they were not getting their money's worth in the form of city services and that their copious tax dollars were instead being wasted on less deserving (Black) people. They felt the establishment was no longer on their side. Many implied that Goode was incompetent and that Northeast residents were inadequately represented in city government. Legislator Hank Salvatore went so far as to formally introduce a secession bill in the state house. Chances for actual secession were remote, but these demands placed additional pressure on the distribution of resources. The Goode administration responded by creating a new municipal service center to serve as a tangible marker of city government commitment to the area, despite the fact that other neighborhoods had greater needs. Still, complaints from Northeast residents persisted. A *Philadelphia Tribune* editorial opined, "The simple truth, we believe, is that Philadelphia's power structure is Black-led now and white folks (many, not most) have a problem with that."[21]

The city tried to shore up some of its financial woes by borrowing more money through bond issues. But when the amount of loans the city requested suddenly doubled between 1989 and 1990, it rang alarm bells and investors balked. The budget deficit ballooned from $32.1 million in fiscal year 1988 to approximately $219 million in 1991. The city's credit rating declined quickly, making it still more expensive to borrow. In an effort to return to solvency, the city increased sales tax by 1 percent, froze wages, and cut benefits. Services declined still more. Goode and other Black politicians were essentially backed into a corner by these financial circumstances. It was difficult to formulate new policies when, by necessity, they had to focus on keeping the lights on.[22]

Controversy raged at the local level over how to "save" Philadelphia. In broad strokes, much of local politics centered around where and how the limited revenue should be spent. The central geographic dilemma pitted downtown against the neighborhoods in the fight for money. In this ongoing conflict, downtown interests were roughly analogous to the establishment, while the neighborhoods generally stood in for grassroots organizations. Black policy makers continued to face pressure from both sides.

Public furor over downtown-focused development rose to new heights in 1979 as Black residents poured into city hall to stage protests over the distribution of government funds. Protesters including leaders like Milton Street were "forcibly ejected" from council chambers. One explained, "We don't want to hear about $73 million here or $15 million there. We want to know how many poor people are going to be put into housing." This conflict continued to play out in the following two decades.[23]

In an atmosphere of scarcity, the stakes over spending priorities escalated. Business interests and much of the local political establishment perceived the central business district as inarguably critical to the metropolitan area's success. Beginning in the late 1970s and continuing into the early 1990s, this belief channeled spending into several interrelated projects that aimed to improve transportation from the suburbs while creating new destinations for tourists and shoppers downtown. The Center City Commuter Connection, commonly referred to as the Commuter Rail Tunnel, tied two separate regional rail networks into one larger system. Business interests joined with construction unions to pursue the project "over the vehement objections of most Philadelphians." Improved rail access spurred nearby investments such as the Gallery shopping complex and the Pennsylvania Convention Center along the Market East corridor. Much of the political support for these developments came in the form of tax abatements, which only exacerbated the city's revenue problems in the short term. But a glance toward Center City left no doubt about the types of changes afoot, as new skyscrapers began to rise higher than William Penn's statue atop city hall. Retaining Philadelphia's professional sports teams also became a symbolic priority linked to the revival of the central business district. As elsewhere, the franchises threatened to relocate in order to secure better facilities. And Philadelphia, like many other cities, shelled out financial concessions to keep the teams in town, even in tough fiscal times. These spending decisions had significant impacts on the everyday lives of Philadelphia's Black population.[24]

Community organizations from Philadelphia's poorer neighborhoods, many of which were predominantly Black, resented the focus on Center City, targeted toward white and middle- and upper-class populations. They felt that addressing the increasingly desperate lived experience of residents in poorer areas should either come first or, at the very least, be pursued in parallel with downtown-focused developments. But, in an atmosphere of austerity, funding was essentially a zero-sum game. For instance, subsidies for the convention center came at the expense of $18 million to aid the city's homeless. Loud voices calling for change persisted despite these realities. Even though activists could not stop the construction of the commuter tunnel, they quickly pivoted to pressing the local government to ensure that the jobs resulting from the downtown development would go to residents of color.[25]

In the transit and utility systems, a sense of crisis emerged from a decade of steep inflation, conflict over management decisions, and deferred maintenance. By the early 1980s, nearly everyone agreed that these critical systems desperately needed investment; the sticking point was where the money would come from. Some officials felt there was no choice but to increase transit fares and utility rates to raise revenue from individual consumers. But they met resistance from lower-income residents who argued they could not possibly afford to get to work or heat their homes if prices rose. The predominantly Black Consumer Education and Protective Association led the charge, arguing that the government could find this money elsewhere through progressive taxation or reappropriation of existing funds. The association also encouraged on-the-ground consumer actions such as paying Southeastern Pennsylvania Transportation Authority (SEPTA) fares with pennies. Local social service organizations set about applying for grants to help their clients with emergency utility needs. Revealing how dire the situation was, community groups demanded that the city guarantee that no resident would die during the winter because they could not afford heat.[26]

Gentrification served as a double-edged sword throughout this period. On the one hand, stabilizing population loss and increasing local tax revenues helped Philadelphia's fiscal situation; wealthier residents, both white and Black, also provided a more attractive market for developers and retailers. On the other hand, Black Philadelphians had begun to sound the alarm about neighborhood "recycling" as early as the 1960s, with the redevelopment of Society Hill. In subsequent years, gentrification and displacement spread to areas such as Spring Garden and Queen Village. By the 1980s and 1990s, demographic shifts and increased property values pushed even more Black residents out of additional neighborhoods such as Powelton Village in West Philadelphia. As Councilman John Street saw it, no one was safe. He explained, "Every Black neighborhood in this city could be jeopardized by recycling. These areas will be new ghettos. New rundown dilapidated neighborhoods where Black and poor people will live on the outskirts of what is now center city." Street was not wrong.[27]

For many Black Philadelphians, public policy decisions during the 1980s and early 1990s endangered their livelihoods, if not their very lives. Cuts to social spending collided with resident concerns about crime and an emerging War on Drugs to increasingly concentrate state intervention in Black communities through policing.

Survival remained the prime focus of poorer Black Philadelphians. Black folks hustled, discrediting loud conservative claims about Black dependency and lack of work ethic. They increasingly combined more sources of income to make ends meet during tough times. Fifi Mazzccua of North Philadelphia is a case in point. She lived in a Philadelphia Housing Authority–owned row house and worked as a caretaker for an elderly man. But, on top of that, family members paid her to care for four great-grandchildren. Others paired inadequate public assistance grants with part-time work, juggled staggered shifts at multiple employers, or sold goods or services on an informal basis. Because more and more of the city's jobs were in the service sector and paid low wages, these strategies only became more common.[28]

As economic restructuring proceeded apace and employment discrimination endured, Philadelphia City Council aimed to ameliorate conditions for Black workers. In response to the loss of manufacturing jobs, they enacted the country's first plant closing legislation in 1982. This law required larger firms to offer their employees sixty days' notice of closure. City council also pushed for affirmative action measures for hiring more Black police officers as well as allotting a set aside amount of city contracts to minority firms. Over the course of the 1980s, the racial income gap closed somewhat but remained substantial. The average Black Philadelphian still only earned 60 percent as much as their white counterpart. The poverty rate for individual Black men actually worsened during this time period.[29]

Philadelphia's sanitation workers, who were predominantly Black, provide an instructive example of the tenor of the time. They initiated a strike in 1986, but the Goode administration could not easily increase city spending to pay sanitation workers more. After twenty-one days, the strike ended without a wage increase, when the union voted to return to the job. Soon after, the administration decreased the size of sanitation worker crews, leading to the loss of fifteen hundred jobs. This treatment was a far cry from the comfortable contracts that the predominantly white police and firefighter unions had long received, or even from the city's begrudging negotiations with the teacher's union when pressured by recurrent strikes. When dealing with organized labor, city officials seemed to apply a double standard based on race and class. The sanitation workers' experience foreshadowed even more difficult times for municipal unions in the years ahead.[30]

Public health and safety were a part of the larger spending and revitalization conversation, but only because emerging crises demanded political attention. To start with, Philadelphia's well-established troubles with gang violence and drug abuse reached new heights as crack cocaine entered the marketplace. At roughly the same time, already marginalized populations began to contract the AIDS virus. These newer challenges heightened the city's deep stratification along racial and class lines.

Drug pushers and gang affiliations had long plagued Black Philadelphia. By the mid-1980s, drug markets gained new prominence due to the introduction of cheap crack cocaine, a greater influx of narcotics from Central and South America, and the more prevalent use of firearms. In addition, the continued erosion of stable working-class employment led more youths to turn to the illicit economy just to get by.[31]

Black residents made up over half of the population that had contracted AIDS by the mid-1980s, but they were not well served by white-oriented gay activist organizations. Absent any robust response from the local government, Black organizations like Delta Sigma Theta sorority tried to fill in with resources such as counseling. Upon taking over responsibility for the city's AIDS programming, Black union official David Fair noted, "Despite all the vows, commitments and sincere promises of several years, nothing, nothing, not a single penny, is being spent to stop the spread of the disease among the poor and non-white." Other activists criticized the city for "dumping" AIDS patients in nursing homes in Black neighborhoods.[32]

In a broader sense, the problem of Black poverty was increasingly diverted to and contained by a stronger carceral state. The local implementation of the War on Drugs disproportionately affected young Black men in Philadelphia, further aggravating extant racial discrimination in the criminal justice system. Corrections was one of the few areas where the state of Pennsylvania enthusiastically spent more money during the 1980s. Plagued by overcrowded prisons, legislators built new ones but still could not keep up with the supply of prisoners. When drug enforcement lagged, it was because there was no more room in the jails. Overcrowding was bad enough that prisoners were occasionally released. On one such occasion, the *Philadelphia Daily News* reflected racialized fear of prisoners as it told readers to prepare for "Philadelphia's Vietnam." Space in addiction treatment programs was even more scarce. Policy makers at the federal, state, and local levels diverted public funds from education and other social support programs to bolster law enforcement and detention facilities.[33]

Similar dynamics marked struggles over the embattled Philadelphia Public Schools. Recurring teacher strikes tested public patience, while physical infrastructure continued to deteriorate. The banks that schools were forced to turn to for loans demanded greater fiscal discipline. That requirement, combined with declining aid from both federal and state government, resulted in large teacher layoffs in the summers of 1980 and 1981. Soon, educators were asked to concede benefits that had already been written into their current contract, and they walked out again in September 1981. The conflict took on a sharp racial dynamic. By this time, fully 70 percent of the system's students were Black, but the teachers union was still predominantly white. Many white taxpayers resented supporting the seemingly ineffective education of a population that they viewed as undeserving. Many Black parents felt strongly enough about continuing their children's education that they were willing to cross picket lines. Teachers unions, often portrayed as greedy, bore much of the public blame for the school system's larger structural issues.[34] (See Fig. 7.1.)

Philadelphia was home to storied welfare rights organizing, and these struggles also persisted, revealing the continuing economic insecurity of many women and children of color. Activists, the majority of them Black women, fought a multifront battle, trying to secure higher levels of state support while also protesting reductions in federal spending. The passage of "Thornfare" (named after Governor Richard Thornburgh), which made the

Figure 7.1 Many Black parents and youths felt that recurring conflicts between the Philadelphia Federation of Teachers and the School District of Philadelphia jeopardized their education. Here, they march down the Benjamin Franklin Parkway on the way to city hall.

criteria to receive relief far more onerous, was a particularly bitter pill to swallow because it depended on Milton Street's defection to the Republican Party. Reacting to the Reagan administration's additional proposed cuts to Aid to Families with Dependent Children, Philadelphia Welfare Rights Organization activist Roxanne Jones exclaimed, "After this cold winter we went through, people freezing to death, not having enough money to pay their fuel bills, I call it human genocide. It is inhumane for [Reagan] to talk of cutting any of the programs any more." Not one for idle talk, Jones's organization sued the state of Pennsylvania over welfare eligibility guidelines and work requirements in 1983; she followed up with protests at both the Philadelphia Gas Works and the capitol building in Harrisburg. Yet, the conservative assault on welfare continued. More voters (most of them white) came to perceive welfare as wasteful spending that supported the undeserving poor. The national Democratic Party, aiming more for the political center than the left, eventually worked with Republicans in the mid-1990s to completely overhaul relief programs that had been in place for six decades.[35]

Even seemingly innocuous occurrences, like a family moving to a new home, had the potential to set off a racial calamity. That's what happened when a mixed-race couple, Gerald and Carol Fox, tried to relocate to the predominantly white Elmwood area of Southwest Philadelphia in 1985. An angry mob met them and vandalized their home. Mayor Goode had to declare a state of emergency until tensions subsided. While such incidents had remained common throughout the 1970s, the persistence of the violent defense of white neighborhoods well into the 1980s was a visceral reminder that formidable barriers to racial progress remained.[36]

Philadelphia had long been notorious for toxic police-community relations, drawing not only local but also national attention. Public frustration with police brutality simmered for decades in communities of color, occasionally brought to the boiling point by all-too-frequent cases involving death at the hands of the police. During former police commissioner Frank Rizzo's tenure as mayor in the 1970s, the city made few concessions despite a groundswell in community organizing. The proportion of Black officers on the force actually decreased even as the city's Black population grew, and the federal government dropped its civil rights suit against the city. Under the Green and Goode administrations, possibilities for reform increased. For example, the passage of more restrictive guidelines for police use of firearms cut police shootings of civilians in half in just two years. The city's first Black police commissioner, Willie Williams, served from 1988 to 1992. Yet, high-profile, deadly confrontations between police and residents overshadowed this incremental progress.[37] (See Fig. 7.2.)

In 1985, Philadelphia police had a second major confrontation with the radical Black collective MOVE. Motivated by complaints from neighbors and concerns that MOVE might be stockpiling weapons and/or mistreating children, the police attempted to remove the group from their home on Osage Avenue in West Philadelphia. The effort quickly devolved into a standoff and blockade. In addition to deploying tear gas and bullets, police dropped an incendiary device on the roof of the house. The explosion ignited a fuel tank, and the ensuing fire killed eleven people and reduced a city block to rubble.

The MOVE disaster became only the most extreme manifestation of mutual distrust between Black communities and the Philadelphia police. Worse, it occurred under the watch of a Black mayor and gravely threatened Goode's prospects for reelection. Goode's style of soliciting many opinions while making decisions on his own, in this case, had tragic consequences. Other Black leaders grew increasingly critical of Goode in the aftermath of the bombing; an investigatory commission went so far as to call his administration's actions "grossly negligent." Meanwhile, contractors bungled the reconstruction of the homes that had been destroyed, adding to the woes of displaced families. Decades later, the MOVE incident still overshadowed Goode's broader legacy when city council moved to name a street after him.[38]

Figure 7.2 State Representative David P. Richardson was on the leading edge of Black activists elected to office in Philadelphia, representing the Germantown area in the state house from 1973 to his death in 1995. He appears here at a demonstration of around one thousand residents outside the Philadelphia Police Department's Fourteenth District Station.

Another high-profile case involved the ongoing legal saga of Mumia Abu-Jamal. A revered radio journalist, former Black Panther, and supporter of MOVE, Abu-Jamal was convicted of murdering a police officer in the early 1980s. Officer Daniel Faulkner had pulled over Abu-Jamal's brother, William Cook, for a traffic violation in the middle of the night. In the ensuing struggle, both Abu-Jamal and Faulkner sustained gunshot wounds; Faulkner died shortly thereafter. Witnesses claimed to have seen Abu-Jamal pull the trigger. But procedural problems plagued the trial, and many felt Abu-Jamal was judged due to his political opinions rather than any evidence of the alleged crime. The guilty verdict came with a death sentence (later changed to life without parole in 2011). His conviction touched off a decades-long social movement that sought to free him while also raising larger questions about due process and the death penalty. Abu-Jamal remained an active author and radio contributor from inside prison. Overall, his case serves as a highly visible, ongoing example of how the justice system failed Black Americans.[39]

Meanwhile, a majority of Philadelphians of all races were concerned about their personal safety and desired more effective policing. The city thus faced a difficult situation of trying to simultaneously rein in police powers while also effectively fighting crime and responding to public pressure. This pressure to calm a frightened public only further exacerbated the difficulty in finding funds for social programs and neighborhood investment.

During the 1980s and early 1990s, many white Philadelphians came to view the local Democratic Party as dominated by the concerns of Black residents. For their part, the Black electorate was more divided than in previous election cycles. This racial dynamic, alongside general frustration with the state of the city, led to the 1991 mayoral election of Ed Rendell. Even with a white mayor in office, Black policy makers continued to play critical roles in city governance. This was especially true of John Street, city council president at the time, who served as mayor after Rendell termed out.[40]

Rendell was a former district attorney with a tough-on-crime reputation, which appealed to many residents as their concerns about street crime persisted. His comeback from election defeats during the 1980s also appealed to Philadelphians who were partial to an underdog. Rendell cast himself in the role of a savior who could reach beyond sharp racial divides. The International Ladies Garment Workers Union, for instance, endorsed him because he was "best suited to turn this city around." While other candidates seemed racially polarizing, union leader Joseph Fisher explained that Rendell "has a record—through more than a decade of public service—of being a friend of the city's African-American and Hispanic communities. He is the only candidate whose track record actually demonstrates an ability to unite all of the people of Philadelphia." Implicit in Fisher's statement was the assumption that Rendell could count on strong white support.[41]

John Street, meanwhile, became city council president in 1992. Notorious for engaging in a fistfight with Fran Rafferty on the council floor in 1981, he was still often regarded as unpredictable a decade later. Yet, his leadership effectively kept city council, a traditionally unruly body, relatively in order and in line with the Rendell administration. Street had a deep understanding of the city's finances and was regarded by one journalist as the Black politician most "willing to make decisions that might actually be good for the entire city, not just for black neighborhoods." This assessment downplayed the establishment's continuing influence on Black officials throughout the 1980s and 1990s.[42]

Rendell and Street faced not only tough economic circumstances but also the outright takeover of some city functions by the state and federal governments. Those transfers of power, though temporary and partial, compromised Philadelphia's political independence. In effect, this meant that even as Black voters and officials gained leverage, the political possibilities narrowed in ways that diluted their influence. Black politicians had even less maneuvering room between the conflicting interests of the establishment and everyday people.

No easy solutions to the overall fiscal crisis were in sight. Borrowing was no longer feasible—the city had a junk bond rating, and one local bank demanded no less than a 29 percent interest rate. Tax increases also seemed impossible because residents already felt short-changed in services, even as they paid some of the highest municipal-level taxes in the nation. Some form of state assistance was unavoidable, but many Philadelphians were loath to succumb to the extreme level of oversight that a financial control board had exercised over New York City in the 1970s. Street led efforts to establish a state control board called the Pennsylvania Intergovernmental Cooperation Authority (PICA), with hopes that the name would signal partnership rather than supplication. PICA had better standing than the city with financiers and could thus access credit and issue bonds at much more favorable rates. In turn, the city had to obtain PICA approval of a five-year financial plan. This funding mechanism served as a stopgap solution while officials worked toward major spending reductions in the budget.[43]

The local role in administering housing and education programs, which both primarily served Black residents, was also in flux. Concerns about corruption, patronage practices, and overall mismanagement at the Philadelphia Housing Authority went back decades. Many tenants faced deplorable living conditions and a huge percentage of units stood vacant. Those trends culminated in a federal takeover of the housing authority for a year in 1992. Even this drastic action seemed to make things worse, and the vacancy rate increased. Federal officials next cajoled Rendell and Street into taking prominent roles in the authority. As always, race was front and center. Rendell admitted in a candid moment that "the two things that have driven PHA over the past three or four years have been patronage and the black issue. Many of the blacks [hired] are incompetent. Many of the white contractors absolutely fuck the tenants and skimp on everything because they know there's no oversight." Though Rendell made it sound recent, politicians' supporters getting jobs in city agencies and loose accountability had long characterized city government. The main difference was that now city employees were much more likely to be Black.[44]

The public school system also continued to struggle, plagued by high dropout rates, low test scores, and, perhaps most important, a toxic reputation among middle-class families that the city hoped to retain. These issues, combined with a budget crisis, led to state lawmakers passing a resolution to take over control of Philadelphia's system in 1998. Political wrangling over funding commitments and the extent of privatization delayed the actual takeover until late 2001.[45]

Philadelphia could not address its sizable deficit without major concessions from the twenty-five thousand workers that comprised four municipal unions. These included the Fraternal Order of Police, Fire Fighters Local 22, AFSCME District Council 47, which represented white-collar workers, and AFSCME District Council 33, which represented blue-collar workers and was predominantly Black. Negotiations over contracts in the summer of 1992 took on the semblance of war. AFSCME leader Jim Sutton told thousands of workers gathered outside city hall, "We intend to fight with every ounce of strength that we have in our bodies. And I say to you, Ed Rendell, if you think that L.A. had a bad time, mess with District Council 33. If you don't play by the rules, we will take whatever action we have to take!" Though exaggerating in front of his members, Sutton's reference to a potential riot underscored the conflict's racial and class contours. The strategic arsenal of the city, meanwhile, included: "The injection and heightening of racial divisiveness among the different unions, the pitting of union against union so that members of one would begin to hate members of another, the ceaseless ratcheting up of layoff notices, [and] notices of the city's intent to privatize certain time-honored union functions." In preparation for the possibility of an ugly strike, the city stockpiled supplies like toilet paper and tried to identify likely targets for sabotage.[46]

Months of back-and-forth with the unions finally culminated in a very brief strike, with John Street serving as an intermediary. Citywide public opinion, a crucial variable, was largely against the unions. Black Philadelphians, though, remained staunchly on the side of labor. They objected to a fiscal crisis being settled on the backs of workers in a time of rising income inequality. Board of Education employee Larry Richardson told the *Philadelphia Tribune*, "There is enough money in this city so that [Rendell] does not have to ask for givebacks from city workers." The unions ultimately backed down on requested wage increases, accepted lower health care contributions, and agreed to changes on work rules. The Rendell administration got most of what it wanted in cost reductions. A *Philadelphia Tribune* editorial framed the deal as a compromise and mused pragmatically, "It would be nice if we continued to enjoy the good economic times that precipitated formerly generous contract proposals. But we don't, and everybody must change with the times."[47]

Budget aside, the Black community now flexed considerable power over city appointments. Black leaders routinely pressed the Rendell administration to appoint Black officials in highly visible roles, and they were overwhelmingly successful—"racial acceptability" became an important hiring criterion. For the first time, Philadelphia had both a Black police commissioner (Richard Neal) and a Black fire commissioner (Harold Byrd Hairston) in addition to strong representation in elected office. But still frustrating were many white people's perceptions of racial considerations in hiring. The *Tribune* noted that "the not so subtle inference that Black support for a candidate can only be based on skin color and not credentials or capability is both inaccurate and offensive."[48]

Black political support was, by this time, absolutely necessary in citywide contests. Even though he had a high approval rating overall, Rendell's reelection still depended on maintaining a "fragile coalition" with Black politicians. He hoped to avoid a potential challenge from a Black candidate, perhaps State Representative Dwight Evans, that he might not survive. Glowing national press that emphasized Rendell's fiscal and downtown successes could also serve as a liability with Philadelphia voters more concerned about neighborhood issues.[49]

To address these constituencies, Rendell staffers zealously pursued an empowerment zone designation from the federal government. Community groups collaborated on a plan targeting three areas: the Parkside area of West Philadelphia, North Philadelphia west of Broad Street, and the American Street corridor. The Philadelphia-Camden bid prevailed, guaranteeing $100 million in federal funding over the next decade to aid neighborhood development. This prize helped secure Rendell's reelection as mayor in 1995. Over time, the program succeeded in decreasing poverty and unemployment rates, but the creation of new businesses and jobs proved much more elusive.[50]

John Street won a five-way race for the Democratic mayoral nomination in May 1999, staving off two other Black candidates (John F. White Jr. and Dwight Evans) as well as the first female candidate (Happy Fernandez). He attributed his success to communicating "a message of hope, not a message of fear" and having the "broad-based support of every ethnic group in the city."[51]

In contrast to the near-monolithic Black support needed to elect Goode as mayor, by the 1990s, Black voters had more choices than ever. This was a mixed blessing. The division of Black support between Lucien Blackwell and George R. Burrell Jr. enabled Rendell's 1991 election. In 1996, Philadelphia Grass Root Political Network leader Omjasisa Kentu warned, "Blacks in Philadelphia don't have time for all this infighting and division among themselves" because it distracted attention from defending legislative priorities from conservative assault. Even these internal divisions, though, reflected the longer trajectory of Black politics in Philadelphia.[52]

As Black politicians reached the highest levels of office in Philadelphia, race continued to pervade almost every issue. "Everything we do as African-Americans is political, and we've got to recognize that," advised union leader Thurston Hyman. Greater influence at the ballot box ran parallel to persistent grassroots activism and struggles for survival.[53]

The sequence and timing of mayoral administrations in this era led to unfortunate racial optics: relative financial stability under white mayors Green and Rendell, compared to fiscal crisis under Black mayor Goode. That rendering ignores the fact that Goode made most of the budget decisions during Green's term. It also discounts the critical role of timing. Goode's terms aligned with the years when accumulated policy decisions, economic transitions, and demographic trends put the most distance between city revenues and obligations. Rendell's tenure in the 1990s conversely benefited from more favorable demographic trends and momentum in the development of the city's service economy.

Although representatives of Philadelphia's progressive social movements had ascended to powerful positions by the 1980s, the contingencies of ongoing urban crisis pulled their governance away from the left and toward the center. In a climate of austerity, the general mode of governance was triage. Race and class still often dictated policy priorities, but the project of balancing budgets was increasingly wrapped in the seemingly neutral language of market logic and framed as an absolute necessity. Residents continued to resist service reductions and downtown-focused redevelopment. But the relentless drive toward fiscal discipline robbed Black Philadelphians of the resources they were due.[54]

For most Black Philadelphians, greater political leverage within the city establishment did not translate into improvements in lived experience. One journalist explained, "In Philadelphia a Black mayor, a Black mayor-elect, two Black police commissioners, a Black schools superintendent and a Black city council president have contributed to the city's history, but a Black man still can't catch a cab on Broad Street." A comparison of the findings of W.E.B. Du Bois's *The Philadelphia Negro* with the state of Black Philadelphia a century later wondered, "How can Black people live in a city for 100 years and see very little change in some aspects of their lives?" As the twentieth century ended, Black politics in Philadelphia had transformed the city in ways that would have been difficult for previous generations to even imagine.

Having secured a seat at the table, Black communities still had to push hard to impact the distribution of resources and power.[55]

NOTES

1. Robert W. Sorrell, "Introduction," in *The State of Black Philadelphia, 1983* (Philadelphia: Urban League of Philadelphia, 1983), 3.

2. Gary, Indiana, and Cleveland, Ohio, paved the way for major cities electing Black mayors in 1967. Among the ten largest U.S. cities at the time, Detroit and Los Angeles elected Black mayors in 1973, Washington, DC, in 1975, and Chicago in 1983. Population figures based on Philadelphia city in Bureau of the Census, "Table 56 Summary of Social Characteristics: 1980," in *Census of the Population: 1980*, vol. 1, Characteristics of the Population, pt. 40, Pennsylvania (Washington, DC: GPO, 1983), 20; Bureau of the Census, "Table 58 Race by Sex: 1980," in *Census of the Population: 1980*, vol. 1, Characteristics of the Population, pt. 40, Pennsylvania (Washington, DC: GPO, 1983), 58. Though the Asian American population in Philadelphia grew throughout the 1980s, many new arrivals migrated from places like Vietnam, Korea, and Cambodia and could not initially vote. On the longer-standing community of Chinese descent in Philadelphia, see Kathryn E. Wilson, *Ethnic Renewal in Philadelphia's Chinatown: Space, Place, and Struggle* (Philadelphia: Temple University Press, 2015).

3. Most official tallies of Puerto Ricans or Latinos such as those recorded by the census were likely drastic undercounts. My estimate is a conservative compromise between census figures and local leaders' estimates that took into account other data sources. See Juan A. Albino, "Report on the Puerto Ricans in the City of Philadelphia," American Friends Service Committee, June 1973, box 4, folder 1, MSS 116 Hispanic Federation for Social and Economic Development, Historical Society of Pennsylvania. On the general background of Puerto Ricans in Philadelphia, see Carmen Teresa Whalen, *From Puerto Rico to Philadelphia: Puerto Rican Workers and Postwar Economies* (Philadelphia: Temple University Press, 2001); Víctor Vázquez-Hernández, "From Pan-Latino Enclaves to a Community: Puerto Ricans in Philadelphia, 1910–2000," in *The Puerto Rican Diaspora: Historical Perspectives*, ed. Víctor Vázquez-Hernández and Carmen Teresa Whalen (Philadelphia: Temple University Press, 2005), 88–105. On Puerto Ricans' political trajectory, see Alyssa Ribeiro, "'The Battle for Harmony': Intergroup Relations between Blacks and Latinos in Philadelphia, 1950s to 1980s" (Ph.D. diss., University of Pittsburgh, 2013), 230–247.

4. For background on such organizing, see Alyssa Ribeiro, "'Asking Them and Protesting': Black and Puerto Rican Civic Leadership in Philadelphia Neighborhoods, 1960s–1970s," *Pennsylvania History: A Journal of Mid-Atlantic Studies* 86, no. 3 (Summer 2019): 359–382; Alyssa Ribeiro, "Forgotten Residents Fighting Back: The Ludlow Community Association and Neighborhood Improvement in Philadelphia," in *Civil Rights and Beyond: African American and Latino/a Activism in the Twentieth-Century United States*, ed. Brian D. Behnken (Athens: University of Georgia Press, 2016), 172–194; Ribeiro, "Battle for Harmony"; Eric C. Schneider, Christopher Agee, and Themis Chronopoulos, "Dirty Work: Police and Community Relations and the Limits of Liberalism in Postwar Philadelphia," *Journal of Urban History*, May 1, 2017.

5. Andrew Feffer, "The Land Belongs to the People: Reframing Urban Protest in Post-Sixties Philadelphia," in *The World the 60s Made: Politics and Culture in Recent America*, ed. Van Gosse and Richard Moser (Philadelphia: Temple University Press, 2003), 88–89;

On Rizzo's particular appeal to white Philadelphians, see Timothy J. Lombardo, *Blue-Collar Conservatism: Frank Rizzo's Philadelphia and Populist Politics* (Philadelphia: University of Pennsylvania Press, 2018).

6. Richard A. Keiser, *Subordination or Empowerment? African-American Leadership and the Struggle for Urban Political Power* (New York: Oxford University Press, 1997), 109–110; "Human Rights Agenda: Black Political Convention Focus '79," January 1979, box 22, folder 9, accession 580 Tenant Action Group, Special Collections Research Center, Temple University Libraries; Tommie St. Hill, "Hispanic Community Claims It's Ignored," *Philadelphia Tribune*, May 14, 1980; William J. Green, "A Historic Commitment of Conscience to the People of Philadelphia," 1979, reproduced in Mary Ellen Balchunis, "A Study of the Old and New Campaign Politics Models: A Comparative Analysis of Wilson Goode's 1983 and 1987 Philadelphia Mayoral Campaigns" (Ph.D. diss., Temple University, 1992), appendix C, 178–179, 182, 185.

7. John F. Bauman, "W. Wilson Goode: The Black Mayor as Urban Entrepreneur," *Journal of Negro History* 77, no. 3 (Summer 1992): 148.

8. Bauman, "W. Wilson Goode," 147; Bruce Ransom, "Mayor W. Wilson Goode of Philadelphia: The Technocrat," *National Political Science Review* 2 (July 1990): 183–184.

9. The coalition called itself the "Draft Goode Committee." Balchunis, "Study of the Old and New Campaign Politics," 8; Bruce Ransom, "Black Independent Electoral Politics in Philadelphia: The Election of Mayor W. Wilson Goode," in *The New Black Politics: The Search for Political Power*, ed. Michael B. Preston, Lenneal J. Henderson Jr., and Paul L. Puryear, 2nd ed. (New York: Longman, 1987), 269.

10. Ransom, "Black Independent Electoral Politics," 268–276; Mike Mallowe, "The Friends of Wilson Goode," *Philadelphia Magazine*, December 1985, 128; Richard A. Keiser, "The Rise of a Biracial Coalition in Philadelphia," in *Racial Politics in American Cities*, ed. Rufus P. Browning, Dale Rogers Marshall, and David H. Tabb (New York: Longman, 1990), 67.

11. Mallowe, "Friends of Wilson Goode," 130; Keiser, *Subordination or Empowerment?* 121.

12. Lisa Levenstein, *A Movement without Marches: African American Women and the Politics of Poverty in Postwar Philadelphia* (Chapel Hill: University of North Carolina Press, 2009); Ribeiro, "Asking Them and Protesting"; Mallowe, "Friends of Wilson Goode," 130; "Black Women in History: Dr. Clayton, First Black, First Woman to Head City's Schools," *Philadelphia Tribune*, February 8, 1983; Bureau of the Census, "Table 58 Race by Sex: 1980."

13. Mallowe, "Friends of Wilson Goode," 199 (quote), 203, 130–131; W. Wilson Goode and Joann Stevens, *In Goode Faith: Philadelphia's First Black Mayor Tells His Story* (Valley Forge, PA: Judson, 1992); W. Wilson Goode, *Black Voters Mattered: A Philadelphia Story* (Cork: BookBaby, 2018).

14. Jodine Mayberry, "Abscam," *Encyclopedia of Greater Philadelphia*, Rutgers University, 2016, available at https://philadelphiaencyclopedia.org/archive/abscam/; Keiser, *Subordination or Empowerment?* 112; Jane Eisner, "Anderson's Staff Backs Angel Ortiz," *Philadelphia Inquirer*, October 5, 1983; William Sutton and Russell Cooke, "Goode Backs Angel Ortiz for Pearlman's Seat," *Philadelphia Inquirer*, June 14, 1984; Feffer, "Land Belongs to the People," 88; "List of Members of Philadelphia City Council since 1952," Wikipedia, September 6, 2018, available at https://en.wikipedia.org/w/index.php?title=List_of_members_of_Philadelphia_City_Council_since_1952&oldid=858343595.

15. Robert P. Inman, "How to Have a Fiscal Crisis: Lessons from Philadelphia," *American Economic Review* 85, no. 2 (May 1995): 382; Anthony S. Twyman, Leonard N. Fleming,

and Thomas Fitzgerald, "Lucien Blackwell, Fighter for the Working Class, Dies," *Philadelphia Inquirer*, January 25, 2003; Kevin J. Mumford, "The Trouble with Gay Rights: Race and the Politics of Sexual Orientation in Philadelphia, 1969–1982," *Journal of American History* 98, no. 1 (June 2011): 56–71; Molly Eichel, "Mayor Nutter Praised Former Councilman John C. Anderson. Who Was He?" *Philadelphia Inquirer*, September 26, 2015, available at https://www.inquirer.com/philly/blogs/real-time/Mayor-Nutter-praises-former-Councilman-John-C-Anderson-who-was-he.html; Inga Saffron, "Changing Skyline: John C. Anderson Apartments, LGBT-Friendly and Urban-Friendly," *Philadelphia Inquirer*, January 16, 2014, available at https://www.inquirer.com/philly/home/20140117_Changing_Skyline__John_C__Anderson_Apartments__LGBT-friendly_and_urban-friendly.html; For more background on LGBTQ activism, see Marc Stein, *City of Sisterly and Brotherly Loves: Lesbian and Gay Philadelphia, 1945–1972* (Philadelphia: Temple University Press, 2004).

16. Richard Rys, "In Search of Milton Street," *Philadelphia Magazine* (blog), May 15, 2006, available at https://www.phillymag.com/news/2006/05/15/in-search-of-milton-street/; Feffer, "Land Belongs to the People"; Matthew J. Countryman, *Up South: Civil Rights and Black Power in Philadelphia* (Philadelphia: University of Pennsylvania Press, 2006), 317–322; Thomas J. Sugrue, *Sweet Land of Liberty: The Forgotten Struggle for Civil Rights in the North* (New York: Random House, 2008), 493–494, 525–526; David Fattah, "The House of Umoja as a Case Study for Social Change," *Annals of the American Academy of Political and Social Science* 494 (1987): 37–41; "House of Umoja Is 16 Years Old," *Afro American* (Baltimore), September 15, 1984.

17. Ransom, "Mayor W. Wilson Goode"; Joseph P. Blake and Joseph Grace, "Hispanic Panel Breaks with Goode," *Philadelphia Daily News*, March 29, 1989; Israel Colon, "The Puerto Rican Experience under Mayor Wilson Goode," in *The Dinkins Administration and the Puerto Rican Community: Lessons from the Puerto Rican Experience with African-American Mayors in Chicago and Philadelphia*, ed. Institute for Puerto Rican Policy (New York: Institute for Puerto Rican Policy, 1990), 10, 11.

18. Mallowe, "Friends of Wilson Goode," 205.

19. Bauman, "W. Wilson Goode," 144; Jerrilyn McGregory, "The Greening of Philadelphia," *Pennsylvania Folklife* 44, no. 1 (1994): 27–35; Domenic Vitiello and Michael Nairn, "Community Gardening in Philadelphia: 2008 Harvest Report," October 2009, 26–47, Urban Agriculture and Community Food Security Research and Practice, available at https://sites.google.com/site/urbanagriculturephiladelphia/harvest-reports; William W. Sutton Jr., "City Deficits May Force Higher Taxes," *Philadelphia Inquirer*, December 23, 1986.

20. Roger D. Simon, *Philadelphia: A Brief History* (Philadelphia: Temple University Press, 2017), 78–79, 99–100; Carol Jenkins, "The Miracle or the Mirage of Local Governance? Mayor Rendell and the Philadelphia Fiscal Crisis" (Ph.D. diss., Temple University, 2000), 78; M. Howard Pell, Jeffrey L. Schmeizer, and Ira L. Weinberg, "Philadelphia Income Tax on Wages, Salaries and Net Profits," *CPA Journal* 51, no. 1 (January 1981): 52; "Philadelphia Wage Tax Up," *New York Times*, January 6, 1945.

21. Matthew Smalarz, "The 'White Island': Whiteness in the Making of Public and Private Space in Northeast Philadelphia, 1854–1990" (Ph.D. diss., University of Rochester, 2016), 287–335; "Racism Breeds Stupid Ideas," *Philadelphia Tribune*, March 1, 1988.

22. Marc Duvoisin, "The Oversight Board: A New Heavy in the Budget Drama," *Philadelphia Inquirer*, May 5, 1991; Inman, "How to Have a Fiscal Crisis," 378.

23. Feffer, "Land Belongs to the People," 67, 80–83; Jim Davis, "Protesters Criticize Low Priority Given Decent Housing at CD Hearings," *Philadelphia Tribune*, January 26, 1979.

24. Jacob I. Kobrick, "'Let the People Have a Victory': The Politics of Transportation in Philadelphia, 1946–1984" (Ph.D. diss., University of Maryland, 2010), 342–343; Harry Kyriakodis, "Single Most Transformative Investment? The Commuter Rail Tunnel, Now Turning 30," *Hidden City Philadelphia* (blog), November 7, 2014, available at http://hiddencityphila.org/2014/11/single-most-transformative-investment-the-commuter-rail-tunnel-now-turning-30/; Simon, *Philadelphia*, 108–109; Aaron Cowan, *A Nice Place to Visit: Tourism and Urban Revitalization in the Postwar Rustbelt* (Philadelphia: Temple University Press, 2016), 101–127.

25. Brian A. Kane, "Beds for Conventioneers, Not for Homeless," *Guardian*, April 26, 1989.

26. Nina Virzi, "Proposal to Utility Emergency Service Fund Grant Case Assistance," February 1, 1983, box 7, folder 23, MSS 116 Hispanic Federation for Social and Economic Development, Historical Society of Pennsylvania; Philadelphia Urban Coalition, "City-Wide Groups Demand City Emergency Fuel Program," n.d., box 16, folder 11, MSS 114 Spanish Merchants Association, Historical Society of Pennsylvania.

27. Simon, *Philadelphia*, 111; "Streets Fight Recycling," *Philadelphia Tribune*, March 6, 1979.

28. Buzz Bissinger, *A Prayer for the City* (New York: Vintage Books, 1999), 302; Max J. Pfeffer, "Work versus Welfare in the Ethnic Transformation of a Philadelphia Labor Market," *Social Science Quarterly* 78, no. 2 (June 1997): 452–471.

29. Keiser, *Subordination or Empowerment?* 112; Francisco L. Rivera-Batiz, "The Economic Status of Racial and Ethnic Minorities within the Metropolitan Area," in *Work, Wages, and Poverty: Income Distribution in Post-Industrial Philadelphia*, ed. Janice Fanning Madden and William J. Stull (Philadelphia: University of Pennsylvania Press, 1991), 115; Michael Leeds and Janice Fanning Madden, "The Region's Poverty Rate during the 1980s," in Madden and Stull, *Work, Wages, and Poverty*, 85–88.

30. Keiser, *Subordination or Empowerment?* 120; Smalarz, "White Island," 320–322.

31. Elijah Anderson, "The Emerging Philadelphia African American Class Structure," *Annals of the American Academy of Political and Social Science*, no. 568 (March 2000): 55–56.

32. Dan Royles, "Taking It to the Streets: AIDS, Race, and Protest in Philadelphia," *Pennsylvania Legacies* 16, no. 1 (Spring 2016): 27; "Counseling on AIDS," *Philadelphia Tribune*, May 26, 1989; Robin L. White, "Critic Heads AIDS Panel," *Philadelphia Tribune*, November 27, 1987; Douglas P. Dabney, "City-Run AIDS Shelter Opens; Draws Fire," *Philadelphia Tribune*, January 6, 1987.

33. A cap on the number of inmates was instituted as part of a consent decree in 1986. Brian McKenna, "Philly Prisoner Release Order Spurs Hysteria," *Guardian*, June 29, 1988; David Zucchino, "As City Jails Overflow, Drug Problems Fester," *Philadelphia Inquirer*, April 10, 1992; Allen Hornblum, "Never Enough Jail Cells to Restore Law and Order," *Philadelphia Inquirer*, March 9, 1993.

34. Jon Shelton, *Teacher Strike! Public Education and the Making of a New American Political Order* (Urbana: University of Illinois Press, 2017), 172–182.

35. Levenstein, *Movement without Marches*, 31–63; Countryman, *Up South*, 258–294; Kim Gallon, "The Blood Demonstration: Teaching the History of the Philadelphia Welfare Rights Organization," *Pennsylvania Magazine of History and Biography* 139, no. 1 (2015): 82–101; Sugrue, *Sweet Land of Liberty*, 525.

36. William K. Stevens, "Philadelphia Neighborhood Torn by Racial Tension Starts to Simmer Down," *New York Times*, December 1, 1985.

37. Ribeiro, "Battle for Harmony," 207–221; Karl E. Johnson, "Police-Black Community Relations in Postwar Philadelphia: Race and Criminalization in Urban Social Spaces, 1945–1960," *Journal of African American History* 89, no. 2 (2004): 118–134; Schneider, Agee, and Chronopoulos, "Dirty Work"; U.S. Commission on Civil Rights, *Police Practices and Civil Rights: Hearing Held in Philadelphia, Pennsylvania, February 6, 1979; April 16–17, 1979*, vol. 1: Testimony (Washington, DC: Government Printing Office, 1979); Nicole J. Maurantonio, "Crisis, Race, and Journalistic Authority in Postwar Philadelphia" (Ph.D. diss., University of Pennsylvania, 2008), 227, 230–231; Keiser, *Subordination or Empowerment?* 111–112; "Willie Williams, Former Philly, L.A. Police Commissioner, Dead at 72," *Philadelphia Magazine* (blog), April 27, 2016, available at https://www.phillymag.com/news/2016/04/27/willie-williams-philadelphia-police-commissioner-dead/.

38. Bauman, "W. Wilson Goode," 152; Mike Mallowe, "The November of His Years," *Philadelphia Magazine*, November 1985; Audrey Clement, "From Bad to Worse as the Trash Piles Up," *Guardian*, July 23, 1986; Mallowe, "Friends of Wilson Goode," 127; Jenice Armstrong, "Renaming a Philadelphia Street after Former Mayor Wilson Goode Is a Really Bad Idea," *Philadelphia Inquirer*, September 17, 2018, available at https://www.inquirer.com/philly/columnists/jenice_armstrong/jenice-armstrong-wilson-goode-street-name-20180917.html. For extended coverage of the MOVE incident, see Robin Erica Wagner-Pacifici, *Discourse and Destruction: The City of Philadelphia versus MOVE* (Chicago: University of Chicago Press, 1994); Charles W. Bowser, *Let the Bunker Burn: The Final Battle with MOVE* (Philadelphia: Camino Books, 1989); Hizkias Assefa and Paul Wahrhaftig, *The MOVE Crisis in Philadelphia: Extremist Groups and Conflict Resolution* (New York: Praeger, 1988); Margot Harry, *"Attention, MOVE! This Is America!"* (Chicago: Banner, 1987).

39. Van Gosse and Kavita Philip, "Mumia Abu-Jamal and the Social Wage of Whiteness," *Radical History Review*, no. 81 (Fall 2001): 7.

40. Bauman, "W. Wilson Goode," 154; Simon, *Philadelphia*, 106.

41. "Rendell Gets Key Union Backing," *Philadelphia Tribune*, April 9, 1991.

42. Liz Spikol, "A History of Violence: Philadelphia Political Brawls," *Philadelphia Magazine*, May 15, 2016, available at https://www.phillymag.com/news/2016/05/15/philadelphia-political-brawls/; Bissinger, *Prayer for the City*, 192–193.

43. Kim Phillips-Fein, *Fear City: New York's Fiscal Crisis and the Rise of Austerity Politics* (New York: Metropolitan Books, 2017); Jenkins, "Miracle or the Mirage," 98–106; Pennsylvania Intergovernmental Cooperation Authority, "Annual Report for Fiscal Year 1992," October 31, 1992, 1–2, available at https://www.picapa.org/docs/OW/AR_FY92.pdf.

44. "Stop Playing Politics with Poor People and Housing," *Philadelphia Tribune*, June 19, 1992; Michael deCourcy Hinds, "Housing Agency's Problems Deepen as U.S. Rescue Effort Proves Futile," *New York Times*, June 9, 1993; Bissinger, *Prayer for the City*, 255.

45. Richard Jones, "Phila. Schools Forestall Takeover: Two Banks Came Forward with Enough Borrowing Power to Take the District through Next School Year," *Philadelphia Inquirer*, May 29, 1998; Susan Snyder and Marc Schogol, "City Agrees to School Takeover: Schweiker, Street Ready for 'a Full Partnership,'" *Philadelphia Inquirer*, December 22, 2001.

46. Bissinger, *Prayer for the City*, 167, 164, 155.

47. Wayne Browne, "Trib Poll: Is Rendell Fair to Unions?" *Philadelphia Tribune*, September 29, 1992; Bissinger, *Prayer for the City*, 209–210; Vincent Thompson, "New Contract Marks End of an Era," *Philadelphia Tribune*, October 9, 1992; "Committed Leaders Deserve Our Praise in Settling Strike," *Philadelphia Tribune*, October 9, 1992.

48. Bissinger, *Prayer for the City*, 416; Vincent Thompson, "Neal Is Named City's Top Cop," *Philadelphia Tribune*, August 21, 1992; Vincent Thompson, "First Black Named Fire Commissioner," *Philadelphia Tribune*, June 26, 1992; "The Realities of Race in Selecting a Superintendent," *Philadelphia Tribune*, June 14, 1994.

49. Bissinger, *Prayer for the City*, 371. For one example of national coverage, see Dale Russakoff, "Another Kind of Help; Philadelphia Mayor Offers Message of Hope, Calls for Major Policy Change to Aid Cities," *Washington Post*, March 20, 1994.

50. Vincent Thompson, "Community Groups Welcome Empowerment Zone: $100 Million Will Be Funneled to Philly and Camden," *Philadelphia Tribune*, December 23, 1994; *Empowerment Zone and Enterprise Community Program: Improvements Occurred in Communities, but the Effect of the Program Is Unclear* (Washington, DC: U.S. Government Accountability Office, September 2006), 122, available at https://www.gao.gov/new.items/d06727.pdf.

51. "John Street Calls for 'Unity': Democratic Nominee Eyes November Elections," *Philadelphia Tribune*, May 21, 1999.

52. Robin Leary, "Power Play! John Street and Dwight Evans Call the Shots; Now, Some Are Firing Back," *Philadelphia Tribune*, April 9, 1996.

53. Vincent Thompson, "Leaders Outline Agenda for Future," *Philadelphia Tribune*, October 6, 1992.

54. Feffer, "Land Belongs to the People," 89–90.

55. Barnett Wright, "The Philadelphia Negro 1899–1999: Before, during, and after W.E.B. DuBois," *Philadelphia Tribune*, December 7, 1999, 2, 38.

8

The Insurgent Nature of Black Politics in Contemporary Philadelphia

Stephen J. McGovern

The most prominent feature of urban politics in most American cities during the latter half of the twentieth century was the broad influence wielded by a governing coalition led by downtown-oriented business elites. At a time when cities were suffering from a devastating loss of jobs and residents due to deindustrialization and suburbanization, such regimes emphasized the virtues of promoting an emerging postindustrial economy based on commerce, finance, real estate, information, technology, and innovation that would be centered in the downtown core. A downtown-centric revitalization strategy, they promised, would generate an abundance of jobs and tax revenue that would then flow to outlying neighborhoods throughout the city.[1]

Although downtown-oriented regimes clearly worked to the advantage of white business leaders as well as other groups with a direct stake in urban redevelopment, such as the building trades, these regimes were typically biracial or multiracial and often led by Black or Latino mayors. The chief executive officers of major corporations, managing partners of prestigious law firms, and heads of department stores, medical centers, and universities understood that, to pursue their progrowth agendas over the long term, they needed the governmental authority that could come only by securing the consistent support of a majority of the voting public in cities with rising minority populations. In the early years of regime politics, therefore, white business elites appealed to African American politicians and voters by vowing to back various civil rights measures. Later on, they committed to supporting affirmative action policies that provided government jobs and contracts to people of color. As time passed, business leaders became adept at using their considerable stockpile of material resources to enlist the cooperation of Black politicians and key groups within the Black middle class through the strategic deployment of selective incentives and "small opportunities." In this way, biracial (or multiracial in some places) regimes enabled public officials and private groups to come together around a common agenda and govern effectively.[2]

Philadelphia fit the mold of regime politics during this period. The leaders of large corporations, banks, real estate development firms, utilities, hotels, and hospitals, and the many enterprises that provided services to these entities, joined forces in advocating for the rejuvenation of Center City, Philadelphia, as the best hope for stimulating the economic growth and revitalization of the entire city. With the once-massive manufacturing sector severely diminished after decades of deindustrialization, most politicians—white and nonwhite—had come to view a downtown-centric strategy as the only viable path. The city's first Black mayor, Wilson Goode (1983–1991), presided over a governing coalition that vigorously supported commercial office development, culminating in an unprecedented transformation of the downtown skyline. His successor, Ed Rendell (1992–2000), continued to prioritize the redevelopment of Center City by energetically promoting the arts, culture, entertainment, and tourism.[3]

But, while Center City thrived under downtown-oriented regimes, the rest of the city suffered. The burgeoning postindustrial economy produced employment opportunities, but it was a bifurcated labor market featuring high-skilled, high-paying jobs for professionals and managers at one end of the spectrum and a larger segment of low-skilled, low-paying jobs at the other end. Downtown growth also generated tax revenue, but not nearly enough to respond to the overwhelming needs of numerous increasingly distressed neighborhoods. Philadelphia, like so many other U.S. cities that pursued a similar path to economic growth, was characterized by uneven development. A flourishing business district ringed by a tight band of prosperous residential neighborhoods was surrounded by a much larger swath of urban blight and concentrated poverty.[4]

The turn of the twenty-first century witnessed a rebellion of sorts. The city's leading Black politician at the time, John Street, who had served as president of the city council during most of the 1990s and who had worked closely with Mayor Rendell, declared that it was time for the city to change course. He was elected mayor in 1999 promising to redirect scarce resources away from downtown and toward its long-neglected neighborhoods. It was a natural turn for Street, who came out of a time-honored tradition of neighborhood-oriented Black politics. Attention to community needs and constituent services was built into his political DNA. Under his Neighborhood Transformation Initiative, the city issued $295 million in bonds to fund a massive campaign to arrest blight through the demolition of thousands of abandoned and derelict buildings, the assembly of large parcels of vacant land, and the conveyance of those parcels to nonprofit and for-profit developers who would produce a mix of subsidized and market-rate housing. However, Street's ambitious plan to transform destitute neighborhoods raised anxiety about mass evictions and gentrification, much like discredited urban renewal programs of the past, while failing to generate enough resources to overcome extensive blight. The Street administration was also hampered by FBI investigations into reports of widespread corruption in city government and subsequent indictments of several high-profile officials.[5]

Notwithstanding some of the disappointments associated with the Street administration (2000–2008), African American and Latino citizens still had reason to believe that city hall would continue to pursue a more neighborhood-oriented agenda going forward. A number of broad social and political changes were beginning to spur shifts in local politics. In the political economy realm, a wave of mergers and acquisitions had resulted in the relocation or closing of corporate offices in many cities that, in turn, contributed to a decline in organized business advocacy in city politics. As the clout of once-potent groups such as the Greater Philadelphia Chamber of Commerce waned, the downtown-led regime no longer seemed as formidable. At the same time, many cities like Philadelphia began to experience an influx of young college-educated individuals attracted by job opportunities in the growing postindustrial economy and the social and cultural amenities of urban life. This "creative class" was more inclined to embrace progressive politics and thus offered a potential counterweight to a somewhat weakened business sector.[6]

Like John Street, Michael Nutter was an experienced Black politician who, for many years, represented a struggling district as a member of city council. But Nutter was even better positioned to take advantage of recent changes in the city's political landscape. He had acquired a reputation as a tireless advocate of good government and ethics reform. As a member of city council, Nutter had been a leader in fights for campaign finance reform, a more transparent process for awarding city contracts, and the establishment of an independent board of ethics. His candidacy for mayor in 2007 resonated with voters who had grown weary of a scandal-plagued city hall. In a diverse and crowded five-candidate field, Nutter won the Democratic primary with an impressive 37 percent of the vote, performing equally well in Black and white wards. An analysis of the election results by the *Philadelphia Inquirer* concluded that Nutter's biracial support "made history" for a mayoral primary election in the city.[7]

Mayor Nutter (2008–2016) honored his commitment to advancing integrity in city government by successfully pushing for a more orderly and rational approach to policy making. He led the battle to overhaul the city's archaic zoning code and moved decisively to restore the City Planning Commission as the primary driver of urban development. Under his watch, the city adopted its first comprehensive plan since 1960. However, Nutter was a victim of bad timing, taking office just a few months before the onset of the Great Recession of 2008, which necessitated deep and unpopular budget and programmatic cuts. Meanwhile, Nutter responded to a surge in gun violence by directing his police force to adopt more aggressive tactics, including a greater reliance on pedestrian stops and frisks. The mayor contended that his emphasis on law and order worked, pointing to a 37 percent decline in the city's homicide rate between 2007 and 2014. Finally, while Nutter was a champion of deliberate city planning, as opposed to the city's previous tendency to allow developers to shape land use decision-making on an ad-hoc basis, he was unabashedly progrowth and content to foster new construction where market demand was strongest. Accordingly, Nutter returned to the practice of earlier administrations by emphasizing the revitalization of Center City. Massive projects were authorized on Market Street East, University City (just west of the downtown business district), and the two waterfronts. While Center City prospered, sprawling sections of the city remained blighted. Philadelphia's 26 percent poverty rate was the highest among the ten largest U.S. cities.[8]

There were voices within the Black political establishment in favor of robust governmental action to confront chronic poverty and deepening inequality. Wilson Goode Jr., the son of the former mayor, successfully promoted a number of notable progressive policies from his position as an at-large member of city council, including fair lending and community reinvestment regulations for local banks and workforce diversity mandates for firms with city contracts.[9]

But another strain of Black politics in the city remained immersed in the factional battles of the Democratic Party machine. Some of the leading Black politicians of the era, such as Councilwoman Marian Tasco and State Assemblyman (and, later, Congressman) Dwight Evans, were renowned for their ability to sway electoral outcomes through their power base in Northwest Philadelphia. An endorsement from their organization, the Northwest Coalition, which could be counted on to turn out large numbers of voters on Election Day, often proved decisive in energizing a campaign and charting a course to victory. Another longtime practitioner of relationship-based, machine-oriented politics was Councilwoman Jannie Blackwell, who held her third district seat between 1992 and 2020. She raised eyebrows across the city in 2005 by opposing campaign finance and ethics reform bills advocated by then councilman Michael Nutter. Blackwell justified her stance by insisting that minority contractors would be disadvantaged in bidding for city contracts if they were required to reveal campaign donations.[10]

Perhaps the most important representative of a transactional approach to city politics during the first two decades of the twenty-first century has been Darrell Clarke, who succeeded Street as the district council member from North Philadelphia in 2000 after Street was elected mayor. Clarke then continued to follow the path of his mentor by becoming city council president in 2012. He soon developed a reputation as a master of legislative politics and a shrewd dealmaker. Major interest groups, especially within the real estate industry, courted his favor, often with generous campaign contributions. For his part, Clarke became an enthusiastic backer of economic development in his district, pointing to the revitalization of North Philadelphia as his proudest accomplishment. Residents have been more ambivalent. Many have expressed anxiety about gentrification and some have protested against what they see as Temple University's encroachment into their neighborhood. Clarke has sought to expand opportunities for citizens to participate in city policy making through community-based budget hearings and public forums, but he has also shied away from the progressive impulse to use city government energetically as a means of redistributing income and wealth. He asserted: "I believe genuinely that the best social program is a good job. I would hope that, at a certain point in time, we don't have to have a sustained, broad-based social-service network." Philadelphia's poverty rate has barely fluctuated over the past two decades even as parts of the city have experienced increased prosperity.[11]

The lack of progress in responding to fundamental problems affecting the city over an extended period of time raises questions about the nature of politics in Philadelphia. For example, what accounts for the ongoing electoral appeal of governing coalitions that consistently favor downtown revitalization over neighborhood redevelopment? Why did so many voters in marginalized neighborhoods continue to support the downtown-oriented regime? Why was there an apparent dearth of oppositional activism?

One theory emphasizes the substantial base of material resources and organizational cohesion of downtown-led regimes in contrast to the relative dearth of resources of fledgling neighborhood-based movements that are often riven by racial, ethnic, cultural, and class divisions. That uneven playing field gives progrowth elites a decisive advantage in building alliances with key interest groups in communities of color that, in turn, help consolidate nonwhite electoral support.[12]

Another theory drills deeper into the imbalance of power explanation by highlighting how white-dominated interests have systematically oppressed Black community organizations and institutions in the past with lasting consequences for contemporary political activity. Structural racism thus largely accounts for Black political quiescence in the face of persistent neglect by downtown-oriented regimes.[13]

A third approach to explaining the puzzle of low levels of Black opposition to progrowth coalitions focuses on political leadership within the African American community. Some scholars contend that Black mayors are generally motivated to contain grassroots protest, or, better yet, prevent its emergence in the first place, to minimize any possible threat to their authority and then do so by deploying various techniques to mollify populations that might otherwise vent their discontent through community organizing, street protests, or even violence. Others examine how some Black politicians seek to divert attention away from structural and institutional problems requiring extensive governmental intervention by harping on discourses that stress the limitations of individuals and the desirability of self-help initiatives. Still others point to the practice of Black politicians allied with downtown-oriented regimes relying on appeals to racial pride and solidarity as a means of delivering votes on Election Day. Both discursive strategies have the effect of subduing incipient protest.[14]

A final explanation for the relative paucity of oppositional politics in Black and Latino neighborhoods in recent decades concerns the nation's turn toward fervent law enforcement starting in the 1970s. With crime rates on the rise, governments at the federal, state, and local levels adopted a much tougher approach to ensuring public safety. However, overzealous policing and prosecution fell disproportionately on communities of color and soon yielded the highest incarceration rates in the world. The many adverse impacts on young Black males have been particularly harsh. Mass incarceration has severely undermined their potential to complete their education and find gainful employment. It has ripped apart families and depleted community institutions. Moreover, the expansion of the carceral state has had crucial consequences for the vitality of democracy. It has undermined civic and political engagement by stifling voices of dissent and undercutting community-based activism and the development of organized protest movements. All of this begets political passivity in marginalized communities and reinforces the inclination of Black mayors to cooperate with business-led regimes that provide a means for reasonably effective governance, although at the substantial price of perpetuating racial and economic inequities throughout the city.[15]

In sum, many factors help explain the persistence of urban regimes that tolerate and even exacerbate uneven development and profound inequality. Many of these factors help account for the surprising lack of oppositional activism at the grass roots. And yet, notwithstanding the powerful demobilization forces at work in Black and brown communities in Philadelphia, some nascent community-based organizing began to surface after 2000. A coalition of affordable housing providers pressed capably for a land bank and housing trust fund. And as poverty rates remained stubbornly high despite a thriving economy in Center City, a vibrant living wage movement erupted.[16]

But the most sustained and effective organizing centered around the issue of criminal justice. By the 2010s, years of passivity were giving way to a heightened level of concern and action with respect to racial injustice within the criminal justice system. Activism aimed at combating racist policing and prosecutorial practices that had fueled mass incarceration began to emerge and intensify.

To a large extent, Philadelphia's reputation as a city of law and order can be traced to one individual. Frank Rizzo grew up on the white working-class streets of South Philadelphia, joined the police department in 1943, and rose through its ranks to become commissioner during the tumultuous 1960s before being elected and reelected as mayor in the 1970s. He remained a major political presence in the 1980s, running unsuccessfully for mayor two more times before dying of a heart attack in the midst of yet another mayoral campaign in 1991.[17]

Rizzo held power at a time of escalating crime and racial tension, and he vowed to crack down on the criminals he felt posed a singular threat to the future of the city. He took pride in his image as a fierce crime fighter, jauntily placing a nightstick in his cummerbund at prominent social events and calling himself "the toughest cop in America." However, Rizzo's aggressive policing tactics provoked intense opposition from other quarters of the city. The police department was notorious for trampling on the constitutional rights of citizens, particularly residents of African American neighborhoods. Police brutality was widespread during the Rizzo years, and Black people bore the brunt of the punishment.[18]

Rizzo cast a long shadow over Philadelphia's criminal justice system. Police officers revered him, grateful for his willingness to defend them against sharp criticism from civil rights and Black Nationalist leaders. They also appreciated his efforts to nurture a powerful union of police officers. Today, as *Philadelphia Magazine* put it, the "Fraternal Order of Police maintains Rizzo's legacy by protecting cops against attempts to punish them for misconduct to a degree that no other public-sector union can." Moreover, a generation of politicians took note of how a forceful approach to law and order could advance one's political career. Prominent figures such as Arlen Specter and Ed Rendell used the district attorney's office as a springboard to higher office. The city's first female district attorney, Lynne Abraham, who served from 1991 until 2010, was known for her zealous prosecutorial style and frequent requests for the imposition of capital punishment, a practice that led to her being dubbed "the deadliest DA." Even some of the city's most notable Black politicians followed the tough-on-crime tradition pioneered by Rizzo. Michael Nutter's unapologetic support for the aggressive use of police stops and searches is an example. Veteran civil rights and criminal defense attorney, David Rudovsky, offered this assessment of the culture that developed around law enforcement: "In Philadelphia, we had as law-and-order people as you could have as prosecutors.... It was kind of the epicenter [of] we'll lock up as many people as we can. We had the highest ... per capita jail population of any major city in the country by far.... Very harsh criminal justice policies."[19]

The turn toward more intensive law enforcement in Philadelphia, and throughout the United States, has generated ample debate among scholars and policy makers with respect to its effects on crime rates. But what have become increasingly indisputable are the costs of punitive policing and prosecution on individuals, families, and communities that have been targeted by the criminal justice system.[20]

When contemplating how the emphasis on crime control over a long period of time has affected daily life, a useful starting point is the fact that Philadelphia has the highest incarceration rate of any of the largest cities in the United States. One of every three Black men in the city experiences jail at some point in their lifetimes. The toll on these individuals in terms of lost opportunities and future prospects is immense. The staggering costs then ripple out to affect family, friends, classmates, coworkers, and neighbors. While the impact of the deepening carceral state did not attract much attention in the media in its early years, people in impacted communities could not help but notice. One longtime criminal defense attorney observed: "[Since] ... the 1970s ... we have just been dropping more and more human beings into jail cells and while maybe the nightly news and a lot of big newspapers didn't notice it, people were noticing it in their jobs.... And they were noticing it in their churches. And they were noticing it in the bills that they had to pay for prisons." Community leaders like Reverend Gregory Holston of the United Methodist Church in North Philadelphia reflected on the economic costs of mass incarceration:

> If you take young black men out of a community in the tens of thousands what does that do to a community? How much economic wealth have you taken out of the community when you do that? Cause those young men were working and many of them, they would be providing income in some way to their families, to their children, to their parents. And so the economic loss and not having their presence of working in the community—devastating.

Reverend Holston proceeded to discuss how mass incarceration affects family life and, particularly, children:

The social costs of being taken away from your children. I've pastored for 18 years and I had taught seven years in the Philadelphia school system. I can tell you children who don't get to see their family, it deeply affects them. I have seen young people literally when I would mention, tell me about your father, they would fall under the table in tears, talking about how much they missed their father, because they did not have their presence in their lives. I've heard parents who would lie to their children and say or lie to their grandchildren and say their father was away for a little bit and he'll be back instead of telling them the devastation that they'll be in prison for the next 20 years.

The myriad costs of the carceral state extend beyond the period of incarceration. After release, returning citizens struggle to adjust to their new lives in searching for employment, resuming their education, and reconnecting with their families. One formerly incarcerated person, who went on to become a prominent activist in the city, recalled how a landlord reneged on a lease that he was about to sign upon discovering his criminal conviction: "There's a social stigma around a criminal record. So . . . it's hard to find apartments. . . . I felt so powerless in that moment. Here I am a person who's trying to do all of the right things. I serve the community. I'm working. I just want a decent place to live and y'know it was yanked from under my feet because of someone else's stereotype of who I was. And I was hurt. And so I have a lot of personal experiences of being discriminated against."[21]

Many persevere and manage to once again become productive members of the community, but others falter in trying to overcome setback after setback. For some, persistent limited opportunities and pervasive discrimination yield frustration and sometimes desperation that leads back to criminal activity. Reverend Holston comments on the high risk of recidivism:

My wife and I talk all the time, my brothers-in-law, they all went to jail. Her brothers all went to jail. Our nephews all went to jail. They're coming out now, and they're in their 30s, but they went in when they were 14, 15, and 16. And they're coming back with no skills, with no education. And many of them are going back to the same issues and getting re-arrested again. It's my brother-in-law. It's people my age. My nephews. And now it's their children. . . . The same pattern of incarceration remains. I don't know what you say? What do you say about this onslaught that has occurred in our communities?[22]

Given the widespread and long-term costs of mass incarceration, it might be reasonable to expect some political opposition. But, for many years, intensive policing and prosecution did not spark much resistance within communities that absorbed the heaviest burden, for two reasons. First, some neighborhoods had suffered from steadily rising crime rates since the 1950s, and so residents may have welcomed a stronger commitment to law enforcement. Second, as the costs of mass incarceration mounted, a profound sense of demoralization set in among those whose primary encounter with the state had been through an oppressive criminal justice system. It is hardly surprising that many who are directly and indirectly affected by the carceral state would perceive little value in participating in local politics. Alienation and withdrawal from the polity became the norm.[23]

Nevertheless, some resistance to carceral state policies and practices came from within the criminal justice system. Criminal defense and civil rights attorneys recognized the threats posed to citizens and communities and litigated tirelessly on a case-by-case basis to uphold the Constitution and advocate for a less punitive approach to law enforcement. In 2008, for example, David Rudovsky filed a class action lawsuit to address the dismal conditions and overcrowding in the city's jails. Two years later, he and the American Civil Liberties Union (ACLU) of Pennsylvania sued the Philadelphia Police Department to challenge the spike in unconstitutional stops and frisks that overwhelmingly involved Black and Latino Philadelphians. The filing of the lawsuit alone drew attention to the issue. When the Nutter administration agreed to sign a consent decree and subject the police department to an ongoing monitoring of stops and frisks by civil rights attorneys and the federal district court, that further enhanced the potential for expanding public awareness. Local newspapers made a habit of reporting on the city's progress in reducing illegal stops and frisks over the next several years. Such media scrutiny helped illuminate what many residents of overpoliced neighborhoods had deemed to be a serious problem.[24]

Meanwhile, the capacity of residents of overpoliced neighborhoods to call attention to problems they were witnessing firsthand from encounters with the police expanded with the advent of cell phones. Videos of police abuse and brutality provided incontrovertible evidence in a courtroom to counter a narrative that had mostly been controlled by a testifying police officer. Such videos also spread through the mainstream media and, more important, through social media coverage—a process that raised awareness about an issue that victims of police misconduct knew all too well. In this way, cell phones began to empower residents to carry out their own monitoring of the police department, record incidents of police misconduct, and tell their own stories.[25]

Victims of the carceral state were beginning to find other ways to advocate for change by the first decade of the twenty-first century. Although mass incarceration exerted a powerful demobilizing effect over an extended period, interviews with activists showed "it also means that some have a level of awakening about how the system truly works that others don't." And, while some felt a crippling despair, others never gave up their faith that change was possible: "African-American people have always been our most creative in the center of most of our oppression. And so that's happening now. And people are responding. So there is hope for real change. And as we move and organize for that change, we are always the ones who kind of set the pace." After serving a fifteen-year prison sentence, Reuben Jones joined with other incarcerated and formerly incarcerated men to form an organization called Frontline Dads in 2002 to help fathers rebuild relationships with their children. Jones then used that formative experience to pursue other forms of political advocacy, a path that led to his group's successful drive to convince the city council to pass legislation in 2011 to discourage employment discrimination against returning citizens. The so-called ban-the-box law prohibited employers from asking job candidates on employment applications whether they had previously been convicted of a criminal offense.[26]

Burgeoning concerns about the criminal justice system within urban communities received a substantial boost in 2010 with the publication of Michelle Alexander's pathbreaking book, *The New Jim Crow*. Even criminal justice professionals who had been very sympathetic to criticisms about punitive policing and prosecution had not fully grasped the magnitude of the crisis surrounding mass incarceration. District Attorney Larry Krasner did not recall using the phrase "mass incarceration" before he read Alexander's book. *The New Jim Crow* opened up the floodgates to a stream of highly regarded publications documenting the brutal impacts of mass incarceration, including Bryan Stevenson's *Just Mercy*, John Pfaff's *Locked In*, James Forman's *Locking Up Our Own*, and Emily Bazelon's *Charged*, all of which strengthened fledgling mobilization drives in numerous neighborhoods.[27]

Perhaps the most important spark for mass-based protest around the criminal justice system in Philadelphia was the police shooting of a young Black man, Michael Brown, in Ferguson, Missouri in 2014. Criminal defense attorney David Rudovsky characterized the incident as "a big event" and one that generated "a huge reaction" in the city. Reverend Holston remembered:

> It was galvanizing. It was a sense that after the Obama, or still in the Obama administration, and still having an African-American president, things still haven't changed much in terms of police conduct. And for some it was a wake-up call. For others it was a very galvanizing moment, particularly for young people who thought, I remember them saying clearly: "We thought you had taken care of this. Why are we still dealing with this as an issue?" And so that movement galvanized us back here in Philadelphia.

The jury verdict exonerating Officer Darren Wilson in Brown's death triggered an outpouring of protest. Thousands spilled out onto Philadelphia's streets that night.[28]

Reverend Holston emphasized that the protests surrounding the events in Ferguson did not fade away. Rather, they motivated young people, in particular, to organize for the long haul: "In the days after [the Brown verdict] many of these young people filled my church for three or four days coming to mourn about what happened and to cry and to organize. And many of those young people are involved in organizations across the city, organizing around criminal justice, are coming out of that movement." Holston himself was a prominent leader of POWER (Philadelphians Organized to Witness, Empower, and Rebuild), a potent, faith-based coalition founded in 2010 to build grassroots power to effect policy changes at the state and local levels. It had been in the vanguard of successful campaigns to establish a living wage for airport workers and increase state funding for public education. But events in Ferguson prompted POWER to shift its agenda to criminal justice reform by demanding an end to police stops and frisks, a fully funded Police Advisory Commission, and a reduction in the city's jail population.[29] (See Fig. 8.1.)

Many activists in Philadelphia point to the Black Lives Matter movement as a vital factor in drumming up public support for an overhaul of the criminal justice system. One called it, "the modern civil rights advocacy group of our time." Another activist asserted that the Black Lives Matter movement "really changed the conversation about criminal justice and racial injustice and policing and who's locked up and why and who's targeted. . . . It's also part of lifting up the consciousness of people in Philly."[30]

The city of Philadelphia had already taken steps with respect to addressing problems with its police department. In response to media reports revealing a 50 percent increase over the previous year in officer-involved shootings in 2012, Police Commissioner Charles Ramsey, one of the city's most prominent Black officials, requested in 2013 that the federal government's Department of Justice (DOJ) undertake a formal review of his department's use of lethal force. Ramsey also mandated the video recording of all interrogations in homicide cases and halted the department's practice of detaining suspects who had not been charged for longer than thirty-six hours. The following year, Ramsey initiated a pilot program requiring a limited number of police officers to wear body cameras while on duty. Finally, in the wake of the crisis in Ferguson and following the release of the DOJ report finding that the Philadelphia Police Department had relied excessively on the use of deadly force, Mayor Michael Nutter established a police community oversight board to consider ninety-one recommendations made by federal investigators. The reform initiatives apparently caught the eye of Presi-

Figure 8.1 Black congregations have been at the forefront of activism to reform the Philadelphia Police Department.

dent Barack Obama, who named Commissioner Ramsey as cochair of his own Task Force on Twenty-First Century Policing in December 2014.[31]

Ramsey is credited with being proactive in promoting the external review of local practices and instituting some new policies. However, other experts were underwhelmed by the police department's limited efforts to respond to the DOJ's "very critical report." Moreover, by all accounts, the Nutter administration dragged its feet in complying with the consent decree signed in 2011 to reduce substantially the unconstitutional stops and searches that disproportionately target people of color. A 2015 report filed with the federal district court concluded that the police had made over two hundred thousand stops during the preceding year, about the same number as in 2011, and 37 percent of those stops were conducted without reasonable suspicion, down only marginally from 47 percent in 2011.[32]

If progress toward reforming the police department was rather tepid during the Nutter administration, there was even less interest in addressing another major aspect of the criminal justice system. There appeared to be no significant policy initiatives or even any sustained discussion around mass incarceration for much of the time that Nutter was in office. The one exception took place at the tail end of the Nutter years when various criminal justice stakeholders learned about a grant opportunity sponsored by the MacArthur Foundation aimed at encouraging municipalities to reduce their jail populations. A consensus formed in favor of applying for a $150,000 planning grant in February 2015. In the process of collecting data for the grant application, the district attorney's office, the Defender Association of Philadelphia, the courts, the probation office, the police department, and other offices with a stake in the criminal justice system were surprised to discover that Philadelphia's incarceration rates were the highest of the ten largest cities in the United States. The chief defender of the city's Defender Association, Keir Bradford-Grey, recalled: "It really just started as an exploratory thing. Hey, where are we? And we found that we were really bad. So then it was we *really* need to do this." The effort paid off when the MacArthur Foundation awarded the city a planning grant to continue its initiative to identify strategies to lower its jail population. This represented the first significant move by the Nutter administration to address the problem of mass incarceration.[33]

Meanwhile, activists associated with a growing number of community-based organizations had already been paying close attention to incarceration rates in the city and state. A group called Decarcerate PA was created in 2011 to oppose plans to construct three state prisons at a time when Governor Tom Corbett was slashing $1 billion in funding for public education. Although that campaign failed, it focused attention in Philadelphia on the dichotomy between expenditures on prisons versus those on schools and how excessive spending on the former perpetuates the school-to-prison pipeline. In 2015, when Councilman Bobby Henom announced a bill to purchase land and build a new $300–$500 million jail to replace the aging and decrepit House of Corrections, a coalition of community-based organizations mobilized in opposition. No one denied the need to shut down the House of Corrections, where conditions were abysmal. But activists contended that no new jail was needed because large numbers of people incarcerated in Philadelphia were behind bars prior to trial simply because they could not afford to post bail. Accordingly, if the city found ways to reduce pretrial detention rates through bail reform, it could shutter the House of Corrections and avoid having to build an expensive new jail. The savings could then be redirected to public schools and communities adversely affected by decades of mass incarceration.[34]

The initial response to the activists was not encouraging. The Nutter administration had supported the new jail and most members of city council saw it as a done deal. But the controversy flared at the same time that the School Reform Commission was planning to close nearly two dozen schools over considerable public opposition. The coalition against the new jail mounted a strenuous campaign, testifying at council sessions on numerous occasions for the rest of the year and meeting privately with wavering council members. They asked: "Do you want to publicly support spending $300–$500 million on a new jail while the city can't fully fund its schools? Do you want that out there as your position?" Social media messaging on the tension between spending on prisons and spending on schools also proved productive, as members of city council began to reassess their previous stands.[35]

Perhaps the most effective tactic in the battle over the proposed new jail was the coalition's engagement in electoral politics. The mayoral election of 2015 was in full swing and activists seized on the opportunity to press the issue about mass incarceration and raise the profile of criminal justice reform in Philadelphia.

For most of his long tenure as an at-large member of Philadelphia's city council, Jim Kenney never distinguished himself as a proponent of criminal justice reform. He was not a member of the public safety committee or any other committees that required him to pay close attention to issues involving policing and prosecution and so rarely had occasion to take any prominent stance on such matters. When he did, his positions were likely to reflect the more conservative attitudes of his white working-class electoral base. For example, he opposed early efforts to establish a civilian board to oversee police activity, and, in comments to a reporter in 1999, he objected to burdening police officers with too many restrictions regarding the use of force: "I mean, come on, you can't use flashlights, you can't use clubs on the head, you can't shoot anybody. What's next? Are we going to hand them feather dusters?"[36]

However, many working within the criminal justice sector in Philadelphia observed that Kenney's views evolved over time. A veteran criminal defense attorney, David Rudovsky, casts light on Kenney's transformation:

> He was a South Philadelphia politician. But I can tell you he came to our office when he was on city council . . . in 2013. We had worked on a couple of things together. And he said, "Why are we locking up people for marijuana in Philadelphia?" Because it was typically 90 percent black kids . . . despite the fact that marijuana is used equally by whites and blacks. You look at the data every month—5,000 arrests, 90 percent black. He said, "Down by the stadiums [in a predominantly white section of South Philadelphia], the white kids are smoking dope all the time. Nobody does anything." He said, "I want to get an ordinance in city council decriminalizing small amounts of marijuana. Would you help us?"

Rudovsky proceeded to note the irony of a white city councilman, who had traditionally taken moderate or conservative positions on criminal justice issues, now advocating a bill to decriminalize the possession of small amounts of marijuana over the objections of a Black mayor, a Black district attorney, and a Black police commissioner. Kenney introduced his bill in 2014 and then secured a veto-proof majority of city council to go along before persuading a reluctant Mayor Nutter to sign the bill after agreeing to a minor compromise.[37]

Kenney's leadership on the marijuana decriminalization bill might seem like a thin foundation for staking a claim as a progressive advocate of criminal justice reform in the 2015 mayoral election. But he used that experience to address broader concerns about the relationship between mass incarceration and poverty. Kenney argued that locking up tens of thousands of Black males, often for low-level, nonviolent offenses, had severely impaired their capacity to finish school and secure decent jobs, with tragic consequences for entire communities. Any serious effort to remedy concentrated poverty, therefore, required sustained attention to mass incarceration.[38]

An early indication of Kenney's commitment on this issue came before he even announced his candidacy. At a meeting with reporters and editors of the *Philadelphia Inquirer*, he was asked about his proudest legislative accomplishments. Kenney singled out the marijuana law, noting the sharp drop in arrests: "It's not the marijuana issue that's important. It's the criminal-record issue that's important. If you want people having an actual shot at improving their lives, an arrest record is a piano on their back." It is hardly a coincidence that Kenney gave a speech extolling the benefits of decriminalizing marijuana on the same day that he formally announced his candidacy for mayor.[39]

Activists concerned about mass incarceration sought to capitalize on Kenney's expressed desire to rethink the city's long-held preference for punitive law enforcement. Early in the campaign, an activist asked him at a public meeting whether he would commit to opposing the city's plan to construct a new jail. He said yes. Activists quickly tweeted out the message that Kenney was the first prominent mayoral candidate to reject the jail.[40]

Using candidate forums to press mayoral candidates to take clear stands on important issues became a favorite tactic of grassroots activists in 2015. For instance, the faith-based organization, POWER, hosted a forum in which it posed various questions about the criminal justice system. Reverend Gregory Holston recalled that Kenney promised to end the controversial police policy of stop and frisk, which had been disproportionately deployed in Black and Latino neighborhoods. POWER vowed to hold Kenney accountable for his promise.[41]

Kenney's pronouncements on mass incarceration, police reform, and poverty, along with a host of other high-profile issues, struck a chord with voters. He assembled a broad-based electoral coalition consisting of his old base of blue-collar workers and building trades unions along with millennials, LGBTQ groups, and immigrant justice organizations, while adding substantial support from many Black voters impressed with his determination to attack concentrated poverty through criminal justice reform. Kenney coasted to victory in the Democratic Party primary in May 2015, defeating a prominent Black state senator, Anthony Hardy Williams, and the former district attorney Lynne Abraham by wide margins before handily winning the general election in November.[42]

Eager to ease police-community tensions during his campaign, Kenney had promised to halt the practice of stop and frisk. "If [I'm] mayor, stop and frisk will end in Philadelphia, no question," he said. Kenney was thus acceding to demands from Philadelphians who felt subjected to overly zealous policing and called for an end to pedestrian stops and frisks. Police disproportionately administered this tactic in Black and Latino neighborhoods, which reinforced popular perceptions of a racially biased police department. But only six weeks into his administration, Kenney adopted a more nuanced position. He explained that police officers would continue to employ the tactic but only when they had a reasonable suspicion of illegal activity. Civil rights attorney David Rudovsky had no objection to the mayor's clarification, commenting that a stop and frisk conducted in accordance with the Constitution was a legitimate policing tool. Many others, however, saw the move as an unacceptable retreat from a solemn vow. In April, citizens vented their anger at a series of demonstrations in Center City. One protester declared: "It's only happening, pretty much, to minorities and poor people. I'm really mad at Kenney for backing down. He ran saying he was going to stop stop and frisk, and now he's backing down."[43]

Notwithstanding Kenney's somewhat clumsy handling of the stop-and-frisk issue at the outset, his administration actually began to make progress working behind the scenes. Indeed, the turnaround from the previous administration was quite striking. After Mayor Nutter entered into the consent decree in 2011 authorizing periodic and detailed reviews of the police department's stop-and-frisk practices by the ACLU with ongoing federal court supervision, the city simply failed to impose policy changes that would reduce the number of pedestrian stops, in general, and the number of illegal stops, in particular. Rudovsky observed that the police department did some retraining, "but they never implemented internal accountability measures that would make a difference. I mean you got to sanction the officer eventually. More importantly, you got to sanction the sergeant who's reading every one of those forms and not doing anything about it." After a sixth report over a five-year period showing little improvement, civil rights attorneys were close to seeking a court order holding the city in contempt.[44]

The new administration under Mayor Kenney brought a palpable change in direction regarding stop and frisk. In accounting for the policy switch from Nutter to Kenney, Rudovsky suggested that the threat of court sanctions hanging over the new administration may have been a factor. He speculated that pressure from the Black community to honor his campaign pledge also mattered. But, in the end, Rudovsky asserted that Kenney "also knew it was the right thing to do" and that he genuinely "want[ed] a change." He further explained: "They started putting in these accountability measures. So they had a very good person in the department reviewing cases, seeing where multiple offenders, police officers, were regularly stopping people without cause." Implicit bias training and more frequent audits by supervisors resulted in a 35 percent decline in pedestrian stops during Kenney's first year in office. After two years, the number of pedestrian stops dropped by 50 percent along with a similar decrease in the percentage of illegal stops.[45]

However, while police stops declined dramatically, African Americans in Philadelphia were still much more likely to be detained temporarily than white people. According to the 2018 ACLU report, Black people, who make up 44 percent of the city's population, accounted for 69 percent of all stops during the first half of 2017. Mary Catherine Roper of ACLU Pennsylvania elaborated: "So they've reduced the number of stops, but when you look at the stops that are happening and who's being stopped in what neighborhood, we have put out report after report after report saying you've got these very white neighborhoods where most of the people being stopped are black. What's going on there?"[46]

In addition to people of color being differentially affected, another lingering problem with the police department's deployment of stop and frisk was the remarkably low "hit rate." The initial justification for the sudden jump in stop and frisk during the Nutter administration was to counter a rise in gun violence. But only an infinitesimal percentage of police stops led to the recovery of a gun or other contraband. Most police stops were motivated by quality-of-life offenses that generally did not necessitate a full-fledged stop and frisk. The weak justification for pedestrian stops, combined with the racially biased manner of its implementation, continued to undermine the legitimacy of the police in many Black and brown communities.[47]

Another major issue that aroused the ire of many Philadelphians concerned the excessive use of force by some police officers. The issue had seized the nation's attention in 2014 following the shooting of Michael Brown in Ferguson, Missouri. Additional police shootings of young Black men in Louisiana and Minnesota, in July 2016, sparked six consecutive nights of street protests in Philadelphia organized by local Black Lives Matter activists seeking to block traffic and disrupt police activity. The protesters' rhetoric was militant and incendiary. A leader of the marches, Asa Khalif, declared: "Our method at times may be frowned upon, but we get results. We're not dumping on anyone who decides to have candlelight vigils, but we want action. If we don't get no justice, you don't get no police." The "weekend of rage" against the Philadelphia Police Department alienated some advocates of policing reforms who preferred a more restrained approach and prompted counterprotests to support the police. A few months later, however, the *Philadelphia Inquirer* published an op-ed essay by Harvard Law professor Randall Kennedy praising the Black Lives Matter movement for exposing structural racism within the criminal justice system while urging the movement to listen to insightful criticism and be more flexible.[48]

The problem of officer-involved shootings hit home a year later when Officer Ryan Pownall of the Philadelphia Police Department shot and fatally wounded a Black man, David Jones, as he ran from a pedestrian stop. Pownall had detained Jones after he had observed him riding a dirt bike "in a reckless manner." During an ensuing pat down, the two men began to struggle and Jones reached for a gun in his waistband. An eyewitness said that Jones then dropped his gun and fled. Pownall shot Jones in the back. Jones's gun was found on the ground 30–40 feet from his body. Pownall was put on desk duty while the police department conducted a lengthy investigation. The incident ignited a new series of street protests demanding that Pownall be dismissed and subjected to criminal prosecution. Police-community tensions escalated again later that summer after a demonstration and counterdemonstration involving Confederate monuments in Charlottesville, Virginia, resulted in the killing of a demonstrator by a white supremacist. Thousands of Philadelphians marched down Broad Street in solidarity with protesters in Charlottesville and to highlight "manifestations of white supremacy in Philadelphia."[49] (See Fig. 8.2.)

The surge in officer-involved shootings around the United States called attention to the issue of how police officers accused of misconduct are disciplined. The police commissioner may discipline such officers, perhaps suspending or even terminating them, but under the terms of the city's contract with the police union, the Fraternal Order of Police, such officers tend to receive highly favorable treatment in arbitration hearings by arbitrators approved by the Fraternal Order of Police, resulting in their reinstatement with back pay and overtime and their records being wiped clean after a two-year period of good behavior. Activists charged that the city's chronic failure to discipline rogue police officers eroded public confidence in the police department.[50]

Given Mayor Kenney's professed interest in reforming the criminal justice system, some observers believed that he might have been willing to reassess those arbitration rules when the police union contract expired in 2017. ACLU Pennsylvania's Mary Catherine Roper asserted, "I gotta tell you the one thing he could do but he hasn't shown the guts to do it any more than any of the preceding six mayors have had the guts to do it is seriously renegotiate that police contract and the disciplinary provisions." Other advocates of police reforms, however, pointed to the difficulty of a prounion

Figure 8.2 Street protest near city hall against the proliferation of police shootings.

mayor challenging labor-management procedures that had been in place for years—and a challenge not just to any municipal union but to one long regarded as wielding considerable clout in city politics. With this in mind, it appears that Kenney invested little political capital in renegotiating the arbitration rules applicable to police officers accused of misconduct; the new contract included only one minor change to those rules. Reformers within the activist community seem to recognize that they, too, may have missed an opportunity to apply pressure on the mayor and push for at least some improvements and others vowed not to make the same mistake when the current police contract expires.[51]

In addition to police-community relations, Kenney made it a point to talk, on a regular basis, about mass incarceration and its crippling effects on city residents and communities while he campaigned for mayor, so advocates of criminal justice reform were eager to see how he would react once in office. Planning to address mass incarceration had gotten a jump-start in the waning days of the Nutter administration when the city won a small planning grant from the MacArthur Foundation in May 2015. In April 2016, Philadelphia was chosen from among a field of 191 applicants to develop a plan to cut its jail population by 34 percent over the next three years while identifying and correcting racial biases in policing and prosecution. Partners from across the city's criminal justice system worked together to formulate and implement nineteen strategies to (1) steer appropriate nonviolent offenders away from the criminal justice system through diversion programs; (2) establish alternatives to cash bail; and (3) assist those already in prison to return to their communities more quickly and effectively.[52]

Early bail review was probably the most important proposal aimed at reducing the city's jail population, particularly in light of Philadelphia's poor record regarding pretrial detention. Policy makers working on the MacArthur Foundation grant discovered that the average stay in pretrial detention in Philadelphia was 95 days, or four times the national average. A new program in municipal court provided people who had been held after five days on low-level bail another hearing that typically resulted in their release, perhaps with electronic monitoring or entering into diversion programs that required treatment instead of a criminal conviction. One inside source stated, "Early bail review really helped a lot. If you had to pick one initiative that made the biggest impact, I think it's that." One year after receiving the MacArthur Foundation's implementation grant, the city had lowered its jail population by 12 percent from 7,486 in April 2016 to 6,603 in March 2017.[53]

That being said, no one in the Kenney administration believes that the job has been completed. Although seventeen of the nineteen strategies developed through the MacArthur Foundation grant process have been implemented, the city has yet to carry out its goal of ending cash bail or making headway on the development of a pretrial risk assessment tool in place of cash bail. As a result, 23 percent of those incarcerated in the city's jails are simply awaiting trial. Moreover, far too many Philadelphians remain on probation and parole, where any kind of violation threatens to send them back to jail. Most glaringly, incarceration in Philadelphia continues to exhibit striking racial disparities. African Americans, who made up 43 percent of the city's population in 2018, constituted 68 percent of the city's jail population.[54]

Jim Kenney's election, as is often the case in urban politics, clearly played a significant role in deciding who wields power in the public sphere. But periodically other citywide elections take on a comparable, or even higher, level of significance. The race for district attorney in 2017 turned out to be that kind of election.

Activists understood the importance of district attorneys because of their discretion in deciding whether to charge someone with a crime and in recommending appropriate sentences. In their view, district attorneys had played a critical role in constructing the carceral state; the next district attorney in Philadelphia could be pivotal in helping dismantle it. Sarah Morris, a codirector of the Youth Art and Self-Empowerment Project, which organizes on behalf of juveniles confined in adult prisons, emphasized how meaningful the upcoming district attorney's race would be for many residents: "When there's a mayoral election, a presidential election, or voting for a state rep, it can be hard to understand how that concretely is going to impact what's happening in your neighborhood. But so many people have been impacted by the courts and the jails and prisons and probation in Philly, I think it's easier for people to make the connection of what it would mean to have a different prosecutor."[55]

Color of Change, a national organization that had been supporting progressive candidates for district attorney in other American cities, reached out to local activists in late 2016 about convening a meeting of grassroots groups with a stake in criminal justice reform. The response was enthusiastic. A wide array of organizations representing formerly incarcerated people, immigrants, students, sex workers, LGBTQ individuals, civil rights activists, criminal defense professionals, and millennials who had been active in Bernie Sanders's presidential campaign came together to discuss their ideas for a new direction. A collaborative spirit prevailed: "We all had this bigger vision of what a progressive DA could mean to this city and we're going to put individual agendas aside and really try to push this unified message of what we want to see in a DA candidate." Members from the newly established Coalition for a Just DA began to consult with experts, asking specific questions about prosecutorial discretion, sentencing guidelines, juvenile incarceration, and bail reform with the intention of developing a compelling platform.[56]

That platform included a call for aggressive measures to reduce the city's jail population, end cash bail, stop incarcerating young people as adults, eliminate the death penalty, challenge police abuse and brutality, address persistent racial disparities throughout the criminal justice system, and halt collaboration between immigration enforcement and the police, the DA's office, and the courts.[57]

At this early stage of the race, the Coalition for a Just DA had not yet settled on a candidate. There had been some discussion about whether to challenge the incumbent district attorney, Seth Williams, the first Black district attorney of Philadelphia, or simply try to force Williams or other challengers to commit to a progressive platform. But then Williams, who had been under federal investigation for bribery and extortion, announced on February 10, 2017, that he would not seek reelection. Initially, many reformers turned to Keir Bradford-Grey, the first African American to head the city's Defender Association, but she soon decided to remain in her position. This flurry of events opened the door to the unconventional candidacy of Larry Krasner.[58]

As a longtime criminal defense attorney with a penchant for representing radical activists associated with entities like the Occupy Wall Street and Black Lives Matter movements, Krasner did not have the typical résumé that leads one to run for district attorney. When asked why he decided to take the leap, he replied, "I ran for district attorney, simply put, because I view the system as a wreck." More broadly, Krasner detected recent changes in city politics that benefited his candidacy. The Democratic Party with its emphasis on "old-school, patronage power," seemed to be on the decline and might opt to remain on the sidelines in this race. Meanwhile, constituencies that were inclined to support him, notably, poor and working-class people of color who had been harmed by the carceral state, would be energized.[59]

Krasner benefited from his capacity to stand out from the rest of the field—and in a positive way. He made no attempt to tack to the center to appeal for votes. Instead, he adhered to his progressive convictions, lashing out in colorful, uncompromising terms against the criminal justice system. "I have seen, in essence, a system that has completely run off the rails," he said. "A place with a mad zeal for the highest charge, for the highest level of conviction, a culture that can find no flaw in police misconduct, that is drunk on the death penalty. It's like watching a car crash in slow motion for 30 years."[60]

At first, the other candidates struck back. Krasner recalls the first candidate forum as being pivotal: "The most important moment in the campaign, frankly, was when all the other candidates jumped on me and said 'Ha-ha-ha, look at the lefty criminal defense lawyer. He's obviously bad.' And thereby they all focused attention on me." But Krasner was able to speak with the authority and confidence of someone who had been immersed in the criminal justice system for three decades and thoroughly understood its flaws. As it became clear that he was winning over the audience, not to mention capturing the lion's share of media attention, other candidates shifted to the left. As civil rights attorney David Rudovsky put it, "Everyone tried to be more progressive than the next." But that worked to Krasner's advantage because only he could say that he had been calling for progressive change for so many years.[61]

The most significant factor weighing in favor of Krasner's campaign was the candidate's strong support at the grass roots and, particularly, within communities of color. Community-based organizations were inclined to support Krasner from the start because of his unique history, personal connections to many activists, and progressive vision. One well-known Black activist and attorney described Krasner as "the blackest white guy he had ever known." So the multiple groups associated with the Coalition for a Just DA quickly swung into action. They prepared a questionnaire for all the candidates and then circulated a fact sheet on where each stood on crucial issues. POWER disseminated a report card for each candidate. They also sponsored their own candidate forum in which formerly incarcerated people and their families took the lead in asking questions. Most important, activist groups organized sweeping door-to-door canvassing drives. The law obligated 501(c)(3) organizations to conduct nonpartisan canvasses that stressed the critical role of the district attorney and encouraged people to register and vote. ACLU Pennsylvania reached out to its base of twelve thousand members and used its resources to hire formerly incarcerated individuals to knock on doors. POWER, another 501(c)(3) organization, operated a phone bank staffed by fifty volunteers over a seven-week period that resulted in over one hundred thousand phone calls and sixteen thousand live conversations. Reclaim Philadelphia organized the most extensive canvass drive, and one that explicitly endorsed Krasner. It trained dozens of volunteers to knock on over fifty thousand doors during a two-and-a-half month span. Reclaim Philadelphia targeted neighborhoods that had been particularly affected by the crackdown on crime over the years, discovering that on some streets seven of ten households reported having had someone "directly affected by the justice system, whether they were stopped by the police or profiled, or stopped and frisked, or they knew someone in their family or friends who have been. So this isn't an abstract issue for people. They have a direct understanding of it. They understand how it derailed their lives."[62]

The impact of the various canvassing drives was substantial. Voter turnout in an off-year election in Philadelphia had averaged only 17 percent in recent years, but POWER reported that 54 percent of the people it reached through its phone bank voted on Election Day. Similarly, Reclaim Philadelphia maintained that turnout in the lower-income and blue-collar neighborhoods of color that it had targeted was unusually high. On Election Day, Krasner won by a lopsided eighteen-point margin, easily defeating his six opponents. A columnist for the *Philadelphia Inquirer* described the election as "a revolution on behalf of poor, marginalized" Philadelphians.[63]

Almost immediately following Krasner's victory in the general election in November, the Coalition for a Just DA announced its intention to hold regular meetings with the new district attorney to keep him accountable for his sweeping campaign promises and called for full transparency with respect to prosecutorial decisions, including those involving racial disparities. Krasner did not disappoint, agreeing to meet personally every month with representatives from about two dozen organizations invested in criminal justice reform. Subgroups also formed around specific issues such as bail reform, juvenile justice, diversion programs, immigration, and reentry and began to meet with policy staffers in the DA's office. Activists expressed considerable satisfaction with what they called a "co-governance model" that emphasized sustained and meaningful input from community groups in the policy-making process. For African Americans and Latinos who had long been overlooked on policing and prosecutorial matters, the change in process was remarkable.[64] (See Fig. 8.3.)

Advocates of criminal justice reform were delighted with Krasner's first one hundred days in office. He moved decisively to transform the culture at

Figure 8.3 District Attorney Larry Krasner meets with residents at a local barbershop.

the office through extensive personnel changes and numerous policy initiatives. On just his fourth day on the job, Krasner surprised many by firing thirty-one staff members after having undertaken a review of the six-hundred-member district attorney's office to determine who would be more inclined to support the new mission of making the office less hierarchical, more transparent, and more committed to reducing incarceration rates.[65]

With respect to policy changes, the first few weeks brought a slew of headline-grabbing announcements. In his inaugural address, Krasner reaffirmed his campaign promises to eliminate the death penalty, work to end the use of cash bail, and slash the city's jail population. On January 12, Krasner expressed skepticism over the paucity of prosecutions regarding officer-involved shootings. Since 2010, police officers in Philadelphia had been associated with fifty fatal shootings; in every case, the DA's office declined to prosecute. Krasner asserted, "This ain't fair, this is biased" and promised that his office would be more diligent in undertaking investigations and prosecutions. In September, Officer Ryan Pownall, who had fatally shot a Black man in the back as he fled from a pedestrian stop in 2017, was charged with criminal homicide, making him the first Philadelphia police officer to be indicted since 1999.[66]

On January 25, Krasner stated his intention to protect undocumented immigrants facing minor charges from being seized and deported by agents of Immigration and Customs Enforcement when they appear in city courts. He established a new position staffed by an attorney who would develop new protective policies and train assistant district attorneys.[67]

On February 15, Krasner and Mayor Kenney published an op-ed piece faulting Philadelphia's past practice of criminalizing drug addiction and thus exacerbating the crisis of mass incarceration. The two pledged to expand the city's drug court capacity and opportunities for obtaining assistance through treatment programs instead of being imprisoned.[68]

At a well-publicized event on February 21, Krasner announced that he had instructed prosecutors to no longer request cash bail for people accused of twenty-five low-level, nonviolent offenses such as driving under the influence, prostitution, resisting arrest, and some burglaries. The district attorney stated that holding people who pose no flight or security risk in jail for weeks or months until their trial because they cannot afford to post bail is "simply not fair." The new policy was expected to affect about four thousand cases per year, or about 10 percent of the DA's caseload.[69]

Krasner also worked behind the scenes to carry out promised reforms. For example, in accordance with a 2011 U.S. Supreme Court decision that mandatory life sentences without parole given to juvenile offenders were unconstitutional, the DA's office moved quickly to review the cases of 315 juvenile lifers from Philadelphia and within two months had resentenced 127 of those individuals; some who had been in prison for decades were offered time served and released. The district attorney also reinvigorated the conviction integrity unit by hiring a well-respected supervisor and adding several quality attorneys to its staff. The unit is now reviewing numerous cases where there may be innocents incarcerated or where sentences imposed are demonstrably unjust.[70]

Finally, in what the *Philadelphia Inquirer* described as "perhaps the boldest set of policies yet of his two-month tenure," Krasner made public a five-page memo given to the three hundred prosecutors in the DA's office instructing them to offer shorter prison terms in plea deals to nonviolent offenders—indeed, sentences below the lowest range outlined in the state's sentencing guidelines. In addition, the office would no longer prosecute a variety of nonviolent cases, including marijuana possession absent an intent to sell or prostitution prior to a third arrest. The memo also called on prosecutors to detail how much a requested sentence would cost taxpayers. According to the memo, one year in prison costs taxpayers $42,000—roughly equivalent to the annual salary of a teacher or police officer. In justifying the policy changes, Krasner explained in his memo that "over-incarceration . . . tears the fabric of defendants' familial and work relationships" and, by swallowing up huge sums of scarce resources, has "bankrupted investment in policing, public education, medical treatment of addiction, job training, and economic development—which prevent crime more effectively than money invested in corrections."[71]

By and large, reactions to Krasner's first year as Philadelphia's district attorney were quite positive. David Rudovsky, for instance, offered this assessment: "I've got to tell you, he's really done it. Everything he talked about—civil forfeiture, bail, lengthy sentences, the juvenile lifers is a great example . . . prosecuting police . . . juvenile justice, some restorative justice initiatives, the death penalty gone. Every one of the major things he talked about he's made some initiatives. . . . So I give him high marks."[72]

Meanwhile, work proceeded on other fronts beyond the DA's office. Pursuant to the MacArthur Foundation grant, officials representing multiple interests within the criminal justice system continued to implement policies to reduce incarceration as well as racial and economic disparities in the criminal justice system. Progress in addressing overincarceration is undeniable. The city's jail population stood at 8,301 in January 2015 when the MacArthur Foundation grant process started; by April 2019, the jail population had fallen to 4,638, exceeding the ambitious 34 percent goal set by the foundation at the outset. City officials aimed for a 50 percent decline in the jail population by 2020. Progress toward remedying racial and economic inequities has been slower, but it remains a top priority. Speaking of the latest grant from the MacArthur Foundation, Keir Bradford-Grey, the head of the Defender Association of Philadelphia, declared: "Criminal justice reform is the civil rights movement of our time, and this award will help us to address the racial disparities that plague our system."[73]

Not that all advocates have been entirely satisfied. Some viewed Krasner's early achievements as low-hanging fruit, some of which were secured with a simple signature. Many have been concerned about the slower pace of change since Krasner's first year in office and, especially, the lack of progress on certain major issues such as the promise to end cash bail. Activists lament the fact that so many low-income people continue to languish in jail awaiting trial only because they cannot afford to post bail, particularly when a growing body of research questions whether the existence of bail has any discernible impact on the likelihood of people returning for scheduled court dates or committing other offenses.[74]

Resistance to progressive reforms from other quarters of the criminal justice system has been more pronounced. John McNesby, the president of the Fraternal Order of Police, charged that Krasner's pursuit of criminal justice reform has come at the expense of keeping Philadelphians safe. He asserted that a 10 percent increase in the city's homicide rate since 2017 is attributable to the DA's turn away from strict law enforcement. Krasner countered that the uptick in the homicide rate has been the result of drug-related shootings arising from a nationwide opioid crisis, while pointing out that violent crime in general is down 5 percent and the overall crime rate has been stable.[75]

A countervailing power in response to opponents of criminal justice reform lies within the vast network of grassroots, community-based organizations that ignited the reform movement in the first place. Activists have not been shy about promising a new round of mobilization if needed, and one directed not just at Krasner's opponents but at Krasner himself should he falter in delivering on his promises. One activist put it this way: "I don't want to say this is a threat, but there's always at some point going public to complain about [issues such as the lack of progress on bail reform]. . . . We stand for . . . accountability. And while we're very happy generally, there's stuff that I think could be improved. And we'll say that publicly." The stress on accountability was a sentiment that was echoed by numerous other activists.[76]

Looking to the future, reform-minded activists anticipate operating within a variety of venues and forums to advance their mission. Engagement in citywide elections has already paid huge dividends with respect to the mayoral race in 2015 and the DA race in 2017, and so campaign organizing will remain a part of the activists' arsenal, including city council and even judicial elections. In addition, civil rights attorneys have long utilized the courts as a mechanism to apply pressure, and they have signaled some frustration with a slowdown in progress regarding the police department's use of stop and frisk and, especially, the persistence of racial disparities in its implementation. The lack of substantial compliance with the consent decree on this critical issue might warrant a motion for contempt against the city.[77]

Activists have developed closer ties to certain members of city council in recent years and many see that institution as a potentially fruitful venue for seeking further reforms. Many are looking for additional ways to exploit the city council's inherent but often underutilized powers, such as their control over appropriations, their ability to investigate and publicize issues by holding hearings, and, of course, their power to enact legislation. To illustrate, advocates of bail reform persuaded the city council to hold hearings in 2018 on the city's practice of retaining 30 percent of all posted bail, even if an individual was acquitted or the bail was posted by a community bail fund. The hearings raised awareness about a practice that soon came to be seen as indefensible and the city then abolished the practice. On a more far-reaching issue, many activists are determined to find ways to use the considerable savings from declining incarceration rates for community reinvestment. How such savings might be reinvested in communities over the decades is a large issue that looms over the city and will likely be contested in multiple political forums in the years ahead.[78]

A number of lessons emerge from the case study of criminal justice reform about the changing condition of Black politics in Philadelphia. To start, citizens appear to be less reliant on established figures within the Black community to provide leadership in addressing hard issues. Instead, there is a growing inclination to take matters into their own hands, manifested by a marked rise in the level of grassroots mobilization over the past decade.

With respect to the issue of criminal justice, the swelling of mass-based political activity has hardly been confined to Philadelphia. It is part of a nationwide trend and reflects a broad and deep-seated dissatisfaction with the myriad and painful costs associated with the country's decades-long determination to get tough on crime through aggressive policing, prosecution, and incarceration. The devastation that this approach has brought to countless Black and brown communities has precipitated a wide-ranging reform movement.

But insurgency around the criminal justice system has been especially pronounced in Philadelphia. Grassroots organizing there began among individuals who were most impacted by the carceral state—incarcerated and formerly incarcerated people themselves along with family members, friends, and neighbors. It spread with the emergence of the Black Lives Matter movement and its powerful and sustained attack on racist practices and policies within the police department. Street protests, demonstrations, and rallies inspired the development of new community-based organizations dedicated to policy advocacy and electoral change.

The increasing presence of grassroots politics by the mid-2010s had significant ramifications for conventional politics in Philadelphia. It impelled the candidacies of progressive politicians like Jim Kenney and Larry Krasner, whose decisive electoral victories for mayor and district attorney, respectively, further energized the reform movement. Their actions once in office yielded important changes in criminal justice policy and practice.

Still, obstacles remain. Some of the most intractable issues such as how to discipline rogue police officers, the continuing use of cash bail in far too many cases, and the need for viable programs to facilitate the reentry of formerly incarcerated citizens have yet to be resolved. Even progressive politicians like Kenney and Krasner have faltered in trying to devise workable solutions. But the vital activist community pledges to maintain its pressure on policy makers, even as activists themselves sometimes diverge on the appropriate path forward. The key point is that there has been a shift in local power dynamics in Philadelphia, at least with respect to the issue of criminal justice reform—power appears to be flowing not just from the top down but also from the bottom up.

The looming question is whether the politics of criminal justice reform during the 2010s represents a model for how the city might address additional long-standing problems of racial injustice as well as inequities related to other critical categories of identity. For much of the past half century, Philadelphia has struggled over the issue of urban development. Its preferred downtown-centric strategy of revitalization has produced uneven results at best, leaving hundreds of thousands of its citizens in a state of chronic poverty.

Abundant evidence suggests that Mayor Kenney recognizes the inadequacy of the downtown-centric approach. He frequently calls attention to the persistence and even immorality of poverty and how it impedes progress for all Philadelphians. Kenney's signature policy imposes a stiff tax on sugary drinks, not so much to address public health problems, such as obesity, diabetes, and heart disease, but as a means to fund three ambitious programs to reduce poverty: (1) a major expansion of pre-K education; (2) equitable civic space development centering on the reconstruction of parks, playgrounds, recreation centers, and libraries in underserved neighborhoods (also known as the Rebuild Initiative); and (3) the establishment of "community schools" that would offer an array of social services in addition to traditional classroom learning.[79]

However, Kenney has waffled at other times when confronted by potent groups with a stake in maintaining business power and white privilege. For example, developers have strenuously resisted proposals for a tax on all new construction to fund affordable housing production. And union leaders have fought efforts to promote racial diversity within the predominantly white building trades. Because both groups still hold considerable sway in city politics, Kenney has so far refrained from taking positions on either issue.[80]

But whereas, in the past, the downtown-led regime would invariably prevail in light of the striking imbalance of power between downtown and neighborhood groups, with the relative political passivity of the latter, today the situation is quite different. In the current political landscape, residents of Black and Latino communities are no longer content to sit back and allow city leaders to assume responsibility for dealing with seemingly intractable issues. Rather, an increasingly engaged citizenry is more likely to take the initiative through a variety of mechanisms ranging from disruptive protest to skilled policy advocacy and possibly transformative electoral campaigns. While the downtown business establishment has declined in terms of resources and organizational capacity, the constellation of community-based organizations has expanded and found ways to collaborate effectively. Given these shifts, the potential for citizens in Black and Latino communities to exercise more influence in Philadelphia over issues of urban development, poverty, job access, housing, education, and criminal justice appears to be on the rise.

NOTES

1. Clarence N. Stone, *Regime Politics: Governing Atlanta, 1946–1988* (Lawrence: University Press of Kansas, 1989); Clarence N. Stone and Heywood T. Sanders, eds. *The Politics of Urban Development* (Lawrence: University Press of Kansas, 1987); Stephen J. McGovern, *The Politics of Downtown Development: Dynamic Political Cultures in San Francisco and Washington, D.C.* (Lexington: University Press of Kentucky, 1998); John Mollenkopf, *The Contested City* (Princeton, NJ: Princeton University Press, 1983).

2. Stone, *Regime Politics*; Raphael Sonenshein, *Politics in Black and White: Race and Power in Los Angeles* (Princeton, NJ: Princeton University Press, 1993).

3. Richard A. Keiser, *Subordination or Empowerment? African-American Leadership and the Struggle for Urban Political Power* (New York: Oxford University Press, 1997); Stephen J. McGovern, "Mayoral Leadership and Economic Development Policy: The Case of Ed Rendell's Philadelphia," *Policy and Politics* 25, no. 2 (1997): 153–172.

4. David W. Bartelt, "Renewing Center City Philadelphia: Whose City? Which Public Interest?" in *Unequal Partnerships: The Political Economy of Urban Redevelopment in Postwar America*, ed. Gregory D. Squires (New Brunswick, NJ: Rutgers University Press, 1989); Carolyn T. Adams, David W. Bartelt, Jon Elesh, Ira Goldstein, and Nancy Kleniewski, *Philadelphia: Neighborhoods, Division, and Conflict in a Postindustrial City* (Philadelphia: Temple University Press, 1991); Buzz Bissinger, *A Prayer for the City* (New York: Random House, 1997).

5. Stephen J. McGovern, "Philadelphia's Neighborhood Transformation Initiative: A Case Study of Mayoral Leadership, Bold Planning, and Conflict," *Housing Policy Debate* 17, no. 3 (2006): 529–570; Editorial, "A Look at Mayor Street's Legacy: Lots of Gain, More Pain," *Philadelphia Inquirer*, December 30, 2007, C6.

6. Saskia Sassen. *The Global City: New York, London, Tokyo* (Princeton, NJ: Princeton University Press, 1991); Elizabeth Strom, "Rethinking the Politics of Downtown Development," *Journal of Urban Affairs* 30, no. 1 (2008): 37–62; Richard Florida, *The Rise of the Creative Class: And How It's Transforming Work, Leisure, and Everyday Life* (New York: Basic Books, 2002); Eugenie L. Birch, *Who Lives Downtown?* (Washington, DC: Brookings Institution, 2005); Jeannie Haubert and Elizabeth Fussell, "Explaining Pro-Immigrant Sentiment in the U.S.: Social Class, Cosmopolitanism, and Perceptions of Immigrants," *International Migration Review* 40, no. 3 (2006): 489–507; Jamie Peck, "Struggling with the Creative Class," *International Journal of Urban and Regional Research* 29, no. 4 (2005): 740–770; Stephen J. McGovern, "Mobilization on the Waterfront: The Ideological/Cultural Roots of Potential Regime Change in Philadelphia," *Urban Affairs Review* 44, no. 5 (2008): 663–694.

7. Patrick Kerkstra, "Ethics Grows as a Concern for Voters," *Philadelphia Inquirer*, April 1, 2007, B1; Thomas Fitzgerald, "On Nutter's Horizon," *Philadelphia Inquirer*, May 20, 2007, A1; Michael Matza, "How Nutter's Win Made History," *Philadelphia Inquirer*, May 17, 2007, A13.

8. Chris Hepp, "Nutter Looks to Legacy," *Philadelphia Inquirer*, October 13, 2014, B1; Julia Terruso, "How Has Mayor Nutter Done during His Tenure?" *Philadelphia Inquirer*, February 8, 2015, B1; Suzette Parmley, "Why Market East Is Becoming the New Hot Area

for Millennials," *Philadelphia Inquirer,* July 3, 2016, E5; Jacob Adelman, "Drexel Plans a University City," *Philadelphia Inquirer,* March 3, 2016, A1; Inga Saffron, "New Attempt to Develop Waterfront," *Philadelphia Inquirer,* April 4, 2013 (website); Maria Panaritis, "City: Poverty Programs Beginning to Help," *Philadelphia Inquirer,* November 21, 2015, B1.

9. Wendy Ruderman and David Gambacorta, "Wilson Goode Jr. Talks about His Election Defeat, What's Next," *Philadelphia Daily News,* May 21, 2015, 5.

10. Chris Hepp, "Black Coalition Backing Kenney," *Philadelphia Inquirer,* April 7, 2015, B1; Chris Brennan, "Krasner Picks Up Key Ward Leaders and More PAC Support for DA," *Philadelphia Inquirer,* May 2, 2017 (website). Troy Graham, "William H. Gray III Helped Empower Black Politicians," *Philadelphia Inquirer,* July 8, 2013, A1; Holly Otterbein, "The Penna. Primary's Big Winners and Losers," *Philadelphia Inquirer,* May 17, 2018, A4; Michael Currie Schaffer, "On Ethics, Blackwell Won't Back Down," *Philadelphia Inquirer,* November 16, 2005, B1. Ironically, the Northwest Coalition was formed in the 1970s in reaction to a Democratic Party that was perceived as phlegmatic and unresponsive to Black interests. As an insurgent organization, it provided crucial support for the election of William Gray to Congress in 1978 and Wilson Goode to the mayor's office in 1983. Over time, however, the Northwest Coalition itself became a major player in the city's Democratic Party machine.

11. Stone, *Regime Politics*; Troy Graham, "Darrell L. Clarke: A Most Purposeful, Accidental Politician," *Philadelphia Inquirer,* February 1, 2012, A1.

12. Stone, *Regime Politics.*

13. Cynthia Horan, "Racializing Regime Politics," *Journal of Urban Affairs* 24, no. 1 (2002): 19–33; Neil Kraus, "The Significance of Race in Urban Politics: The Limitations of Regime Theory," *Race and Society* 7 (2004): 95–111.

14. Phillip J. Thompson III, *Double Trouble: Black Mayors, Black Communities, and the Call for a Deep Democracy* (New York: Oxford University Press, 2006); Michael B. Katz, "Why Don't American Cities Burn Very Often?" *Journal of Urban History* 34, no. 2 (2008): 185–208; Adolph Reed Jr., "Demobilization in the New Black Political Regime: Ideological Capitulation and Radical Failure in the Post-Segregation Era," in *The Bubbling Cauldron: Race, Ethnicity, and the Urban Crisis,* ed. Michael P. Smith and Joe R. Feagin (Minneapolis: University of Minnesota Press, 1995).

15. Michelle Alexander, *The New Jim Crow: Mass Incarceration in the Age of Colorblindness* (New York: New Press, 2010); Marie Gottschalk, *Caught: The Prison State and Lockdown of American Politics* (Princeton, NJ: Princeton University Press, 2015); Amy Lerman and Vesla Weaver, *Arresting Citizenship: The Democratic Consequences of American Crime Control,* (Chicago: University of Chicago Press, 2014); Traci Burch, *Trading Democracy for Justice: Criminal Convictions and the Decline of Neighborhood Political Participation* (Chicago: University of Chicago Press, 2013); Pamela Oliver, "Repression as Crime Control: Why Social Movement Scholars Should Pay Attention to Mass Incarceration as a Form of Repression," *Mobilization* 13, no. 1 (2008): 1–24.

16. Larry Eichel, "A New Push for Affordable Housing," *Philadelphia Inquirer,* February 17, 2006, B3; Anthony Twyman, "Street Hails New Housing Trust Fund," *Philadelphia Inquirer,* August 4, 2005, B4; Jane M. Von Bergen, "Fight for $15 Hourly Minimum Wage Hits Streets in Phila. and Nationwide," *Philadelphia Inquirer,* November 11, 2015, A13.

17. Timothy J. Lombardo, *Blue-Collar Conservatism: Frank Rizzo's Philadelphia and Populist Politics* (Philadelphia: University of Pennsylvania Press, 2018); Joseph R. Daughen and Peter Binzen, *The Cop Who Would Be King: The Honorable Frank Rizzo* (Boston: Little, Brown, 1977).

18. Donald Janson, "Rizzo Wins Race in Philadelphia," *New York Times*, November 3, 1971, A1; Lombardo, *Blue-Collar Conservatism*.

19. Steve Volk, "John McNesby's Massive Influence on Philadelphia Policing," *Philadelphia Magazine* (February 2019), available at https://www.phillymag.com/news/2019/02/23/john-mcnesby-fop-police-philadelphia/; Tina Rosenberg, "The Deadliest DA," *New York Times*, July 16, 1995, 21; Barbara Boyer, "Nutter, Ramsey Hail Success of Phila. Anticrime Effort," *Philadelphia Inquirer*, December 31, 2008, A1; Mary Catherine Roper (deputy legal director, American Civil Liberties Union of Pennsylvania), personal interview, January 18, 2019; David Rudovsky (partner, Kairys, Rudovsky, Messing, and Feinberg), personal interview, January 24, 2019. Arlen Specter was subsequently elected to the U.S. Senate where he represented the state of Pennsylvania from 1980 until 2010. Ed Rendell was the mayor of Philadelphia from 1992 until 2000 and then governor of Pennsylvania from 2003 to 2011.

Many activists have noted Philadelphia's desire to lock people up. "Philadelphia has had a long history of district attorneys and just actors in the criminal justice system that have been pretty explicit about their crackdown mentality on communities.... At least in our city, the criminal justice system is used as a billy club to get people in line, make sure that they follow orders." Rick Krajewski (organizer, Reclaim Philadelphia and Philadelphia Coalition for a Just DA), telephone interview, January 14, 2019.

20. John Eck and Edward Maguire, "Have Changes in Policing Reduced Violent Crime? An Assessment of the Evidence," in *The Crime Drop in America*, ed. Alfred Blumstein and Joel Wallman (New York: Cambridge University Press, 2000); George L. Kelling and William J. Bratton, "Declining Crime Rates: Insiders' Views of the New York Story," *Journal of Criminal Law and Criminology* 88, no. 4 (1998): 1217–1231.

21. "Philadelphia 2018 Safety and Justice Challenge Fact Sheet," *Safety and Justice Challenge* (John D. and Catherine T. MacArthur Foundation), fact sheet, 2018, available at www.safetyandjusticechallenge.org/challenge-site/philadelphia/; Larry Krasner (district attorney, city of Philadelphia), personal interview, March 5, 2019; Rev. Gregory Holston (executive director, POWER), telephone interview, January 31, 2019; Reuben Jones (founder, Frontline Dads), personal interview, February 2, 2019.

22. Keir Bradford-Grey, (chief defender, Defender Association of Philadelphia), personal interview, January 17, 2019; Holston interview.

23. Curtis Jones (member, Philadelphia City Council), personal interview, March 5, 2019; Cathy J. Cohen, *Democracy Remixed* (New York: Oxford University Press, 2010); Burch, *Trading Democracy for Justice*; Lerman and Weaver, *Arresting Citizenship*.

24. Emilie Lounsberry, "Lawyers Sue Again over Prison Overcrowding in Philadelphia," *Philadelphia Inquirer*, April 30, 2008, B1; Troy Graham, "U.S. Lawsuit Targets Philly's 'Stop-and-Frisk' Policy," *Philadelphia Inquirer*, November 5, 2010, A1; Jeremy Roebuck, "Civil Rights Group: Stop-and-Frisk Still Targets Minorities," *Philadelphia Inquirer*, February 25, 2015, A1.

25. Paul Hetznecker (president, Defender Association of Philadelphia), personal interview, January 9, 2019; Hannah Sassaman (policy director, Media Mobilizing Project), telephone interview, February 4, 2019; Dean Wilson and Tanya Serisier, "Video Activism and the Ambiguities of Countersurveillance," *Surveillance and Society* 8, no. 2 (2010): 166–180.

26. Sassaman interview; Holston interview; R. Jones interview; Troy Graham, "Philadelphia Council's 'Ban the Box' Criminal-Background Bill Passes," *Philadelphia Inquirer*, April 1, 2011, B1.

27. Bryan Stevenson, *Just Mercy: A Story of Justice and Redemption* (New York: Spiegel and Grau, 2014); John F. Pfaff, *Locked In: The True Causes of Mass Incarceration—And How to Achieve Real Reform* (New York: Basic Books, 2017); James Forman, *Locking Up Our Own: Crime and Punishment in Black America* (New York: Farrar, Strauss and Giroux, 2017); Emily Bazelon, *Charged: The New Movement to Transform American Prosecution and End Mass Incarceration* (New York: Random House, 2019). It is hard to overestimate the impact that Alexander's book has had in promoting grassroots activism in Black and brown communities all over the United States. In time, *The New Jim Crow* may come to be seen as having the same catalytic effect on mass-based protest as Betty Friedan's *The Feminine Mystique* and Rachel Carson's *Silent Spring* did on the women's movement and environmental movement, respectively.

28. Rudovsky interview; Holston interview; Julia Terruso, Tricia L. Nadolny, and Mike Newall, "Protests, Pleas for Calm outside City Hall after Ferguson Announcement," *Philadelphia Inquirer*, November 25, 2014, A1.

29. Holston interview.

30. Hetznecker interview; Sarah Morris (codirector, Youth Art and Self-Empowerment Project), telephone interview, January 23, 2019.

31. Sandy Bauers, "Ramsey Seeks Study on Police Use of Force," *Philadelphia Inquirer*, May 29, 2013, B1; Aubrey Whelan and Craig R. McCoy, "Ramsey Orders Changes on Interrogations, Holding Suspects," *Philadelphia Inquirer*, December 20, 2013, A2; Aubrey Whelan, "Philadelphia Police to Test Body Cameras for Six Months," *Philadelphia Inquirer*, December 2, 2014, B1; Claudia Vargas, "Nutter Names 24 to Police Community Oversight Board," *Philadelphia Inquirer*, April 18, 2015, B1; Aubrey Whelan, "Ramsey, Presidential Task Force in Policing to Begin Work," *Philadelphia Inquirer*, December 23, 2014, B2.

32. Rudovsky interview; Julie Wertheimer (director of criminal justice, managing director's office, city of Philadelphia), personal interview, January 29, 2019; Roper interview; Roebuck, "Civil Rights Group."

33. Mark Houldin (policy director, Defender Association of Philadelphia), personal interview, January 22, 2019; Keir Bradford-Grey (chief defender, Defender Association of Philadelphia), personal interview, January 17, 2019; Wertheimer interview.

34. Morris interview; Tricia L. Nadolny, "Phila. Considering Replacing House of Corrections," *Philadelphia Inquirer*, May 19, 2015, B1; Krajewski interview.

35. Wertheimer interview; Morris interview; C. Jones interview.

36. Chris Hepp, "Kenney Called Passionate, Loyal to a Fault, Driven to Do Right," *Philadelphia Inquirer*, May 6, 2015, A1.

37. Rudovsky interview; Chris Hepp, "Phila. Pot-Decriminalization Law Signed," *Philadelphia Inquirer*, October 2, 2014, B1.

38. Wertheimer interview.

39. Claudia Vargas, "Kenney's Agenda—With Success in '14, Looking to His Next Race," *Philadelphia Inquirer*, January 1, 2015, B1; Chris Brennan, "Kenney Ahead of Mayoral Rivals on Pot Law?" *Philadelphia Inquirer*, February 4, 2015, B1; Chris Hepp, "Kenney Formally Enters Race for Phila. Mayor," *Philadelphia Inquirer*, February 5, 2015, B1.

40. Morris interview.

41. Holston interview.

42. Jeff Gamage, "Supporters Celebrate Kenney Win: Many See the Candidate as a Progressive Coalition-Builder," *Philadelphia Inquirer*, May 20, 2015, A9; Chris Hepp, "Landslide: Kenney Romps in Philly Mayor's Race," *Philadelphia Inquirer*, May 20, 2015,

A1; Chris Brennan and Julia Terruso, "Kenney Coasts to Victory," *Philadelphia Inquirer*, November 4, 2015, A1.

43. Julia Terruso, "Kenney More Nuanced on Ending Stop and Frisk," *Philadelphia Inquirer*, February 18, 2016, B3; Tommy Rowan, "Rallying around a Day of Action," *Philadelphia Inquirer*, April 15, 2016, B1.

44. Rudovsky interview; Julia Terruso, "ACLU: City Police Frisks Still Flawed," *Philadelphia Inquirer*, March 23, 2016, A1.

45. Rudovsky interview; Chris Palmer, "Philly Police Decreasing Use of Stop-and-Frisk, Officials Say," *Philadelphia Inquirer*, April 22, 2017, A1; William Bender and Michele Tranquilli, "Police Stops Fall Sharply, but Gap Seen," *Philadelphia Inquirer*, April 22, 2018, A1. Although there was a new police commissioner, Richard Ross, Rudovsky credited Kenney, not Ross, for the policy change: "And that administration came in and things started to change. More Kenney than Ross. Ross is a decent guy, but still old school to some extent." Rudovsky interview. Julie Wertheimer, director of criminal justice in the managing director's office, concurs: "It was a very clear directive from the mayor to the commissioner from the beginning." Wertheimer interview.

46. Bender and Tranquilli, "Police Stops"; Roper interview; see also, Samantha Melamed, "Study: High Rates of Stop and Frisk Even in Philly's Lowest Crime Black Areas," *Philadelphia Inquirer*, October 3, 2017, B1.

47. Rudovsky interview.

48. William Bender, "Bearing Angry Message," *Philadelphia Inquirer*, July 10, 2016, A8; Emily Babay, "A Sixth Day of Marching Here," *Philadelphia Inquirer*, July 12, 2016, A6; Jason Nark, "Coalition Leads the City's Most Controversial Protests," *Philadelphia Inquirer*, July 12, 2016, A6; Mike Newall, "Protesters' Inflamed Rhetoric Offers Some the Excuse They Want to Turn Away," *Philadelphia Inquirer*, July 13, 2016, B1; Aubrey Whelan and Jason Nark, "Hundreds Turn Out to Support Police," *Philadelphia Inquirer*, July 14, 2016, B1; Randall Kennedy, "Black Lives Matter, the Next Stage of the Civil Rights Movement," *Philadelphia Inquirer*, December 4, 2016, C1.

49. Chris Palmer, "Shot in the Back," *Philadelphia Inquirer*, July 28, 2017 (website); Adia H. Robinson, "Protesters Disrupt Plans," *Philadelphia Inquirer*, August 8, 2017, B6; Aubrey Whelan and Adia H. Robinson, "Thousands Rally in Solidarity," *Philadelphia Inquirer*, August 17, 2017, A4.

50. Franklin E. Zimring, *When Police Kill* (Cambridge: Harvard University Press, 2017); Volk, "John McNesby's Bully Pulpit"; Krasner interview.

51. Roper interview; Volk, "John McNesby's Bully Pulpit"; Sassaman interview; Will Bunch, "Police Deal Is a Moment Missed," *Philadelphia Inquirer*, August 23, 2017, A13; Sara Mullen (associate director/advocacy and policy director, American Civil Liberties Union of Pennsylvania), personal interview, January 18, 2019; Holston interview.

52. Chris Hepp, "$3.5M for City to Cut Jail Count," *Philadelphia Inquirer*, April 13, 2016, A1.

53. "Philadelphia 2018"; Wertheimer interview; Ben Austen, "On the Inside," *New York Times Magazine*, November 4, 2018: 42–47, 64–65; Houldin interview; David Gambacorta and Samantha Melamed, "Jail Reform Advances as City Inmate Counts Dip," *Philadelphia Inquirer*, April 13, 2017, B1.

54. Wertheimer interview; "Philadelphia 2018 Safety and Justice"; Samantha Melamed, "Study Finds Overuse of Probation, Parole in PA," *Philadelphia Inquirer*, April 25, 2018, A4; "Philadelphia's Jail Population," June 2018, available at https://www.phila.gov/media/20200422121305/June-2018-Public-Piktochart-Report.pdf.

55. Austen, "On the Inside"; Krajewski interview; Morris interview.

56. Sassaman interview; Mullen interview; Morris interview; Bradford-Grey interview; Houldin interview.

57. Holston interview; Morris interview.

58. Morris interview. Williams was indicted on twenty-three charges in March 2017 and, ultimately, pled guilty to one count of bribery. He was sentenced to a five-year prison term. Jeremy Roebuck, "Harsh Words and Five Years," *Philadelphia Inquirer*, October 25, 2017, A1.

59. Volk, "John McNesby's Bully Pulpit"; Krasner interview.

60. Julia Terruso, "Krasner Says He's the True Reformer," *Philadelphia Inquirer*, May 4, 2017, B1.

61. Krasner interview; Krajewski interview; Rudovsky interview.

62. Holston interview; Morris interview; Sassaman interview; Mullen interview; Krajewski interview.

63. Holston interview; Krajewski interview; Chris Brennan, "Krasner Wins DA Race," *Philadelphia Inquirer*, May 17, 2017, A1; Will Bunch, "Larry Krasner Wins Primary for DA," *Philadelphia Inquirer*, May 18, 2017, A15.

64. Julie Shaw, "Activists Call for Krasner to Quickly Transform Office," *Philadelphia Inquirer*, November 10, 2017, B2; see also, Sassaman interview; R. Jones interview; Krajewski interview.

65. Chris Palmer, Julie Shaw, and Mensah M. Dean, "Krasner Lets 31 Go in Culture Change," *Philadelphia Inquirer*, January 6, 2018, A1; Chris Palmer and Julie Shaw, "Krasner: 'The Coach Gets to Pick the Team,'" *Philadelphia Inquirer*, January 10, 2018, B3.

66. Chris Palmer, "An Oath for Change," *Philadelphia Inquirer*, January 3, 2018, A1; Mensah M. Dean, "Krasner Questions Lack of Charges in Police Shootings," *Philadelphia Inquirer*, January 13, 2018, A1; Chris Palmer and Julie Shaw, "Ex-Officer Is Charged in On-Duty Shooting," *Philadelphia Inquirer*, September 5, 2018, A1.

67. Chris Palmer, "DA Moves on Link of Charges, Deporting," *Philadelphia Inquirer*, January 26, 2018, B1.

68. Jim Kenney and Larry Krasner, "Criminalizing Crack Addiction Was a Mistake," February 15, 2018, available at http://www.philly.com/Philly/Opinion/Commentary; Aubrey Whelan, "Connections, Not Arrest," *Philadelphia Inquirer*, March 17, 2018, B5.

69. Chris Palmer, "Phila. DA Won't Seek Cash Bail in Some Crimes," *Philadelphia Inquirer*, February 22, 2018, A1.

70. Samantha Melamed, "Krasner Acts Quickly on Juvenile Lifers," *Philadelphia Inquirer*, February 23, 2018, B1; Samantha Melamed, "An Ongoing Quest for Exoneration," *Philadelphia Inquirer*, January 12, 2018, A1; Rudovsky interview. Philadelphia had the dubious distinction of having sentenced more minors to life in prison without any chance of parole than any other jurisdiction in the United States; Melamed, "Krasner Acts Quickly."

71. Chris Palmer, "Krasner Issues Directives to Limit Incarceration," *Philadelphia Inquirer*, March 16, 2018, A1; Krasner interview.

72. Rudovsky interview; R. Jones interview; Holston interview.

73. "Philadelphia's Participation in the Safety and Justice Challenge," available at www.phila.gov/programs/philadelphia-safety-and-justice-challenge. In all, the MacArthur Foundation has invested $7.65 million in Philadelphia as part of its $148 million national campaign—the Safety and Justice Challenge—to prompt a wholesale rethinking of prosecution and incarceration in the United States. City of Philadelphia, "City Awarded $4 Million by MacArthur Safety and Justice Challenge," press release, Octo-

ber 24, 2018, available at https://www.phila.gov/2018-10-24-city-awarded-4-million-by-macarthur-safety-and-justice-challenge/.

74. Roper interview; Houldin interview; Wertheimer interview; Krajewski interview.

75. Chris Palmer, "Police Union Head Unloads on DA," *Philadelphia Inquirer*, January 26, 2019, B4; Philadelphia Police Department, Crime Maps and Stats, 2019, available at www.phillypolice.com/crime_maps_stats/.

76. Mullen interview; Holston interview; Sassaman interview.

77. Holston interview; Rudovsky interview.

78. Sassaman interview; Krajewski interview; Samantha Melamed, "Court Will Not Keep 30% of Bail," *Philadelphia Inquirer*, October 11, 2018, B1; R. Jones interview.

79. Claudia Vargas, "Kenney Signs Sugary Drink Tax into Law," *Philadelphia Inquirer*, June 21, 2016, B1.

80. Holly Otterbein and Chris Brennan, "Kenney Tries to Avoid Tax Veto," *Philadelphia Inquirer*, September 12, 2018, B1; Solomon Jones, "Council Is Right: More Than a Promise Is Needed," *Philadelphia Inquirer*, May 20, 2018, C4.

Appendix

TABLE A.1 PHILADELPHIA POPULATION: 1880–2019

Year	Total	African American	Percentage African American
1880	847,170	31,699	3.7
1890	1,046,964	40,374	3.9
1900	1,293,697	62,613	4.8
1910	1,549,008	84,859	5.5
1920	1,823,779	134,229	7.4
1930	1,950,961	219,599	11.3
1940	1,931,334	250,880	13.0
1950	2,071,605	376,041	18.2
1960	2,002,512	529,240	26.4
1970	1,948,609	653,791	33.6
1980	1,688,210	638,878	37.8
1990	1,585,577	631,936	39.9
2000	1,517,550	655,824	43.2
2010	1,526,006	661,839	43.4
2019	1,584,064	690,652	43.6

Source: U.S. Census data.

Contributors

Stanley Keith Arnold is Associate Professor of History at Northern Illinois University.

David A. Canton is Director of the African American Studies Program and Associate Professor of History at the University of Florida.

Clem Harris is Assistant Professor of History at Utica College.

Timothy J. Lombardo is Associate Professor of History at the University of South Alabama.

Stephen J. McGovern is Professor of Political Science at Haverford College.

Abigail Perkiss is Associate Professor of History at Kean University.

Alyssa Ribeiro is Assistant Professor of History and Black Studies at Allegheny College.

Heather Ann Thompson is Collegiate Professor of History and African American Studies at the University of Michigan.

James Wolfinger is Dean of the College of Education and holds a joint appointment as Professor in the Department of Curriculum and Instruction and the Department of History at St. John's University.

Illustration Credits

Map 1
Credit: Temple University Press.

Map 2
Credit: Philadelphia Streets Department.

Figure 1.1
Credit: Adapted with permission of the New York Public Library.

Figure 1.2
Credit: State Archives of Florida.

Figure 1.3
Credit: Reprinted with permission of the *Bladen Journal*.

Figure 2.1
Credit: *Philadelphia Tribune*.

Figure 2.2
Credit: *Philadelphia Tribune*.

Figure 3.1
Credit: Samuel D. Holmes Collection, Charles L. Blockson Afro-American Collection, Temple University Libraries, Philadelphia, PA.

232 / Illustration Credits

Figure 4.1
Credit: Special Collections Research Center, Temple University Libraries, Philadelphia, PA.

Figure 4.2
Credit: Special Collections Research Center, Temple University Libraries, Philadelphia, PA.

Figure 5.1
Credit: Special Collections Research Center, Temple University Libraries, Philadelphia, PA.

Figure 5.2
Credit: U.S. Congress.

Figure 6.1
Credit: Special Collections Research Center, Temple University Libraries, Philadelphia, PA.

Figure 6.2
Credit: Special Collections Research Center, Temple University Libraries, Philadelphia, PA.

Figure 6.3
Credit: Special Collections Research Center, Temple University Libraries, Philadelphia, PA.

Figure 7.1
Credit: Photograph by Robert L. Fox, April 17, 1979, *Evening Bulletin* Photograph Collection, Special Collections Research Center, Temple University Libraries, Philadelphia, PA.

Figure 7.2
Credit: Photograph by Jack Tinney, September 4, 1981, *Evening Bulletin* Photograph Collection, Special Collections Research Center, Temple University Libraries, Philadelphia, PA.

Figure 8.1
Credit: POWER.

Figure 8.2
Credit: POWER.

Figure 8.3
Credit: Philadelphia District Attorney's Office.

Index

NOTE: *Page numbers in italics refer to illustrations.*

Abraham, Lynne, 195, 205
Abu-Jamal, Mumia, 177–178
ACLU (American Civil Liberties Union), 198, 205, 206, 212
Africa, Delbert Orr, 152
African American activism: agitation as tool for, 55–56; Black clergy and, 124, 140; campaign organizing, 216; community basis for, 16, 123–124, 125, 128, 217, 218; growing independence in, 64–66, 71; and racial identity, 107; radicalism in, 76, 78, 84, 88; and real political change, 9–10. *See also* Black electoral power; boycotts; criminal justice reforms; demonstrations, marches, and rallies; grassroots movements; Moore, Cecil B.
African American culture and identity, 5, 101, 103–104, 107, 139
African Americans: allegiance to Democratic Party, 92; contributions by, 63–64; factors in lack of opposition, 193–194; loyalty to the GOP, 61, 68, 69; political activism by, xi, 182; purchase of homes by, 53–55
African American women: in city government, 166; and growth of Philadelphia's Black population, 4, 13–14; in housing movement, 145; as important voting constituency, 57–59; political activism by, 27, 49, 52; on Republican City Committee, 60; and welfare spending, 175
Alexander, Michelle, *The New Jim Crow*, 199, 222n27
Alexander, Raymond Pace: alignment with the Democrats, 89; appointment to Court of Common Pleas, 121–122; on Cecil Moore's criticisms, 106, 112n29; desegregation resolution by, 104; as lawyer and activist, 5, 7, 61–62, 66–67, 97–98, 132n13; media defense of, 108; photograph of, *99*; political survival of, 121; racial allegiance defended by, 107; Republican activities of, 68; on slave heritage of, 107; support of Black banks, 69; support of Nix for Congress, 115
Alexander, Sadie Tanner Mossell: appointment to city government, 67; as lawyer and activist, 5, 7, 62, 97–98, 132n13; media defense of, 108; photograph of, *99*; racial allegiance defended by, 107
Anderson, Carol, 49
Anderson, Dorothy, 123

anti-lynching campaigns, 17, 29–30, 32, 34–35, 86
Arlene, Herbert, 117
Asbury, John C., 4, 50, 56, 59, 62–64, 66–68
Asbury bill, 59–60, 61, 65

bail reform, 202, 209, 214–217
Ball, Gilbert, 22, 23
Banks, Cecily, 106
Barber, J. Max, 55, 56, 80
Barkley-Brown, Elsa, 27–28
Barr, Cadwallader, 59–60
Bass, Harry W., 4, 22–23, 26, 35–36, 43n17
Bass Amendment (House Bill 298), 23–24, 25
Bazelon, Emily, *Charged*, 199
Berry, William H., 21–23
Bird, Crystal Dreda. *See* Fauset, Crystal Bird
Birth of a Nation, 39, 52–53
Black banks, 33, 69, 77
Black electoral power: and the balance of power, 15, 16, 18, 30, 32–33, 36–37, 49, 56, 113, 120; bloc voting in, 32, 37, 71, 120, 123; and city's political structure, 133n18, 139; community basis for, 16; and Democratic control of Philadelphia, 7; in election of Krasner, 209–212; and hegemony of GOP bosses, 19; and ouster of reform administration, 38–39, 48; and preservation of civil rights, 4; and reapportionment, 126; response to Vote White, 136–137; rise in, x–xi; single-party democracy's effect on, 123; successes in West Philadelphia, 142; support of Roosevelt, 86; weakening of, 122, 123, 178; working within the Democratic Party, 142. *See also* elections
Black Lives Matter movement, 2, 9, 200, 206, 207, 210, 217
Black Nationalism, 124, 125, 126–128, 129
Black Political Forum (BPF), 129, 142, 147, 148, 149
Black politics: and coalition for Black empowerment, 157; as collective activity, 28; and community control, 147; critical realignment in 1932–1945 of, 76; and the Democratic Party, 5–6, 92, 120–121; development of Black political organizations, 57, 114; and expansion of power, 23; and Great Migration, 4; growing reliance on grassroots mobilization, 217; independents under Cecil Moore, 124–128, 129; populism and civil rights in, 128; protest politics of the 1960s, 7–8; Rizzo and Black empowerment, 137, 143, 146, 157. *See also* African American activism; Black electoral power; Black Nationalism; grassroots movements
Black Power activism, 125, 129, 139, 140
Black Progressives, 16, 28–29, 30, 33, 38, 44n22
Blackwell, Jannie, 192
Blackwell, Lucien, 166, 167, 181
Blankenburg, Rudolph, 25, 26, 39, 48
Bowser, Charles, 8, *148,* 149–150, 154, 155, 163–164
boycotts, 8, 51–52, 104, 139
BPF. *See* Black Political Forum
Bradford-Grey, Keir, 202, 210, 215
Brancato, Anne, 78
Branche, Stanley E., *105*
Briggs, Cyrill, 65
Brill, Frederick, 91
Broderick, Raymond, 153
Brown, Michael, 199–200, 206
Brumbaugh, Martin Grove, 50
Bullock, Riley, 54
Burrell, George R., Jr., 181

Campbell, James, 24
Carmichael, Stokely, 140
Catto, Octavius V., 3, 18, 20
CCTR. *See* Citizens Committee for Tenants Rights
Certaine, Joe, 168
Charlottesville demonstration, 207
charter change amendment. *See* Home Rule Charter
Chicago as Black Mecca in politics, 32, 43n17, 69, 70, 71, 183n2
Chudoff, Earl, 114
Churchville, John, 124
CIO. *See* Congress of Industrial Organizations
Citizens Republican Club (CRC), 48, 50, 55–56, 59, 66
city employment of African Americans: in the 1980s, 166, 181; and the city charter, 117; in the early twentieth century, 49; King's police appointments, 18–19; underrepresentation in, 61, 62–63; under the Vare machine, 58, 62, 66, 69, *70,* 71;

of women, 166; and working-class support of patronage, 116
city governance in the 1980s and 1990s: and advancement of Black businesses and professionals, 166; appointments of African Americans, 166, 181; challenges faced by, 162–163, 167, 169–171, 178, 179, 180, 182; entrenched politics and, 168–169; federal empowerment zone funding, 181; foreshadowing of Black control, 164; gay rights, 167; gentrification and new ghettos, 172–173; police-community relations, 176–178; poverty, jobs, and welfare, 173, 175; public health and safety, 18, 174–175; public school system's struggles, 175, 180; and Puerto Ricans, 163, 166, 183n3; race and class as persistent issues, 176, 182; transit and utility systems, 171; union pressures, *175*, 175, 180–181; urban development and housing, 171–172, 179–180. *See also* Goode, Wilson; Rendell, Ed; Street, John
civil rights: the Alexanders' work for, 97–98; Black Progressives' efforts to protect, 28–29; coalitions formed to fight for, 84; and commitment to the Black community, 108; congressional districting victories and, 127; Democratic Party's indifference to, 89–90; emergence of radicalized activism for, 104; housing and, 147; poverty and, 146; Rizzo as threat to, 142. *See also* African American activism; Bass amendment; criminal justice reforms; desegregation; equal employment opportunity; equal rights
Civil Rights Acts, 24, 127
civil rights liberalism, 3, 15–16, 113, 123–124
civil rights movement, 40n3, 124, 144, 215
Clark, Joseph Sill, Jr., 7, 92, 97, 98, 116, 117, 137
Coalition Against Police Abuses (CAPA), 151
coalitions, multiracial: 1970s mobilization of, 151–152; Black alliances with white progressives, 149, 150; business interests in, 189–190; as critical, 164; factionalism and demise of, 113; and Philadelphia's first Black mayor, 157; and political power, 9; in postwar Philadelphia, 98; of Progressives and Black elites, 28–29; Rizzo and the opportunity to build, 138–139; and the role of Latinos in, 163
Coates, Thomas C., 66

Cole, Solomon, 20
Coleman, Joseph, 101, 166, 167
Colored Protective Association, 4, 54
Colored Republican Central Committee, 39, 48
Commission on Human Relations, 7, 95, 98, 103. *See also* Alexander, Raymond Pace; Alexander, Sadie Tanner Mossell
congressional election campaigns, 33–36, 66–67, 81, 114–120, 125–126, 133n18. *See also* Nix, Robert N. C., Sr.
Congress of Industrial Organizations (CIO), 83, 89, 117
Congress of Racial Equality, 124, 139
Consumer Education and Protective Association, 172
Cooper, Richard A., 26, 43n17, 48
Corbett, Margaret, 58, 60, 61
Corbett, Tom, 202
corruption, 6, 15, 20–21, 77, 167, 179–180, 191
Council of Organizations on Police Accountability and Responsibility, 141, 163, 164
Countryman, Matthew, 98, 111n22, 123, 134n23
Cowdery, Martin, 54
CRC. *See* Citizens Republican Club
Creditt, William A. (Rev.), 28, 29, 31–32, 45n29
crime, 140–141, 178, 192, 197, 203–204
criminal justice reforms: and accountability, 216; and arbitration rules, 207–208; bail reform, 202, 209, 214, 215, 216, 217; critiques of, 215–216; fair treatment, 10; under Goode, 176; grassroots organizing for, 217–218; Krasner and, 210, 212–215; policy reforms, 201–202. *See also* antilynching campaigns; law and order politics
criminal justice system: Black Lives Matter and, 200; Brown's murder and injustice in, 199–200; and discrimination, 178, 194; district attorneys and, 209–210; funds spent on, 174–175; life after incarceration, 196–197, 217; mobilization for changes in, 198–200; overpolicing, 140, 141, 152, 194, 198, 205; racial disparities in, 195, 209, 215; support of white mobs, 53. *See also* lynchings

Dabney, A. P., 63
Davis, Jim, 155

Dawson, William L., 7, 120
DCC. *See* Democratic City Committee
Deal, Alphonso, 151, 152, *153*
deindustrialization, 7, 138, 157, 189, 190
Democratic City Committee (DCC), 142, 149
Democratic Party: achieving majority, 7; African American leadership in, 89–90; African Americans' move to, 16, 68–69, 71, 76, 79–80, *80*, 81, 119; and control of city hall, 18, 92, 97; demise of independent voices in, 120–121; emergence of Roosevelt coalition, 70; factional battles in, 192; and importance of winning Pennsylvania, 83; and independent voices, 126; and the Jim Crow South, 4; losses to Republicans in 1960s, 128; postwar leadership change in, 91; reformers *versus* stalwarts in 1958, 114–120; retaking of the state legislature, 86; segregationist wing of, 83; slating policy change, 115–116; voter intimidation by, 20; voter registration of African Americans, 166; weakness in Philadelphia of, 77–78; white power in, 138; zenith of power in Pennsylvania, 122
demonstrations, marches, and rallies: in 1967, 139; Black Progressives' 1912 rally, 29; at Girard College, 105, *105*; held by African American women, 60; March on Washington movement, 6; against modifications to stop and frisk policy, 205–206; over downtown development, 171; over police brutality, 156, *177*, 206, 207, *208*; police brutality during, 38–39; proposed march against Roosevelt, 87; at Rizzo's inauguration, 143; school issues, *175*; squatting campaigns, 163; in support of Republican candidates, 48; in the Whitman neighborhood, 154
Dennis, Shirley, 145–146, *148*
Department of Justice (DOJ) report on policing, 200, 201
De Priest, Oscar, 69, 70
desegregation, 53–55, 98, 101
Deutsch, Isaac, 51
Dickerson, G. Edward, 28, 56, 60, 64, 66, 67, 132n13
Dilworth, Richardson, 7, 92, 115, 117, 122, 137, 139, 149
disenfranchisement, legal, 3, 16, 36, 40

"Don't Buy Where You Can't Work," 51, 84, 88
"Double V" campaign, 6, 88
Douglass, Frederick, 1, 17
Du Bois, W.E.B., 16, 27, 30, 44n22, 95; *The Philadelphia Negro*, 3, 18–19, 182
Duffy, Thomas S., 21

Earle, George H., Jr., 25, *80*, 81, 85
Easton, J. M., 52
economy, postindustrial, 189, 190, 196. *See also* urban development
elections: Black Nationalism in, 124–125; general elections, 36–37, 56, 58, 59; gubernatorial elections, 21–23, 81; presidential elections, 1–2, 32–33, 128. *See also* congressional election campaigns; local and state elections; mayoral elections
employment: corruption and government posts, 35; defense spending and, 86–87; for returning Black soldiers, 39; wartime demands and, 6, 13; in Wilson's federal government, 37; in WPA projects, 85–86. *See also* city employment of African Americans
equal employment opportunity, 3, 7, 10, 62, 116. *See also* job discrimination
equal protection under the law, ambiguity of, 20
equal rights, legislation for, 4, 5, 59–60, 61, 65, 71, 81
Evans, Dwight, 192
Executive Order 8802, 6, 87

Fair, David, 174
Fair Employment Practices Committee (FEPC), 6, 87, 88, 89, 90–91, 92
Farmer, James, 105
Fattah, Chaka, 168
Faulkner, Daniel, 177–178
Fauset, Arthur Huff, 5, 79, 84, 88, 89, 132n13
Fauset, Crystal Bird, 5, 79, *80*, 84, 85, 87–88, 90, 132n13
Feffer, Andrew, 164
Fellowship Commission, 122, 132n17
Fellowship House, 5, 88, 90–91
FEPC. *See* Fair Employment Practices Committee
Fifteenth Amendment, 19, 20, 37
Finnegan, James, 116

Fisher, Joseph, 178
Fletcher, Benjamin, 78
Foglietta, Thomas, 150
Forman, James, *Locking Up Our Own*, 199
Fourteenth Amendment, 19–20
Fourth Congressional District (Philadelphia): dissolution of, 126; special election in, 114–120, 133n18
Fox, Gerald and Carol, 176
Franklin, John Hope, 31, 43n17
Fraternal Order of Police, 151, 180, 195, 207, 215
Freeman, Andrew G., 103

Garvey, Marcus, 65
gay rights, 167
gentrification, 172–173, 191, 193
gerrymandering, 113, 127
Gibson, Kenneth, 138
Gipson, Stephen, 22
Girard College, integration of, 8, 104–105, 126, 140
Goode, Wilson, Jr., 192
Goode, W. Wilson, Sr.: accomplishments as mayor, 168–169; administration of, 166; background of, 165; Bowser's campaign and, 149; as city manager, 164–165, 167; and downtown development, 190; election as mayor, 8, 9, 156–157, 165–166, 168, 220n10; fiscal crisis under, 182; and MOVE bombing, x; police reform under, 176; and public housing, 146–147
Gordon, Lena Trent, 49, 58, 60, 61
grassroots movements: to address housing and policing issues, 163; Black mayors' containment of, 194; and criminal justice reform, 216, 217; and election of district attorney, 209–211; factors inhibiting, 193–194; fight for equality by, 9; use of candidate forums, 204. *See also* criminal justice reforms
Gray, William H., Jr., 115, 220n10
Great Depression, 5, 76–77
Great Migration, 4, 13–14, *14*, 16, 17, 19, 49, 57. *See also* Second Great Migration
Great Recession of 2008, 192
Green, William, III, 143, 149, 155, 164, 176, 182
Green, William "Bill," 114–116, 117, 120, 122, 127, 131n5
Green, William Howard, murder of, 156

Grim, Webster, 21–23
Guffey, Joseph, 78

Hahn, Steven, 28
Hall, Charles B., 60, 61, 66
Hamilton, Shirley, 166
Hart, Samuel, 63, 64
Hatcher, Richard, 138
Haynes, Pamala, 143
Heacock, Elwood, 55
Henom, Bobby, 202
Henry, Ed, 66, 132n13
Hickok, Lorena, 77
Hill, Louis, 149
Hodos, Jerome, 26
Holmes, Samuel D., *80*
Holston, Gregory, 196–197, 199, 200, 204
Home Rule Charter, 7, 95, 117, 136–137, 154–155
Hoover, Herbert, 68–69, 77, 81
Housing Association of the Delaware Valley (HADV), 145, 146
housing in Philadelphia: and African Americans' purchase of homes, 53–55, 77, 96, 98–99, 100; competition for, 19; fight for public housing, 5, 139, 144–148, 157; during fiscal crisis, 171; Great Depression and, 5, 77; Great Migration and, 53–54; overcrowding and calls for safety in, 83–84; shortages in, 91, 96. *See also* tenants' rights
Huff Fauset, Arthur. *See* Fauset, Arthur Huff
Hyman, Thurston, 182

Jackson, Maynard, 138
Jeffries, Martha, 78
Jewish Americans, 31–32, 37, 45n29, 51, 83
Jim Crow: Democratic Party and, 4; intersection with migration and urbanization, 30; proliferation of, 30. *See also* Alexander, Michelle, *The New Jim Crow*; Great Migration; racism; segregation; violence, racial
job discrimination, 5, 6, 19, 86, 91. *See also* city employment of African Americans; equal employment opportunity
John Mercer Langston Club, 66
Jones, A. I., 50
Jones, David, murder of, 207
Jones, Reuben, 199

Jones, Roxanne, 168, 175
juvenile delinquency, 101, 118, 124
juvenile incarceration, 209, 210, 214, 215, 224n70

Keim, George, 18
Kellogg, Charles, 30
Kelly, John B. "Handsome Jack," 78, 82
Kelly, Robin D. G., 101
Kendrick, W. Freeland, 61, 62, 63
Kennedy, Randall, 207
Kennedy, Thomas, 84
Kenney, James "Jim," 9, 203–206, 207–208, 209, 217, 218
Kentu, Omjasisa, 181
Kenyatta, Muhammad, 149
Keystone Party, 23, 25–26, 27, 33, 35
Khalif, Asa, 206
King, Martin Luther, Jr., 105, 124
King, Samuel L., 18
Kousser, J. Morgan, 127
Krasner, Larry, 9, 199, 210–214, *213*, 216, 217
Ku Klux Klan, 39, 52, 102

labor unions, 63, 82–83, 84–85, 131n5, 173–174, 180, 218
La Follette, Robert, 33, 37, 66
Latinos: activism by, 127, 194, 218; on the city council, 166; Goode and, 166, 168; Krasner's reforms and, 212; and the police, 198, 204, 205; in regime politics, 189; Street administration and, 191. *See also* Puerto Rican population
law and order politics, 141, 147, 194, 195, 196. *See also* Rizzo, Frank
Lawrence, David, 122
Layton, S. Willie, 49, 58–59, 60, 61, 63
Leader, George, 121
Lloyd, Mark Frazier, 112n29
local and state elections: in the 1880s, 18; in the 1920s, 57, 58–59, 60–61, 79; in the 1930s, 81; in the 1950s, 116; in the 1960s, 126; in the 1970s, 138, 148
Locke, Alain, *The New Negro*, 65
Logan, Thomas S., 140
Lombardo, Timothy, 129
Longstreth, W. Thacher, 143
lynchings, 30–31, 53. *See also* anti-lynching campaigns

MacArthur Foundation grants, 201–202, 208, 215, 224n73
Mackey, Harry, 67
Malcolm X, 7, 124, 125
Mallowe, Mike, 166, 168
Marston, David, 164
Martin, Edward, 91
Martin, Isadore, 55, 62
mass incarceration: coalition protests against, 202–203; and demoralization, 197–198; drug addiction treatment instead of, 174, 214; and juveniles, 209, 210, 214, 215, 224n70; in Philadelphia, 202, 221n19; progress in reducing, 215; resistance to, 198; socioeconomic costs of, 194, 196–198, 204, 214–215. *See also* criminal justice reforms; criminal justice system; MacArthur Foundation grants; Philadelphia Police Department
mayoral elections: of 1880–1881, 38–39; in 1915–1935, 38–39, 56, 58, 82; in 1959–1975, 122, 127, 129, 142–143, *144*, 148–150; in 1983–1999, 156–157, 165, 168, 178, 181, 190; in 2007–2015, 191, 204–205; election of African Americans, 137–138, 155, 183n2; Philadelphia's first Black mayor, 156–157
McCoach, Billy, 65
McKenzie, Edward, 20
McNesby, John, 215
middle-class and elite African Americans: Black criticism of, 123–124; Moore's challenge to, 104, 106; moving into all-white neighborhoods, 96, 98, 99, 100; Progressives, 16, 28–29, 30, 33, 38, 44n22; in the Republican Party, 48, 49–50; success in the North, 49; views toward Southern migrants, 15; white views of, 59. *See also* Alexander, Sadie Tanner Mossell; Fauset, Arthur Huff; Moore, Cecil B.
Moore, Carolyn Davenport, 6, 88, 92
Moore, Cecil B.: alignment with militant activism, 7, 104, *120*; attacks on the Alexanders by, 7, 108; background of, 102, 118–119; challenge to leadership of, 106–107; confrontations with Rizzo, 140; criticism of Mount West Airy, 106, 111n22; death of, 167; election to city council, 148; electoral defeats for, 118–120, 126–127, 128; factors in rise of,

114; influence in Black politics, 125; and integration of Girard College, 105–106, 126; leadership style of, 129, 132n13; legacy of, 130; mayoral campaign of, 139; on Nix for Congress, 115; and North Philadelphia, 103–104; popularity of, 126; and race pride, 125–126; at rally, *105*; switch to the Democratic Party, 123; weakening of, 129
Moore, E. W. (Rev.), 28, 29
Moore, J. Hampton, 56, 58, 60, 81
Morris, Sarah, 209
Morrisette, Maude, 49, 58, 61, 63
MOVE, raids and bombings of, ix–x, 152, 154, 168, 176
Myrdal, Gunnar, 98–99; *An American Dilemma*, 95–96

National Association for the Advancement of Colored People (NAACP), 4, 24, 29, 53, 122, 125–126, 143. *See also* Philadelphia Chapter of the NAACP
National Independent Political League, 29, 38–39
National Negro Congress (NNC), 5, 84–85, 88
New Deal policies, 76, 81, 82, 85, 86, 91, 92, 129
New Negro movement, 5, 16, 65–66
Nichols, Henry, *105*, 106–107, 108
Nineteenth Amendment, 49, 57
Nix, Robert N. C., Sr.: Black support for, 121; as Democrat, 90; education and reputation of, 115; election to Congress, 7, 9, 36, 71, 119–120, 121, *121*, 126, 127; and hope for Black representation, 114; and national civil rights legislation, 133n17
NNC. *See* National Negro Congress
Norris, Austin, *80*
North City Congress (NCC), 139, 141
Northern urban centers: building of a Black political culture in, 16; comparison of Black populations in, 32–33; as locus of civil rights struggle, 40; racism and violence in, 19, 53; recruitment of Southern Black labor to, 13
North Philadelphia, 102, 103, 193
Northwest Coalition, 192, 220n10
Nutter, Michael: Bowser and, 8; election of, 9, 191; law and order policies of, 192, 196; and marijuana decriminalization bill,

204; and mass incarceration, 201–202; and police monitoring, 198, 200, 201, 205; reform goals for city government of, 191–192; and revitalization of Center City, 192

Obama, Barack, 1–2, 201
Ortiz, Angel, 166, 167
Owens, Chandler, 59

Parks, John W., 50
Pennsylvania Equal Rights Law (1935), 5, 81
Pennsylvania Intergovernmental Cooperation Authority (PICA), 179
Pennsylvania state legislature: African American representation in, 8, 22, 26, 81, 85, 126–127, 142, 168; anti-segregations laws passed by, 3; Bass Amendment (House Bill 298), 24; equal rights legislation, 5, 55, 59–60, 71, 81; and fair housing legislation, 122, 123, 145
Penrose, Boise, 22, 23, 25, 33, 37–38, 60
Pepper, George, 66, 67, *68*
Perry, Bertha, 60
Perry, Chris (reporter), 106
Perry, Christopher (editor), 37, 38, 48, 50. *See also Philadelphia Tribune*
Petshek, Kirk R., 116
Pfaff, John, *Locked In*, 199
Philadelphia: and African American political history, 3; diverse manufacturing environment in, 76; early firsts in Black representation, 43n17; fiscal crises in, 85, 138, 162, 169–171, 178, 180–181, 182, 192; gentrification and new ghettos, 172–173; growth in Black population of, 2–6, 8, 9, 13, 28, 96, 109n3; Home Rule Charter for, 7, 95, 117, 136–137, 154; law and order reputation of, 196, 202; as Northern city with largest Black population, 14, 32–33; postindustrial Democratic control of, 113; reapportionment in, 126, 127; revitalization of, 189, 190, 192, 216–217; as shipbuilding center, 86–87, 90; as slow to elect Black politicians, 137–138; unemployment in, 5, 77, 86, 90; urban crisis in, 9–10; WPA projects in, 85. *See also* city employment of African Americans; city governance in the 1980s and 1990s; criminal justice system; Democratic

Philadelphia *(Continued)*
Party; Goode, Wilson, Jr.; Great Depression; Great Migration; housing in Philadelphia; Krasner, Larry; labor unions; Nutter, Michael; Rendell, Ed; Republican Party; Rizzo, Frank; urban development

Philadelphia Chapter of the NAACP, 55, 88, 92, 102, 108, 126, 129

Philadelphia City Council: activists' closer ties with, 216; and ban-the-box legislation, 199; diverse representation on, 166, 167; in the early twentieth century, 36, 43n17, 90; Moore's election to, 148; Street's leadership on, 178–179. *See also* Alexander, Raymond Pace; Blackwell, Lucien; Coleman, Joseph; Kenney, James "Jim"; Moore, Cecil B.; Nutter, Michael; Shepard, Marshall, Sr.; Street, John

Philadelphia Commission on Human Relations, 95, 97, 98, 103

Philadelphia Housing Association, 91, 145, 146, 147. *See also* Housing Association of the Delaware Valley

Philadelphia Housing Authority, 146–147, 179

Philadelphia Inquirer: on elections, 20, 26, 212; indictment of the police department by, 151; on Krasner's criminal justice policies, 214; on Nutter's biracial constituency, 191; op-ed on structural racism, 207

Philadelphia Police Department: accountability measures implemented in, 206; actions taken to increase oversight of, 200, 203; Black congregations and, *201*; Black officers' support of Rizzo, 142, 150–151; clashes with African Americans in the 1960s, 8; disciplinary measures, 217; hiring of Black officers, 18, 173; indictment of, 151; stop and frisk policy, 192, 198, 200, 204, 205–206, 212, 216, 223n45; voter intimidation by, 20; "weekend of rage" against, 206–207. *See also* criminal justice reforms; MOVE; police brutality and abuse; Rizzo, Frank

Philadelphia Rapid Transit Employees Union (PRTEU), 88–89

Philadelphia Tribune: on the 1920 presidential election, 56; advertisements in, 65–66, 67, *68,* 69, *70;* on African Americans' contributions to Philadelphia, 63–64; on African Americans in North Philadelphia, 71, 103; on an all-Black slate, 125; on Black leaders, 23, 106, 107; on the Black vote, 48–49, 64, 137, 155; on congressional opportunities, 68; on electing a Black mayor, 138; endorsements by, 143, 149–150; on failure of Progressives' promises, 48; founding of, 50; letters to, 31–32, 58, 154–155; on meritocracy in government, 61; on need for fair treatment, 62; praise for African American women, 57–58, 61; on racial perceptions in hiring, 181; Republican support from, 80; on Rizzo's policies, 141–142, 153, 154; on the union deal during fiscal crisis, 180–181; on white protest under Black control, 170. *See also* Perry, Christopher; Williams, G. Grant

PICA. *See* Pennsylvania Intergovernmental Cooperation Authority

Plessy v. Ferguson, 24

police brutality and abuse: and Black activism, 198; Black activism and, 3, 9; and coalition for Black empowerment, 157; criticism of, 48; Deal's fight against, 151, 152, *153;* disciplining of police, 207; Green's actions to address, 155–156; against MOVE, 152; protection from, 15; protests against, 2, 139–140, 156, *177,* 206, 207, 215; under Rizzo, 141, 151, 176, 195; shootings of young Black men, 156, 199–200, 206–207; and working-class residents, 124

police-community relations, 8, 176–178, 206–207

political power: Black Philadelphians' achievement of, 8, 26, 36–37, 49, 120, 125, 157; congressional power of African Americans, 34–35; control of jobs and, 117; racial tensions, 15. *See also* African American activism; Black electoral power; Black politics; Bowser, Charles; Democratic Party; regime politics; Republican Party

Porter, George D., 38–39, 48

postwar liberalism, 95–96, 98–99, 104–108

poverty: attempts to address, 9, 128, 173, 175, 192, 218; and civil rights, 146; and incarceration, 174

Powell, Adam Clayton, Jr., 7, 119, 120
POWER (Philadelphians Organized to Witness, Empower, and Rebuild), 200, 204, 211, 212
Pownall, Ryan, 207, 213
Progressive reform movement, 4, 16–17, 21, 32, 40n4, 43n16
Progressives, 25–27, 35, 36, 37. *See also* Black Progressives
progressive social movements. *See* city governance in the 1980s and 1990s; Krasner, Larry; Progressive reform movement
PRTEU. *See* Philadelphia Rapid Transit Employees Union
public health and safety, 8, 173–174
public housing. *See* housing in Philadelphia
public school system: Black activism for reforms in, 3, 7–8, 139–140; community schools in, 218; defunding of, 202–203; and redlining, 91; strikes against, *175*, 175
Puerto Rican population, 8, 163, 164, 166, 168, 183n3
Purvis, Robert, 17

race riots, 31, 53–54
racial discrimination: after incarceration, 197; and antidiscrimination ordinances, 167; commission created to tackle, 95; in the criminal justice system, 174, 194, 206; in defense industries, 86, 87; pervading Philadelphia, 88, 95, 102, 182; post-war continuation of, 91; public housing and, 154; by the South Street Business Association, 51–52
racial justice, fight for, 17–18, 95–96, 104, 106
racial tensions, 8, 15, 28, 51–52, 103
racism: in the early twentieth century, 71; fascism and, 95; housing movement's fight against, 144–146, 147; increases in, 15, 19, 52–53; of the Republican leadership, 71; structural racism and regime politics, 193–194, 207; in the urban North, 19, 36; of white Progressives, 16, 27–28. *See also* criminal justice system; desegregation; labor unions; racial discrimination; Rizzo, Frank; segregation; violence, racial; Wilson, Woodrow
Rainey, Joseph, Jr., *80,* 132n13
Ramsey, Charles, 200, 201

Randolph, A. Philip, 6, 59, 63, 84, 87
Reagan, Ronald, administration of, 175
reform movements, 15, 18–19, 115, 116–117. *See also* criminal justice reforms; Progressive reform movement
regime politics, 189–190, 191, 193–194, 218
Rendell, Ed, 178, 179–182, 190, 195, 221n19
Republican City Committee, 60, 61
Republican Party: and the 1910 gubernatorial election, 21–23; and the Bass Amendment, 24, 25; Black disaffection with, 5, 16, 17–21, 25, 76; Black support for, 38–39, 48, 58, 61, 80, 143; and the congressional campaign of 1912, 35; control of local and state government by, 85, 91; courting of Black population and migrants by, 15, 18–19; dominance in Philadelphia, 23, 57; ignorance of African American problems, 5; loss of executive power by, 122–123; and power shifts in Philadelphia, 6–7; preservation of power by, 36–37; shift in racial foundations of, 123; Specter and, 128; weakening in Philadelphia of, 81. *See also* Alexander, Raymond Pace; Citizens Republican Club; Fauset, Crystal Bird; middle-class and elite African Americans; Street, Milton; Vare political machine
Residents Advisory Board (RAB), 145–146, 147–148, 153
Reynolds, Hobson, 5, 81–82, 132n13
Reynolds, Nellie, *148*
Reynolds v. Sims, 127
Rhodes, E. Washington, 63, 65–66, 67, 69, 80, 132n13
Richardson, David P., 8, 168, *177*
Richardson, Larry, 180
Rizzo, Frank: African American support for, 150–151, 154; attempt to oust, 164; Black clergy and, 140–141; Black electoral challenge to, 148–149; Black Nationalism and rise of, 129; and change to city charter, 136, 154–155; and charges of police brutality, 141; grievances filed against, 150; law and order politics of, 195; and MOVE, 152; national reputation of, 137; as police commissioner, 137, 139; primary challenge to Goode, 165; and public housing, 144–145, 146, 153; racism of, 136, 140, 142, 151, 153–154, 154; repudiation of regime of, 155–156; rise of, 8

Roosevelt, Franklin Delano: African American support for, 5, 81, 83, 89; and the Democratic Party in Philadelphia, 18, 70–71; Executive Order 8802, 6, 87; Guffey's assistance to, 78; reelections of, 83, 89; Rhodes's warnings against, 80–81. *See also* New Deal policies
Roosevelt, Theodore, 18–19, 32, 33
Roper, Mary Catherine, 206, 207
Rose, Sam, 117
Roster, Edgar, 67
Rudovsky, David, 196, 198, 199, 203, 205–206, 211, 215, 223n45

Salvatore, Hank, 170
Sawyer, Henry, 117
Schermer, George, 96, 100
Schmidt, Harvey N., 117–118, 119
Scott, Amos C., 48, 50, 51–52, 55–56, 60, 61, 66
secession movement, 169–170
Second Great Migration, 6, 95–96
segregation, 3, 57, 59–60, 62, 64, 82
Sesqui-Centennial International Exposition, 62–63
Seventh Ward, 14, 20, 21, 26, 36, 38, 39, 53, 57
Shapp, Milton, 126, 156
Shedd, Mark, 139
Shepard, Lorenzo, 149
Shepard, Marshall, Sr.: activism of, 5, 132n13; background of, 78–79; as a Democrat, 80, 83; election to the state legislature, 81; Nix and, 115; opposition to the Democratic Party, 121; Roosevelt's appointment of, 89; support for Schmidt's candidacy, 118; support of Roosevelt by, 79
Shepard, Marshall Lorenzo, Jr., 125
Shields, Jesse, 117
Silcox, Harry, 18
Sinclair, William A., 24, 29–30, 37
Smalls, Leonard M., 128
Smith, Ellison "Cotton Ed," 83
Smith, Louis, 124
Smith, Thomas B., 48, 49
Southern Black migrants, 13–14, 15. *See also* Great Migration
Southern Democrats, 5, 16, 36, 37, 39, 83, 86, 119. *See also* Wilson, Woodrow
South Street Business Association (SSBA), 51–52

Sparks, John, 67
Specter, Arlen, 122, 128, 195, 221n19
SSBA. *See* South Street Business Association
Stanford, Max, 124
Steffens, Lincoln, 77
Stein, Abram, 55
Stein, Gilbert, 146
Stemons, James Samuel, 28
Steptoe, Lamont, 2
Stevens, Andrew F., Jr., 48, 50, 51–52, 54–55, 59
Stevens, Andrew F., Sr., 50
Stevenson, Bryan, *Just Mercy*, 199
Still, William, 17
Stokely, Bill, 18
Stokes, Carl, 138
Stone, Chuck, 150; "An Authentic American Racist," 154
stop and frisk policies, 192, 198, 200, 204, 205–206, 212, 216, 223n45
Street, John, 8, 9, 167, 172, 178–179, 180, 181, 190–191
Street, Milton, 154, 156, 168, 170, 175
strikes, 6, 78, 83, 88–89, 173
Student Nonviolent Coordinating Committee (SNCC), 124, 140
Sullivan, Leon, 7, 101, 106, 118, 124
Sulzberger, Mayer, 32, 37
Sutton, Jim, 180

Taft, William Howard, 32, 33
Tasco, Marian, 192
Tate, James, 127, 128, 140, 144
taxation, 9, 150, 162, 169–170, 171, 172, 179, 189, 218
Tayoun, James, 167
Tenant Action Group, 163, 164
Tenants League of Philadelphia, 84
tenants' rights, 146, 147, 157
Tener, John K., 21–23, 26
Thirtieth Ward, 14, 28, 57, 58, 64–65, 67, 68
"Thornfare" legislation, 174
Tindley, Charles Albert, 28, 62
Trapp, H. J., 117
Trotter, William Monroe, 37
Truman, Harry S., 89, 97
Tucker, C. Delores, 8
Tyson, John R., 59

urban development: downtown development, 171, 189, 190, 192; efforts to

address poverty, 192, 218; gentrification and, 193; regime politics in, 189–190, 191, 193–194; Society Hill redevelopment, 172; urban renewal programs, 7, 144
Urban League, 4, 53
Urban League, *State of Black Philadelphia*, 162
U.S. Civil Rights Commission, 156
U.S. Congress, African Americans in, 2, 7, 33–34, 36. *See also* Nix, Robert N. C., Sr.
U.S. Supreme Court, 24, 85, 104, 153, 214

Vann, Robert L., 81
Vare, Edward, 22, 35, 56, 64
Vare, William, 25, 35, 56, 64, 66–67, 69, 70, 79
Vare political machine: attempt to defeat, 66–67, 68; and Black votes, 64, 66, 69, 70; corruption and racism of, 61, 66, 71; domination of local politics by, 56; and equal rights, 65; and jobs for African Americans, 58, 62, 64, 66, 69, 70, 71
violence, racial: as an American story, 4; during the Great Migration, 30–31, 40; increase in, 15; during mayoral campaigns, 38; in Northern cities, 53; pattern of, 40; in the transit sector, 89; and white homeowners' resistance to Black neighbors, 96–97, 98
voter intimidation, 20–21

Walker, Zachariah, 24–25, 28, 29
Walker-Bryan, Lela, 27, 28
Waring, Everett J., 26
Washington, Booker T., 17, 29–30
Washington, Walter, 138

Weems, Robert, 49
Weiner, Charles R., 125
Wells, Ida B., 17
Welsh, Garrett, 20
Wesberry v. Sanders, 127
West Mount Airy, 7, 99, 100–101, 103, 104, 110n10, 110n13
White, Arbertha, 79
White, George H., 4, 29, 33–36, *34*
White, Julian St. George, 62, 66
White, Walter, 87
Whitman Park housing project, 144, 145–146, 147, *148,* 152–154, 156
Wiebe, Robert, 29
Wiley, Rosetta, 145–146
Wilkins, Roy, 105, 119, 129
Williams, Anthony Hardy, 205
Williams, G. Grant, 50–52, 54, 56, 57, 60
Williams, Hardy, 142, *144,* 148, 163
Williams, Seth, 210, 224n58
Williams, Willie, 176
Willkie, Wendell, 86
Wilson, S. Davis, 82, 84
Wilson, Woodrow, 32–33, 36–37, 39, 53, 58, 78
Woodard, Kathryn, 125
Woodson, Carter G., 102, 103
working-class African Americans, 4, 63, 113, 123, 125, 172
World War II, 86–87, 90
Wright, C. E., 55
Wright, Richard R., Jr., 27, 28, 37, 57, 69

Young, Coleman, 138

Ziegler, John, 156

www.ingramcontent.com/pod-product-compliance
Lightning Source LLC
Chambersburg PA
CBHW060947230426
43665CB00015B/2102